DATE DUE

BRODART, CO.   Cat. No. 23-221-003

GUNS AND BUTTER

International Political Economy Yearbook
Volume 14

Series Editors
Christopher May and Nicola Phillips

GUNS AND BUTTER

The Political Economy of International Security

edited by
Peter Dombrowski

LYNNE
RIENNER
PUBLISHERS

BOULDER
LONDON

Published in the United States of America in 2005 by
Lynne Rienner Publishers, Inc.
1800 30th Street, Boulder, Colorado 80301
www.rienner.com

and in the United Kingdom by
Lynne Rienner Publishers, Inc.
3 Henrietta Street, Covent Garden, London WC2E 8LU

Library of Congress Cataloging-in-Publication Data
Guns and butter : the political economy of international security /
editor, Peter Dombrowski.
    p. cm. — (The international political economy yearbook ; v. 14)
    Includes bibliographical references and index.
    ISBN 1-58826-312-6 (hardcover : alk. paper) — ISBN 1-58826-338-X
(pbk. : alk. paper)
    1. Security, International.   2. International economic relations.
3. Industrial mobilization.   I. Dombrowski, Peter J., 1963–   II. Series.
JZ6005.D66 2005
355'.033—dc22

2005000413

British Cataloguing in Publication Data
A Cataloguing in Publication record for this book
is available from the British Library.

Printed and bound in the United States of America

The paper used in this publication meets the requirements
(∞)   of the American National Standard for Permanence of
Paper for Printed Library Materials Z39.48-1992.

5 4 3 2 1

Contents

Acknowledgments

Producing an edited volume is always a collective effort, and this one is no different. If anything, this project required even more collaboration than usual given the topic and the number of institutions involved in compiling the volume. First and foremost, Sue Eckert and Bill Keller deserve special mention. At virtually every step along the way, both Bill and Sue provided wise counsel and inspiration, in addition to material support from the Ridgeway Center for Security Studies at the University of Pittsburgh and the Watson Institute for International Studies at Brown University, respectively. I could not have managed to complete this volume without their efforts.

Various people at the Naval War College were also supportive, including Alberto Coll and Jonathan Pollack. Both helped ease my way through the bureaucratic and organizational thickets involved in carrying out a collaboration among a federal institution, professional associations, and private universities. Andrew Ross, as always, provided substantive and practical expertise that kept me on the right path. At various times Cheryl Reilly, Mitch Ewing, Shirley Wilkins, Pauline Gagne, and Mary Ann Hall pitched in with expertise and assistance. Laura Goss Miller, then my intern and now a friend and co-author, worked tirelessly to ready the first draft for Lynne Rienner Publishers. In the final stages, my colleagues at the Naval War College Press, Pel Boyer, Phyllis Winkler, and Lori Almeida, remained patient and supportive as I struggled to complete this manuscript while still working my "day job" as editor of the press.

The International Studies Association, the Political Economy of Development Program at Brown University's Watson Institute, and the Ridgeway Center for Security Studies all provided financial, administrative, and in-kind support for holding a two-day workshop where participants shared their initial draft papers. Many people at these institutions were helpful: Ellen Carney and Sheila Fournier at the Watson Institute and Kelley McDevitt at the Ridgeway

Center stand out. I would be remiss if I did not mention Tom Biersteker for allowing us to use the Watson Institute facilities for the crucial workshop (not to mention his critical comments that helped clarify my thinking) and Barbara Stallings for generously providing much needed financial assistance.

Readers and commentators were numerous in addition to those already mentioned: Joshua Goldstein and Andrew Ross must be especially acknowledged, as well as our workshop reporters, Edward Wagner and Peter Romaniuk.

Phil Cerny was a driving force behind the entire project. It was Phil's idea that I edit this volume, and he participated in all events associated with the project. Although we had a few rocky moments along the way, I am nothing but thankful for his good grace and intellectual leadership. The general editors of the IPE Yearbook series, Nicola Phillips and Christopher May, took a chance on having this volume relaunch the series under their watch; both provided useful comments and suggestions. I am most grateful.

Finally, Lynne Rienner Publishers did its usual superb job. Lynne Rienner herself was instrumental in shaping the volume's content and themes; it was and is a pleasure to work with someone so enthusiastic and knowledgeable—not to mention patient. Lisa Tulchin waded through more than a few frantic e-mails as the manuscript came together.

As always, no one but myself is responsible for errors or omissions.

—Peter Dombrowski

The Political Economy of International Security

Peter Dombrowski

Students of public and international affairs have long recognized the depth and complexity of the relationship between security and economic affairs. Authors as diverse as Alfred Thayer Mahan, Norman Angell, Karl Polanyi, Jacob Viner, Herbert Feis, and a host of others all incorporated both economics and security into their analyses.[1] Yet throughout much of the middle to late twentieth century, and with a few prominent exceptions (e.g., Knorr 1973, 1978; Baldwin 1985; Gilpin 1975), mainstream international relations scholars tended to specialize in either security or economic issues. The theories, methods, and research programs of the two areas rarely coincided.

In recent years, however, interest in the intersections between security affairs and international economics has once again increased among both academic researchers and policymakers. Developments in both scholarship and the world of public policy and politics have called into question Cold War truisms about the primacy of security over economics and, more generally, the analytic and practical separation of the two areas. Scholars have begun reintegrating security studies and the study of international political economy (e.g., Kirshner 1998), thus broadening the substantive and theoretical boundaries of both fields.[2] As the chapters in this volume will demonstrate, integration has had the practical effect of increasing the realms in which scholars have been able to link the two issue areas and academic specializations.

Policymakers in particular have addressed the economic implications of emerging security threats and, conversely, the security implications of economic phenomena like globalization. Already, public officials have collapsed some of the remaining artificial boundaries, as much out of necessity as conviction. The United States has taken both military and economic steps to protect its national interests in a world characterized by more lethal terrorist threats, the proliferation of nuclear, biological, and chemical weapons, the spread of dual-use commercial technologies, and the profusion of failed or failing states. Current events have thus reinforced the illogic of separating the so-called low politics of economics from the high politics of war and peace.

The extent to which other countries share, and shared, the U.S. view of the global security environment or what constitutes appropriate policy responses to this environment, is uncertain.[3] We know that some countries have greeted U.S. efforts to use economic statecraft in the war on terror—not to mention the prosecution and the aftermath of the Iraq War—with skepticism. Many European analysts criticized continuing economic sanctions against Saddam Hussein's regime. Now, with efforts under way to reduce the debt load on post-Saddam Iraq, attract foreign investors, and bring in international firms to bid on reconstruction contracts, many countries remain suspicious that the U.S. focus on economic and commercial issues stems from expediency, war profiteering, and opportunism. Yet the European Union and its members have drawn upon their commercial and financial strengths to help cope with political instability, both real and projected, in its own near-abroad, including the Mahgreb, the Balkans, and central Europe during the early stages of the post-communist transition.

Complicating matters is the open question of whether current security challenges are new or simply more virulent manifestations of long-term trends. It could be argued, for example, that Islamist terrorism is, at least in part, a by-product of late-twentieth-century economic globalization. Even the events of September 11, 2001, can be understood as another link in a chain of events dating back to the first Bush administration. Osama bin Laden and Al-Qaida did not simply enter the public consciousness one September morning. Al-Qaida had been waging an undeclared war against the United States and its allies for over a decade (Benjamin and Simon 2002, pp. 219–293).

This volume explores how fields of international security and international political economy intersect by asking: What are the sources of continuity and change in the relationship between security and economics at the beginning of the twenty-first century?

Continuity and Change

For virtually all social phenomena, the search for the sources of continuity and change occupies a central position within the scholarly discourse. This is especially true with regard to evolutions of the global economy and the interstate system. Rather than exploring the large and diverse literature that exists on global transformation,[4] this introduction will discuss the major themes related to continuity and change in global society that underlie chapters written for this volume.

The following pages introduce possible changes in the overarching international environment, with an emphasis on how those factors influence the global economy; the theoretical and conceptual innovations that international political economy (IPE) and security studies scholars have developed to understand and explain these developments will be examined in much more detail in Chapter 2, in which Norrin Ripsman undertakes a critical survey of the realist literature linking political economy with national and international security.

The contributions to this volume focus on five parameters of potential change within the international political, economic, and security subsystems. No single chapter examines all five dimensions and no chapter author would agree with this summary of the issues.

State Sovereignty

Although state sovereignty remains an essential pillar of contemporary politics, there is growing evidence that the nature of sovereignty has been eroded both in specific cases and as a general norm (Krasner 2001; Biersteker and Weber 1996). As in the past, powerful states remain willing to violate sovereignty norms in the pursuit of their own economic and security objectives. Often, they operate with only cursory legal and political justifications. They are aided by international organizations, created in part to provide and manage global public goods in the collective interest of members, to impinge upon the formal sovereignty of individual members. Hence International Monetary Fund (IMF) and World Bank programs habitually supersede the judgment of domestic political leaders and technical experts. The United Nations Security Council has increasingly invoked a norm of humanitarian intervention to justify action even against the explicit wishes of the parties involved in the conflict. In the Kosovo crisis, the North Atlantic Treaty Organization even managed to overcome the traditional caution of its membership to intervene against Serbia.

Recent events have contributed to a further erosion of state sovereignty. With the announcement of the so-called Bush Doctrine, a declaratory policy of preemption, preventive war, and regime change, the United States has asserted both its right and its willingness to intervene militarily in the face of perceived global threats from rogue states and terrorists. Despite widespread international opposition to the U.S. position, other states, including Russia, Austria, and France, have hinted that they too are prepared to strike terrorists and other adversaries preemptively. As the recently issued report of the UN Secretary-General's High-Level Panel argues, even the United Nations may support preemption, providing decisions are made under UN auspices and in general accordance with the principle of just war theory (United Nations 2004).

In the economic sphere the implications are less stark, but with policies like the Millennium Challenge Account the Bush administration has assumed a more aggressive stance toward using foreign aid as a tool of economic state-craft. Indeed, if fully implemented the United States may be embarking on a period of unprecedented economic coercion in the service of national security ends. As will be discussed by Steven Hook and David Rothstein in Chapter 8, the United States has also used its long-standing security assistance programs more aggressively since September 11, 2001, to reward members of the various "coalitions of the willing." Beneficiaries include countries, like Uzbekistan, that have been willing to provide bases for the Afghan campaign, as well as countries, like Pakistan, the Philippines, and Indonesia, that face internal threats from Al-Qaida.

Powerful European and Asian states have also used economic statecraft to further their own political and diplomatic aims. Underlying security concerns have motivated the policies of the European Union and its member states toward postcommunist Europe, while Japan's relatively generous foreign aid programs have a great deal to do with its perceived need to maintain stability in key economic partners across Asia.

In each case, there is a fine line between cooperation in pursuit of common goals and active interference in the affairs of sovereign states. Moreover, whether other countries will emulate the recent aggressive military and economic interventionism of the United States remains to be seen. It may be that interventionist economic and military policies represent short-lived and understandable U.S. reaction to the horrific attacks of September 11. The willingness of other countries to intervene in the affairs of other states may be less important than the fact that they themselves are affected by the aggressive use of both security and economic instruments by the United States.

Global Governance and Institutional Capacity

Global governance has been a long-standing theme in international relations in various incarnations, from dreams of world government to the more modest focus on international regimes (Krasner 1983), epistemic communities (Haas 1990), and transnational networks of nonstate organizations (Florini 2000, 2003).[5] While none of the chapters in this volume focus explicitly on global governance, several imply the importance of international cooperation for controlling conflicts. More positively, many global public goods are beyond the power and desire of individual nation-states to provide; only collective action among nation-states facilitated by international institutions or hegemonic leadership has the political capacity and material resources to provide such goods in sufficient quantity and quality. At the intersection of security and economic policies are transnational phenomena with adverse consequences for global security that cannot be handled by individual states or even small groups of states.

At both the state and interstate levels, then, we have seen renewed interest in building governance capacity, especially with regard to increased responsibility and accountability on the part of social actors at all levels of society. States are increasingly held responsible for harboring terrorists, turning a blind eye toward domestic groups with ties to terrorists, or exploiting resources, regions, and peoples. Accountability means risking unilateral or multilateral military intervention or the use of economic coercion such as sanctions or embargoes, or both. It also means channeling official development assistance and the programs of the international financial institutions, including the World Bank and the International Monetary Fund, to build or rebuild the governance capacities of states. International organizations have thus reoriented their own policies to ensure that they use governance as an independent variable in determining the suitability of particular countries for grants and loans.

As Virginia Haufler explains in Chapter 4, even multinational corporations are sometimes being held accountable for their behavior in conflict-torn regions. For many host countries it is no longer sufficient for corporate investors to offer capital and expertise in return for access to cheap labor, abundant raw materials, and lax regulatory regimes; they must also play a role in maintaining local security and brokering deals among conflicting factions. Transnational activists encourage corporate responsiveness by applying political pressure to become more conscious of the political, social, and increasingly, security implications of business decisions.

Public and Private Responses

In a related trend first brought to prominence by Susan Strange and John Stopford (1991), alliances among and between states and firms have become common within the international political economy; there is a mutual interdependence between states and firms on a range of issues. For many years the United States remained officially and ideologically opposed to alliances between the public and private sectors to accomplish public purposes in the international system. U.S. opposition to public-private alliances has often been breached in practice, however. Commercial banks and other financial services firms, for example, were assigned important roles in managing the third world debt crisis of the late 1970s and early 1980s (Dombrowski 1996).

States like France, Germany, and Japan, not to mention upwardly mobile middle-income countries like South Korea, have long promoted national champions and work closely with private firms to serve both commercial and national ends. More recently, the United States has caught up with its economic competitors by increasing the public use of the private interest (Schultze 1977). U.S. government agencies such as the Trade and Development Agency and the Overseas Private Investment Corporation seek to encourage U.S. overseas trade and investment by working closely with corporations.

In the security realm, this dynamic is evident in the defense industrial sector, the targeted sanctions regime, and the growing demand for corporate responsibility among others areas. The U.S. government has (re)discovered that it cannot accomplish all of its foreign and security policy objectives if it relies solely on its own resources. The demands of the revolution in military affairs for technological innovation in weapons and systems are far too great to be funded solely from government military research and development accounts. Large commercial firms often dominate the most innovative business sectors—in communications, computing, and information processing, for example—and so the U.S. military draws heavily upon commercial and dual-use technologies for developing and acquiring cutting-edge, first-generation weapons systems necessary to conduct information age warfare (Dombrowski, Gholz, and Ross 2002).

U.S. Hegemony and Unipolarity

For better or worse, the international security system is unipolar and will remain so for the foreseeable future.[6] No single nation or even group of nations can challenge U.S. military supremacy using conventional military forces. As has been commonly noted, the United States currently spends more on defense than the next twenty-five or so largest militaries in the world combined. There are, however, practical limits to U.S. power, as the aftermath of the Afghan and Iraq wars suggests. The U.S. military is relatively large, well funded, technologically sophisticated, and therefore powerful. But it would be sorely pressed, given current force levels, to wage more than one Iraq-sized adventure simultaneously or to use its overwhelming technological lead effectively in insurgencies and civil wars.

Further on the horizon remains the possibility that other states will decide to balance U.S. power either individually or collectively. Already the European Union has taken steps toward developing it own military capabilities, while countries like France and Russia have hinted at their willingness to lead efforts to neutralize and contain U.S. power. Much depends, however, on the willingness of other countries to forgo the advantages of free-riding and bandwagoning in the face of a global hegemon. Balancing would constitute an expensive and unpredictable course sure to inflict domestic and international costs on participating states.

On the economic front, the United States is much less dominant than in military matters. The European Union is now the single largest market in terms of purchasing power. Meanwhile, China has achieved economic growth rates that far exceed those in the United States and, for that matter, the rest of the world. The United States remains *primus inter pares* but often has to rely on suasion and "salami" tactics rather than on overwhelming material superiority. Since the Doha trade round and talk during the late Clinton years of rebuilding the global financial system architecture, the United States has only devoted intermittent attention to sustaining and expanding global economic cooperation. On related areas such as environmental politics it has played the role of spoiler.

Yet the post–World War II international economic institutions, despite many modifications, continue to place the United States in a privileged position vis-à-vis other states and nonstate actors. Whether due to voting rules that effectively give the United States veto power over IMF decisions or the singular ability of the United States to opt out of international agreements, the United States is often able to avoid the constraints imposed on most other nations. The United States also maximizes its economic strength by pursuing a self-conscious policy of bilateralizing as many economic relationships as possible. The exercise of structural power remains one of the most powerful mechanisms for achieving U.S. policy objectives in both the economic and security realms.

To many contributors to this volume, much of the changing relationship between economics and security could be traced to developments with roots extending long before the outbreak of the global war on terror. If anything, they concentrated on long-term tectonics, what Charles Tilly has called "large processes" (1989), such as globalization, to account for recent changes in the behavior of states and other international actors.

Even more tenuous, from the perspective of several authors, is the claim that the relationship between international security and economic affairs itself is shifting. Rather, there is some evidence that what you find depends on where you look. In brief, recent scholarship has shed light on new issues because only in recent years have scholars developed analytic tools and empirical data. Hence, for example, in Chapter 5, Colin Kahl explores the ecological sources of conflict by summarizing a literature that has exploded due to new scholarly interest. Ecological factors, then, have not necessarily become more important as source of conflict, but rather scholars have conducted the in-depth research into past and ongoing conflicts to examine the phenomena. In a similar fashion, in Chapter 4, Virginia Haufler delves into the corporate accountability phenomenon's migration from issues like "blood diamonds" to public and private demands that firms play a larger role in ensuring contributing to peace in countries where they invest.

Yet major changes may be afoot. The primary source of conflict and driving force underlying the acquisition of force is not the challenge of revisionist or rogue states specifically, but nonstate actors, namely terrorist groups with global reach and associated socioreligious movements, including radical Islam. The second Iraq war aside, much of the global war on terror targets nonstate actors, often in conjunction or partnership with other nonstate actors. The United States and its allies cannot, by themselves, track the sources and destinations of terrorist funds. Instead they must rely heavily on the cooperation of private financial service firms. In attempting to stabilize and rebuild failed and failing states, governments recognize the limited reach of official development assistance. They understand both the essential role of humanitarian nongovernmental organizations in alleviating suffering and the absolute necessity of private capital for promoting economic growth. In short, wars and internal conflicts today are not solely interstate affairs.

Such findings echo the literature on the relationship between economic development and conflict. Traditionally, development specialists treated both the domestic and international security environments as exogenous. Today, more scholars recognize that the prospects for sustained economic growth and general prosperity are undermined by security threats. Internal conflicts dampen the willingness of multinational investors to do business. Civil wars, insurgencies, and terrorists also erode the confidence of local businesses, leading to pathologies such as capital flight. Worse still, high government expenditures on weapons and security diminish the resources available for infrastructure investments, education spending, and other government programs. The World Bank and the International Monetary Fund, for example, have recognized this and sought to wean recipient countries off the military treadmill. Governance in all forms, including the greater control over the level of expenditures on security, has become a cause for concern with these world bodies.

In sum, there are obviously many long-standing trends and processes in the global economy that are affecting the shifting terrain for economic and security policies. Globalization, however it is defined, is neither new nor unprecedented in world history. But the unipolar nature of the international security system is unprecedented and the military gap between the United States and its potential challengers is large and growing. Reconciling a multipolar global economy with a unipolar security system will be one of the foremost challenges facing the world in the coming decades.

The extent to which the 2001 terrorist attacks on New York and Washington (and the subsequent wars in Afghanistan and Iraq) will affect how these longer-term trends develop in the coming years, remains unknown. Globalization may be slowed—either through the increased costs associated with more extensive security measures or through the more skeptical views of some about the impact of globalization on political instability, regional conflict, and the ability of nonstate actors to operate across national borders. On the other hand, the lack of medium-term consequences for the U.S. national economy or the global economy as a whole may have demonstrated once again the resiliency of markets.

Volume Organization

This volume brings together chapters by scholars working at the intersection of economics and security. The main purposes are to survey the state of the field, encourage further scholarly exchanges, and improve interactions between academics and the analytic and policy communities charged with crafting national strategies in a changing global security environment. Taken individually and as a whole the chapter contributions will help

- set an agenda for further scholarly engagement between security studies and international political economy;
- provide a resource on the "state of the art" for those researching in this area or broadening their own scholarship to include insights from other subfields; and
- stimulate innovative thinking about the security and economic challenges facing the global community.

The contributions span a wide range of topics, from research traditional to security studies to arguments more often found in the IPE literature.

The volume is divided thematically into three parts. Part 1 explores emerging issues in the international political economy of security. Part 2 considers various dimensions of U.S. policies toward the political economy of security. Part 3 helps sketch the future of the global security and economic environments and explains how individual perspectives on economics and security may be shifting.

Political Economy and International Security: New Intersections

One of the areas where the research agendas of the security studies and international political economy communities have traditionally overlapped is in the domestic sources of military power. Historical research has demonstrated that one reason why states were able to outlast other competing types of polities (from empires to city-states to city leagues) was that they were a superior organizational form for extracting resources and transforming them into useable instruments of power (from large standing armies to advanced military technologies such as oceangoing warships). In Chapter 3, Emily Goldman and Leo Blanken provocatively examine how the emergence of the information age economy may shift the balance of power between states and nonstate actors in the production of security.

Some analysts have speculated that in an information-based economy, nonstate actors have new opportunities to compete with states, not directly by acquiring the traditional instruments of military power, but rather indirectly through the adoption of asymmetric strategies. Challengers to the status quo will not attempt to match the conventional military resources of the United States or the other major powers. Rather, they will adopt tactics, technologies, and strategies that leverage inexpensive, commercial, dual-use weapons against the strengths of great powers. In the information age, this often means exploiting the reliance of great powers on information-processing, telecommunications, and sensor technologies, perhaps by launching cyber attacks against military and civilian targets.

If the military advantages of advanced industrial societies are being challenged by the transition to a postindustrial economy, weak and failed states find themselves in dire straits. Many are unable or in some cases unwilling to maintain the basic level of internal security necessary to promote economic growth and development, much less technological innovation. Local insurgencies, warlords, and terrorists have frightened foreign investors and made it increasingly difficult for these states to enjoy the benefits of economic openness and globalization. Moreover, as the Taliban's rule in Afghanistan demonstrates, weak or failed states have provided potential refuges and breeding grounds for terrorists.

Virginia Haufler argues that in response to this negative cycle, multinational corporations have come under pressure to perform a critical stabilizing role that was once the sole province of states. Taking a cue from the corporate social responsibility movements found in some Western nations, firms are assuming conflict mediation roles that may be incompatible with their narrowly understood corporate missions, but that may be a necessity for businesses operating in some of the world's most desperate environments. Both home and host countries may be willing to cede powers, and even a measure of their own sovereignty, to firms that will use their own resources, expertise, and commercial leverage to intervene in civil wars. Public-private cooperation, then, seeks to reduce conflict and mediate between warring parties.

As the information age economy has changed the nature of security production and as economic globalization has helped thrust multinational corporations into the limelight in developing countries, another even older theme has reemerged. Scarcity as a potential producer of violence and conflict has long been a focus of both the IPE and security literatures as scholars have theorized endlessly about the relationship between resource scarcity and violent conflict. In Chapter 5, Colin Kahl performs a valuable service by providing a conceptual framework for sorting through the competing claims of scholars.

In Chapter 6, Christopher Hughes investigates the impact of the war on terror and associated U.S. policies on Japan's foreign and security policies. He concludes that Japan has shifted some of its policies to support U.S. positions. It has done so, however, in a way that reflects Japan's unique foreign and security traditions, specifically Japan's decisions to de-emphasize military force and assert the primacy of economic statecraft. Thus Japan contributes to the war on terror by supporting nation building and focusing foreign assistance programs on frontline countries. In the end, however, Hughes detects developments suggesting that Japan, over time, will move toward a more positive view of military instruments.

Chapter 6 differs in that it examines in detail how U.S. policies have influenced the positions of other governments; as such, it provides a transition to Part 2, which discusses U.S. policies and the emerging political economy of security. The chapter demonstrates that even countries outside the immediate area of operations for the war on terror can and do attempt to translate U.S. objectives into contributions that reflect their own foreign policy traditions. Given this, we find a need for more scholarship and policy analyses of how changes in U.S. international and regional security priorities in the period since September 11, 2001, have been accepted, modified, or rejected by both allies and adversaries. The same holds true for international and regional organizations.

As a whole, the chapters in Part 1 examine issues of enduring importance. By these accounts, change in the international security environment, when it occurs, is slow and uneven. Even in the case of Japan responding to the war on terror, pressure by the U.S. government and an increasing recognition of the threat environment resulted in a modification of the long-standing focus on human security rather than the wholesale revision of Japan's security posture. Further, with the exception of the implications of postindustrial development for the vulnerability of military powers, these issues do not generally attract the full attention of U.S. policymakers.

U.S. Policies and the Emerging Political Economy of Security

Part 2 focuses on changing U.S. policies vis-à-vis the political economy of security. The underlying assumption is that the challenge of global terrorist groups and rogue states seeking or potentially seeking weapons of mass destruction has altered the political, economic, and military strategies of the United States and thereby helped provoke change in the overall global security environment. On a range of issues the United States has shifted course in ways that may force other countries and international institutions to adapt their own policies and reconsider their own values.

Academic interest in U.S. grand strategy has revived in recent years in part due to the efforts of scholars like Barry Posen and Andrew Ross (1996–1997) to systematically explore the links between strategic choices and policy outcomes. As John Lewis Gaddis has recently argued, the Bush administration's September 2002 national security strategy "could be the most important reformulation of U.S. grand strategy in over half a century" (Gaddis 2002, p. 56). Nearly all efforts to analyze U.S. grand strategy, including recent contributions by Robert Art (2003) and innumerable others, pay relatively less attention to the economic dimensions of U.S. strategic choices than to the political and military implications. In this volume, however, Lars Skålnes, in Chapter 7, attempts to link the military-strategic components of U.S. strategy with their economic analogues. Working from a realist perspective on national and international security, Skålnes argues that in an era of primacy, "U.S. policymakers may not be able to integrate economics and security in statecraft." Why? Because in the relative absence of international threats, at least of the sort posed by a competing superpower, domestic politics will determine outcomes. If Skålnes is correct, current efforts to more closely link security and economic policies in order to wage the global war on terror are doomed to fail.

In Chapter 8, moving from the overarching U.S. strategic perspective to the specific policy instruments available to the U.S. government, Steven Hook and David Rothstein analyze U.S. participation in the contemporary global arms market. They focus on U.S. policies because the U.S. share of the global market meets or exceeds the combined shares of all other exporters. Specifically, they argue that since September 11, 2001, the United States has increased its security assistance to countries allied with itself or otherwise essential to fighting the war on terror. In the short term, arms sales shore up both friendly regimes and the domestic defense contractors being asked to invest in new weapons systems and technologies in a time of relatively low levels of defense spending.

For the rest of the world, these changes are critical. The United States, year in and year out, is the world's largest exporter of weapons. For other arms-producing states seeking to save their own domestic jobs and ensure the continued vitality of their own defense industrial sectors, the U.S. export drive is threatening. Russia is perhaps the prime example of this dynamic as it struggles to earn hard currency from arms exports while competing directly with U.S. arms producers.

For those countries and even terrorist groups facing adversaries armed with U.S. weapon systems, arms transfers can shift the power calculus. Here the commercial interests of U.S. defense firms appear to coincide with U.S. national security objectives. On the downside, the ever-increasing volume of weapons loose in the world, including not just U.S. exports but those of other countries as well, fuels the fires of many long-standing conflicts.

In Chapter 9, Sue Eckert examines how the U.S. government works with private firms to meet its security objectives[7] with regard to protecting the nation's critical infrastructure. With roughly 85 percent of critical U.S. infrastructure in private hands and the September 11, 2001, attacks graphically demonstrating the vulnerabilities of public and private facilities, private cooperation is a necessity in the post–September 11 world. Eckert recounts the important but seldom told story of how the Clinton and Bush administrations struggled to create a useful set of institutions and processes for facilitating public-private partnerships. In particular, she focuses on the promise and pitfalls of the Information Sharing and Analysis Centers (ISACs), which were created to assist with the "voluntary gathering, analyzing, and dissemination of information to and from infrastructure sectors and the federal government."

While focused on a U.S. case, Chapter 9 offers useful insights into the problems facing all advanced industrial societies in coping with terrorism. In particular, Eckert identifies "impediments to cooperation" between private enterprise and government entities that will be familiar to most involved in homeland security. They provide a useful starting point for developing policy solutions and guiding cross-national comparisons.

A Window on the Future

This first chapter in Part 3 challenges many theoretical and methodological orthodoxies and offers new ways for framing discussions about the international environment and looking to the future. In Chapter 10, one of the most provocative and innovative contributions to this volume, Mark Boyer and his colleagues at the GlobalEd project challenge readers to think about security through the eyes of the young. Using data from a series of surveys funded by the U.S. Department of Education, the authors explore how middle and high school students think about security. Surprisingly, they find evidence that today's youth have a much broader conception of security than most adults, including academic specialists in international affairs and national security. Especially noteworthy is their finding that economic security is high on the list of concerns for children.

How long such beliefs will hold and how they will affect individual and collective decisions as the young grow into adulthood remain to be seen. Boyer and colleagues argue there is persuasive evidence in the literature of socialization that early beliefs are enduring and will indeed influence political activities in the future. If their conclusions are accurate, we can look forward to the closer marriage of security and political economy issues as today's youth assume the mantle of leadership.

In Chapter 11, I revisit the themes explored in this volume to tease out the policy implications for the United States and other countries as the relationship between security and policy shifts still further, and as our understanding of the meaning of this shift advances. The focus on policy stems from a belief held by most of the contributors to this volume, a belief in "useable knowledge" and the need to bridge the gap between theory and practice, scholarship and policy analysis, that so often stymies efforts to improve people's lives in times of change, challenge, and stress.

Conclusion

The task of reintegrating security studies more closely with the subfield of international political economy is a long and uncertain process. Yet if Norrin

Ripsman is right, there is a great deal of hope, because even realist scholars have long recognized the importance of political economy. What is required is a better appreciation for the traditions of both security studies and international political economy as well as a certain amount of skepticism about claims that the two fields are seldom united.

This volume offers research demonstrating how fruitful such efforts can be. Much depends on developments in the "real" world of government policymaking and changing global structures and relationships. The continued evolution of long-term macro processes like economic globalization and more recent developments like the emergence of global terrorism are forcing policymakers, the military, corporate leaders, not to mention journalists and academics, to consider more seriously whether it was ever appropriate to treat economics and security as entirely separate spheres of human activity.

Notes

I would like to thank Ellen Frost and two anonymous reviewers for their suggestions and comments on earlier versions of this chapter. The views expressed here are mine alone; they do not necessarily represent those of the Naval War College, the U.S. Navy, the Department of Defense, or any other government agency or department.

1. Not to mention Marxists of all bents, including most prominently Lenin in his book *Imperialism: The Highest State of Capitalism.*

2. Chapter 2, Norrin Ripsman's contribution to this volume, presents an excellent summary of this literature, so the scholarly debates over the relationship between economics and security and the scholarly differences between the approaches of security studies and international economy will not be rehearsed here.

3. The late Susan Strange was one of the first and most impassioned observers of the different perceptions and scholarly interests of American academics and those from Europe and elsewhere. See, for one example, Strange 1983.

4. For particularly noteworthy examples of this vast literature, see Gilpin 1981; Ferguson and Mansbach 1996; and Castells 1996.

5. For various perspectives on global governance see, for example, Waltz 1999; Reinecke 1997; and Hirst and Thompson 1995.

6. For a set of articles dealing with many of the major issues associated with unipolarity, see Kapstein and Mastanduno 1999.

7. In this respect, Eckert's contribution bears a familial resemblance to Virginia Haufler's chapter on corporate conflict resolution.

2

False Dichotomies: Why Economics Is High Politics

Norrin M. Ripsman

As a result of globalization and the increasing salience of global terrorism, it is now commonplace for observers to assert that a sea change in the pursuit of national security has occurred (e.g., Cha 1999; Mandel 1999; Kugler and Frost 2001; Flynn 2002). Not only is the nature of security threats changing, these observers assert, but the traditional distinction between economics as "low politics" and national security as "high politics" is no longer appropriate (for a critical review of this emerging literature, see Ripsman and Paul 2005). After all, in the contemporary era, states must secure themselves in a variety of new ways, including interrupting the sources of terrorist financing, providing economic assistance to poorer areas to prevent them from becoming terrorist breeding grounds, and protecting vulnerable commercial and military networks from sabotage (see, e.g., van Creveld 1999, pp. 394–408; Ohmae 1994; and Lipschutz 2000).

In this chapter, I argue that such arguments, while not incorrect, overstate the degree to which economic considerations and national security were ever separable. Although the security studies literature has been dominated by the traditional distinction attributed to realists between high and low politics, this distinction has always been no more than a caricature of realism. It has been considerably overdrawn, even if one uses a narrow definition of security, for several reasons.[1] First, it ignores the economic underpinnings of military might and national security that many realists themselves acknowledge as essential components of national power. Second, it exaggerates the independence states have both from the international economy and from domestic political opposition when mobilizing economic resources in support of security objectives. Finally, it glosses over the potential for states to achieve national security objectives in an interdependent world economy by using economic instruments, such as economic sanctions and economic incentives.

This chapter systematically attacks the myth that economics do not affect national sovereignty and therefore must take a backseat to "security" matters. First I explore the sources of the realist hierarchy of issue areas. Next, drawing upon both the classical geopolitics literature and a growing contemporary literature on the political economy of security, I identify a unique set of "political economy" issues that have a direct bearing on national security calculations. I then demonstrate that even the classical realists who supposedly propagated the inaccurate hierarchy of issue areas and the neorealists who allegedly perpetuated it, acknowledge the economic underpinnings of security. Thus the conception of high politics and low politics that has defined the security studies literature is a mere caricature of realism that leading realists would disavow. Finally, I consider the implications of reintegrating economics and national security policy in the contemporary era of globalization and global terrorism.

The Hierarchy of Issue Areas

Political realists contend that, in an anarchic international system, in the absence of a central authority with an enforcement mechanism to regulate state behavior, states must be prepared to protect themselves from others who may have designs on their resources or territory. They must therefore arm and forge alliances in order to preserve their sovereignty. Since the threat of force and the potential for war are always present under anarchy, realists argue that national security and sovereignty protection take precedence over all other national goals, including the promotion of national wealth, the pursuit of ideological ambitions, or other social achievements. They assert, therefore, a hierarchy of issue areas. Matters of defense and national security merit the designation "high politics" and are privileged above all other economic, political, and social matters of state, which are designated "low politics" (for a discussion of this hierarchy of issue as a defining feature of realism, see Keohane and Nye 2001, p. 20). Thus, in Edward Hallett Carr's view, states do not quite face a "guns" versus "butter" dilemma. Economic welfare is a luxury that only secure states can afford:

> The question asked never takes the form, Do you prefer guns or butter? For everyone (except a handful of pacifists in those Anglo-Saxon countries which have inherited a long tradition of uncontested security) agrees that, in case of need, guns must come before butter. The question asked is always either, Have we already sufficient guns to enable us to afford some butter? or, Granted that we need x guns, can we increase revenue sufficiently to afford more butter as well? (1946, p. 119)

Perhaps because of its privileged position within the realist worldview, the security studies literature—more than any other subfield of international relations—has been dominated by political realism. As a result, economic considerations have traditionally received very little consideration by security theorists (see Mastanduno 1998, pp. 825–854; Blanchard, Mansfield, and Ripsman 1999, pp. 1–14; Kirshner 1998, pp. 64–91; and Kapstein 1992). Looking back on fifty years of research on security studies, for example, Michael Mastanduno observed that "the study of economic statecraft, and economic issues more generally, tended to be conducted separately from the study of military statecraft, and national security issues more generally" (1998, p. 826). And Jonathan Kirshner lamented that, as a result of the Cold War, "in contemporary International Relations theory, there exists a sharp distinction between international political economy and security studies" (1998, p. 64). As I shall demonstrate in the next section, however, this dismissal of political economic issues by the security studies community is unfortunate, since it ignores essential components of state power, several economic instruments that national security establishments have at their disposal, and important political economy dilemmas that they must face when mobilizing resources and manpower in pursuit of national security.

False Dichotomies: The Economic Underpinnings of National Security

Wealth and Military Power

The first and most fundamental problem with the traditional hierarchy of issue areas is that it ignores the economic roots of power. Mercantilists have long contended that "money is the sinews of war," because wealth converts rather fluidly into military power (Baldwin 1985, pp. 72–77; Earle 1986, pp. 217–261). In the age of divine-right monarchs employing mercenary armies, wealthier states could afford larger and better-equipped armies. With the introduction of national military conscription after the French Revolution, the size of a state's military apparatus no longer depended as directly on national wealth. Nonetheless, as Napoleon observed, "an army marches on its stomach" (van Creveld 1977, p. 40). The ability to feed, clothe, train, and equip the armed forces—all of which require economic resources—can play a decisive role in combat. Moreover, in the modern era, wealthier states tend to have more to invest in research and development of weapons technologies, which can yield a decisive advantage on the battlefield.

A state's ability to secure itself is not affected only by aggregate wealth. It also requires access to a wide array of resources (often called "strategic goods") and weapons that can enable it to sustain a war effort (on strategic goods see Culbertson 1924; Emeny 1936; Hessel, Murphy, and Hessel 1942; Staley 1937; Haglund 1986, pp. 221–240; and Blanchard and Ripsman 1996, pp. 225–246). These include foodstuffs, metals and minerals used in weapons production, oil and other fuels, and a wide range of other materials essential to sustaining agriculture, industry, and the military in wartime. They also require adequate supplies of labor, machinery, and infrastructure. Consequently, one of the most important dilemmas of "high politics" that states must face is an economic one: Should they attempt to produce as many of these strategic goods as possible domestically, by striving for autarky, or should they trade for them on the international market? The pursuit of autarky—to the extent that it is possible—entails both economic costs, since it promotes economic inefficiency, and strategic costs, since it requires the state to produce defense goods that it may not have the resources, infrastructure, or know-how to produce (see Milward 1965, 1977; and Staley 1937). (Consider, for example, the inferior-quality synthetic oil that Germany had to produce during World War II, due to its lack of domestic crude oil supplies, or the strategic costs that would accrue to a country like Canada if it produced its own fighter aircraft instead of purchasing state-of-the-art U.S.-built F-18s.) Trading for defense goods, though more economically efficient, is risky, however, since adversaries may be able to terminate shipments or interfere with deliveries from other states during wartime, like the German U-boat campaign did to Allied supply convoys in the Atlantic during the early phases of World War II.

The resource acquisition dilemma is part of a broader political economy dilemma with profound security implications: whether to organize the national economy in accordance with the principles of economic nationalism or those of economic liberalism (see Earle 1986, pp. 217–261; and Baldwin 1985, chap. 5). An economic nationalist strategy, designed to protect domestic industries from foreign competition through the use of both subsidies and trade barriers, may ensure that a defense industrial base exists to serve the national security effort when needed. It may also promote economic distortions and inefficiencies that reduce national wealth and can therefore hamper the pursuit of national security. An economic liberal strategy, based on the free market, specialization, and comparative advantage, helps to maximize national wealth and consequently the aggregate resources that the state can devote to national defense (see, e.g., Lake 1992, pp. 24–37). Nonetheless, a free market approach will also rationalize the economy. Consequently, it has the adverse effect of extinguishing uncompetitive national industries that produce defense-related goods less efficiently than do foreign suppliers, which means that the state cannot count on them to supply the war effort if it is cut off from international supplies.

National wealth, resource allocations, and the structure of economic activity can thus have important consequences for national security. Moreover, since no state—not even the United States or the Soviet Union after World War II—possesses all required resources within its national borders, no state is completely autonomous of the international market, which has profound implications for military strategy.

Trade Dependence and Military Strategy

Since all states depend on foreign trade at least to some degree, economic considerations can have a profound influence on national security policies in preparation for war and wartime military strategies. Much of the business of national security aims to acquire secure access to foreign resources that would not be interrupted in the event of war. Indeed, the primary purpose of colonization was to obtain exclusive ownership and control of overseas resources.[2] Similarly, states can prepare for war by tying the economies of smaller nearby states to their own in order to safeguard access to their exports. They can accomplish this by offering them extremely favorable terms of trade that could not be matched on the international market, as Nazi Germany did in southeastern Europe before World War II (Hirschman 1945). Alternatively, as Imperial Japan did in its "Co-Prosperity Sphere" in the 1930s, they could coerce smaller neighbors militarily or conquer them to guarantee access to their exports in the event of a broader war (Barnhart 1987). In a more benign fashion, states could forge military and economic alliances with key suppliers.

In wartime, trade dependence and the need to supply the war effort encourage military strategists to target the enemy's economic base as a complement to—or perhaps even a replacement for—battle preparations. As British strategist B. H. Liddell Hart argued, grand battles pitting the bulk of the combatants' forces against each other are physically, economically, and morally exhausting for both victor and vanquished. Conversely, an indirect approach, targeting the adversary's economic infrastructure—that is, supply lines, fuel depots, shipments of overseas strategic goods, and the like—can overcome both the enemy's will and capability to resist, thereby achieving victory more efficiently (Hart 1967, pp. 351–365). Thus, for example, a strategy of naval blockade—which aims to deny the adversary access to critical overseas strategic goods shipments—can paralyze the adversary's war effort (Mahan 1941, pp. 91–98). Indeed, the Allied victory in World War II was expedited by the wide British blockade of the North Sea, which deprived Germany of the food, oil, coal, and rubber it needed to continue fighting (Grebler and Winkler 1940, pp. 5–23). Similarly, the Germans nearly knocked the British out of World War II with their sustained submarine commerce-raiding campaign, targeting Allied supply convoys in the North Atlantic (Gretton 1977, pp. 128–140). Although it has not been used as effectively in a major war, the strategy of strategic bombing—bombing industrial sites, supply depots, infrastructure, and population centers behind enemy lines in an attempt to defeat the enemy without a decisive battle on the ground—is the airborne analog of naval blockade and commerce raiding (Brodie 1959, pp. 79–106; MacIsaac 1976; Pape 1996).[3]

To complement these physical measures to undermine the enemy's supply efforts, economic strategists can wage economic warfare. Economic warfare entails two broad categories of activities (Wu 1952; Milward 1977, chap.

9). First, national strategists can impose export embargoes to deny the enemy access to their own strategic resources and manufactures. Second, they can attempt to deprive the enemy of imports from neutral suppliers. Although, as Eugene Gholz and Daryl Press observe, neutral countries frequently benefit from supplying belligerents in war (2001, pp. 1–57), either they can be dissuaded from supplying the enemy through diplomatic and military pressure or their supplies can be diverted through preemptive buying.

Thus, far from being a trivial concern, economic considerations play a significant role in war-fighting strategy and doctrine, because states are not as autonomous of the international market as the security studies literature conventionally assumes.

The Political Economy of War Mobilization: Domestic Political Aspects

States are also not as autonomous domestically as the distinction between economics and high politics implies. Governments do not have automatic access to domestic resources; they must mobilize the money, manpower, industrial capacity, and materials necessary to sustain a war effort. They must ensure, however, that the domestic costs of war mobilization are not too onerous for the population or powerful societal groups, or they will risk a revolution, like those in Germany and Russia as a result of World War I, which will undermine national security goals (see Barnett 1992, pp. 3–4).[4]

National security establishments therefore face two political economy dilemmas of utmost importance. The first involves financing the war effort—the focus of the emerging field of defense economics (see, e.g., Hartley and Sandler 1995; and Kennedy 1983). Direct taxation, which can provide needed revenue without creating a burden of indebtedness, is the most reliable means of raising revenue. As the tax burden begins to bite, however, it can inspire domestic political opposition to the war effort and the government, thereby undermining the military effort. Conversely, debt financing, using both domestic and foreign debt instruments, offers the advantage of tapping into voluntary suppliers of capital. In the event of a long and costly war, though, debt financing can lead to a heavy burden of indebtedness that ultimately saps state power (Kapstein 1992, pp. 16–19). This is an important reason for the British and French decline after the two world wars, when they became mired in debt to the United States.

The second dilemma involves raising the manpower, matériel, and industrial contribution to fuel the security apparatus. States can do so within the context of existing state-society relations, by using their existing power resources and policy instruments to levy what they can for the war effort. Such an "accommodational strategy" entails the fewest political costs for the state, but, as Michael Barnett observes, it is frequently unable to satisfy all the state's national security requirements during a severe crisis. Thus, states are frequently compelled to pursue "restructural strategies" that alter state-society relations in order to generate a greater domestic contribution to national defense. Either the state can coercively increase its power vis-à-vis society in order to extract a greater contribution, or it can negotiate further limits on state power in exchange for the even larger voluntary contribution it can obtain through liberalization. Coercion, of course, is risky, since it can lead to both domestic resistance and inefficiency. Liberalization, though, erodes state capacity and therefore constrains a state's ability to mobilize for future wars. Thus, Barnett observes that the autonomy of the Egyptian and Israeli national security executives eroded as a result of the domestic political bargains they struck between the 1967 and 1973 Arab-Israeli wars (Barnett 1992).[5]

Thus, war mobilization, the quintessential exercise of "high politics," is fundamentally dependent on matters of political economy that the security studies literature wishes to consign to the category of "low politics." But some authors (Trubowitz 1998; Fordham 1998; Solingen 1998; Narizny 2003b; Nolt 1997) go even further, arguing that not only is the state's ability to respond to international threats dependent on domestic political economic factors, but even the way it defines the national interest is a product of the underlying economic interests of society. They contend that key economic interests and sectors compete for the direction of the ship of state to advance their own political and economic interests. What they perceive as a threat, whom they perceive as friend and foe, and how they adapt their grand strategies to respond will therefore be determined not only by the politics of the international system, but also by the composition of the ascendant domestic political coalition.[6] Thus, although others (e.g., Lobell 2003; Rowe 1999b) argue that domestic coalitional politics are themselves largely the product of international factors and therefore not properly seen as isolated domestic matters, it may be difficult to distance "high" politics from its "low" politics roots.[7]

The dependence of states on both domestic support and international sources of supply in order to meet their security needs not only complicates war mobilization and military strategy, it also creates opportunities for states to achieve their strategic goals through economic statecraft rather than military force. If states can manipulate economic interdependence by deepening international economic ties, imposing economic sanctions, or offering economic inducements, they can create incentives for others to behave consistently with their security objectives.

Interdependence and International Conflict

Commercial liberals maintain that when economic interdependence between states is high, the likelihood that they will use force to settle their differences declines (Blainey 1988, chap. 2; Angell 1933; Keohane 1990, pp. 186–187). Their argument is that, when trade and investment flow freely across national boundaries, the opportunity costs of war in terms of economic exchange are so high as to make war an unattractive option.[8] Furthermore, trade is more efficient than force as a means of extracting resources and wealth from territory, especially since nationalism and modern technology make conquest unprofitable in the contemporary era (for a dissenting view, see Liberman 1996). Thus, they conclude that liberal states can attain their national security objectives economically rather than militarily, by erecting a liberal international trading regime.

Although there has been a spate of recent tests of the commercial liberal claim, there is still insufficient empirical evidence either to support or to refute it. Some quantitative studies have indeed shown a powerful link between interdependence and reduced international conflict (Oneal, Oneal, and Maoz 1996, pp. 11–28; Oneal and Russett 1999, pp. 1–37; Oneal and Russett 1997, pp. 267–293; Polachek 1980, pp. 55–78). Other empirical studies—both quantitative and qualitative—however, show either no clear relationship between interdependence and conflict (Barbieri 1996, pp. 29–49; Ripsman and Blanchard 1996–1997, pp. 4–50) or even some support for the neorealist counterclaim (Waltz 1979, p. 138) that economic interdependence can actually promote interstate conflict (Barbieri 1996; Gasiorowski 1986, pp. 23–38). Still others maintain that intervening variables, such as future trade expectations, the domestic regime types of the trading partners, or their membership in preferential trading institutions, determine the effect that interdependence has on conflict (see, for example, Copeland 1995, pp. 5–41; Papayoanou 1995, pp. 42–76; Mansfield, Pevehouse, and Bearce 2000, pp. 92–118).

These discrepant findings may be explained by the lack of consistency with which these studies operationalize the variable "economic interdependence" (see Ripsman and Blanchard 2000, pp. 57–85; Blanchard and Ripsman 2001, pp. 95–127; and Blanchard and Ripsman 1996, pp. 225–246). According to Robert O. Keohane and Joseph S. Nye, interdependence is characterized not merely by economic interconnectedness, but also by economic relations that are mutually costly to break. States are *vulnerable* if they would suffer significant long-term costs if normal economic relations were to be disrupted, but only *sensitive* if policy options are available to them that would mitigate long-term costs (Keohane and Nye 2001, pp. 8–19; Jones 1984, pp. 17–63; Blanchard and Ripsman 1996, pp. 225–246).[9] In other words, economic interdependence refers to the importance of economic relations to national economies and the magnitude of costs that would accrue in the event of their termination. Most of the empirical tests of commercial liberalism, however, use different measures of either sensitivity or mere interconnectedness—including trade as a percentage of gross domestic product, aggregate bilateral trade, foreign investment as a percentage of national income, and the share of foreign currencies as percentage of a state's total reserves (see, e.g., Polachek 1980, pp. 55–78; Gasiorowski and Polachek 1986, pp. 709–729; Domke 1988; de Vries 1990, pp. 429–444; Mansfield and Bronson 1997, pp. 94–107; Oneal, Oneal, and Maoz 1996, pp. 11–28; and Barbieri, 1996, pp. 29–49)—that are not materially equivalent, nor do they fully capture the essence of economic interdependence.[10] Others include measures of the strategically more significant vulnerability interdependence (Gasiorowski 1986, pp. 23–38; Ripsman and Blanchard 1996–1997, pp. 4–50). It is difficult to reconcile the results obtained using these very different independent variables, and clearly, more carefully coordinated research is needed (for a concerted attempt to fill this gap, see Mansfield and Pollins 2003). Nonetheless, it remains plausible that international economic exchange may have some effect on national security decisions.

Economic Sanctions

The condition of economic interdependence gives national security executives another policy tool: they can threaten or impose economic sanctions on another state in order to alter its security policies. Indeed some of the recent applications of economic sanctions have had explicit security goals, including to punish states for testing nuclear weapons (India and Pakistan in 1998), to prevent rogue states, such as Iraq, from obtaining nuclear capability, to contain or terminate regional conflicts (the UN strategy in West Africa), and to punish aggression (UN sanctions against Iraq in 1990) (on these and other episodes, see Cortright, Lopez, and Gerber 2002). Economic sanctions entail a disruption of ordinary economic relations—for example, a reduction in financial aid or loans, restrictions on foreign trade or investment, or the seizure of assets—in order to compel a target state to comply with political demands. Sanctions are designed to operate in two ways. First, they impose economic costs on the target state and its leadership, thereby creating international economic incentives to modify its policies.[11] Second, they cause domestic economic deprivation in the target state, thereby generating domestic political pressure for the target government to comply with the sanctioner's demands, or perhaps domestic efforts to overthrow the existing government and replace it with one that will comply (Losman 1979, p. 1; Pape 1997, pp. 90–136, esp. pp. 93–94).

As with commercial liberalism, empirical tests have yielded conflicting conclusions about the efficacy of economic sanctions. Some researchers, such as Gary Hufbauer, Jeffrey Schott, and Kimberly Elliott, conclude that sanctions can achieve their stated purposes as frequently as 35 percent of the time (see Hufbauer, Schott, and Elliott 1990; Doxey 1987; and Daoudi and Dajani 1983). Their optimism is bolstered by high-profile cases of apparent sanctions success, such as Western sanctions against the South African apartheid regime. Moreover, as David Baldwin argues, sanctions can achieve important political objectives—such as deterring third parties from taking unwelcome actions—even if they fail to achieve their stated purposes (Baldwin 1985, pp. 130–144; Lindsay 1986, pp. 153–173).[12] Conversely, studies by Robert Pape and others maintain that economic sanctions are rarely effective at achieving important security objectives; when they do appear to "succeed," it is usually an artifact of either military or political pressure or the insignificance of the demands made (Pape 1997, pp. 90–136; Haass 1997, pp. 74–85; Knorr 1977a, pp. 99–126; Galtung 1967, pp. 378–416). Sanctions pessimists further justify their skepticism with reference to high-profile failures, such as the forty-year U.S. sanctions regime against Cuba and the twelve-year international sanctions regime that failed to bring about either compliance or political change in Iraq. A third group of scholars occupies the middle ground, arguing that sanctions succeed only when the right international and domestic political conditions are present (Blanchard and Ripsman 1999, pp. 228–264; Kirshner 1997, pp. 32–64) or when the sanctioner possesses enough economic power to impose heavy economic costs on the target state.[13]

Despite this muddled empirical record, the increasing use of economic sanctions by the United States and the international community in the post–Cold War era—both in place of and in tandem with traditional military and political instruments—indicates that the realms of economics and security are integrally linked.

Economic Incentives

In addition to coercive economic sanctions, the need for states to reach beyond their borders to finance and supply war also presents an opportunity for national security establishments to purchase security with economic incentives and foreign aid.[14] These incentives can take two forms. Short-term trade, financial, or technology transfers can be exchanged for immediate and limited policy changes in a sort of quid pro quo with the target government (Drezner 1999, pp. 188–218). Alternatively, longer-term preferential trading arrangements can be extended in the hope of influencing the target state's policies in the medium to long term. In the latter case, the "influence effect" occurs over time, as domestic groups in the target develop vested interests in continuing the economic relationship and pressure the government to avoid policies that endanger it (Hirschman 1945, pp. 14–40; Abdelal and Kirshner 1999, pp. 119–156; Long 1996, pp. 77–106; Newnham 2002). Both these strategies offer the target state a reward for compliance, rather than a punishment for noncompliance; therefore, they can, in principle, achieve their purposes without engendering the hostility and resistance that economic sanctions can inspire (Baldwin 1971, pp. 19–39). Moreover, an incentives regime is relatively easy to maintain, since third parties have no incentives to interfere, as they do with economic sanctions.[15]

Very little systematic empirical testing has been conducted on the efficacy of economic incentives (see Baldwin 1989, chaps. 4, 7). The research that has been done, however, demonstrates that it is much more difficult to achieve important political objectives with incentives than it is with coercive economic and political instruments (see especially Drezner 1999, pp. 188–218). Two recent episodes, however, provide some evidence that economic inducements may indeed serve national security purposes. The inclusion of economic incentives to cement the Bosnian peace accord indicates that economic payoffs can help stabilize a civil war (Väyrynen 1997, pp. 155–181). And the U.S. and Japanese use of financial and technological incentives to forestall the construction of a weapons-grade nuclear facility by the government of North Korea was able to contain North Korean nuclear aspirations, at least for a few years (Snyder 1997, pp. 55–82; Newnham 2003). Thus, under the right circumstances, economic statecraft may be able to contribute quite a bit to the pursuit of national security.

Realist Writings and the Political Economy of National Security

To this point, I have demonstrated the inappropriateness of the false dichotomy between economics and high politics that dominates the security studies literature, since economic factors play a central role in matters of security and defense. In this section, I will show that even realists have recognized the economic underpinnings of security and identified them clearly in their writings.[16]

To begin with, the same classical realists and geopoliticians who are said to have privileged national security over economics nonetheless identified national wealth and industrial capacity as a component of national power. In his seminal discussion of "the elements of national power," for example, Hans Morgenthau lists natural resources and industrial capacity as essential prerequisites of great power status (Morgenthau 1985, pp. 130–139; Organski and Kugler 1980, chap. 2; Knorr 1977b, pp. 183–199; Knorr 1973; Jones 1971, pp. 164–186). John Mearsheimer, recognizing that "the more resources a state has at its disposal, the more likely it is to prevail in war," considers wealth an important building block of "latent power," which may be harnessed by the state to build military power (2001, pp. 57–82). And Fareed Zakaria observes that wealth not only allows states to pursue broader security interests, but also conditions national leaders to do so (1998).

In this regard, the proponents of realist power transition and hegemonic war theory contend that the engine that drives the competition for hegemony in the international system is the differential economic growth rates of the great powers. As the leading state of the international system maintains its

global interests, the economic burden of overextension serves as a drag on its power. Meanwhile, challengers—who are not economically overextended—may emerge to vie for leadership of the international system as a result of a growth of their population, industrial capacity, wealth, and military might. The result is frequently a hegemonic war (see Gilpin 1981; Organski and Kugler 1980; and Kennedy 1987). Thus, for realists, the determinants of relative power and military conflict—the bread and butter of high politics—are often economic.

Structural realists, or neorealists, also implicitly accept the economic foundations of military power in their debate with liberals over the difficulty of international cooperation. Liberals maintain that international economic cooperation is possible and even likely, as states will recognize that they all stand to gain. Neorealists reject this liberal view that international politics and economics are positive games. Instead, they contend that cooperation in international politics is difficult, even in matters of "low politics," such as trade or investment, because states seek relative gains, as opposed to absolute gains. They do so, neorealists argue, because of the security externalities of trade and investment. Since the gains of economic exchange are distributed unevenly and since increased wealth leads to increased power, states are unwilling to allow potential competitors in an anarchic environment to gain at their expense (Grieco 1988, pp. 485–507; Mearsheimer 1994–1995, pp. 10–11). For this reason, Joanne Gowa maintains that trade is most likely to flow within alliances, rather than across them, and is likely to be higher when the polarity of the international system dissuades alliance defection so that states do not need to fear that the security externalities of economic exchange will be used to benefit a rival alliance (1994).

Thus, even realists recognize that national security is at least partially rooted in economics. Indeed, a careful reading of the leading realist scholars would put the false dichotomy to rest. Morgenthau, for example, writes that "it is necessary to distinguish between, say, economic policies that are undertaken for their own sake and economic policies that are the instruments of a political policy—a policy, that is, whose economic purpose is but the means to the end of controlling the policies of another nation." Such economic policies "must be judged primarily from the point of view of their contribution to national power" (1985, p. 36). Carr similarly took pains to debunk the "illusory separation of politics from economics." To this end, he commented, "The contrast is not one between 'power' and 'welfare,' and still less between 'politics' and 'economics,' but between different degrees of power" (1946, pp. 119–120). Waltz thus concludes that "the distinction frequently drawn between matters of high and low politics is misplaced. States use economic means for military and political ends; and military and political means for the achievement of economic interests" (1979, p. 94). And in his treatise on offensive realism, Mearsheimer affirms:

Survival is the number one goal of great powers according to my theory. In practice, however, states pursue non-security goals as well. . . . Offensive realism certainly recognizes that great powers might pursue these non-security goals, but it has little to say about them, save for one important point: states can pursue them as long as the requisite behavior does not conflict with balance-of-power logic, which is often the case. Indeed, the pursuit of these non-security goals sometimes complements the hunt for power. . . . Furthermore, greater economic prosperity invariably means greater wealth, which has significant implications for security, because wealth is the foundation of military power. (2001, p. 46)

Clearly, the dominant interpretation of the hierarchy of issue areas represents a misreading of realism and therefore a distortion. Realists do prioritize matters of national security and sovereignty. But this does not necessarily consign all matters of economics, the environment, or social policy to the basket of "low politics." Instead, realists treat any instrument or policy that may affect national security ends as matters of "high politics" (for a recent realist statement of this position, see Miller 2001, pp. 13–42).

The Economic Roots of National Security in an Age of Globalization and Global Terrorism

Recognizing that economics and national security are heavily intertwined, there are several features of the contemporary era that shape the political economy of national security in the twenty-first century: the phenomenon of globalization, the changing nature of warfare, and the rise of global terrorism.[17]

The contemporary era has been labeled one of globalization, where the scale of economic activity transcends the nation-state and is organized on a global scale.[18] Economic globalization basically refers to two parallel phenomena that have increased in magnitude since World War II. The first is economic interdependence, which I have already discussed. The second, which poses a different set of challenges for the national security apparatus, is transnationalism, which refers to the increased ease with which goods, services, and business entities can cross national boundaries due to revolutionary advances in communication and transportation technologies (see Frieden and Rogowski 1996, pp. 26–27).[19] The increasingly transnational organization of economic activity in the contemporary era should have profound implications for national sovereignty and national security policy. While much has been written on transnationalism's assault on sovereignty and national autonomy in the economic realm, very little research has been done to date on its implications for national security.[20] It stands to reason, however, that as corporate investment, decisionmaking, production, marketing, and sales take place across national borders and involve shareholders, managers, and laborers from multiple countries, the ability of states to pursue the economic nationalist/autarkic security policies discussed above erodes. After all, what constitutes a *national* defense company that should be cultivated and protected to ensure an adequate national defense supply base in case of war? One that operates on national territory, even if it is largely foreign-owned, or one that is nationally owned but operates abroad with foreign managers and workers? (For a similar point, see Reich 1990, pp. 53–64.) Thus, in a globalized world, states often have less control over the production and distribution of defense-related goods and technologies than do multinational corporations (Goldblatt et al. 1997, pp. 277–279).

Furthermore, the growing dependence of the military and the civilian economy on computer technology and the increasing speed with which people, goods, services, and information cross borders create a host of new national security concerns with which states must deal. These include enhanced risks of terrorism, electronic sabotage, and large-scale illegal immigration (see, e.g., van Creveld 1999, pp. 394–408; Mandel 1999; Rosso 1995, pp. 175–207; and Weiner 1994, pp. 394–412). As a result, states must increasingly define national security goals in terms of economics. In particular, they must protect their commercial networks from infiltration and sabotage; they must monitor a growing amount of interstate commercial transactions to prevent illegal money laundering and the transfer of money and deadly weapons to the hands of terrorists or rogue states; they must be more vigilant at international borders and transportation centers to prevent the smuggling of human cargo and explosives; and they must persuade people worldwide that it is safe to conduct business, lest terrorist groups and other international outlaws paralyze the global economy with fear.[21] Thus, some, such as Stephen Flynn (2002), contend that national security activities in the contemporary era must consist of data mining, trade inspections at border crossings, commerce protection, and the issuance of tamper-proof identity cards.

Moreover, in the post–September 11, 2001, environment, when not only the United States but also the Western world in general and other states—such as Russia and China—face global terrorism as their principal threat, national security becomes a matter of winning hearts and minds, rather than one of defeating traditional foes on the battlefield. The economic dimension of counterterrorism is therefore considerable (Livingstone 1989, pp. 77–106; Crenshaw 1990, pp. 113–126). In addition to locating and tracking down terrorist groups, national security establishments must also try to counter the appeal of terrorism, which means that, where appropriate, they must help to improve the economic circumstances of disaffected populations.[22] In this regard, the wealthy industrialized countries must not only increase foreign aid to the breeding grounds of global terrorism, but also encourage less corrupt governments in these regions that will allow economic assistance to reach those most in need. For, as Samuel Huntington contends, "governments that fail to meet the basic welfare and economic needs of their peoples and suppress their liberties generate violent opposition to themselves and to Western governments that support them" (quoted in Mousseau 2002–2003, p. 7). Furthermore, they must provide like-minded governments in these regions with the economic and technological means to monitor local groups of extremists and combat local terrorist cells. Finally, they must use economic incentives and economic sanctions to reward regional governments that assist in the fight against terrorism by restructuring their economies to reduce radical socioeconomic inequalities and prod along those who do not (see Cronin 2002–2003, pp. 30–58, esp. pp. 56–57).

Thus the economic dimensions of security have maintained importance in the twenty-first century and have grown more complex. Clearly, it would be a gross error to cling to the traditional distinction between economics and high politics in the modern world.

Conclusion: An Increasingly Inappropriate Distortion

Even with a minimalist, traditional definition of national security, the distinction between national security as "high politics" and economic affairs as "low politics" is artificial and inappropriate. States are not as autonomous from either the international market or the domestic political economy as they would have to be for this distinction to be useful. They are dependent on the international market for many of the resources and weapons, as well as much of the financial resources needed to safeguard national security. They also cannot take domestic resources for granted when mobilizing for defense, lest they engender a domestic revolt that could undermine national security to a greater degree. Consequently, the political economy of defense mobilization is of utmost importance to national security policy. Furthermore, national dependence on international sources of supply and the domestic political economy creates the potential to achieve security goals through economic means, such as economic sanctions, incentives, or the deepening of international trade. Thus economic considerations can be central to the pursuit of national security in the contemporary era of globalization and new security threats, as they have been in earlier eras.

As we have seen, though, political realists and neorealists did not actually intend to divorce economics and national security. Instead, they acknowledged that wealth promotes military power and that economic policy can complement defense policy. Thus the realist hierarchy of issue areas has been greatly exaggerated by the security studies literature to exclude economic matters, which has led to an unwarranted dismissal of the political economy of national security. As a result, the "reemergence" of the political economy of security in the post–Cold War era is not as novel or radical a departure as we may be led to believe.

Notes

This research was supported by research grants from the Social Sciences and Humanities Research Council of Canada and the Quebec government's Fonds pour la Formation de Chercheurs et l'Aide à la Recherche. I thank Peter Dombrowski, Eugene Gholz, Korina Kagan, Colin Kahl, T. V. Paul, and participants at the workshop "The Political Economy of the New Security Environment," Watson Institute, Brown University, Providence, R.I., May 2003, for their helpful comments on earlier drafts of this chapter. I also thank Héloise Blondy, Richard Choi, and Kate Muller for their research assistance.

1. For the case that security must be interpreted narrowly so as to include only threats to national sovereignty and matters of war and peace, see Walt 1991; and Miller 2001. Others (Dixon 1994; Ayoob 1997; Klare and Thomas 1994) argue, however, that the concept of security must be broadened to include economic and ecological threats, as well as threats to individuals and groups.

2. Eugene Staley (1937, pp. 24–26) observes, however, that control of resources is less important than access. Therefore, since the enemy can blockade shipments from colonial possessions during wartime, colonial resources a state possesses may be less valuable than those it purchases from a neighboring ally or neutral supplier.

3. It is possible that modern technology has made strategic bombing more effective, as suggested by two campaigns against Iraq and the war against Serbia.

4. As these revolutions demonstrate, state autonomy from domestic attitudes in the national security realm does not depend solely on regime type. Even authoritarian states can be dependent on key domestic groups. Conversely, even democratic states can be autonomous of domestic opposition in matters of national security (see Ripsman 2002).

5. Barnett suggests a third option, "an international strategy," which pertains more directly to war financing, as I discuss above.

6. Kevin Narizny (2003a) is more nuanced, arguing that domestic economic interests constrain strategic responses, rather than define the threat situation.

7. I (Ripsman 2002) also contend that, in high-threat situations, domestic interests tend to defer to national security policy executives, which minimizes the impact of domestic political economic squabbling over policy.

8. This, of course, presumes that war necessarily interrupts economic relations between combatants. For a recent study that suggests otherwise, see Barbieri and Levy 1999.

9. For the argument that only mutual vulnerability can be considered interdependence, see Baldwin 1980; and Waltz 1970.

10. Such measures may indicate the magnitude of a state's exposure, but not the actual costs that would accrue in the event of a disruption, since they do not consider the availability of alternate sources of supply or the importance of the goods traded (Blanchard and Ripsman 1996).

11. This is especially the case with targeted economic sanctions that aim to impose costs on the leadership of the target state and not its population (Cortright and Lopez 2002).

12. Indeed, publicly stated objectives may amount to no more than a smokescreen concealing the true purposes of sanctions. In his reexamination of British sanctions against Rhodesia, for example, David Rowe (1999a) indicates that British leaders had not in fact desired to topple Ian Smith's regime with their oil embargo. Instead, they had merely wanted to send a signal of resolve to the African members of the British Commonwealth that would not be so strong as to invite retaliation from South Africa.

13. Kim Nossal (1994), for example, argues that only great powers can expect to influence target state behavior with economic sanctions.

14. For a recent study focusing on the use of economic incentives in the high politics area, see Bernauer and Ruloff 1999.

15. Third parties can often supply sanctioned states at better-than-market prices, which can defeat a sanctions regime (Crumm 1995).

16. Of course, economic and political liberals have long recognized that economics and security are intertwined. That is why Adam Smith recognized that a wealthy nation is also a secure nation and the Manchester liberals assumed that free trade would reduce international conflict (see Earle 1986; and Dawson 1926). Since realist writings have dominated the security literature, this section will confine itself to a discussion of realists who challenge the alleged hierarchy of issue areas.

17. My purpose here is not to examine all of the changes that globalization and modernity bring to the pursuit of national security. Instead, my focus is on how globalization both complicates and increases the importance of the *economic* dimension of national security. For a broader discussion of the impact of globalization on the pursuit of security, see Cha 1999.

18. This definition of globalization is both an economic one and a spatial one, drawing on Frieden and Rogowski 1996, pp. 25–27; Goldblatt et al. 1997, pp. 269–285; Cerny 1995; and Cha 1999, p. 392. There are also political definitions of globalization focusing on the ability of the state to adjust to economic changes, social definitions, which assess the winners and losers in a globalized world, and cultural definitions, which define globalization in terms of changing identities (see Hülsemeyer 2003, pp. 3–4).

19. For more political definitions of transnationalism, see Keohane and Nye 1973; and Risse-Kappen 1995.

20. Some notable exceptions include Cha 1999; Kugler and Frost 2001; van Creveld 1999; and Mandel 1994. It should be noted, however, that the predictions of this emerging literature do not fully conform to the experience of national security apparatus in the 1990s and 2000s (Ripsman and Paul 2003).

21. The impact of the September 11, 2001, terrorist attacks is instructive in this regard. Not only did they hurt global stock prices immediately, but over the longer term they also devastated the international airline industry—sending some national airlines into bankruptcy—damaged consumer confidence, and sent shock waves through the global economy.

22. Of course, since the majority of the September 11 bombers were from Saudi Arabia, a rather wealthy country, the link between poverty and terrorism might be exaggerated (see Mousseau 2002–2003, esp. pp. 7–8; and Pipes 2001–2002). Moreover, billionaire Osama bin Laden is also not waging his war against the West for economic reasons. Nonetheless, it seems plausible that Al-Qaida's appeal would diminish among much of the Islamic world if the region's poor were not to perceive as sharp an income gap between themselves and the Western world.

PART 1

Political Economy and International Security: New Intersections

3

The Economic Foundations of Military Power

Emily O. Goldman and Leo J. Blanken

The fundamental premise of national security studies is the privileged position of the state as the key purveyor of violence. Commonly, the very form of the nation-state is justified as the unit of political organization that achieves the most efficient economy of scale for generating violence (Bean 1973; Vries 2002). Since the 1970s, advances in information, communication, and transportation technologies, and the process of globalization they foster, have reduced the comparative advantages enjoyed by states in accumulating wealth and power and monopolizing the means of destruction. Seen from this vantage point, the events of September 11, 2001, are one of the most vivid examples of the empowered nonstate actor,[1] particularly because the events fall within the security domain. A nonstate group inflicted a level of destruction normally associated with a state without donning the other encumbrances of that political organizational form. Predictions that terrorists might one day acquire weapons of mass destruction foreshadow even greater nonstate empowerment.

Terrorism is not a new phenomenon, but it has assumed a more devastating scope. More Americans were killed in the attacks on the World Trade Center than in two separate Iraq wars with one of the largest conventional armies in the world. That nonstate actors are relatively invulnerable to common tools of deterrence and defense, while the economic infrastructure that underwrites state power has become more vulnerable, has fueled claims that in the information age, technology is eclipsing the territorial state.

Have globalization and information technology altered the distribution of capabilities for violence, empowering nonstate actors like terrorist and criminal organizations? Are the economies, societies, and militaries of highly networked, high-tech-dependent countries more vulnerable to disruption and destruction because their critical infrastructures are networked through computers? Does information technology favor organizational forms that hierarchical state bureaucracies find difficult to adopt?

It is premature to declare that the information age has supplanted the industrial age, in the way that the age of agriculture passed into history with the emergence of new sources of energy, like steam and electricity, derived from fossil fuels. However, information has become a much larger part of the mix of resources—along with land, labor, and capital—for generating wealth and power. The questions are whether the links between economic power, the capacity to do harm, and vulnerability have been altered in important ways today in light of the informational underpinnings of advanced societies, and whether long-standing relationships between economic capacity and military capability still hold. Are once-impotent adversaries being transformed into formidable foes?[2]

We argue that nonstate actors possess some distinct advantages over nation-states, such as their invulnerability to common tools of coercion. Yet they sacrifice the ability to sustain an effective attack even against the soft and inviting targets of modern urban society. There is a difference between producing and sustaining destruction. The informational infrastructure of modern societies, economies, and militaries produces vulnerabilities for states, yet the very infrastructure that makes states vulnerable is necessary in order for states to sustain modern military operations. Although changes in the relationship between economics and security in the information age have empowered nonstate actors, states retain distinctive advantages because of, rather than in spite of, the economic infrastructure that supports their power.

To make our case, we compare the relationship between economic capability and military power in the industrial and information ages. We examine how the information age has affected warfare, and the conditions under which states retain their advantages in waging war. Because we are situated precisely at the transition between the industrial and information ages, the ability of organizations to adapt is critical. In this area states suffer some disadvantages, but these are not debilitating. We evaluate the factors affecting the military potential of states and nonstates and conclude that lack of sustainability means that nonstate actors can only punish a state's vulnerable socioeconomic targets, not erode its preeminence as the modal political unit in the foreseeable future.

Economic Capability and Military Power in the Industrial Age

Our understanding of the relationship between economic capability and military power was established in the context of a system dominated by state actors. Security studies approaches have been shaped by the subfield's privileging of the externally sovereign Westphalian state and its counterpart, the internally sovereign governmental state, as the most important units of analysis. This partiality is grounded in historical reality: for 500 years states have reserved to themselves the right to carry out large-scale public violence, and private actors have rarely possessed significant military means (Spruyt 2002). Current leading approaches to the study of military power in the international relations subfield remain grounded in the state.

Economic power does not translate directly into military power, but the material basis of military strength has traditionally been a starting point for assessments of military potential, and economic capacity has been treated as a necessary condition for the ability to inflict significant harm since the advent of the industrial age.[3] Paul Kennedy observed in 1987 the strong correlation between the productive and revenue-raising capacities of states and their military strength (p. xvi).

Kennedy's remarks echo the neomercantilist proposition that economic capacity is a core foundation of military power (Dorn 1963, p. 7; Heckscher 1936; Viner 1948).[4] Large-scale modern warfare in the industrial age, best exemplified by the two world wars, illustrates the mercantilist position. Prevailing in lengthy wars of attrition depended not only upon the military forces a state could initially muster but also upon its ability to mobilize the underlying economic and industrial capacity of the state to produce combat power during war. War was not just a military conflagration but also a contest among entities that strove to understand and exploit the relationship between combat and economics.

The rise of the state itself as a form of political organization is largely viewed through the lens of war. Empires were too busy with coercion to provide a sound economic base, and city-states were too busy focusing on economic gain to provide adequate protection. Nation-states carried the field by balancing the twin tasks of coercion and capital accumulation (Tilly 1990, pp. 22–29). States survive by waging wars, and wars are expensive. States generated revenue by taxing their subjects, or by borrowing. Whatever the sovereign's choice, robust economies are to be preferred to weak ones; a healthy economy is a source of power, and is therefore also a target (see Chapter 2).

Tangible economic assets, like volume of gross national product or size of defense industry, of course yield only a partial understanding of a state's military capacity. Intangibles, like a state's organizational ability and administrative competence to efficiently employ the resources at its disposal, are crucial, as are superior training and morale, which often compensate for inferior weaponry (van Creveld 1991, chap. 20). Countries also differ in their will to achieve military strength, and in the ability of leaders to impose costs on society (Milward 1977). Finally, the strategic environments of countries place different demands on armed forces (Geyer 1986). Even if a country possesses a comparatively small economy and weak technological base, these may still be sufficient for defending its territory from neighbors that are similarly equipped.

With the dawn of the nuclear age, the concept of economic "war potential" lost its relevance, because modern weapons had made wars of attrition a thing of the past. The prospect of massive nuclear strikes and counterstrikes epitomized initial mobilization advantage and made all discussions of subsequent mobilization moot. Rather than discard the concept of war potential entirely, Klaus Knorr (1978) argued for adapting it to current conditions. The logic of mutual deterrence moved the locus of conflict below the nuclear level, and as the Cold War superpowers embarked on an arms race, the ability of the economy to sustain peacetime mobilization to support defense potential became critical. The concept of "defense potential" focused on a wider spectrum of defense efforts, including the ability to sustain a peacetime military establishment and to recover from a nuclear attack. Only the most robust economy could develop and produce large numbers of complex weapons systems, while only the most prescient planners could at the same time address the vulnerability of the economic and social base.

If a shift from agricultural to industrial modes of production altered the foundations of military power, then logically, the shift from the industrial to the postindustrial age should affect how international actors leverage different types of resources to increase their potential to inflict harm. By the end of the Cold War, for example, it appeared as if the Soviet Union had reached a high level of industrial maturity. In one key indicator of industrial capacity, steel production, the Soviet Union was producing 160 million tons per year in 1985, as compared to 74 million tons produced by the United States. Still, in the 1980s, even Soviet military strategists realized that their country could not keep pace with the West and began writing about a military-technical revolution that they believed was under way in the West.

The information age is altering the economic foundations of modern advanced societies, while globalization has dramatically increased international flows of goods, services, people, and money, improving access to information, technology, and their military applications. The information age presents new opportunities for states, but also new targets of vulnerability that can be exploited by empowered nonstate actors.[5]

Economic Capability and Military Power in the Information Age

The relationship between wealth and power has changed as societies transition to the information age. Manuel Castells argues that technology does not determine society but that "the ability or inability of societies to master technology, and particularly technologies that are strategically decisive in each historical period, largely shapes their destiny, to the point where we could say that while technology *per se* does not determine historical evolution and social change, technology (or the lack of it) embodies the capacity of societies to transform themselves" (1996, p. 7).

Socioeconomic change creates new military capabilities that can shift the relative influence of international actors (Organski 1958, 1968; Organski and Kugler 1980). Industrialization changed the pool of critical resources available to states, the capacity of states to utilize the human and material resources they possessed, and hence their capacity to wage war effectively. It dramatically increased the level of productivity that could be extracted from any given population and hence the capacity of states to generate wealth and wage war. Those states with a larger working- and fighting-age fraction of their total population could realize more productivity from industrial technology, become more powerful, and wage war more effectively (Organski and Kugler 1980, pp. 8–9, 33). As industrial technologies and practices diffused to more and different states, those with the resources to exploit the new methods for economic productivity and military effectiveness gained international influence. Although there may be a lag time between socioeconomic transition and how quickly militaries adapt, after the industrial revolution the correlation between industrial and military power was very high.[6]

The information revolution suggests that the process of improving resource utilization does not end with industrial maturity.[7] By fueling globalization, the information revolution enables states to increase productivity and enhance economic capacity by accessing new markets, expanding international trade, and increasing foreign direct investment (Castells 1996, p. 142). E-mail dramatically reduces the communications costs of doing business. The information revolution has also enabled some states to build remarkably advanced and lethal militaries that have produced extremely skewed results on the battlefield.

States have been resilient in the face of technological change, and despite the increasingly rapid diffusion of information, states still shape the political space within which information flows (Keohane and Nye 1998; Herrera 2004). Yet state power has been diminished too. States have lost much of their control over monetary and fiscal policies, which are often dictated by global markets (Castells 1996, pp. 245, 254). The rapid movement of currency in and out of countries by currency speculators can extract a devastating cost on those that do not have large currency reserves. States no longer monopolize scientific research. The Internet allows a global scientific community to exchange information on topics that can be easily exploited by terrorist organizations (Castells 1996, p. 125). The Internet has made it impossible for states, dictatorships as well as democracies, to monopolize the truth (Castells 1996, pp. 384, 486–487). Nor can they monopolize strategic information (Keohane and Nye 1998)—the information that confers great advantage only if competitors do not possess it—because states no longer control encryption technologies.

Most critically, information technology (IT) has made the most technologically advanced and powerful societies, by traditional indices, the most vulnerable to attack. A distinguishing hallmark of the information age is the "network," which exploits the accessibility and availability of information, and computational and communicative speed, to organize and disseminate knowledge cheaply and efficiently (Harknett 2003). The strength of the network lies in its degree of connectivity. Connectivity can increase prosperity and military effectiveness, but it also creates vulnerabilities. Information-intensive military organizations are more vulnerable to information warfare because they are more information-dependent, while an adversary need not be information-dependent to disrupt the information lifeline of high-tech forces. Information-dependent societies are also more vulnerable to the infiltration of computer networks, databases, and the media, and to physical as well as cyber attacks on the very linkages upon which modern societies rely to function: communication, financial transaction, transportation, and energy resource networks. It would be foolish for a well-financed and motivated group not to attack the technical infrastructure of an adversary.

The same forces that have weakened states have empowered nonstates. The information revolution has diffused and redistributed power to traditionally weaker actors. Terrorists have access to encryption technologies that increase their anonymity and make it difficult for states to disrupt and dismantle their operations (Zanini and Edwards 2001, pp. 37–38). Global markets and the Internet make it possible to hire criminals, read about the design and dissemination of weapons of mass destruction, and coordinate international money laundering to finance nefarious activities (Kugler and Frost 2001; Castells 2000, pp. 172, 180–182). Terrorists can now communicate with wider audiences and with each other over greater distances, recruit new members, and diffuse and control their operations more widely and from afar. Nonstate actors also have increasing access to offensive information warfare capabilities because of their relative cheapness, accessibility, and commercial origins (U.S. General Accounting Office 1996; Office of the Undersecretary for Defense for Acquisition and Technology 1996). Globalization, and the information technologies that undergird it, suggest that a small, well-organized group may be able to create the same havoc that was once the purview of states and large organizations with substantial amounts of resources.

Reliance on information technology also creates vulnerabilities for nonstate actors. Computers centralize information, and confiscation of them by law enforcement agencies can undercut terrorist operations; law enforcement and intelligence agencies are becoming increasingly adept at monitoring communications equipment—cell phones, satellite phones, and the Internet—for digital traces (Zanini and Edwards 2001, pp. 39–40). Finally, the same global communications networks so adeptly exploited by terrorist and criminal groups can facilitate coordination among law enforcement and intelligence

Table 3.1　Advantages and Disadvantages of States and Nonstates

	Industrial Age	Information Age
States	*Advantaged* by centralized power and economies of scale for industrial production	*Advantaged* by ability to create and dominate information infrastructure *Disadvantaged* by susceptibility to disruption
Nonstate actors (terrorists)	*Disadvantaged* by inability to generate wealth and power, or to exploit industrial production resources	*Advantaged* by decentralized power and ability to exploit information infrastructure *Disadvantaged* by inability to sustain attack

agencies worldwide to apprehend terrorists and gain valuable information about their future operations. Robert Keohane and Joseph Nye (1998) point out that the collection and production of intelligence information is very costly and that states still retain significant advantages over nonstates in this area.

Table 3.1 summarizes the capabilities and vulnerabilities of states and nonstate actors in the industrial and information ages. The difference between these two ages is that the industrial age skewed power toward states at the expense of nonstate actors, while the information age simultaneously advantages and disadvantages states and nonstate actors.

The different capacities of states and nonstates are also illustrated in Figure 3.1. Vulnerability is plotted along the x-axis and capability plotted along the y-axis. In the industrial age, states possessed high capability and low vulnerability to nonstate actors, while nonstate actors possessed the reverse—

Figure 3.1　Capability and Vulnerability in the Information Age

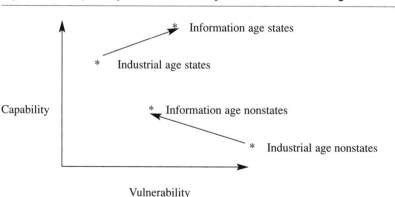

high vulnerability to the coercive capacity of the state and low capability to threaten the state. In the information age, states have moved higher on the capability scale to the extent that they can leverage information technologies to generate greater violence. But they have also moved rightward, increasing their vulnerability precisely because they are more reliant on networks. Nonstate actors have moved upward and toward the left, increasing their capabilities to inflict harm on states while decreasing their vulnerabilities to state coercion because information technologies afford them an unprecedented degree of coordination capability, global reach, and anonymity.

War and Destruction in the Information Age

We have examined the impact of information technology on the capabilities and vulnerabilities of states and nonstate actors. Now we focus on the consequences of these changes for waging war. The information age has increased the availability and affordability of information, information technologies, and information age weapons, and created new vulnerabilities for advanced information-dependent societies. The availability of off-the-shelf commercial technologies benefits smaller states and nonstate actors, to be sure, but only the wealthiest and most powerful states will be able to leverage information technology to launch a "revolution in military affairs." The ability to gather, sort, process, transfer, and disseminate information over a wide geographic area to produce dominant battle-space awareness will be a capability reserved for the most powerful (Keohane and Nye 1998). In this respect, information technology continues trends already under way in the evolution of combat that have enhanced the military effectiveness of states. IT makes conventional combat more accurate, thereby improving the efficiency of high explosive attacks.

On the other hand, IT also continues trends in warfare that circumvent traditional military forces and that work in favor of weaker states and nonstates. Like strategic bombing and countervalue nuclear targeting, efforts to destroy or punish an adversary by bypassing destruction of its armed forces and directly attacking its society, predate the information technology age. Techniques of information warfare provide attackers with a broader array of tools and an ability to target more precisely and by nonlethal means the lifelines upon which advanced societies rely: power grids, phone systems, transportation networks, and airplane guidance systems. Not only is information a means to boost the effectiveness of lethal technologies, but it also opens up the possibility of nonlethal attacks that can incapacitate, defeat, deter, or coerce an adversary, attacks that can be launched by individuals and private groups as well as by professional militaries. Warfare is no longer the exclusive province of the state.

Some analysts remain skeptical that terrorists can overcome the technical and financial hurdles to inflict a highly damaging cyber attack (Soo Hoo, Goodman, and Greenberg 1997; Weimann 2004). They argue that terrorists are more likely to use IT for organizational rather than for offensive purposes (Zanini and Edwards 2001, pp. 46–50). Others point out that computer systems are remarkably resilient to attack, that sensitive military systems, the classified computers of intelligence agencies, and the Federal Aviation Administration's air traffic control system are physically isolated from the Internet (Lewis 2002). Yet private sector targets and critical infrastructure systems are far less secure, while the next generation of terrorists are growing up in a digital world and may see far more potential and have far more capacity for cyberterrorism (Weimann 2004). Globalization suggests it will be easier for the IT skills of the few to be leveraged by the many, while studies of military diffusion show that a successful demonstration of a new form of warfare is a major impetus to its spread (Goldman and Eliason 2003).

The conceptual categories laid out in Table 3.2 clarify the relationships between information technology and warfare.[8] The state has a significant advantage only in Cells I and II.

Cell I captures the characteristics of traditional warfare and cyber-enhanced physical attack. Information technologies augment conventional attack, as enablers of existing technologies, by boosting the ability to find targets,

Table 3.2   Domains of Information Warfare

Means of Attack	Target of Attack	
	Physical	Cyber
Physical (hurling mass and/or energy)	*I – Traditional War and Cyber-Enhanced Physical Attack* Bombing military or civilian facilities; conventional warfare or terrorism	*II – Blast-Based Information War* Physical strikes on information infrastructure (e.g., September 11, 2001, attacks impacted cell phone switching area); EMP from directed-energy weapons that destroy or disrupt digital services
Cyber (hurling information)	*III – Cyber-Enabled Physical Attack* Attacks on aircraft navigation system; spoofing air traffic control system; attacks on specialized digital devices that control electrical power and dam floodgates	*IV – Nonlethal Information War* Denial-of-service attacks, worms, logic bombs inserted into information systems, defacing websites

directing fire to targets, as well as facilitating planning and communication among one's own forces. In several post–Cold War military engagements, including those in the Persian Gulf, Kosovo, and Afghanistan, states used information technologies extremely effectively in battle to support and enhance traditional destructive warfare.

Cell II captures the idea that the information systems that undergird the operations of modern-day societies and military organizations can be directly targeted through physical attack. Blast-based information war targets information systems with firepower. Physical attacks with conventional munitions on command and control targets, as well as on civilian critical infrastructure, such as electrical power generation and transmission systems, have been hallmarks of recent Western military campaigns. A new category of firepower—directed-energy weapons—uses high-power microwaves to disable electronic targets, in contrast to traditional jamming equipment that blocks communications devices from functioning but does not physically damage them. The new generation of directed-energy weapons "is meant to emulate the sort of damage that nuclear EMP [electromagnetic pulse] can inflict upon electronics but at far less range, with more control of the damage and without all the ancillary physical destruction and radioactivity" (Schiesel 2003, pp. E1, E5).

Cell III, cyber-enabled physical attack, captures the destruction of physical targets by means of attacks on underlying technical systems. These attacks may be lethal, destroying lives and property, although only indirectly so. Recent attention has been directed toward the potential for terrorists to use the Internet to target specialized digital devices, namely the distributed control systems and supervisory control and data acquisition systems that throw railway switches and adjust valves in pipes that carry water, oil, and gas. Increasingly, these digital control devices are connected to the Internet and lack rudimentary security. Moreover, utilities worldwide allow technicians to remotely manipulate digital controls, and information on how to do this is widely available (Gellman 2002, pp. 6–7).

Cell IV captures the pure form of information warfare—combat waged solely within the domain of information and information systems—which is nonlethal. The tools are "digital" and the targets include an enemy population's beliefs, an enemy leadership's beliefs, and the economic and political information systems upon which society relies to function.[9] The information age opens up the possibility of coercing and deterring adversaries, and influencing and shaping the strategic environment in nonlethal ways. Cyber operations that target an adversary's digital systems or coordination capacity (military or societal) rather than their physical assets will disrupt, not destroy. Yet disruption can be combined with physical attack to produce destruction and defeat.

As states become more capable in executing cyber-enhanced physical attack (Cell I) and blast-based information warfare (Cell II), with the United

States dominating the global battlefield in conventional weapons, foreign governments and nonstate actors are likely to resort to asymmetric strategies, like Cell III and Cell IV types of information warfare, terrorism, and weapons of mass destruction. These are ways of balancing the odds against a conventionally superior opponent. For weaker actors that cannot marshal the physical capability necessary to harm or influence more powerful adversaries, these methods of attack are likely to become strategies of choice. Particularly given an adversary with a highly informatized society and military, it makes logical sense to target the information systems of the adversary that provide intelligence about the opponents' tactics and strategy, that exercise command and control over, and direction of, capabilities and assets, and that undergird the functioning of the adversary's society and economy. It would be foolish to conclude that because there has not yet been a recorded instance of a major cyber attack, there will never be one. How many people were surprised by the events of September 11, 2001?

Adapting to Conflict in the Information Age

More than in any previous era, the obstacles to acquiring leading-edge technologies have fallen significantly. The physical limits on capabilities and resources that precluded states from modernizing their militaries in the past no longer exist. In the preindustrial age, changes in the distribution of capabilities between and among nations took a long time. Efforts by one nation to increase its relative capabilities, either through territorial conquest or alliance formation, gave rise to a sufficiently even distribution of capabilities to prevent any one nation from subjugating others by means of war. This process was upset by the industrial revolution. The adoption of industrial technology provided nations with a far more rapid accretion in capabilities. Still, the roots of national power lay in natural resources and plant investment, which were very costly.

Information power differs from industrial power in the speed with which it is likely to spread. Globalization accelerates this process. States unable to sustain a large modern defense industrial and technological base, as well as nonstate actors, can rely on the international transfer of arms for access to advanced weapon systems. External sources of advanced technology have grown to include not only direct transfers of military technology from abroad, but purchases of advanced components and equipment from world commercial markets, and technology diffusion from the state's civilian industries. Buying off the shelf allows states and nonstate actors to obtain sophisticated equipment quickly.

But access to hardware is not enough. Organizations must be able to integrate and exploit the hardware, which requires specific human skill sets and the adaptation of organizational structures and processes.[10] During periods of rapid technological change, the ability to maintain or augment one's military power depends upon one's "transformational" potential, or how effectively one can absorb new technologies and implement accompanying practices. Indicators like defense expenditures or financial assets tell us little about transformational potential. Andrew Krepinevich (1994) compared French and German military expenditures during the interwar years and showed that France enjoyed a clear lead for nearly the entire period. Yet it was Germany that transformed its military to execute the blitzkrieg form of war and defeat France. In the same period, U.S. and Japanese naval budgets were constrained, in the former case by the Great Depression and in the latter case by bureaucratic subservience to the Japanese army. Nevertheless, both transformed their battle-fleets and made the aircraft carrier the central offensive strike element. How much of a threat or challenge a particular modernizing military or terrorist group represents depends in large part on its capacity to assimilate new technologies and leverage new capabilities.

Success in the information age depends upon the ability to exploit information to produce wealth and wage war,[11] and as in earlier periods, actors possess differing capacities. The size of a state's information industry is one indicator that it is developing into an information society and that its military is transitioning from an industrial to an informational one (Baocun 2001, p. 148). Taiwan's growing commercial high-tech sector and highly educated work force have bolstered its military prowess in Asia (Bitzinger and Gill 1996, p. 36). Tiny Singapore's highly developed information technology and communications sector has allowed this country to modernize its military by exploiting IT (Huxley 2004; *Singapore 2000*, pp. 125–126).

Although a well-educated population that is familiar with information and communications technology facilitates absorption of technologically sophisticated systems by the military, wider societal familiarity with and receptivity to computers (Foster and Goodman 2000; Demchak 2000) is not a necessary condition for transformation. Roger Cliff, in his analysis of China's human capital base, argues that "absolute numbers of scientists and engineers may be more important than numbers as a proportion of total population, and in this regard China compares more favorably with other countries" (2001, p. xii). The important factor is whether the society can sustain a high-tech sector and whether scientists and engineers are effectively recruited from it into the military.

The ability to exploit information age technologies to wage war requires organizational adaptation. Richard Bitzinger and Bates Gill argue that the existence of a huge military-industrial complex, a large military research and development infrastructure, and an expanding commercial high-tech base are not enough for China to be able to exploit the current revolution in military affairs (1996, p. 21). A variety of historical, organizational, managerial, technical, and political factors present hindrances,[12] much in the way that although Taiwan possesses many technological and economic precursors to a deep revolution in military affairs, political and bureaucratic constraints have impeded full exploitation of this potential capability (Mulvenon 2004). Organizational structures that facilitate the free flow of information are better positioned to take advantage of current information-related military innovations. This explains the push in the U.S. military toward greater information sharing, more jointness, flatter command and control structures, reduced hierarchy, and more decentralized command and control.

Information is something that states, organized for success in the industrial age, do not have a comparative advantage in exploiting. John Arquilla and David Ronfeldt argue that the information revolution is strengthening the network form of organization over hierarchical forms, that nonstate actors can organize into networks more easily than traditional hierarchical state actors, and that the master of the network will gain major advantages over hierarchies because hierarchies have a difficult time fighting networks (2001, pp. 1, 15).

States are run by large hierarchical organizations with clearly delineated structures and functions. By contrast, a more efficient organizational structure for the knowledge economy is the network of operatives, or "knowledge workers" not bound by geographic location. This is precisely the type of organizational structure being adopted by terrorist groups as they adapt to the information age.

There is evidence that adaptation is quicker in flat hierarchies or matrix organizations than it is in the steep pyramidal hierarchies that run the modern nation-state; that flatter networks have a much shorter learning curve than do hierarchically networked organizations (Areieli 2003). The higher the hierarchy, the faster it operates if it is doing something it has already foreseen and thus for which it is prepared. If, on the other hand, a scenario requires the development of new processes that were not foreseen, the flatter organization is better at learning. Matrix organizations are more creative and innovative.[13] According to Castells, the performance of a network depends on two fundamental attributes: "its *connectedness,* that is its structural ability to facilitate noise-free communication between its components; its *consistency,* that is the extent to which there is sharing of interests between the network's goals and the goals of its components" (1996, p. 171). On both criteria, large state bureaucracies suffer serious disadvantages.

Table 3.3 summarizes the factors influencing the military potential of states and nonstate actors today. Many of the debates on information warfare center on the resiliency, or recoverability, of states. It is simply not clear how susceptible to collapse the information infrastructure, society, and economic base of the United States are, if attacked in earnest. Many theorists argue that the integrated grids and networks are extraordinarily vulnerable to attacks at critical points, and that attacks will reverberate with special force through the fragile, liberal society (Molander, Riddile, and Wilson 1996; Lake 2000; Triplett 2000).

Richard Betts (2002) calls this "the soft underbelly" of U.S. primacy (see also Byman and Waxman 1999). Specifically, Betts points out that in such situations the defender, despite overwhelming preponderance of military power, is asymmetrically eroded due to the inability to deter a nonstate opponent, coupled with the enormous cost of defending itself everywhere at once. In short, if a major power is inordinately vulnerable in the information age, and if nonstate actors can wage a sustained campaign, then we might conclude that the future looks grim for the major powers of the world.

The truth is that we simply do not know the extent to which the information age has altered the recoverability of advanced, wealthy economies. The Y2K scare played on the fear of the delicacy and interconnectedness of information systems, and yet failed to produce any noticeable effects. Major and extended blackouts in the northeastern and midwestern United States and in Canada in the summer of 2003 (which would have been a major coup if accomplished by a terrorist group) failed to produce the mayhem, crime, and social dislocation of lesser blackouts in the 1970s. The dynamics of such a complex system as the United States, or a similarly advanced state, preclude a clear answer.

Other significant factors are the economic capacity and knowledge paths of terrorist groups. States are frequently in the business of generating large-scale violence; to generate violence, however, weapons are needed. States are then

Table 3.3   Military Potential of States and Nonstates

Factors Affecting Military Potential	States	Nonstate Actors
Economic capacity	Indigenous research and development; technology transfers	External linkages; consumer technology
Organizational constraints/obstacles	High; steep hierarchical organizational structures with entrenched interests and bureaucratic rivalry innovate slowly	Low; flat organizational structures are more creative and adaptable
Knowledge paths	Social networks	Supplier networks; common training
Normative constraints	Taboos against certain practices	Few taboos
Globalization	Increases diffusion and levels playing field	Increases access and empowers
Vulnerability	High	Low
Ability to sustain military operations	High	Low
Ability to recover from attacks	?	High

confronted with the classic economic problem of "make or buy."[14] Nonstate actors usually are forced to rely on buying. They gather whatever conventional weapons are available, through whatever means possible, and apply them as best they can.[15]

How does the information age alter this scenario? Besides monetary support from external sources, "consumer technology" is a source of economic capacity. This is best described by Betts (2002, p. 25), who writes: "Nineteen men from technologically backward societies did not have to rely on home-grown instruments. . . . They used computers and modern financial procedures with facility, and they forcibly appropriated the aviation technology of the West and used it as a weapon" (see also van Creveld 1991, p. 306). In the liberal, informatized world, weapons are everywhere if one is able to see the correct combination of consumer technologies. Though information technology has been diffused to and exploited by nonstate actors in the past (such as the printing press), it has never been used to generate large-scale violence—a significant development.

Attacking the Base: Sustainability and Vulnerability

The transition from the industrial to the information era has undercut many of the strengths we have traditionally associated with great power status. For nonstate actors, the information age presents new opportunities that in some cases do not carry with them attendant vulnerabilities. Nonstate actors can employ information technology to project destructive power without having to maintain a large industrial or information infrastructure that itself would present a target. Yet just how susceptible are the social and economic bases of states?

The answer depends on the nature of the trade-off between power and vulnerability. In other words, the greater the industrial base, which provides the material of modern war, the greater the dependence a state has on the fixed and relatively soft targets of modern society (industry and its supporting infrastructure). These targets have been discussed in an operational context (most extensively in the strategic bombing literature), but there has been little effort to link this to the set of broader questions implied above: What advantages accrue to the nation-state and its relatively vast potential for sustained war-making (versus nonstate actors)? What disadvantages accrue to the nation-state in terms of the access to and vulnerability of its economic base during war? Conversely, what advantages and disadvantages do nonstate actors possess or lack in these areas? Additionally, how do these relationships change in light of the transition from the industrial age to the information age?

First we must discuss the relationship between sustained military force and the economic foundations of power. In the industrial age, a positive relationship has commonly been assumed to exist between the ability to sustain military force and the vulnerability of the societal base. This is evident from a brief examination of the evolution of industrial age operational theory regarding the targeting of the economic base of an enemy. The literature, however, frequently conflates two components of an enemy's war-making capabilities: its economic base and its society's will to resist. As will be shown below, punishment aimed at eroding a society's will to resist is rarely successful. Attacking the state's economic base is a viable means of disabling an opponent, but this is only possible after delivering an enormous amount of punishment. As a result, although nonstate actors can remain largely invulnerable to a nation-state's tools of deterrence and defense, this invulnerability is purchased at the cost of sustainability. Without the ability to mount a sustained attack, they will have a difficult time producing significant effects on the economies of modern states.[16]

The U.S. Civil War is sometimes argued to be the first "modern" war—modern in the sense that victory was decided not just by the size, skill, and leadership of the opposing military forces, but also by the burgeoning industrial capabilities of both sides. Not only was this component part of the offensive capabilities of each side, but it also became a target. William Sherman realized that industrial age wars could not be won by solely concentrating on the decisive battlefield engagements of the Napoleonic tradition, but required methodical dismantling of the opponent's economic base. Civil War historian James McPherson has argued that Sherman's campaign prefigured the strategic bombing campaigns of World War II. Sherman "preferred to destroy wealth and property that sustained the enemy army rather than that army itself" (quoted in Castel 2003, p. 421).

French naval policy in the post–Crimean War period also shows a burgeoning appreciation of strangling an opponent's economic base. The French *Jeune Ecole* hoped to embrace the naval technological revolution of the mid–nineteenth century to offset the much larger and more powerful British navy. Their program of commerce-raiding and coastal barrage recognized the British weakness for supplying its population and industries with foodstuffs and raw materials from abroad. Instead of losing the race of battleship procurement, it was wiser to invest in cheaper, faster ships, which could cut off Britain's economic base at the knees (Marder 1940). Once again, the focus was on circumnavigating the tough defensive shell of the opponent, and seeking the soft and vulnerable links in the economic chain.

This thread of strategic thought came into its own with the advent of air power. Early theorists such as Guido Douhet and Billy Mitchell developed operational doctrines that maximized the disjuncture between battlefield success and the erosion of economic capability to sustain a war effort. In a world reeling from the bloody stalemates of the Western front, planners of the interwar period had high hopes for bringing a more decisive instrument of coercion to bear in future conflicts. The logic behind strategic air power flowed directly from Sherman's campaign in Georgia and the French *Jeune Ecole:* evade the enemy's military forces and seek out and cripple the economic base, which is a necessary component for war-making in the industrial age. World War II provided the first and best example of these types of air campaigns, and the punishment of vulnerable targets culminated in Hiroshima, which laid the basis for nuclear deterrence in the Cold War (Quester 1966).

One key problem with these theories is their tendency to conflate two theoretically distinct but empirically intertwined variables: physical economic capabilities and the will to resist (Pape 1996, p. 57). Targeting civilian areas serves the dual purpose of inhibiting the state from replenishing material losses on the battlefield, and inciting the population to cry out for an end to the punishment.[17] It erodes both the physical and the psychological capability of the enemy to resist. It is rarely made clear which is more effective, or if one aim can be achieved without the other. Operationally, the question is often moot. As Hugh Trenchard argued to the British cabinet in 1941:

> If you are bombing at sea, then 99 percent of your bombs are wasted, but not only 99 percent of the bombs are wasted but 99 percent too, of the pilots and of the training which went to produce them. . . . If, however, our bombs are dropped in Germany then 99 percent which will miss the military targets all help to kill, damage, frighten, or interfere with Germans in Germany, and the whole 100 percent of the bomber organization is doing useful work and not merely 1 percent of it. (quoted in Murray 1992, p. 245)

This practical arithmetic suggests that targeting physical economic facilities could produce the desirable externalities of punishing the German people's will to resist. In the age of largely imprecise ("dumb") bombing, it was unimportant which factor had a larger independent effect, since both were being inflicted by the same operational policy.

The most recent and refined progeny of this doctrine is known as "effects-based" operations. Targets are chosen to produce indirect as well as direct effects; these second- and third-order effects are designed to produce nonlinear shockwaves that reverberate through the target society and directly erode the enemy's will and ability to fight (Beagle 2001; Cordesman and Burke 2003). It is hoped that "rather than relying on old approaches of annihilation or attrition, this new way of conducting operations will focus on generating desired effects [as opposed to] objectives or the physical destruction of targets" (Batschelet 2002, p. 2). It is implied in this doctrine that the more complex, interdependent, and concentrated a society is, the more susceptible it is to such attacks.

Recent empirical research has shown, however, that punishment strategies (such as those of Douhet, Schelling, and some "effects-based" planners) rarely work in military conflicts (Pape 1996, 1997–1998). William Arkin

(2001) found in the air war over Kosovo that bombing by the North Atlantic Treaty Organization actually solidified the will of the Serbian populace; only after an extended, intense, and technologically unprecedented strategic bombing campaign did pressure come to bear on Milosevic. T. W. Beagle agrees. After examining four U.S. bombing campaigns (one each from World War II, the Vietnam War, the Gulf War, and Kosovo), he concedes that the air force has been good at generating tactical effects, but less so at the operational or strategic level, concluding that "the most sought-after effects are often psychological in nature, and efforts to improve airpower's capabilities in this area are virtually non-existent" (2001, p. 3).

Rather than being used as a psychological weapon, air power seems better employed in wartime as a tool for degrading the military capabilities of the opponent on, or immediately behind, the front lines. Airpower, despite the claims of proponents, appears to degrade the economy of a state only through a sustained and massive application.[18] This is important for the discussion at hand. If nonstate actors use terrorist attacks against the vulnerable homeland of nation-states, is the target the physical (economic capabilities of the nation-state), or the psychological (the will of the populace to resist the terrorists' demands)? If it is the former, such attacks are likely to succeed only if they are significant and can be sustained.[19] If it is the latter, they may serve just to stiffen the resolve of the opponent.[20] As a result, they are unlikely to succeed in achieving their aims, if these aims include bending powerful nation-states to their will. They may be able to change some aspect of policy, disrupt some aspect of economic or social normalcy, or gain some other minor concessions.[21] But they will not be able to "defeat" a "normal" state, in the military sense, because they do not have the societal, industrial, and financial base to apply a significant amount of force consistently.

Conclusion

Despite more capable nonstate actors and increasing state vulnerabilities, the nation-state retains the optimal economy of scale for generating wealth and violence. The important issues are how states and nonstates have been both empowered and weakened, and how adaptable they are to the exigencies of conflict in the future.

Terrorist groups have proved to be adaptable and flexible, difficult to deter and defeat. Yet the very structures that terrorist groups use to their advantage against deterrence and defense rob them of the ability to sustain their energy on the "battlefield," even if that battlefield is the opponent's domestic landscape. If they were to attain the infrastructure and assets required to seriously undermine an advanced economy such as that of the United States, they would sacrifice the veil of anonymity, which is their greatest advantage. Yet without sustainability, these actors must fall back on a punishment strategy, which is more likely to galvanize the opponent than it is to achieve its goals.[22]

Notes

1. We are concerned with those nonstate actors bent on waging war and violence in the international system. Hence we do not focus on the full range of nonstate actors, including multinational corporations, nongovernmental organizations, and intergovernmental organizations.

2. This is the question posed by David Alberts, John Garstka, and Frederick Stein in *Network Centric Warfare* (1999).

3. This is evident from a perusal of the literature stemming back to Friedrich List and Alexander Hamilton (Earle 1986), up to Paul Kennedy (Kennedy 1987) and Aaron Friedberg (Friedberg 1988), and through the Cold War (Kapstein 1992, p. xiii). For all these theorists, a sizable economic base was a necessary condition for military power. The question was, given a decent economic base, how did the state manipulate its economic potential to extract the maximum amount of military power (or overall national security) from it?

4. This is the notion of neomercantilism versus traditional mercantilism, because it accepts the fact that military power is predicated on the strength of the economy rather than on stored bullion. For a discussion, see Goodwin 1991, pp. 27–29.

5. The impact of improved information technology on the military has of course been noted and studied prior to the advent of the information age. For example, see Dennis Showalter's analysis (1973) of the impact of the electric telegraph on Prussia's command structure.

6. This was because of the tremendous capital investment required to generate a modern mass production industrial base for warfare in the industrial age. The correlation need not be so close in the information age.

7. This is the thesis that Alvin Toffler and Heidi Toffler (1993) adopt when they explain their three civilizations and war forms: agricultural, industrial, and information. For a critique of the Tofflers, see Bunker 1995.

8. This table is adapted from Bishop and Goldman 2003.

9. In this respect, nonlethal information warfare also includes perception management and propaganda. See Zanini and Edwards 2001, pp. 41–44.

10. See Macgregor 2003 for a discussion of how the U.S. military must transform its organizational structure to exploit new technologies.

11. For a more comprehensive analysis of the political, economic, social, cultural, and organizational factors shaping the ability of states to assimilate and master the use of advanced information technologies in the military sector, see Goldman 2004.

12. China suffers from low interconnectedness, high formalism, and low organizational slack. China's military and commercial sectors are segregated, which inhibits cross-fertilization and diffusion of commercial technologies and organizational principles to the defense sector and the ability of the military to benefit from spin-on of locally available commercial technology. Bureaucratic formalism pervades organizational norms such that meeting production quotas is valued over innovation. Central planning reduces organizational slack and surplus capacity for producers to innovate outside the "plan." Finally, incentives in the production of dual use technologies are for lucrative commercial applications and markets, not spin-on efforts to support military modernization.

13. I am indebted to Chris Demchak for bringing these distinctions to my attention.

14. It may serve a state's short-term interest to buy off-the-shelf systems from an ally. This may not be the best long-term solution, however, as the purchaser becomes dependent on the flow of technicians and spare parts. For example, China's aeronautics industries (both military and commercial) have been significantly retarded by their reliance on Soviet equipment (Allen 2000).

15. Under certain specified conditions, nonstate actors can challenge states on the field of battle, even in the industrial age. For discussions, see Taw and Hoffman 1994 and Arreguin-Toft 2001.

16. A single incident of maritime terrorism, if it were to close down one or more hub ports critical to world trade, could have a devastating impact on the global economy. For example, it has been estimated that the global economic impact from a closure of the port of Singapore alone could exceed $200 billion per year from disruptions to inventory and production cycles. Shutting down of ports on the western coast of the United States could cost up to $1 billion a day (Ho 2004).

17. For example, in the strategic bombing campaign of Japan during World War II, U.S. planners had the "strong opinion, that the will of the Japanese people and of its government to resist could be greatly weakened and perhaps destroyed by urban area [incendiary] attacks" (U.S. Strategic Bombing Survey 1946, p. 37).

18. For example, Germany maintained a viable economy during World War II until December 1944 despite roughly 1.8 million tons of bombs having been dropped on it by that point (U.S. Bombing Survey 1945, p. 2; see also the extended discussion in Milward 1965).

19. Osama bin Laden, in discussing the September 11 attacks, argued hopefully for a sustained campaign against the economic base of United States: "These blessed strikes showed clearly that this arrogant power, America, rests on a powerful but precarious economy, which rapidly crumbled . . . the global economy based on usury, which America uses along with its military might to impose infidelity and humiliation on oppressed people, can easily crumble. . . . Hit the economy, which is the basis of military might. If their economy is finished, they will become too busy to enslave oppressed people. . . . America is in decline; the economic drain is continuing but more strikes are required and the youths must strike the key sectors of the American economy" (quoted in Betts 2002, p. 25).

20. Betts argues that terrorist groups may underestimate U.S. resolve, and that when vital interests are at stake, "primacy unleashed may prove fearsomely potent" (2002, p. 35).

21. For an analysis of suicide bombing in particular, see Pape 2003.

22. The attacks of September 11 did serve to galvanize U.S. support for extensive overseas interventions. In a very crude calculus, the terrorists toppled two buildings, and in response, the United States toppled two regimes (those of Afghanistan and Iraq).

4

Foreign Investors in Conflict Zones: New Expectations

Virginia Haufler

Corporate critics have complained for decades that foreign investors have propped up dictators, destabilized governments, abused human rights, and generally worsened a bad situation in many developing countries. The height of this criticism, and its most potent expression, was the divestment campaign to undermine apartheid in South Africa. The campaigners wanted foreign investors to sever ties with an illegitimate regime and withdraw from South Africa. With the end of apartheid and emergence of a "third wave" of democratization and economic reform around the world, a new era ensued in which many developing countries welcomed foreign investors and competed to attract them, hoping to gain the benefits of capital investment, technology transfer, and effective links to global markets. Despite a generally favorable environment for foreign investors in the 1990s, many voices continued to speak out about the dangers of foreign investment in unstable or conflict-ridden states.

The continued concern about the impact of foreign investment in the developing world produces diametrically opposed positions: (1) some take the stance that foreign investment produces or exacerbates conflict, government repression, and corruption, and therefore call for foreign investors to withdraw; (2) others believe that foreign investment produces or facilitates economic development and job creation, and ultimately reduces conflict and corruption, and therefore they call for foreign investors to stay. Both sides assume a link between economic factors and security, but they see it operating in very different ways.

A compromise position has emerged in the past decade, however. Pragmatists have begun to preach a middle course in an attempt to have the best of both worlds: investment and development along with stability and democracy. They argue that foreign investors should stay, but engage in conflict prevention activities. They justify this by claiming it would be beneficial to the

55

local society, that it would demonstrate corporate commitment to responsible action, and also that it simply makes good business sense. This position may be incredibly ingenious, because it gets one of the biggest, most influential actors in a developing country involved in promoting peace. On the other hand, it could also be dangerous, since in essence it promotes the intervention of multinational corporations in the domestic politics of their host countries.

In either case, the issue of business behavior in unstable areas of the world has been on the international agenda for a decade now. Despite the attacks on the World Trade Center, the war on terrorism, and intervention in Afghanistan and Iraq, this attention has barely wavered. As I describe below, a number of corporate conflict prevention initiatives have been launched in the past few years, and interest in this area within the international community has remained high.

Violent conflict typically forces most companies to withdraw from a country if they have a choice of investment locations. Levels of foreign direct investment declined significantly over the past few years, due to a combination of economic slowdown and a loss of business confidence after September 11, 2001 (United Nations Conference on Trade and Development [UNCTAD] 2003).[1] However, there are many situations where the violence is localized, foreign business is not targeted, and production activities can continue to operate successfully, as in the case of oil companies operating in Angola during the civil war there (Berman 2000). Most extractive industries have few other choices of location if they want to continue to develop natural resources. In "failed states," where the government is weak, ineffective, and under attack, the contributions of foreign investors to peace and war may be a central link between economic and security affairs (Berdal and Malone 2000; Ballentine and Sherman 2003).

Is the pressure for corporations to engage in conflict prevention activities a permanent change in expectations about corporate behavior, or simply a policy fad? In order to explore this question, we need to have a better understanding of the factors that led the international community to promote a new role for corporations in conflict prevention. In this chapter, I argue that the corporate accountability movement is in the process of establishing new norms and expectations about corporate behavior, but they are still only weakly institutionalized.[2] Major political actors—states, nongovernmental organizations (NGOs), and international organizations—are attempting to rework the identity of economic actors by promoting the adoption and internalization of corporate social responsibility as a guide to appropriate behavior. Just as state security interests may be shaped by cultural factors, as argued in recent theoretical work in the security field, so too may the "security interests" of corporations (Katzenstein 1996). As I describe in the rest of this chapter, new norms emerged out of debates over corporate social responsibility in other issue areas, such as labor and the environment. These norms were strengthened by the integration of the conflict prevention agenda with those of development and sustainability. Increasing acceptance of the idea of international intervention in response to systematic violations of human rights and humanitarian disasters may have led to creative ideas about the potential use of corporations as new instruments of intervention and conflict prevention. These factors facilitated the creation of new initiatives and policies by states, international organizations, NGOs, and corporations that go beyond the old dichotomous choice between "engagement" and "divestment."[3]

This links the security and political economy fields in ways that have so far been underexplored in the existing literature. Typically, the political economy of security studies has examined the role of industry only by analyzing (1) strategic industries such as oil and the potential threat to national security posed by those who control oil supplies; (2) the arms industry and arms trade, including debates over dual-use technology, and how changes in these sectors might affect military preparedness and military competition with other states; and (3) the linkage of economic competitiveness with security and foreign policy through concepts such as "economic security" or "grand strategy." All of these have contributed greatly to our empirical and theoretical understanding of how political economy and security interact, but they are limited in explaining some of the new developments in which corporations play a significant role in security affairs.

In addition to these traditional analyses, it is useful to explore the relations between state and nonstate actors through a sociological or constructivist lens. Approaches to norms and identity, I argue, can be applied to economic actors, and this has not been a focus so far of theoretical attention (Finnemore and Sikkink 1998). Norms tell us what is appropriate behavior in particular situations for particular actors. Norms are by definition held collectively, and are the product of acquired knowledge, socialization, and historical social development (Weil 2003a, 2003b; Finnemore and Sikkink 1998). They are developed as a collective project through repeated interaction over time, and gain force and effect through institutionalization in law and organizations. An emerging norm may be carried by only a few groups, but given the right environment and effective strategies, it may be adopted by more and more people until it reaches a "tipping point." Many norms are so well internalized that they are uncontested, while others are the subject of continued political debate as they evolve over time (Finnemore and Sikkink 1998; Florini 1996; Weil 2003a, 2003b).

Corporate social responsibility norms are in the early stages of development, but each year they appear to be gaining more force and acceptance (Haufler 2001b). New norms regarding the role of corporations in conflict prevention and peace promotion are beginning to be institutionalized through the programs of leading governments and international institutions. This institutionalization is in its early stages and may yet fail. Nevertheless, the initiatives

launched under the banner of corporate conflict prevention have shown re-
markable resiliency in the face of challenges posed by the war on terrorism, the
challenges of postconflict reconstruction in places such as Afghanistan and Iraq,
and the natural resistance of the private sector to these issues (Banfield, Haufler,
and Lilly 2003). We can see some of these changes reflected in current efforts
by the International Criminal Court to consider corporate culpability in the war
in the Congo, or recent initiatives in the financial sector to mandate that companies borrowing money assess the conflict impact of their major projects.[4]

This chapter discusses trends in corporate social responsibility; the linking of development, sustainability, and conflict agendas; and the evolution of
thinking about intervention. These constitute the environment in which efforts
to integrate corporations into conflict prevention emerged. The chapter then
goes on to explore the evolution of norms regarding corporate conflict prevention in general. It concludes by discussing some of the impact of recent
changes in the security environment on these trends, and speculates about
their longevity and impact.

The Intersection of Corporate Social Responsibility and Conflict Prevention Agendas

There are over 61,000 multinational firms in the world today, with over
900,000 foreign affiliates (UNCTAD 2004). In the past decade, a growing
amount of foreign investment has been going into the emerging markets in the
developing world, though the majority of investment is still located in the
triad countries of the United States, Japan, and the European Union. Many
markets are now dominated by oligopolistic firms, and the largest firms have
revenues that exceed those of a small, industrialized country. As competition
in global markets has increased, corporations have been moving into ever
more socially and environmentally sensitive locations (Christiansen 2002).
Even as corporations have extended their reach farther into new countries,
they have been followed by the eyes of the rest of the world—through activists and modern media. As Deborah Spar has said, corporations are "in the
spotlight" everywhere they operate around the world (1998).

The context of foreign investment has changed dramatically over the past
two decades, and so have expectations about the role of corporations in society (Haufler 2003). We can see these changes most clearly in three areas: (1)
the evolution of corporate social responsibility norms across a diverse set of
issues and policy domains; (2) the merging of conflict prevention, development, and environmental agendas in policy and scholarship; and (3) changing
ideas regarding the conditions under which it is acceptable for the international community to intervene in the domestic affairs of states. These all pro-

vide the context in which corporate conflict prevention has become an important issue on the international agenda.

What exactly do we mean by "corporate conflict prevention initiatives"? One example stems from the international outcry against so-called conflict diamonds mined in West Africa, particularly Sierra Leone. The sale of these diamonds into international markets has provided the funds for continuing rebel and government fighting, and prolonged the bitter conflicts there. The international campaign against conflict diamonds pushed the diamond industry to agree to develop a regime to certify the origin of rough diamonds and regulate the trade (the Kimberley Process). The idea behind this was that industry action was critical to undercutting the continued flow of money to combatants (Smillie, Giberie, and Hazleton 2000). Similar campaigns exist for other commodities, such as coltan and timber, although these so far have not gained the attention of the international community in the way that diamonds did.

Another example is international concern regarding the way in which major extractive industries hire security to protect their people and facilities—hiring the services of either government or private security forces. When these forces committed violence against local populations or were involved in various forms of criminality and corruption, the corporation that used their services found itself accused of collusion. Policymakers in the United States and United Kingdom, where many of these companies were based, became concerned about the attacks on their companies. They responded by facilitating negotiations with activists and companies to develop what became known as the U.S.-UK Voluntary Principles on Human Rights and Security.[5] These establish guidelines for the provision of protection services to companies operating in regions of instability and violence. A number of NGOs are now pressing companies to perform a conflict impact and risk assessment prior to investing in a location and before expanding operations.[6]

Another major area of concern is the way in which tax revenues paid by the extractive sector can be used to fund corruption and continued war. Recently, the World Bank developed a radical new revenue-sharing agreement with governments and oil companies as part of a project to build a Chad-Cameroon gas pipeline. A large percentage of the project revenues would be deposited in a development account for the country, overseen by a group of experts. The purpose of designing this revenue management system was to avoid feeding the corruption that plagues Chad and Cameroon, and limit the ability of existing elites to procure arms to fight a war.

All of these examples demonstrate that corporate conflict prevention has become an area of both concern and action. Policymakers, scholars, and analysts now wonder *how*—not *if*—business should be incorporated into conflict prevention initiatives (Haufler 2001a; Nelson 2000; Guaqeta 2002; International Peace Academy 2001; Sherman 2002).

The Emergence of Corporate Social Responsibility Norms

The initial impetus toward a corporate social responsibility agenda can be traced back to the 1960s, and perhaps before. This is the period of time when U.S. corporations dramatically expanded their presence abroad. By the 1970s, many newly independent developing countries became concerned about the power of multinational corporations, and successfully pressed the United Nations to establish a center to oversee transnational corporations, and to launch negotiations to develop a code of conduct for transnational corporations. After a decade of effort, however, the negotiations were quietly ended without results in the 1980s, when many countries even in the developing world had lost interest and the Reagan administration in the United States declined to continue negotiations (Kline 1985).

What Robin Broad and John Cavanagh (1998) label the "corporate accountability movement" really began with the antiapartheid movement (see also Bendell 2004). As part of this, Reverend Leon Sullivan established guidelines for corporations operating under apartheid. As a member of the board of directors of General Motors, he sought to crack the system from within by pressuring foreign corporations to adopt policies of racial equality within their organizations. The Sullivan Principles, launched in 1977, did not entirely succeed in undermining apartheid from within, but the effort helped establish the principle of corporate responsibility. The second phase of the antiapartheid campaign—the divestiture movement—took those principles further. Major investing institutions such as universities were pressured to divest themselves of their shares in companies with investments in apartheid South Africa.[7]

While the antiapartheid movement demonstrated the potential effectiveness of targeting multinational corporations, it was not until the 1990s that a real "movement" could be said to have begun.[8] Many groups active on issues of the environment, development, health, labor standards, and human rights began to develop guidelines, principles, and codes for multinational corporations to adopt. But their influence was weakened by the diversity of their goals and strategies. Some groups remained intensely hostile to the business community, while others were willing to work with individual companies. Different groups busily advocated on separate and often narrow issues, without sufficient coordination. They were more effective at stimulating consumer awareness of the importance of a specific issue or corporate scandal than they were at developing common standards (Broad and Cavanagh 1998).

By the end of the 1990s, there were a variety of separate and disconnected campaigns against corporate misbehavior, but each narrow and targeted campaign increasingly became linked into larger initiatives. Many international NGOs began to forge relationships with local ones in campaigns against foreign investors that highlighted the ways in which companies undermined labor standards or polluted the environment. At the same time, prominent international advocacy groups, such as the World Wildlife Fund or Amnesty International, began to engage in dialogue with corporations to launch specific voluntary programs in their areas of interest, combining carrot and stick tactics. Within the private sector itself, new corporate social responsibility initiatives were developed in an effort to ward off outside pressure and the threat of potential government regulation (Haufler 2001b). These initiatives carried forward new norms about the appropriate role and behavior of multinational corporations operating in the developing world.

There is mixed evidence so far on the degree to which these new norms have been incorporated into company practice. There are reports of improvement in some areas and continued violations in others—sometimes by the same company. One thing is clear, however: throughout the 1990s, the range of issues, networks, campaigns, and multistakeholder partnerships developing corporate social responsibility programs expanded dramatically. Every major corporation now has a corporate code of conduct; most of them also have adopted internal management systems to implement those codes, often involving external auditing; a number provide regular reports on their activities, similar to financial reports; and many are involved in a variety of partnerships with NGOs, governments, communities, and international organizations. Governments have helped institutionalize some of these changes through policies that provide incentives for positive corporate performance—for instance, through regulatory relief. Consumers and investors are also reinforcing this trend through, for example, investment funds that screen companies on the basis of a number of social and environmental criteria.[9] A recent survey of corporate social responsibility (CSR) experts revealed a number of trends: that CSR is slowly moving into mainstream business (though some experts are more pessimistic about this); that CSR itself is deepening in degree of commitment by the business sector; and that governance (including transparency and integrity) is one of the top CSR issues (Strandberg 2002).

It is against the background of these developments that the debate over corporate complicity in human rights abuses and continued conflict in developing countries emerged on the international agenda. Voices in the international community called for the withdrawal of corporations from investment in countries with illegitimate governments or unstable political environments. They began to debate whether there was a role for corporations in conflict prevention initiatives, and proceeded to develop standards for corporate behavior when they operated in zones of conflict (Haufler 2001a).

Merging of the Development, Environment, and Conflict/Security Agendas

Foreign investment has always been considered a key element in the development of the poorer countries of the world. But the way in which it fits into policy has changed with shifts in the development paradigm. And that paradigm has evolved in significant ways over the past few decades. In the 1960s and 1970s, development theories and policies emphasized investment in infrastructure projects, state intervention in the economy, and import substitution policies that meant selective restrictions on foreign investment. In the 1980s and 1990s, there was a decided move toward liberalization policies that welcomed trade, privatized national infrastructure, and encouraged unrestricted foreign investment. Today, the development agenda emphasizes concerns about state failure, corruption, and the need for "good governance." Along with this has come more attention to the links between development and security, and between environmental degradation and insecurity. This new agenda supports policies that promote both foreign investment and corporate social responsibility.

After World War II, with the establishment of the World Bank, a new development community of practitioners emerged with ideas about how to promote development in poorer states. In these early years, both aid workers and many host governments worked from a state-centric paradigm. Donor governments and agencies financed and implemented projects through the host government and often in partnership with state-owned companies. Many developing countries adopted import-substitution policies, and up to the 1970s many also nationalized, expropriated, or heavily restricted foreign investment. The model of the "strong" developmentalist state such as Japan was attractive to many countries, particularly in East Asia (Fridtjof Nansen Institute 2000 p. 17; Haggard 1990).

Over the past fifteen years, the development paradigm has shifted, both in the donor community and in the developing countries themselves. The "Washington consensus" among the World Bank, the International Monetary Fund, and the U.S. Treasury promoted liberal policies of free trade, deregulation, and privatization as a means to promote economic growth. The rapid globalization of markets swept up regions of the world that had previously been isolated from other economies. Heightened economic competition affected both states and foreign investors, as the former sought to attract investment, and the investors competed with each other for newly opened markets and resources. As investment became a large percentage of financial inflows to many developing countries, many people raised concerns about the concomitant externalities, in the form of both environmental degradation and repression.

A few years after the Berlin Wall fell, the World Bank and others began promoting a new "good governance" agenda. The end of command and control economies, the crises experienced by welfare states, the state-led development of East Asian economies, and the collapse of states in some areas of the world all led the World Bank to examine the role of the state more closely in its 1997 development report. It sought to determine how to increase the capability of states to "undertake and promote collective actions efficiently"

(World Bank 1997, p. 3). Attention was focused on the failures of state capacity in many developing countries, the need for more transparency in their
policymaking, and the negative impact of corruption on development. The
World Bank and others sought to limit rent-seeking by the state through economic reforms, especially privatization and other policies that would limit the
discretionary power of the government. This went along with democracy promotion, which became a significant component of development programs.
The focus on state capacity inevitably linked the development and security
agendas, as there was greater recognition of the role that conflict and corruption play in retarding development.[10] In many ways this new development
agenda was intrusive into domestic politics in ways that would not have been
acceptable during the Cold War. It entailed taking a more active role in promoting political change in many areas of the world.[11]

One of the most prominent lines of research today that links development
and security, and also highlights the role of corporations in both areas, is scholarship on the so-called resource curse, or the "paradox of plenty." The sudden
development of natural resource wealth tends to undermine economic development and industrialization, increase political conflict, and ultimately retard
democratization; it brings failure and not success in both economic and social
terms (Ross 1999, 2000; Collier et al. 2003; Fridtjof Nansen Institute 2000;
Berdal and Malone 2000; Woodrow Wilson International Center for Scholars
and International Peace Academy 2001).[12] For instance, Terry Lynn Karl
(1997) analyzed the role of oil in the political economy of a number of oil-
exporting states, particularly Venezuela, and concluded that when government
owns the petroleum sector (the "petro-state"), it becomes predatory in the collection of "mineral rents." There are few incentives to develop an efficient private sector or effective administrative system. Paul Collier and his colleagues
at the World Bank have conducted empirical research indicating that the more
a country is dependent on one or a few highly valuable commodities for a majority of its export revenues, the more likely it is to suffer from corruption and
underdevelopment (Collier 2000; Collier et al. 2003). One implication of this
is that corporations should be more cognizant of the impact they have on local
politics when they develop new natural resource wealth.

Parallel to this literature is one on the links between environmental degradation and security (see Chapter 5). It is in some ways the opposite of the resource curse approach, positing a link between resource *scarcity* and conflict,
corruption, and weak governance. The development of natural resources can
lead to their depletion, or to the degradation of land and water upon which people's livelihoods depend. Thomas Homer-Dixon and his colleagues have been
at the forefront in this area, exploring the paths through which environmental
degradation and depletion cause or exacerbate differences among groups and
become an important source of domestic conflict (Homer-Dixon 1999; Homer-
Dixon and Blitt 1998; Gleditsch 1998). Homer-Dixon argues that resource

scarcity drives elites to capture existing resources and marginalize others, which becomes a source of grievance. On the other hand, Ken Conca (2002) and others argue that there is a potential to promote peace through environmental cooperation. Most of those exploring this environment-security-peace nexus, however, do not pay particular attention to the role of foreign investors, despite its obvious relevance. Foreign investors who operate in an environmentally sustainable manner may in fact be a critical ingredient of conflict prevention and good governance initiatives (Switzer 2002).

Globalization, led by multinational corporations, is itself posited as a new source of threat to developing countries. Economic transactions span the globe through networks of intermediaries, including both legitimate and illegitimate businesses. These networks may be instrumental in facilitating the use of revenues from resource extraction to fund the purchase of weapons, and provide sustenance to rebels and repressive governments alike, as the issue of "conflict diamonds" has demonstrated (Duffield 2000; Reno 2000; Smillie, Giberie, and Hazleton 2000). Increasingly, these global markets are implicated in transnational organized crime and even terrorism (Williams 2002). Even reputable companies may be incidentally linked into these networks and thus contribute to destabilizing forces.

Norms of Intervention

Nonintervention in the political affairs of a state has been a dominant norm in the international system for centuries. The principle of sovereignty was established with the Treaties of Westphalia in 1648, and enshrined in the United Nations Charter at its founding (Weiss 1996, p. 435).[13] During the Cold War, the United Nations was constrained not to intervene by a narrow interpretation of its Charter. It dealt only with recognized governments, and worked through those governments when it did intervene. During the 1960s and 1970s, the UN supported intervention to free people from colonial domination, but that is all (Jonge Oudraat 2000a, p. 5). The Cold War competition between the United States and the Soviet Union further reinforced this principle, and any violation of it was interpreted in the light of superpower rivalry. Even though the founding of the UN system also enshrined the principles of human rights, there was no enforcement mechanism and no presumption of intervention in cases of gross violations. The Human Rights Charter itself is meant to be signed by states and its principles are to be carried out by national governments. Until the end of the Cold War, intervention of any sort was rare, and when it occurred it was often condemned.

After the end of the Cold War, the United Nations and leading countries such as the United States and other members of the North Atlantic Treaty Organization became more enamored of humanitarian intervention in crises (Jackson 2000). There has been an ongoing debate over when intervention is justified, and by whom (Jonge Oudraat 2000a). Under the UN Charter, the Security Council can ignore nonintervention principles if a problem is a threat to international peace and security—and in the 1990s the Security Council became creative in how it interpreted such threats. "By the end of the 1990s, the idea that states should not be allowed to hide behind the shield of sovereignty when gross violations of human rights take place on their territory had firmly taken root" (Jonge Oudraat 2000a, p. 4). The International Commission on Intervention and State Sovereignty declared there is a "responsibility to protect" those most in need (2001).

The impulse to intervene has been strengthened by the emergence of an international human rights regime. International and regional laws now enshrine the principles associated with human rights. The rights of individuals and the rights of specific groups (including women and indigenous groups) have become entrenched in world politics. The UN now has a Human Rights Commission, which monitors conditions around the world; the U.S. Department of State regularly reports the human rights status of countries; and the Canadian government has adopted "human security" as the basis of its foreign policy. The norms surrounding the human rights regime are now well accepted in theory, although not always in practice. This has made it more likely that governments that violate these norms will be subject to scrutiny and sanctions (Rodman 1997).[14] The United States, for its part, has been quick to impose economic sanctions on a number of countries that have violated various principles of human rights (Jonge Oudraat 2000a). In recent years, the United Nations Security Council has imposed sanctions, for instance on Angola, and then published a report by an expert panel of an investigation of sanctions-busting. These highlight the commitment of the international community to upholding sanctions against incorrigible regimes.

Most states still reject the *unilateral* right to intervene for humanitarian purposes, as reaffirmed by the General Assembly in the past few years.[15] Furthermore, most would agree with the conclusions of the International Commission on Intervention and State Sovereignty, which stated that "sovereign states have a responsibility to protect their own citizens from avoidable catastrophe . . . but that when they are unwilling or unable to do so, that responsibility must be borne by the broader community of states" (2001, p. viii). In other words, it is states that are still expected to protect their own people. The problem in recent years, as noted already above, is that many states do not have the capacity or the will to do so.

The debate over intervention does not admit any role for the private sector. Nevertheless, there may be some spillover to expectations regarding corporations that operate in zones of conflict. To the extent that the private sector is seen as a tool of states and international organizations in their efforts to attain peaceful goals, then there is some room for corporations to become more directly and officially involved in host-country politics. In most regions where conflict occurs, "responsible engagement" has become a significant theme (Bomann-Larsen 2003).

The emergence of corporate social responsibility norms; the linkages now being made among development, environment, and conflict; and changing attitudes toward intervention all set the stage for the intersection of corporate social responsibility and conflict prevention initiatives. This linkage has been made most forcefully by NGOs with an interest in ending the suffering of the victims of war and repression. The idea has been taken up by governments and international organizations that would like to find some way to promote economic development via foreign investment while avoiding the negative externalities detailed in so much of the literature. Certainly, from the point of view of those in the donor and conflict prevention communities, it may seem that foreign corporations are the best-functioning institutions in societies suffering from state failure.

Extractive Industry Revenues: Norm Entrepreneurs and Institutionalization

Martha Finnemore and Kathryn Sikkink (1998) have described how "norm entrepreneurs" promote new norms that eventually are adopted by a sufficiently large number of people that they reach a kind of "tipping point." They may become so widely accepted that they overturn old ways of understanding appropriate behavior, and become institutionalized into society. We have not reached that point in the development of corporate social responsibility norms, particularly for conflict prevention. In fact, there are many factors militating against institutionalization of such norms: the material self-interest of corporations; the rejection by societies of corporate intervention in domestic affairs; competing norms of free markets and of sovereignty; and others. Nevertheless, I describe here recent initiatives regarding the treatment of revenues from natural resource extraction—oil and gas in particular—in terms of norms, norm entrepreneurs, and institutionalization, and speculate on the durability of this trend.

In the era of globalization, politics—not just economics—has become increasingly globalized. Activists today organize in ways that transcend national boundaries, bringing together interested parties across the globe (Lichbach 2002; Keck and Sikkink 1998). While the general statement that "all politics is local" remains true, what has changed is that the local political situation is now visible and of interest to political interests abroad. When local activists become frustrated with their inability to change government policy because domestic political channels are blocked, they bring in pressure from abroad in the form of transnational activist networks, in a "boomerang effect" against the government (Keck and Sikkink 1998). Increasingly, such a boomerang may also be aimed at foreign corporations operating in unstable political areas.

The notion of bringing business into conflict prevention efforts emerged from activism over oil in Angola, diamonds in Sierra Leone, and the use of security forces in Nigeria and Colombia (Global Witness 1998, 1999; Freeman 2000). Norm entrepreneurs such as Global Witness, an NGO, highlighted in the global media the role of specific companies in profiting from turmoil in Africa. The agenda for corporate conflict prevention was set by the groundbreaking report *The Business of Peace,* produced by the Council on Economic Priorities and the Prince of Wales Business Leaders Forum (Nelson 2000). This report made the economic and moral case for why business should view conflict prevention activities as being in their own self-interest. Interest in this topic was reinforced by the United Nations Global Compact. The Global Compact brings together corporate leaders with three agencies of the UN system, in which the businesses commit to nine principles drawn from UN conventions on the environment, labor, and human rights (with anticorruption as a recently added tenth principle). In the first policy dialogue sponsored by the Global Compact, participants from the private sector, international organizations, and NGOs discussed a number of issues raised by the role of business in stimulating conflict and corruption, both directly and indirectly. Through this dialogue, the participants—with UN leadership—were beginning to disseminate new norms about the corporate role in conflict situations (United Nations Global Compact 2002). A policy-oriented literature emerged that attempted to tease out the economic elements of conflict, the potential role for foreign investors in conflict prevention, and the actual practical policies that this might entail (Guaqeta 2002; International Peace Academy 2001; Sherman 2002; Anderson and Zandvliet 2001; Banfield, Haufler, and Lilly 2003).

For the extractive industries—petroleum in particular—two issues relating to the revenues that flow from corporations to host-country governments serve to illustrate recent changes: the debate over the allocation of such revenues within society, and the transparency of those payments to the public. How a government allocates revenue is of course a responsibility of sovereign states, and typically is not considered an issue for external interest or intervention. However, a misallocation or misappropriation of these funds can deepen divisions between different groups within society, as some are advantaged and some are disadvantaged. In the case of natural resources such as oil or diamonds, the revenues can be huge, dwarfing all other sources of income in the country. As a result, the development of natural resource wealth may stimulate competition to control revenues, fueling corruption and strengthening the position of some elite groups within society at the expense of the poor and disenfranchised. The revenues themselves may become what different groups fight over, as greed and grievance combine in ways that lead to state failure (Collier 2000).

Many observers argue that the very secrecy surrounding the payments made by large companies to host governments facilitates corruption. They argue that one mechanism to encourage a better distribution of revenues is for companies to provide the public with information about what they pay in tax revenues and fees to host-country governments. With that information, observers are often able to trace the funds that are "missing" from government coffers, and bring public scrutiny to bear. Transparency and revenue-sharing as issues go hand in hand, and more and more outsiders—NGOs, international organizations, and donor states—are putting pressure on companies to ensure that revenue figures are made public, and that revenue-sharing formulas include a better distribution of wealth for the purposes of development. One barrier to private sector adoption of more transparency is that in many cases contracts with governments forbid disclosure of information about payments; firms that violate this clause may be expelled from the country.[16]

Today, unlike in decades past, the idea has been firmly planted that commercial enterprises, particularly in the petroleum sector, should establish mechanisms to stamp out corruption and ensure that oil revenues are used for wider societal development. Concerns about corruption in international bidding for major oil exploration and development contracts have existed for many decades, but those concerns are subject to global debate today that has not been seen before. The first step in the evolution of concern for corruption was taken in 1977, when the United States passed the Foreign Corrupt Practices Act. It was the only state to have a law banning bribes in commercial activities.[17]

In the 1990s, activists and development specialists began to view corruption as a barrier to development and a precursor to social breakdown. Since the war on terrorism began, corruption has also come to be viewed as an element of security. Transparency International, an NGO dedicated to changing law and regulation regarding corruption issues, launched a highly successful campaign to "name and shame" countries by publishing its annual Corruption Perception Index of the most corrupt political environments. It promotes the negotiation of "integrity pacts" between business and government.[18] Member states of the Organization for Economic Cooperation and Development in 1997 finally passed a convention on combating bribery of foreign public officials in international business transactions. The World Bank, as part of its program of good governance initiatives, began to incorporate anticorruption elements into its development programs, and it supports the idea that both government and the private sector need to provide better information about commercial transactions. As a sign of its commitment to fight corruption, the World Bank has instituted strict rules about its own procurement system and actually debars from doing business with the World Bank those found guilty of bribery (World Bank 1997). The Publish What You Pay Campaign and the UK Extractive Industries Transparency Initiative[19] both aim to increase the transparency of revenue payments. Recently, a group of ten major investors called for extractive companies to be more transparent about the payments they make to governments, arguing that misused funds can pose a significant business risk (ISIS Asset Management 2003).

Another more dramatic example of the convergence of concerns about state failure, changes in norms of intervention and development, and transnational activism is the revenue-sharing agreement that is part of the Chad-Cameroon pipeline project. The World Bank used its leverage in 2001 to structure a gas pipeline project in Chad and Cameroon in a new and innovative way. In return for World Bank participation, the energy companies and governments had to agree to a new kind of project conditionality. Most of the revenue from the gas pipeline development will go into a separate account for improving public services and funding development projects.[20] An "international advisory group" will monitor the use of pipeline profits and ensure a certain degree of transparency. This revenue-sharing agreement may be unique, but others are looking to it as a model for dealing with oil development under weak and ineffectual governments (Bennett 2001; McPhail 2002). In this case, the World Bank was seeking to prevent both corruption and conflict in a major development project in some very poor countries at the same time that it promoted resource development and more equitable distribution of the proceeds.

This brief overview of recent trends reflects the intersection of new norms about corporate social responsibility, and concern over conflict and conflict prevention. Particular norm entrepreneurs, such as leading NGOs, the UN, and the World Bank, have sought to both raise the profile of the discussion of corporate conflict prevention and institutionalize anticorruption and conflict prevention policies. These policies often rely upon the private sector for implementation, and bypass local host governments. By doing so, they transform the relationship between issues of security and economics.

Corporations and Terrorism

A little over a decade ago, we spoke of war in terms of bloodshed between nation-states, with fears of an East-West conflict always in the front of our minds. With the end of the Cold War, the talk turned primarily toward the civil wars and internal conflicts of the "failed states" of the periphery, in which neighbor turned on neighbor. Since September 2001, we speak primarily of the war on terrorism, and how it is linked to the intractable conflicts of the Middle East and the long-running internal conflicts in countries struggling with corrupt or ineffective regimes.

The private sector can directly or indirectly, deliberately or accidentally, aid terrorists through a number of different routes. Companies and individuals within companies may deliberately aid terrorists in whatever way they can, and in this case, they may be operating outside the law. But even legitimate companies can produce products or provide services that are used in terrorist activity, whether they intend to or not. These include armaments, chemicals, financial services, and many other goods and services (Alexander 2004).

There are three main areas in which legitimate business has a direct role in the fight against terrorists: in regulating financial services, in protecting facilities and products from terrorists, and in developing the technological systems that will help defend against terrorists (Alexander 2004; Rothkopf 2002). One of the most stringent actions against terrorism has been the tightening up of regulations about money transfers and financial fraud. The Financial Action Task Force of the Group of Eight countries has established extensive multilateral rules about money laundering, and publishes a list of companies that comply and those that do not. Financial institutions must report to governments any suspicious banking activity by their customers. Recent financial scandals, such as the one involving Riggs Bank and its relationship with Saudi clients, highlight the degree to which the private sector has a role to play in cutting off the sources of financing for terrorists.

The private sector also has a role to play in securing the very products and services they provide legitimately. For instance, the chemical industry produces the materials that can be used to produce a bomb or chemical weapon. Chemical facilities themselves provide a potential target of attack that could make a relatively small explosive into a large disaster; the accidental explosion at Bhopal, India, which killed and sickened thousands, demonstrates the potential risk posed by these facilities. To date, the chemical sector in the United States has resisted efforts to impose security regulations on its production, but many companies have adopted relatively strict security policies on their own, in a form of self-regulation. The transportation sector, particularly airlines, has of course already been subject to increasingly stringent regulations. Many companies have shown themselves to be quite willing to partner with government, especially in the United States, to provide information to assist in security measures, such as sharing customer lists.

Finally, another significant role for the private sector is in developing new technologies that will help detect and prevent attacks. New screening technologies, for instance, have already been developed for the travel industry. The Pentagon began directing money toward the technology sector some years ago, and the Central Intelligence Agency has a venture fund called In-Q-Tel to support innovation in relevant areas.

A number of people have begun calling for the development and institutionalization of public-private partnerships to combat the threat of terrorism. Dean Alexander, in his recent book *Business Confronts Terrorism* (2004), points out how the need to deal with terrorists has pushed government to assist industry, and industry to assist government, in a symbiotic relationship that is not without some tension. In an article titled "Business Versus Terror," David Rothkopf points out that public-private cooperation has been inadequate so far in the United States, and therefore "a vital resource in defending the nation remains underutilized" (2002, p. 58).

The arguments for a public-private partnership in the war on terror mesh well with recent interest in engaging the private sector in conflict prevention. But despite the incentives for integrating industry into both peacebuilding and antiterrorism, the long-term consequences of the war on terrorism may ultimately undermine many of the goals of conflict prevention. The war on terrorism is a return to "high politics," though without the state-centered focus of the past. This may mean that "low politics," including foreign policies that facilitate foreign investment, may be given a lower priority by governments. Certainly the decline in foreign direct investment worldwide over the past two years reduces the possibilities for corporate conflict prevention. Host societies may become increasingly suspicious of foreign investors and place barriers and restrictions on their operations in the name of security (though this has occurred more in the United States than elsewhere). The fight against terrorism itself is already putting a costly burden on producers everywhere, but especially in regions of instability. We may see less commitment to the norm of transparency and more efforts to increase secrecy, and this might affect the ability of corporations to engage in public reporting and local community dialogue. A number of companies have already expressed concern that publishing information about, for instance, their toxic releases might provide terrorists with the information to pinpoint facilities that could then become targets of attack. On the other hand, the effort to sever the link between legitimate business and terrorist financing may actually promote more extensive regulation and self-regulation in this area.

The Future of Corporate Conflict Prevention

Do corporate conflict prevention initiatives actually reduce the potential for conflict? We do not yet have sufficient evidence to make a judgment about their effectiveness. There is no reason to think that widespread adoption of conflict management policies by corporations would not be helpful, and certainly some initiatives, such as the Kimberley Process for diamond certification, appear to have reduced financial resources for continuing conflict in West Africa. But there exist a number of barriers to widespread adoption of corporate conflict prevention that make it difficult for companies, host governments, and activists to pursue this strategy successfully. While numerous persuasive arguments have been made that such policies are in the long-term best interest of corporations, not all company managers are persuaded. Most still operate in a short-term world where the added costs of conflict management outweigh the benefits. There are few immediate political benefits from engaging in anticorruption efforts, transparency, or local dialogue. For instance, British Petroleum stood alone when it published figures on its payments to the Angolan government, and other oil companies and the Angolan government condemned its public reporting. The costs of conflict itself often do not fall on the private sector; after all, foreign investors always have the option to withdraw entirely from politically difficult situations. Government policies so far provide few incentives for positive action by companies, although some are now considering what they might do (Banfield, Haufler, and Lilly 2003).

One of the key barriers to private sector action is of course the host governments, which resist outside interference in their affairs. Many governments have only limited sovereignty, and activist foreign investors may undermine their legitimacy in ways that simply exacerbate instability. Intervention from outside, as Philip Cerny (2005) argues, can create backlashes that further destabilize the environment. It is host governments that have regulatory power over companies, and in response to challenges from the private sector, they can withhold their license to operate in the country. Attempts by private sector actors to contribute to local community development, protect human rights, redistribute resources, or resolve divisions within and between societies have been beset with unintended side effects, insufficient expertise, and accusations about the lack of accountability and illegitimacy of the firms. While it may sound positive to have companies engage in conflict prevention activity—and it certainly sounds bad to have them ignore the impact of their operations on local politics—an official policy of encouraging this may give them license to intervene more directly in host country politics, which may pose more problems than it resolves.

Some of the activist groups that are committed to humanitarian causes remain ambivalent about the corporate presence in developing countries. For many of them, corporations remain a source of political division and grievance, and nothing they can do will ameliorate the negative externalities they impost on host societies. It is not clear that activist NGOs and corporations have much room to reach a consensus on what action to take, and what would be the indicators of success. While the possibilities for corporate conflict prevention are of great interest, there is a possibility that they will go unrealized.

Nevertheless, the international community appears to be inching its way, step by step, toward promoting a more significant role for corporations in the politics of states that have failed to meet the standards of democracy, transparency, and respect for human rights and the environment. This is not to say that corporations are free to intervene directly in the political process. There is still a strong prohibition against, for instance, allowing a company to undermine or overthrow a government. Foreign investors who financially support one political party over another in a democratic system are still regularly condemned (in both developed and developing countries). The intervention proposed here is more indirect and generally accomplished in partnership with actors that have more legitimacy in this realm, such as governments and international organizations. These partnerships would have been unthinkable a few decades ago.

Theories of international relations and international political economy have relatively little to say about the trends and challenges discussed in this chapter. The traditional literature on security has been supplemented by a literature on the "new" security agenda, but this new literature has not done a good job of theorizing a role for corporations. The extensive empirical work on conflict certainly provides us with a better understanding of civil war and instability and the contributions of resource wealth to societal breakdown. Neither of these, however, has engaged directly the literature on conflict prevention, which is a more policy-oriented topic (Crocker, Hampson, and Aall 2001). International political economy has provided us with a way to understand the many facets of globalization, although the scholarly debate over its character, extent, and effects has not reached any consensus (Hirst and Thompson 1995; Keohane and Nye 2000; Stiglitz 2003). This literature also does not wrestle particularly well with the place of multinational corporations in theory and policy. Recent theorizing in a constructivist vein about transactional activist networks and norms provides us with a framework for understanding some of the dynamics of this new agenda, but do not provide answers to some of the practical questions we have about how norms may be transferred by activists to the business community, and how those might interact with other opposing interests and norms.

The dominant motif of the globalization debate has been the power of corporations and the declining capacity of the state (Strange 1996; Greider 1997; Derber 1998; Korten 1995). Liberal policymakers have promoted a minimal role for governments. Many critics decry the weakened authority and ability of governments even as promarket enthusiasts trumpet the ability of the private sector to be innovative, efficient, and forward-thinking. All of these ideas point us toward the business community as both the source of and the solution to current problems, bestowing upon it a certain legitimacy even when it acts outside of its traditional market role (Cutler, Haufler, and Porter 1999).

The idea of corporate social responsibility has been adopted by a wide array of actors in a transnationalized political community. The end of the Cold War and a global war on terrorism provide the space for ideas and options to be considered today that would not have been possible previously. In a seemingly more complex political world, the idea of involving the private sector in areas previously reserved to the state may spread rapidly among policy entrepreneurs, and become a focal point for action (Schelling 1978; Avant 2000; Finnemore and Sikkink 1998). As this trend has expanded in recent years, participants could easily believe that it is a logical extension to move from environmental and labor standards, where most of the action is now, to human rights, corruption, equity, and conflict. Note that this is not about seeking to redefine or reconstitute the capitalist system itself, unlike the claims and demands of many of the antiglobalization activists (Berejikian and Dryzek 2000). The participants are simply redefining behavior at the margins by shifting the focus from corporations as the source of problems, to corporations as the potential source of solutions.

The evolution of expectations regarding corporate behavior in foreign countries seems to have taken much of the private sector by surprise, although the change did not happen overnight. Experts and activists alike now propose higher standards for corporate conduct, expecting them to behave in ways that promote wider normative goals, such as social justice and equality (Kapstein 1998–1999). At the moment, most proposals are still for voluntary action. In the future, will the world community consent to stronger restraints on global corporate behavior? Multilateral investment agreements have failed in the past, for a variety of reasons, and do not appear to be any closer to being concluded than in the past. Narrow agreements are more possible, such as the Kimberly Process for diamond certification. In some ways, these authoritative and traditional legal instruments should be welcomed by the corporate community. The hope is that they could establish clear and stable expectations that would have an authority and legitimacy that purely voluntary actions would never have.

The idea that the private sector could contribute to human rights protection, democratization, and the elimination of corruption turns our notions of world politics upside down. States are supposed to be sovereign and in charge. They are the central actor in world politics, especially on issues of war and peace. Private interests are traditionally viewed as selfish and uninterested in the impact their operations may have on social and political divisions within society. Many people equate globalization with the growing power of multinational corporations. They also equate it with the increasing division of the world into haves and have-nots, exacerbating local and international points of contention. Globalizers believe that economic interests have become so strong that markets replace politics at home and abroad. On the one hand, corporations cannot legitimately perform the functions of governments, and should not be asked to do so. But on the other hand, in dire situations, there might be no other actor able to intervene effectively.

Notes

1. The sharpest downturn in inward foreign direct investment was in the United States, the United Kingdom, and the Netherlands. The unstable or failed states of concern here generally received little foreign direct investment to begin with, and their declines were not quite so dramatic (UNCTAD 2003).

2. Norms are typically defined as "collective expectations for the proper behavior of actors with a given identity" (Katzenstein 1996, p. 5). The whole idea of corpo-

rate social responsibility is an attempt to reshape collective expectations about the proper behavior of multinational corporations (Haufler 2001b).

3. The divestment option is still clearly on the table, however. The international community has put extensive pressure on companies to withdraw from Burma, for instance, where a brutal dictatorship rules.

4. The head of the International Criminal Court has declared an interest in investigating the ways in which corporations took advantage of the conflict in the Democratic Republic of Congo to exploit its natural resources. The UN Commission on Human Rights has also declared a similar interest. A number of businesses in the financial sector, in response to criticism, recently adopted the so-called Equator Principles, which deal with responsible investment behavior.

5. Initially only a handful of companies participated in the early negotiations, but more have now joined, and a number of other governments have also either joined or expressed some interest in joining.

6. Political risk assessment examines how political factors will affect the local operations of an investor in a particular country. Conflict impact assessments examine the other side of this—how those operations affect local politics in ways that may increase political risk (Anderson and Zandvliet 2001).

7. A similar code also was established for U.S. companies investing in Northern Ireland, called the McBride Principles. These are intended to foster religious tolerance and equality.

8. Robin Broad and John Cavanagh (1998) are not entirely certain whether this qualifies as a full-fledged social movement, given the diversity of its aims and membership.

9. Not all of these criteria are what would be considered "progressive." While the social screens that eliminate gun manufacturers and known polluters from an investment portfolio have received a lot of attention, there are also screens based on religious preference, or objections to abortion and family planning.

10. Mark Duffield (2001, p. 2) argues that this is a radical project on the part of the North—the incorporation of conflict resolution and societal reconstruction within aid policy entails a transformation of society and a new form of global liberal governance.

11. The Millennium Development Goals adopted by the UN General Assembly in 2000, and endorsed by the multilateral development banks, do not directly mention any issues related to the political efficacy of regimes. It is in the implementation of programs to achieve these goals that institutional capacity becomes a leading factor.

12. The resource curse is often linked to the "Dutch Disease," in which the sudden vast development of one resource for export leads to an increase in the exchange rate, which makes other sectors uncompetitive and weakens fiscal discipline. The country becomes progressively more dependent on that one resource. The Dutch suffered this problem in the early 1960s in developing its natural gas resources.

13. The character and extent of sovereignty from Westphalia onward has become a subject of intense scholarly debate. See, for instance, Krasner 1999.

14. Mary Robinson has commented that "business leaders were unsure about where their responsibilities for human rights begin and end. They were concerned that by expressing their commitment to international standards such as the Universal Declaration of Human Rights, they would be going beyond their proper role" (Robinson 2003).

15. States in the developing world have spoken out against any intervention at all, even in a humanitarian crisis, since they know that it is the powerful states of the North that probably would be doing the intervening in the South—and not vice versa. China, India, and Brazil have been particularly vocal on this point.

16. British Petroleum made a commitment to fiscal transparency by publicizing the signature bonuses it paid in Angola. The company has made a strong commitment to increase the amount of information it provides publicly about its operations, and to put in place systems to prevent corruption and bribery by its employees (Christiansen 2002). As a result of publishing those bonuses, however, the company stirred up controversy in Angola, among other oil company partners, and among those who criticize the payment of signature bonuses as a form of corruption itself.

17. The U.S. commitment to the Foreign Corrupt Practices Act is being tested today by a major investigation of U.S. companies involved in competition for oil contracts in the Caspian region ("Big Oil's Dirty Secrets" 2003). For more details, see also Tsalik 2003. It will be tested even more in the bidding for contracts to rebuild Iraqi oil facilities. The entire process of contracting out for the rebuilding of Iraq will be subject to extreme scrutiny, but the likelihood of corruption is high. Recently, Transparency International challenged oil companies planning to operate in Iraq to publish what they pay.

18. One innovative initiative is the new nongovernmental organization TRACE ("Transparent Agents and Contracting Entities")—an organization that has established strict standards for anticorruption through due diligence regarding intermediaries to transactions. These include sales agents, suppliers, contractors, and consultants who are essentially certified as to their integrity.

19. George Soros, wealthy financier and philanthropist, funded the launch of the Publish What You Pay Campaign. British prime minister Tony Blair put forward the Extractive Industry Transparency Initiative at the 2002 World Summit on Sustainable Development in Johannesburg. Other governments have joined the campaign, including Italy, Norway, Indonesia, the Central African Republic, France, and South Africa. A number of nongovernmental organizations, the World Bank, and the UN Development Programme have also become involved.

20. The intent was to head off corruption and conflict, though the government of Chad almost immediately used signing bonuses from the oil companies to purchase arms.

5

Plight or Plunder?
Natural Resources and Civil War

Colin H. Kahl

Although the study of international security has long been fixated on war between countries, especially great powers, three-quarters of all armed conflicts
since 1945 have been *within* countries, and the vast majority of these conflicts
have occurred in the developing world (Holsti 1996). The number of civil
wars peaked in the early 1990s and has been declining gradually ever since,
but they remain a scourge on humanity. Indeed, as many people have died as
a result of internal strife since 1980 alone as were killed in World War I (Leitenberg 2003). Armed conflicts have also crippled the prospect for a better life
in many countries, especially in sub-Saharan Africa and parts of Asia, by destroying essential infrastructure, decimating social trust, encouraging human
and capital flight, exacerbating food insecurity, spreading disease, and diverting precious financial resources toward military spending. Compounding matters further, the damaging effects of civil wars rarely remain confined within
the afflicted countries. In the past decade alone, tens of millions of refugees
have spilled across borders, producing significant socioeconomic and health
problems in neighboring countries. Instability has also rippled outward as a
consequence of cross-border incursions by rebel groups, disruptions in trade,
and damage done to the reputation of entire regions in the eyes of investors.
Globally, war-torn countries have become havens and recruiting grounds for
international terrorist networks, organized crime, and drug traffickers (Collier
et al. 2003; Marshall and Gurr 2003).

This chapter examines a crucial component of the political economy of
civil wars: the connection between growing pressures on natural resources,
stemming from rapid population growth and the negative externalities of economic globalization, and armed conflict in developing countries. Recent research suggests that the linkages here are real and important. A number of

high-profile case studies, for example, demonstrate that population growth, environmental degradation, and natural resource competition have interacted in many instances to produce or exacerbate civil and ethnic violence (Baechler et al. 1996; Baechler and Spillman 1996; Homer-Dixon and Blitt 1998; Kahl 1998; Homer-Dixon 1999). Quantitative studies analyzing the correlates of civil wars over the past several decades also suggest that countries that are highly dependent on natural resources (Collier et al. 2003), as well as those experiencing high rates of deforestation, soil degradation, and low per capita availability of arable land and freshwater, have higher than average risks of falling into turmoil (Hauge and Ellingsen 1998; Cincotta, Engelman, and Anastasion 2003, chap. 5).

Despite this growing body of scholarship, analysts disagree as to whether too few or too many resources are the problem. Neo-Malthusians contend that natural resource scarcity makes societies more conflict-prone. Neoclassical economists challenge this view, arguing that greater dangers flow from a local abundance of natural resources. This chapter engages the debate between neo-Malthusians and neoclassical economists as a means of deepening our understanding of the role natural resources play in contemporary civil wars.[1] I argue that many of the arguments put forth by these two approaches are not as opposed as they initially appear, making it possible to pool many of their insights. Much of the apparent tension is resolved once it is recognized that each focuses on different levels of analysis, different types of resources, and different time frames. Neo-Malthusians tend to be most concerned with the problems created by the degradation and depletion of renewable resources (e.g., arable land, freshwater, forests, and fisheries), while neoclassical economists emphasize the challenges emanating from nonrenewable resources (e.g., oil, gemstones, and other valuable minerals).[2] Furthermore, both neo-Malthusians and neoclassical economists agree that problems emerge from natural resource dependence; their apparent disagreements stem mainly from the fact that each emphasizes pathologies at different temporal stages of this dependence. The least contentious point between the two approaches relates to the political context most likely to produce violent conflict. Both generally agree that weak states with authoritarian or transitional political institutions are more likely to experience resource related strife.

I begin by briefly describing the intersection between demographic change, economic globalization, and natural resources. Next, I provide an assessment of the competing arguments advanced by neo-Malthusians and neoclassical economists regarding the relationship between natural resources and civil war. Finally, I draw lessons from this debate for the future. Given projected levels of population growth, economic expansion, and inequality, I conclude that both approaches point to turbulent times ahead unless difficult behavioral and policy changes are adopted.

Pressures on the Planet

The past century witnessed unprecedented population growth, economic development, and environmental stress, changes that continue to this day. From 1900 to 2000, world population grew from 1.6 billion to 6.1 billion. Since 1950 alone, 3.5 billion people have been added to the planet, with 85 percent of this increase occurring in developing and transition countries (World Bank 2003b, p. 7; Worldwatch Institute 2003, p. 67; United Nations Population Division [UNPD] 2003). Worldwide population growth rates peaked in the late 1960s at around 2 percent a year, but the current rate of 1.2 percent still represents a net addition of 77 million people a year. The differential population growth rates of rich and poor countries have also become more pronounced. The current rate in high-income countries is 0.25 percent, compared to 1.46 percent for developing countries as a whole. Moreover, within the subset of the forty-nine *least*-developed countries, the rate is currently 2.4 percent (UNPD 2001, p. 5; UNPD 2003, p. vi).

The global economy has also experienced tremendous growth over the past century. Estimates vary, but the global economy most likely increased twenty to forty times between 1900 and 2000. The tempo of change has been especially pronounced since the end of World War II; between 1950 and 2002, the global economy grew from $6.7 trillion to $48 trillion (UNPD 2001, p. 1; Worldwatch Institute 2003, pp. 44–45). This enormous economic expansion occurred during a time of accelerating globalization and, especially since the 1980s, rising faith in the power of markets and privatization. Economic growth, globalization, and the harnessing of market forces have allowed for average living standards to advance faster than world population growth, improving the quality of life for billions. Nevertheless, the benefits of economic growth and globalization have been unevenly distributed within and across countries and regions (UNDP 2003, p. 16).

In the 1990s, for example, average per capita growth was less than 3 percent (the threshold needed to double incomes in a generation given constant rates of inequality) in 125 developing and transition economies, and 54 of these countries were actually poorer in 2000 than in 1990.[3] More than 1.2 billion people currently live in extreme poverty, defined as an income of less than $1 a day, and a total of 2.8 billion (more than half the population of the developing world) live on less than $2 a day. Although the proportion of people suffering from extreme poverty fell from 30 percent to 23 percent during the 1990s, the absolute number fell by only 123 million, due to a 15 percent increase in the population of low- and middle-income countries. Driving most of this progress was China, which managed to lift 150 million people out of poverty. However, 37 of 67 countries with data saw poverty rates increase in the 1990s and, excluding China, the total number of extremely poor people worldwide *increased* by 28 million. Worst off was sub-Saharan Africa, where per capita income fell by 5 percent and 74 million additional people descended into extreme poverty (producing a regional total of 404 million living on less than $1 a day in 1999). Other key indices of human welfare also reveal a similar pattern: overall progress but also numerous countries falling further behind. Over the past decade, 34 countries had lower life expectancy, 21 countries had a larger portion of people hungry, and 14 had more children dying before age five (UNDP 2003, pp. 2–3, 5, 34, 40–41; World Bank 2003a, pp. 4–5, 9; World Bank 2003b, pp. 1–3).

This pattern is also reflected in widening gaps between rich and poor. In 1960 the ratio between the gross domestic product (GDP) per capita in the 20 richest and 20 poorest countries was 18 to 1; in 1995, the ratio was 37 to 1 (Worldwatch Institute 2003, pp. 18, 88). Between 1980 and the late 1990s, inequality also increased *within* 33 of 66 countries for which there is adequate data available. All told, the richest 5 percent of the world's people now receive 114 times the income of the poorest 5 percent and the richest 1 percent receive as much as the poorest 57 percent. Nonincome measures also point to stark inequalities. A decade ago, children under five in sub-Saharan Africa were 19 times more likely to die than were their counterparts in rich countries, but they are now 26 times more likely to die. Indeed, Latin America and the Caribbean were the only parts of the developing world where disparities in infant mortality compared to rich countries did not widen in the 1990s (UNDP 2003, pp. 5, 39–40).

Rapid population and economic growth over the past century have placed severe and accelerating pressures on natural resources and planetary life-support systems. The traditional Malthusian notion that exponential population growth alone drives strains on the environment has long been refuted; no serious thinkers, including neo-Malthusians, now maintain that human-induced environmental changes are a mere function of numbers. Rather, the relationship between population growth and the environment is mediated by consumption habits, as well as the technologies used to extract natural resources and provide goods and services. The population-environment connection is thus affected by the choices of individuals, firms, and governments, and it is deeply embedded in the processes of economic expansion and globalization.[4]

At both the global and local levels, resource depletion and environmental degradation result from extreme wealth and extreme poverty. The material-intensive and pollution-laden consumption habits and production activities of high-income countries are responsible for most of the world's greenhouse gases, solid and hazardous waste, and other environmental pollution. High-income countries also generate a disproportionate amount of the global demand for fossil fuels, nonfuel minerals, grain, meat, fish, tropical hardwoods, and products derived from endangered species (World Bank 2003a, p. 118; Worldwatch Institute 2003, p. 17; World Resources Institute 2000, pp. 26–27).

Although consumption and production activities by rich countries may be the primary drivers of global environmental challenges, poverty and inequality within developing countries also place burdens on the environment, especially on local renewable resources. Impoverished individuals in developing countries frequently live in the most fragile ecological areas and are often driven to overexploit croplands, pastures, forests, fisheries, and water resources in order to eke out a living. Many have been forced to migrate to marginal areas due to overcrowding on better land. In the past fifty years, the number of people living on fragile lands in developing countries doubled to 1.3 billion,[5] and rural population growth remains higher than average in countries with 30 percent or more of their population on fragile land. Fragile ecological areas, which represent 73 percent of Earth's land surface, have very limited ability to sustain high population densities and are particularly vulnerable to degradation, erosion, flooding, fires, landslides, and climatic change (World Bank 2003a, p. 118; World Bank 2003b, pp. 7–8, 60–67; Worldwatch Institute 2003, p. 17).

Numerous signs suggest that the combined effects of population growth, unsustainable consumption, and extreme poverty are taking their toll on the environment. More natural resources have been consumed since the end of World War II than in all of human history to that point (McKibben 1998, p. 63). The consumption of nonrenewable resources has significantly increased, although consumption has risen at a slower rate than population and economic growth, due to changes in technology. In 2003 the global consumption of fossil fuels (which account for 77 percent of all energy use) was 4.7 times the level it was in 1950 (Worldwatch Institute 2003, p. 34). High-income countries consume more than half of all commercial energy, and per capita energy consumption is five times greater than in developing countries (World Bank 2003a, p. 118). In terms of nonfuel minerals, 9.6 billion tons of marketable minerals (e.g., copper, diamonds, gold) were extracted in 1999, almost twice as much as in 1970. And once again, high-income countries account for the majority of mineral demand (Sampat 2003, p. 113).

In terms of renewable resources, the World Wildlife Fund (WWF) has recently calculated humanity's "ecological footprint" by comparing renewable resource consumption to an estimate of nature's biological productive capacity. A country's ecological footprint represents the total area (measured in standardized global hectares of biologically productive land and water) required to produce the renewable resources consumed and to assimilate the wastes generated by human activities. In 1999, each person on the planet demanded an average of 2.3 global hectares, but countries varied widely in their footprint. On average, high-income countries demanded 6.5 biologically productive hectares per person, compared with 2 hectares for middle-income countries and 0.8 hectares for low-income countries. All told, the global footprint in 1999 amounted to 13.7 billion biologically productive hectares, exceeding by about 20 percent the 11.4 billion hectares estimated to exist. While the ecological footprint approach is only a partial measure of the impact humanity is placing on nature, it does suggest an unsustainable rate of consumption of renewable resources over the long run. Indeed, the WWF calculates that humanity has been running an ecological deficit with Earth since the 1980s (Wackernagel et al. 2002; WWF 2002).

This conclusion is reinforced by signs of growing depletion and degradation of renewable resources. Worldwide, 23 percent of all croplands, pastures, forests, and woodlands (totaling 2 billion hectares) have been affected by soil degradation since the 1950s, impacting the livelihoods of perhaps 1 billion people. Of these lands, about 16 percent are so severely degraded that the change is too costly to reduce, 46 percent are moderately degraded, and 39 percent are lightly degraded (UNDP 2003, p. 10; World Bank 2003b, p. 2). Deforestation has also been rapid over the past century. Worldwide, there were 5 billion hectares of forested area at the beginning of the twentieth century; now there are less 4 billion hectares. One-fifth of all tropical forests have been cleared since 1960, with the bulk of deforestation occurring in developing countries. In the 1990s alone, low-income countries lost 8 percent of their forested area as a result of global and local demand for timber, the conversion of forests into large-scale ranching and plantations, and the expansion of subsistence agriculture (World Bank 2003a, p. 118; World Bank 2003b, p. 3).

Land is not the only resource under siege. Freshwater, which is critical for both human survival and economic development, is becoming increasingly scarce in many areas. Over the past twenty-five years, global per capita water supplies have declined by one-third, and 1.7 billion people in developing regions are currently experiencing water stress (defined as consumption of more than 20 percent of a country's renewable water supply each year). If current trends persist, as many as 5 billion people could face such conditions by 2025 (UNDP 2003, pp. 10, 125; World Bank 2003a, p. 118; World Bank 2003b, p. 2). Finally, about 34 percent of all fish species are at risk from human activities and around 70 percent of commercial fisheries are either fully exploited or overexploited and experiencing declining yields. This is troubling not only from a biodiversity perspective; millions depend on fisheries for employment and 1 billion people worldwide rely on fish as their primary protein source (UNDP 2003, p. 10; World Bank 2003b, p. 3; World Resources Institute 2000, p. 70).

The Connection Between Natural Resources and Civil War

Since the early 1990s, a number of academics and international security specialists have argued that demographic and natural resource pressures pose significant threats to political stability in developing countries. Initially, this discussion was dominated by neo-Malthusians, but more recently a number of scholars working within the tradition of neoclassical economics have entered the fray. Neo-Malthusians and neoclassical economists agree that natural resources can play a role in causing or exacerbating civil wars, but they disagree as to the character of this relationship. Neo-Malthusians contend that population growth, environmental degradation, and scarcity interact to place strains on societies and states, making them more vulnerable to armed conflict. Neoclassical economists, in contrast, argue that abundant supplies of valuable natural resources are more likely to produce strife.

Deprivation and State Failure

Neo-Malthusians argue that rapid population growth, environmental degradation, resource depletion, and unequal resource access combine to exacerbate poverty and income inequality in many of the world's least-developed countries (Merrick 2001, 2002). In stagnant economies, rapid population growth can contribute to declining wages, unemployment, and landlessness, because the labor force expands faster than available jobs. Environmental degradation and depletion can also worsen poverty, especially among those forced by population pressures and unequal land distribution to live on marginal land. Some 3.2 billion people in developing countries live in rural areas, and for many of these individuals, both long-term environmental stress (e.g., deforestation, soil degradation, fish and freshwater scarcity) and short-term natural disasters (e.g., floods, droughts, and the emerging effects of global climate change) pose significant threats to their survival (UNDP 2003, pp. 10, 123–125; UNPD 2002, p. 13; World Bank 2003a, p. 12).

Neo-Malthusians argue that intergroup violence becomes more likely as deprived individuals and social groups engage in increasingly fierce competition over dwindling natural resources and economic opportunities. Deprivation also increases the risk of rebellion against the state by generating a large pool of aggrieved individuals (Homer-Dixon 1991, pp. 104–105, 109–111; Homer-Dixon 1999, pp. 142–147). Norman Myers (1993, p. 22), for example, has argued that people impoverished by population growth and environmental degradation "become desperate people, all too ready to challenge governments through . . . guerrilla groups" (see also Ehrlich and Ehrlich 1990, pp. 178–179; and Matthews 1989, pp. 166, 168).

The civil war in El Salvador that began in the late 1970s and raged throughout the 1980s provides an example of these dynamics. Prior to the outbreak of the conflict, decades of rapid population growth had combined with a highly skewed distribution of farmland to produce acute land scarcity, widespread landlessness, substantial migration to marginal ecological areas, and mounting poverty and inequality. Compounding matters further, by the 1980s, extensive deforestation, soil erosion, and watershed deterioration had undermined food production and hurt the incomes of many poor farmers. As absolute and relative deprivation escalated, so did support for the communist rebellion (Myers 1993, pp. 122–129).

Although early neo-Malthusian conflict claims emphasized absolute and relative deprivation, more recent work acknowledges that deprivation by itself is rarely sufficient to produce large-scale organized violence. The poor often lack the capabilities to rebel, especially in the context of a strong state. Therefore, neo-Malthusians contend that population and environmental pressures are most likely to contribute to internal wars when these pressures also weaken state authority, thereby opening "political space" for violence to occur (Goldstone 1991, 1997, 2002; Homer-Dixon 1991, 1994, 1999; Kahl 2000; Kaplan 1994, 1996).

Demographic and environmental pressures can undermine state authority in a number of ways. First, as population and environmental challenges mount, so will the demands placed on the state from suffering segments of the economy and marginalized individuals, including calls for costly development projects, such as hydroelectric dams, canals, and irrigation systems, subsidies for fertilizer and other agricultural inputs, and employment, housing, schools, sanitation, energy, and lower food prices in urban areas. These demands increase fiscal strains and thus erode a state's administrative capacity by requiring budgetary trade-offs. A state's legitimacy may also be cast in doubt if individuals and groups come to blame the government for their plight (Goldstone 1991, chap. 1; Goldstone 1997, p. 108; Homer-Dixon 1994, pp. 25–26).

Second, population growth, environmental degradation, and resource depletion can undermine overall economic productivity, thereby reducing the revenue available to local and central governments at the very time that rising demands require greater expenditures (Homer-Dixon 1994, p. 25). Neo-Malthusians do not argue that population growth is universally detrimental to the economy. Nevertheless, in countries with stagnant economies, scarce or costly natural resources, dysfunctional markets, and government policies biased against labor, significant population growth can undermine economic productivity. Population growth tends to lower the ratio of capital to labor and the resulting "capital shallowing" can reduce the per capita economic productivity of a society. Rapid population expansion can also increase dependency ratios and make it more difficult for households to educate and pass on capital to children. By creating large numbers of young people who cannot be educated or productively employed, population growth can undermine the productivity of workers and reduce a country's ability to compete in the global economy (Cohen 1995; Kelley 1988; Kelley and McGreevey 1994). Higher dependency ratios also force households to shift a greater proportion of financial resources toward basic consumption, limiting their ability to save. In the aggregate, lower domestic savings rates can undermine investments necessary for long-term economic growth or force public and private actors to borrow from abroad, thereby increasing foreign debt (Ahlburg 1994, pp. 136–137; Lee,

Mason, and Miller 2001, pp. 137–142; Williamson 2001, pp. 124–128). All told, recent models that disaggregate population growth into several components (i.e., population size and density, as well as changes in mortality and fertility, labor force size, and youth dependency ratios) suggest that the net effect of rapid population growth on economic progress in developing countries has been negative, at least since the 1980s (Birdsall and Sinding 2001, pp. 9–10; Kelley and Schmidt 2001).[6]

Environmental depletion and degradation can also have serious adverse effects on countries whose economies depend on natural resources. Agriculture continues to account for nearly a quarter of the GDP of low-income countries, and forestry products and fisheries also make large contributions (UNDP 2003, p. 125). Thus the loss of valuable agricultural land and reductions in crop yields due to soil erosion and desertification, the loss of timber and fuel wood due to deforestation, the collapse of fisheries due to overfishing and pollution, and the loss of hydroelectric power and transportation due to the siltation of rivers and reservoirs can all have damaging economic effects (Homer-Dixon 1991, pp. 94–97).

The communist insurgency in the Philippines demonstrates how the simultaneous strains placed on societies and states can lead to civil strife. An annual population growth rate of around 3 percent, an extremely skewed distribution of arable land, and destructive logging and fishing practices all combined to produce some of the worst deforestation, soil erosion, and coastal degradation in the world. These demographic and environmental pressures worsened poverty and inequality from the late 1960s onward and placed increasing strains on the Philippine state, including escalating demands on the Marcos regime to invest in costly rural and urban infrastructural projects. At the same time, population growth, environmental degradation, and resource inequality ate into domestic savings and undermined economic productivity. This contributed to the debt crisis of the early 1980s, crippling the state's ability to control and service the countryside. As state authority waned and economic insecurity in the countryside grew, poor Filipinos and indigenous communities were driven in ever-increasing numbers into the waiting arms of the New Peoples Army (Kahl 2000, chap. 3).

In addition to increasing the risks of rebellion from below, state weakness sometimes encourages political elites themselves to instigate societal warfare in an effort to cling to power. Ethnic clashes in Kenya in the early 1990s illustrate this dynamic. During the 1980s, population growth averaging 3.4 percent a year combined with soil erosion, desertification, and unequal land access to create an extreme scarcity of arable land, escalating economic marginalization in rural areas, and substantial rural-to-urban migration. As the population of Nairobi and Kenya's other urban centers soared, and related social and economic problems worsened, pressure mounted on President Daniel Arap Moi's regime to forsake monopoly rule by the Kenya African National Union (KANU) and allow multiparty elections. In response to this threat, Moi and many of his close associates set out to discredit the democratization process and consolidate their control over the valuable and fertile Rift Valley by orchestrating a series of tribal clashes that left 1,500 dead and hundreds of thousands homeless. To implement this strategy, KANU elites capitalized on and manipulated a set of demographically, environmentally, and historically rooted land grievances between the Kalenjin, Maasai, and other pastoral groups, and the Kikuyu, Kissii, Luhya, and Luo farming communities that had moved on to traditionally pastoral land during the colonial and postcolonial periods (Kahl 1998; Kahl 2000, chap. 4).

The genocide in Rwanda exhibited similar patterns of state exploitation on a much larger scale. In 1992 the internationally sponsored Arusha Accords called on President Juvénal Habyarimana's Hutu regime to open up the government to greater participation by Tutsis. In a bid to maintain control, Hutu extremists organized militias and fomented anti-Tutsi sentiment among Hutus. After the suspicious death of Habyarimana in a plane explosion in April 1994, extremists unleashed a wave of violence against Tutsis and moderate Hutus that left hundreds of thousands dead. Population and land pressures in Rwanda were critical to the ability of Hutu elites to execute this vicious campaign. Between 1985 and 1990, Rwanda's annual population growth rate was 3.3 percent, and prior to the genocide, Rwanda ranked as Africa's most overcrowded nation. These demographic pressures combined with overcultivation and soil erosion to generate an acute scarcity of land, a substantial problem given the predominantly rural nature of Rwanda's economy (Percival and Homer-Dixon 1995). An increasing number of uneducated and underemployed youths began to look for any means of improving their condition. There was thus a large pool of desperate individuals who were susceptible to anti-Tutsi propaganda and easily directed by extremists to kill and drive off their neighbors. As Gérard Prunier (1995, p. 4) notes, "The decision to kill was of course made by politicians. . . . But at least part of the reason why it was carried out so thoroughly by ordinary rank-and-file peasants . . . was a feeling that there were too many people on too little land, and that with a reduction of their numbers, there would be more for the survivors" (see also Ohlsson 1999, chap. 4).

Honey Pots and the Resource Curse

Neoclassical economists advance a set of claims that, on the surface at least, appear to turn neo-Malthusian arguments on their head. Resource abundance, rather than scarcity, is argued to be the bigger threat to political instability. One claim centers on so-called honey pot effects. According to this view, abundant supplies of valuable local resources create incentives for rebel groups to form and fight to capture them. This can spawn attempts by regional warlords and rebel organizations to cleave off resource-rich territories or violently hijack the state. Once seized, valuable natural resources fuels conflict

escalation by allowing the parties to purchase weaponry and mobilize potential recruits (Ross 2003, pp. 15–26; Ross 2004). In short, profit-seeking motivates and empowers insurgents in resource-rich countries. As Paul Collier
(2000, pp. 4, 21) argues, "rebellion occurs only when rebels can do well out
of war. . . . Rebellions either have the objective of natural resource predation,
or are critically dependent upon natural resource predation in order to pursue
other objectives. These, rather than objective grievances, are the risk factors
which conflict prevention must reduce if is to be successful" (see also Collier
and Hoeffler 2001; and Collier et al. 2003). Echoing these sentiments, Indra
de Soysa (2000a, p. 26) contends that "greed rather than grievance (at least in
terms of the availability of natural resources is concerned) is likelier to generate armed violence" (see also de Soysa 2000b; le Billon 2001; and Ross
1999).

The conflicts in Sierra Leone and the Democratic Republic of Congo (the
former Zaire) demonstrate the honey pot effect in action. The Revolutionary
United Front (RUF), a group formed by disgruntled Sierra Leone officials and
supported by Liberia's Charles Taylor, invaded Sierra Leone from Liberia in
1991. The RUF was chiefly interested in capturing the country's mineral
wealth. Indeed, its first act was to seize control of the Kono diamond fields and
throughout the conflict the RUF sustained its operations with diamond revenues (Klare 2001, pp. 191, 199–202; Renner 2002, pp. 22–26). In the Congo,
the attempt by local actors and neighboring armies to profit from the country's
valuable supply of diamonds, gold, copper, coltan, and timber resources was
not the initial source of turmoil. Nevertheless, plunder eventually became a
powerful contributor to the escalation and endurance of one of the bloodiest
wars in recent memory (Renner 2002, pp. 26–31).

Like the deprivation claims advanced by neo-Malthusians, honey pot arguments locate the origin of violence in the incentives of societal actors. By
themselves, however, these incentives are not enough to explain violence;
strong, capable states should be able to prevent, deter, or repress attempts to
seize natural resources before they escalate to all-out war (Collier et al. 2003).
In other words, like grievance-based clashes, greed-based ones are more
likely when states are weak.

Picking up on this basic insight, some neoclassical economists argue that
natural resource abundance also produces weak states via a set of developmental pathologies known collectively as the resource curse (Auty 1998b;
Ross 1999). Economically, abundant natural resources are said to contribute
to economic stagnation over the long run through a number of crowd-out effects sometimes referred to as Dutch Disease. "The core of the Dutch Disease
story is that resource abundance in general or resource booms in particular
shift resources away from sectors of the economy that have positive externalities for growth" (Sachs and Warner 1999, p. 48). When capital and labor
focus on booming natural resource sectors, they are drawn away from other

sectors of the economy, increasing their production costs. These economic distortions slow the maturity of nonresource tradable sectors, harm their competitiveness, and thereby inhibit the kinds of economic diversification, especially an early period of labor-intensive manufacturing, that many neoclassical economists suggest are vital for long-term growth (Auty 1998b, 2001; Sachs and Warner 1995, 1999, 2001). It is also argued that overreliance on exports of minimally processed natural resources makes countries vulnerable to declining terms of trade and the highly volatile nature of international commodities markets. In the absence of a diverse array of exports, especially manufactured goods that tend to have more stable prices, resource-rich countries are prone to dramatic economic shocks when prices for primary commodities inevitably crash (Ross 1999).

Beyond the economic distortions created by local resource abundance, there is also a political dimension to the resource curse. The most common political argument focuses on problems associated with "rentier states." States that accrue a significant amount of revenue from natural resource exports they directly control are prone to developing corrupt, narrowly based authoritarian or quasi-democratic governing institutions. When states capture enormous rents from natural resources, they face far fewer incentives to bargain away greater economic and political accountability to the populace in exchange for broader rights of taxation (Auty 1998b, 2001; Karl 1997; Ross 1999, 2001). Instead, natural resource wealth can be used to maintain rule through patronage networks and outright coercion. The institutional makeup of rentier states therefore reduces the prospects for broad-based, benevolent economic and political reform, weakening the state over the long term and generating substantial societal grievances. These conditions are ripe for violent revolt (de Soysa 2000a, 2000b; Reno 1998; Ross 2003).

There appears to be strong cross-national evidence for the developmental problems associated with the resource curse. Statistical analyses suggest that countries that are highly dependent on primary commodity exports have, on average, lower rates of economic growth and more unequal distributions of income (Sachs and Warner 1995, 2001). Underdevelopment and poor governance, in turn, can generate grievances and open political space for organized violence. For example, many oil-exporting countries, including Algeria, Angola, Ecuador, Indonesia, Iraq, and Nigeria, have historically been prone to authoritarianism, corruption, periodic social protests, and violence (see, for example, Watts 2001). Recently, some have also expressed fears that Dutch Disease and rentier-state pathologies could pose significant threats to the future stability of post-Saddam Iraq. If an equitable system is not established to manage and distribute the country's oil wealth among the various regions and religious and ethnic communities, it could have a corrupting influence on future political institutions, put any new government's legitimacy at risk, and spur bloody competition between Shiites, Sunnis, Kurds, and Turkmen (Tierney 2003).

Scarcity vs. Abundance

Neo-Malthusians and neoclassical economists seem to advance polar-opposite views. The former see too few natural resources as the problem while the latter see too many resources as the curse. Thus, while neo-Malthusians would be concerned about the potentially destabilizing effects of demographic, economic, and environmental trends, especially in the world's least-developed countries, neoclassical economists might argue that rising demographic and environmental pressures will create incentives for countries to diversify their economies away from natural resource dependence, ultimately making them more prosperous and stable. Upon deeper reflection, however, the arguments advanced are not as incompatible as they first appear.

First, natural resource scarcity and abundance as conceptualized by neo-Malthusians and neoclassical economists are not opposites. They can, and often do, exist at the same time at different levels of analysis. The vast majority of troublesome resources discussed by neoclassical economists (oil, gemstones, valuable metals, timber, etc.) are abundant locally *but scarce globally*, something neo-Malthusians are careful to point out (Pearce 2002, p. 40). Indeed, it is the global scarcity of these resources that make them so valuable and thus such huge prizes to seize through violence.

Second, abundance can produce scarcity. The extraction and production activities centered around locally abundant (and usually nonrenewable) resources can lead to environmental degradation and scarcities of *other* (usually renewable) resources, and the synergy may lead to violent conflict. In Bougainville, Papua New Guinea (PNG), for example, a local abundance of copper led to huge mining operations, resulting in both disputes over unequal distributions of the revenue, and grievances stemming from environmental degradation and scarcity. Copper was discovered on Bougainville in the 1960s, and in the 1970s extensive cooperation began between the PNG government and the London-based mining company Rio Tinto Zinc (RTZ). The Panguna copper mine run by the company soon became one of the largest mines in the world. Not surprisingly, the mine became incredibly important to the revenue of the national government, producing 16 percent of PNG's internally generated income and 44 percent of its exports since 1972. Nevertheless, Bougainvilleans grew increasingly resentful of the fact that mining revenues went to RTZ (80 percent) and the national government (20 percent), and that many of the mining jobs went to workers from other parts of PNG. Compounding matters, poisonous tailings and chemical pollutants stemming from mining operations destroyed local fisheries, contaminated drinking water, and undermined crop production, threatening the livelihoods of local landowners. When the national government and RTZ ignored Bougainvillean concerns, local landowners started a sabotage campaign against the mine, and the conflict soon escalated to a guerrilla war against troops of the national government (Böge 1992; Klare 2001, 195–198; Renner 2002, pp. 9, 44–45).

This type of situation is not unique to Bougainville. In Nigeria, revenue streams from the oil-rich Niger Delta have historically filled the coffers of a small minority and propped up a series of repressive regimes. Throughout the 1990s, inequities, environmental degradation, pollution, and health problems stemming from the oil industry generated substantial grievances among local communities in the Niger Delta, including the Ogoni people. In the mid-1990s, the military dictatorship in Nigeria responded to Ogoni protests with repression and the instigation of interethnic violence (Renner 2002, pp. 45–47; Watts 2001).

Finally, abundance and scarcity combine to pose development challenges for resource-dependent countries. In many respects, neo-Malthusians and neoclassical economists speak past each other because they ignore the notions of time and sequence that are implicit in their analyses. To see how both logics may operate and actually reinforce one another, consider three idealized temporal stages in a country whose economy is dependent on local supplies of natural resources: (1) initial abundance; (2) emerging scarcity; and (3) the time at which exploitation of the scarce local resource is no longer economically viable, forcing diversification and a search for alternative supplies and substitutes. Neo-Malthusians and neoclassical economists should *both* agree that the second phase holds the highest risk of internal war.[7]

The logic of the honey pot effect, for example, applies much more during a time of emerging scarcity. After all, when natural resources are consumed or degraded at unsustainable rates, their value increases and rival social groups confront greater incentives to seize them. The renewal of civil war in the Sudan in 1983 provides a clear example here. By the end of the 1970s, environmental stress in northern Sudan, stemming in large part from mechanized farming, increased the value of water, land, and oil resources in the south. Northern elites, acting in support of allied northern mechanized farm owners, pushed south to capture these resources. This posed an enormous threat to the economic and physical survival of southerners, encouraging them to restart the war against the north. As the war raged on, oil exports became central to the north's ability to finance its campaign, encouraging it to seize and exploit oil deposits deeper and deeper into the south (Renner 2002, p. 10; Suliman 1992, 1993). More generally, Michael Klare's research on contemporary resource clashes in Angola, Indonesian and Malaysian regions of Borneo, the Democratic Republic of Congo, Sierra Leone, and elsewhere finds that rising global demand and scarcity-driven price increases provide additional incentives for contending social groups and elites to capture control of valuable mines, oil fields, and timber stands, by force if necessary (2001, pp. 20–21, chap. 8).

If development is viewed as a sequence of temporal stages, a good case can also be made that the developmental pathologies of the resource curse and those emerging from rapid population growth, environmental degradation, and resource scarcity can all occur and interact with one another within the same country over time. During the first stage, when resources are abundant, a country may become highly dependent on them, and elements of Dutch Disease and rentier-state politics may take hold. Then, during the second stage, demographic and environmental pressures may produce growing scarcities and undermine economic and political stability *precisely because* the country developed such a strong dependence on exporting natural resources in the first place. Finally, at the third stage, scarcity and economic crisis may force the government and the private sector to promote diversification as a means of resuscitating growth. This hypothetical sequence suggests that neoclassical theorists tend to focus on the logic involved in the leaps between these temporal stages without sufficiently recognizing the risks of transitional violence during the middle stage emphasized by neo-Malthusians.

By ignoring transitional dangers, neoclassical economists miss important contributors to civil strife. The experience of the world's poorest countries suggests that many are currently stuck in the second stage, where high dependence on natural resources, rapid population growth, environmental degradation, and emerging scarcity conspire to threaten political stability. Recent reports by both the UN Development Programme (UNDP) and the World Bank suggest that the least-developed countries tend to be those that are most dependent on minerals, agriculture, forestry, fish, and other natural resources (UNDP 2003, p. 123; World Bank 2003a, p. 119). Unfortunately, as the UNDP notes:

> Slow world market growth, unchanging technologies and often volatile and declining world prices for these commodities offer much too narrow a base for economic advance. Continued heavy dependence on a handful of primary commodity exports provides no chance of long-term success. This unfortunate situation afflicts much of Sub-Saharan Africa, the Andean region and Central Asia.
>
> Exacerbating these structural problems is rapid population growth, which tends to be fastest in countries with the lowest human development. These challenges can seriously hinder the availability of farmland and increase environmental degradation (deforestation, soil degradation, fisheries depletion, reduced freshwater). (2003, p. 17; see also p. 123)

Different Resources, Different Risks

Different types of natural resources are likely to be implicated in different types of conflict. In fact, a close look at the conflict claims advanced by neo-

Malthusians and neoclassical economists reveals that they are generally not talking about the same resources. Unlike the across-the-board warnings of their predecessors, contemporary neo-Malthusians primarily write of the dangers inherent in the degradation and depletion of renewable resources. In contrast, the logic of the neoclassical honey pot and resource curse applies primarily to nonrenewable mineral resources (with the partial exception of timber).

The broad grievance-based scenarios identified by neo-Malthusians are most likely when international demand, local population dynamics, unsustainable extraction practices, and unequal resource access interact to produce environmental degradation and emerging scarcities of renewable resources. Agriculture, forestry, and fishing contribute much more to employment than do capital-intensive nonrenewable resource sectors. Moreover, access to arable land (or inexpensive food) and freshwater is vital to extremely poor individuals throughout the developing world. Degradation, depletion, and maldistribution of these resources can therefore directly implicate the survival of large numbers of people in rural areas in ways that nonrenewables usually do not. Of course, in some instances, the extraction of nonrenewable resources causes degradation, depletion, or unequal distributions of renewable ones (as the example of Bougainville suggests), but even here it is the impact on the surrounding renewable resource base that is likely to have the widest direct effect on the quality of life and related grievances.

Nonrenewable resources are much more likely to be implicated in the conflict scenarios outlined by neoclassical economists. Nonrenewable resources are likely to be central to violent conflicts in which natural resources themselves are the main prize to be captured, as opposed to conflicts emanating from the more diffuse social and economic effects of environmental degradation and renewable resource scarcity. According to the honey pot logic, the incentive and capability to capture nonrenewable resources are especially high because mineral resources tend to be much more valuable per unit of volume, geographically concentrated, and easily tradable than most renewable resources. These features make nonrenewable resources considerably more "lootable" (le Billon 2001, pp. 569–170). It should come as no surprise, therefore, that the vast majority of honey pot–driven conflicts revolve around oil, diamonds, and other valuable minerals (de Soysa 2000a, pp. 9–10; Ross forthcoming).

Economic and political components of the resource curse also apply much more to countries dependent on the export of nonrenewable resources. Here, several characteristics distinguish mineral-dependent economies and polities from countries dependent on renewables (again, with the partial exception of timber). Mineral countries tend to be economically dependent on a single resource. Consequently, their economies tend to be especially sensitive to price volatility (Karl 1997, pp. 47–48). Furthermore, mining countries are typically dependent on resources that generate extraordinary rents. This is especially true of oil, but is also the case with other minerals. As Jeffrey Sachs and Andrew Warner note, "we should distinguish minerals (which generally have high rents) from agriculture (which generally has low rents). In the same vein, perhaps processed agriculture should be distinguished from primary agriculture" (2001, p. 831).

States in the developing world also exercise sole ownership rights over subsoil assets and, often, public forestlands. This means that export revenue from these resources is not mediated through domestic private actors, but instead accrues directly to the state and allied firms. This differs dramatically from the situation in most countries dependent on exports of agriculture, since these resources tend to be privately owned (even if sometimes highly concentrated). Thus, since government officials have the ability to extract and control unusually high income from nonrenewables, the pathologies of rentier-state politics are likely to be much more acute than in countries dependent on most renewable resources (Auty 1998b, p. 1; Karl 1997, pp. 15, 48–49, 52, 56–57; Ross 1999).

The Importance of the State and Political Institutions

Demographic and environmental pressures are rarely if ever sufficient to produce conflict; there are many countries that experience these pressures yet avoid civil strife. Neo-Malthusians and neoclassical economists generally agree that demographically and environmentally induced civil wars are most likely in countries with weak governments and authoritarian political institutions.

As noted above, strong states are typically able to prevent, deter, or repress large-scale organized violence initiated by potential challengers. Strong states are also less vulnerable to conflicts initiated by state elites themselves, because elites generally feel more secure and are able to advance their interests without risking societywide warfare. State weakness, in contrast, makes the government vulnerable. This increases the prospects of rebellion and secession stemming from societal grievances and the predatory motivations of rebel organizations and regional warlords. A sense of insecurity may also tempt political leaders to instigate widespread intergroup violence as a desperate means of diverting attention, crushing opponents, rallying supporters, and holding on to power (Kahl 1998; Kahl 2000, chap. 2).

Beyond the strength of the state, the character of its governing institutions also matters. Consolidated democracies are unlikely candidates for civil war and are less vulnerable to widespread upheaval during times of crisis. Democracies normally enjoy greater system legitimacy than authoritarian states and are better able to channel grievances into the normal political process. Democratic institutions also increase the transparency of political decisions and place constraints on executive authority, limiting the ability of state elites to instigate violence (Kahl 1998, pp. 90–91; Kahl 2000, pp. 75–80).

Quantitative studies suggest that many consolidated authoritarian states also avoid civil wars. Nevertheless, their stability typically relies on a high degree of coercive power and patronage, and these governments often generate substantial antistate grievances, especially among excluded social groups. Consequently, these states are vulnerable to rapid collapse and civil war during times of crisis or regime transition (Goldstone et al. 2000, pp. 14–16)

All told, when the strength of the state and the character of its political institutions are taken into consideration, it becomes clear that some political contexts are especially vulnerable to demographically and environmentally induced violence. The natural resource–civil war connection is likely to be particularly tight when population growth, environmental degradation, resource scarcity, and the pathologies of the resource curse contribute to state weakness and authoritarian institutions, or when demographically and environmentally induced grievances and honey pot effects occur in the context of states that are already weak and narrow or undergoing rapid regime transition.

Implications for the Future

Over the next half century, the UN medium projection estimates that the world population will increase from 6.3 billion in 2003 to 8.9 billion in 2050 (UNPD 2003). Population growth is projected to slow across the board, but differential growth rates between rich and poor countries are expected to persist. Indeed, by 2050, the population of the high-income countries is expected to be in the midst of a twenty-year population *decline*. In contrast, the population of developing countries is projected to increase from 4.9 billion in 2003 to 7.7 billion in 2050; over the same period, the population of the least-developed countries is projected to more than double, from 668 million to 1.7 billion (UNPD 2003, pp. vi–viii, 1–9).

Economic growth and consumption are also projected to increase in the decades ahead, spurred on by continued economic globalization. The World Bank projects growth in global income of 3 percent per year over the next fifty years, suggesting a fourfold rise in global GDP (to a total of $140 trillion) by midcentury. Historically, higher income is associated with higher levels of consumption. Consequently strains on the environment are likely to accelerate "if there is too little attention to shifting consumption and production patterns" (World Bank 2003b, p. 4).

Although it is impossible to predict the future of any complex system, let alone a future based on the intersection of several complex systems (demographic, economic, political, and environmental), some have offered possible scenarios. Combining UN population growth estimates, Intergovernmental Panel on Climate Change estimates on future carbon dioxide emissions, and

UN Food and Agriculture Organization estimates regarding trends in the consumption of agriculture products (crops, meat, and dairy), forest products (including fuelwood), and fish and seafood, the World Wildlife Fund has projected humanity's ecological footprint forward from 2000 to 2050:

> Based on the UN, IPCC, and FAO reference scenarios, which assume slowed population growth, steady economic development, and more resource-efficient technologies, the world's ecological footprint will continue to grow from 20 per cent above the Earth's biological capacity to a level between 80 and 120 per cent above it. In these scenarios, 9 billion people would require between 1.8 and 2.2 Earth-sized planets in order to sustain their consumption of crops, meat, fish, and wood, and to hold CO_2 levels constant in the atmosphere. (2002, p. 20)

Whether this scenario comes about obviously depends on future consumption habits and available technology. Rapid advances in technology that provide for significant improvements in resource efficiency, for example, could allow for long-term sustainability and continued advances in human welfare; however, without significant technological changes, projected consumption would become unsustainable (WWF 2002, p. 20).

Consumption will likely drive global patterns of resource depletion and pollution, but population growth and poverty will continue to have an important impact at the local level. Even as globalization raises the living standards of some countries and peoples, pockets of extreme poverty and yawning inequalities are likely to persist, placing their own strains on the environment. Current projections suggest that millions of people in the developing world will continue to rely on overcrowded and ecologically fragile lands where there is a real danger of becoming trapped in a vicious cycle of poverty and environmental decline. This is likely to generate substantial challenges for both human welfare and political stability.

Other dangers emerge from the opportunities globalization provides to profit from the control over, and exploitation of, valuable natural resources. As Klare notes:

> The increasing vigor of globalization has . . . contributed to the persistence of resource contests in the developing world. With industrialization spreading to more countries than ever before, the worldwide demand for many basic materials—including minerals, gems, and timber—is growing rapidly, thereby increasing the monetary value of many once-neglected sources of supply. . . . Globalization has also expanded the roster of corporations with both the means and the incentive to procure resources from remote and undeveloped areas—even if this means dealing with warlords and/or transporting valuable commodities through areas of conflict. (2001, pp. 194–195; see also Renner 2002, p. 21)

It should be remembered, however, that none of these demographic and environmental changes will take place in a political vacuum. In this regard, the continued spread of democracy (the political side of globalization) is cause for both hope and concern. Hope springs from the prospect of greater democratic consolidation and the potential for both long-term stability and justice that such consolidation may bring about. However, it is also well documented that the transition to democracy is fraught with difficulties. Sudden democratization puts the political rules of the game up for grabs, potentially threatening existing powerholders and their allies, and may produce substantial increases in political participation prior to the solidification of institutions capable of accommodating new demands. As a consequence, some democratizing states experience periods of turmoil, violence, and backsliding to authoritarianism (Goldstone et al. 2000, pp. 14–16; Zakaria 2003).

Severing the natural resource–civil war connection requires a series of behavioral and policy changes. High-income countries must commit to reducing their unsustainable consumption and pollution habits by altering lifestyles, developing cleaner and more efficient technologies, and assisting developing countries in gaining access to these technologies. Steps must also be taken to ensure noncoercive reductions in population growth. To achieve projected declines in fertility rates, more needs to be done to ensure that individuals in developing countries have greater access to family planning, public health services, and educational opportunities, especially for young girls and women.[8] To mitigate the destabilizing consequences of natural resource dependence, developing countries should be encouraged to diversify their economies by promoting sectors that do not rely primarily on a handful of primary commodities but are still labor intensive. Greater efforts must also be made to provide a more equitable distribution of essential renewable resources, especially land, for those who remain dependent on the environment for their livelihood. Finally, the international community must move beyond the mere promotion of democracy to ensuring that democratic transitions, once started, actually bring about responsive governing institutions. None of these steps are easy, but they are necessary if the international community is to come to grips with one of the greatest security challenges of the early twenty-first century.

Notes

1. A third approach, political ecology, informs the discussion in this chapter but is not reviewed in detail. Political ecology offers a radical critique of neo-Malthusianism and neoclassical economics that draws insights from Marxian theory and postmodernism. Specifically, political ecologists study the way in which international and local political, economic, social, and cultural processes constitute resources as "valuable" and distribute them in certain ways. To the extent that they discuss the natural

resources–civil war connection, the political economy of resource access and control, rather than population growth or natural scarcity, is viewed as central. Political ecologists argue that strife can emerge from attempts by powerful actors to seize and exploit valuable natural resources and from violent acts of resistance on the part of oppressed groups. For a general introduction, see Bryant and Bailey 1997; and Watts 2000. For analyses of the natural resources–violence connection, see Dalby 2002; le Billon 2001; Peluso and Watts 2001; and Suliman 1999. For critiques of this literature, see Kahl 2002; and Vayda and Walters 1999.

2. Renewable resources are natural resources that *theoretically* regenerate themselves indefinitely through normal ecological processes. They can become scarce, however, if they are qualitatively degraded or quantitatively depleted at unsustainable rates. In contrast to renewable resources, nonrenewable resources do not regenerate in time scales that are relevant to human beings, making them for all intents and purposes finite.

3. Of these fifty-four, twenty were in sub-Saharan Africa, seventeen in Eastern Europe and the former Soviet Union, six in Latin America and the Caribbean, six in East Asia and the Pacific, and five in the Middle East (UNDP 2003, p. 3).

4. Neoclassical economists generally have faith in the power of markets and social institutions to head off resource scarcities before they become too acute. The basic economic logic underlying this claim is straightforward: rising prices stemming from increased demand for, or decreased supply of, natural resources forces individuals, firms, and societies to adapt by diversifying, developing cheaper substitutes, deploying conservation methods, and utilizing more efficient means of extraction. Classics in this tradition include Boserup 1965; Simon 1981; Simon and Kahn 1984; and Simon 1992. Although these claims have substantial merit, neoclassical economists tend to be overly optimistic about the prospects for adaptation. Markets and institutions have frequently adapted to population and environmental pressures at the global level and within wealthy industrialized countries, but serious local scarcities, especially of renewable resources, continue to emerge within developing countries for a number of reasons. First, in many developing countries, the markets, property rights, government policies, judicial (contract-enforcing) institutions, basic infrastructure, research facilities, extension services, and human capital required to transform price signals into adaptation are imperfect, absent altogether, or distorted in ways that actually compound resource problems. Second, critical renewable resources such as arable land and freshwater often lack cheap substitutes or easy tech-fixes. This leaves conservation as the major adaptation mechanism. Unfortunately, the economic practices and poverty that drive many environmental pressures in the first place also tend to undermine the capacity of individuals and governments to make timely and expensive investments in conservation. Finally, neoclassical economists tend to underrate the degree to which environmental systems become stressed in nonlinear, rapid, and irreversible ways, producing sudden surprises and scarcities that are difficult to respond to, at least in the short term. Therefore, adaptation, even if it eventually occurs, may be too late to head off significant transitional difficulties and conflicts. See Ahlburg 1998; Homer-Dixon 1995; and Homer-Dixon 1999, chap. 3.

5. This figure includes 518 million in arid regions with no access to irrigation systems; 430 million on land with soils unsuitable for agriculture; 216 million in slope-dominated regions; and more that 130 million in fragile forest ecosystems (World Bank 2003b, p. 60).

6. Neoclassical economists contest the connection between population growth and economic decline. The positive effects emerging from economies of scale, larger labor forces, and induced innovation and technological change are argued to balance

out the negative effects of capital shallowing, higher dependency ratios, and environmental degradation. Moreover, neoclassical economists argue that government policies are much more important than population growth in determining prospects for economic development. Unfortunately, in the world's least-developed countries, government policies have encouraged capital-intensive industries that underutilize abundant supplies of labor. Governments have also adopted other policies ill suited for labor-intensive agricultural sectors, such as high taxes on farm inputs and outputs. Compounding matters, economic policies have tended to overemphasize urban areas at the expense of investments in rural development. Thus, development strategies have often been incompatible with the promotion of economic growth in an environment of rapid population growth. Moreover, "while it can be demonstrated that 'population problems' are largely due to inappropriate government policies, it is also clear that, *given* these policies, population growth can exert a stronger adverse impact" (Kelley 2001, pp. 42–43, emphasis in original). This all suggests that the effects of population growth are likely to vary from context to context. In some cases, the effects may be negligible or even positive. But in other cases, the effects are likely to be negative, sometimes profoundly so. For excellent reviews of the debate over the economic consequences of population growth, see Kelley 2001; and Kelly and Schmidt 2001.

7. Some may object by pointing to the statistical evidence presented by Paul Collier and colleagues (2003) and Jeffrey Sachs and Andrew Warner (1995) that, according to the authors, suggests that the first stage is the most dangerous period. However, both Collier and colleagues and Sachs and Warner measure abundance by calculating primary commodity exports as a percentage of GDP. Ultimately, this is measure of resource dependence, not of abundance. In and of itself, the measure says nothing about resource endowments or changes in those endowments over time. Thus it is perfectly conceivable that resource-dependent countries face higher risks in general, but that risks escalate during the second stage, when scarcities begin to emerge but before the country is forced to break its dependence. For a similar argument, see de Soysa 2000a, p. 11.

8. Absent this access, there is the potential for considerably greater population growth. If fertility rates were to remain at their current levels, for example, the estimated world population in 2050 would balloon to 12.8 billion. And even if women were to have, on average, only about half a child more than the current medium projection assumes, world population could increase to 10.6 billion in 2050 (UNPD 2003, p. vi).

6

A Multidimensional Approach to Security: The Case of Japan

Christopher W. Hughes

Following the events of September 11, 2001, the United States, through the interlinking of the issues of transnational terrorism, the proliferation of weapons of mass destruction (WMD), and the states of the "axis of evil," has fashioned a new global and regional security agenda. The administration of George W. Bush (and particularly the Department of Defense) has labeled this agenda a "war on terror," and prosecuted it by a variety of means. Military power has clearly come to the fore in the U.S. policy response, as witnessed in successive preemptive wars in Afghanistan and Iraq, counterinsurgency operations in the Horn of Africa and the Philippines, and the reinitiation of support for the Indonesian government's tackling of terrorism. The Bush administration has similarly indicated its willingness to confront by military means, if necessary, North Korea's nuclear weapons program.

At the same time, the United States has shown a propensity to support these military efforts with economic power. The degree of long-term U.S. commitment to, and patience with, the intricacies of "state-building" programs in Afghanistan, Iraq, and in other regions of the world remains questionable. Nevertheless, at least over the short term, it appears that the United States has become more willing to distribute humanitarian, economic, and military aid for the reconstruction of "failed states," the regimes of which it has toppled, and for the strengthening of frontline states engaged in the struggle against terror networks and the proliferation of WMD. If the United States does not quite practice state building, then it has certainly rediscovered the importance of Cold War–style economic dispensations in fostering new and existing regimes supportive of itself and its goals across the Middle East, Africa, and East Asia (even if, as indicated by the Millennium Challenge Account, announced in March 2002, and the U.S. National Security Strategy of September 2002, this economic assistance is to come with enhanced conditionality relating to economic liberalization [White House 2002]). Conversely, U.S. policymakers as of late 2004 are once again considering the use of sanctions as a tool of economic power to force North Korea to desist from its nuclear program. Hence, even though the United States stands as a military superpower of unprecedented global and regional reach, and demonstrates an apparent predilection for military means in the first instance in order to realize its security objectives, it has certainly not lost sight entirely of the interrelationship between economics and security.

It is all too apparent that the logic and wisdom of the new U.S. security agenda has undergone heavy questioning and criticism by policymakers in other states, within the United States itself, and by academic observers. The interlinkages among the three components of terror networks, WMD, and the "axis of evil" are yet to be proven, and the assertion of the interlinkages among the component states of the axis remain tenuous. Just as important, the U.S. belief in the primacy of military power in dealing with these security issues has been questioned on grounds of long-term efficacy. It is doubtful whether the application of military power, and thus an essentially technological approach, is capable of resolving the problems of terrorism and the proliferation of WMD, which are more deeply rooted politically, economically, and socially. Indeed, the contention has been that U.S. policy approaches will eventually prove counterproductive, only serving to exacerbate antagonism and sources of threat toward the United States. The Bali bombing in 2002, and further terrorist attacks in Indonesia, Kenya, Saudi Arabia, and Morocco from 2002 to 2004, attest to this argument, not to mention questions of the legality and ethicality of U.S. military actions in Afghanistan and Iraq.

The debate regarding the wisdom of the U.S. war on terrorism is set to rage on, but one certainty is that the new security agenda has forced, and will continue to force, new policy responses from other developed powers and key U.S. allies. U.S.-led military campaigns in Afghanistan and Iraq have thus far produced divergent responses. In Afghanistan, the United States was supported militarily by the United Kingdom, France, and Germany. In Iraq, the main source of military support for the United States was the United Kingdom. However, while these key U.S. allies have been divided over questions of the differing utility and legitimacy of military action in Afghanistan and Iraq, there has been possibly greater convergence among them and divergence from the United States over the importance of state building in these countries. For while the United States has concentrated its efforts on the destruction of regimes and then the rebuilding of the physical infrastructure of states, it is the Europeans who have concerned themselves more with the real intricacies of peacekeeping and state building. The professed objective of the European powers, lacking as they do the raw military power to match that of the United States, is to find within the context of the war on terrorism, and regardless of whether they fully agree with the purported aims and trajectory of

U.S. military strategy, a niche role in future conflict prevention. This role concentrates not just on humanitarian assistance and development assistance, but also on filling the gaps between these two through policies of promoting human resource development and governance structures. The consistency and actual implementation of the European powers' emphasis on state-building efforts is also not without question, but it does demonstrate a keen perception of the connections between economics and security, and one that is often focused at a different level from that of the United States.

The purpose of this chapter, given the divergent views at various times of the U.S. and European powers concerning the relative utility of military and economic power for the pursuit of security ends, is to investigate the impact of the war on terrorism on the security policy of Japan, which stands as another major developed power and key U.S. ally, and historically one of the strongest practitioners of the political economy of security. Japan's case, considered alongside that of the United States and European powers and within the context of the war on terrorism, is instructive in a number of ways to understand the political economy of the new security environment.

First, Japan has been heavily affected by the post–September 11 security environment to the degree that it may precipitate significant, if as yet still incremental, changes in the overall trajectory of its own security policy. Japan on the global level has shared U.S. concerns about the spread of terrorism, and on the regional level these concerns have been reflected in the problems of potential links between Al-Qaida and insurgency in the Philippines and Indonesia. Japan has feared even more the proliferation of WMD in East Asia and beyond. As will be argued later in this chapter, Japan does not accept the full logic of the war on terrorism and its "axis of evil," or the implied linkages between terrorism and WMD, especially between Iraq and North Korea. Nevertheless, Japan is aware that the United States, for its part, increasingly accepts this logic and may act upon it in seeking to constrain North Korea's nuclear program, and that this may then pose severe dilemmas for Japanese security policy in terms of countering North Korea's acquisition of nuclear weapons through military support for its U.S. ally, or through the use of economic engagement.

The second and most crucial way that Japan's case is instructive is not only that the war on terrorism is exerting pressure for change in its security policy, but also that these changes take the form of testing Japan's relative commitment to military and political economy approaches to security. Japan's constitutional prohibitions have highly constrained it as a major military power in the East Asia region and globally in the postwar era. However, beginning in the Cold War period and increasing since, Japan has faced steady pressure domestically and from the United States for the incremental remilitarization of its security policy. Japan's reaction to the events of September 11 was to enact in October 2001 a special antiterrorism law that has enabled it to dispatch successive flotillas of its maritime self-defense forces to the Indian

Ocean in order to provide logistical support for the United States and the military forces of other states engaged in Operation Enduring Freedom in Afghanistan (Hughes 2002). This change is again incremental and provides the maritime self-defense forces with a solely noncombat role. But it does represent the first time that Japan's military has been officially dispatched overseas in wartime; it also represents the acceleration of Japan's remilitarization and is a portent of its increasing willingness to participate in U.S.-led military "coalitions of the willing." Japan has further indicated its potential preparedness to support its U.S. ally militarily by passing on July 26, 2003, a law concerning special measures on humanitarian and reconstruction assistance. This law has enabled the dispatch of a 600-strong unit of the self-defense forces to provide logistical support for U.S. and coalition forces in Iraq and in the surrounding Persian Gulf states.

At the same time that Japan's future military role has once again come into question as a result of the war on terrorism, its use of economic power for security purposes has also been the subject of scrutiny. Japan's constrained potential as a military actor in the postwar era has obliged it to consider the use of economic power to deal with security problems of both a military and a nonmilitary nature. As discussed in more detail below, Japan has articulated conceptions of comprehensive and human security that stress the interrelationship between economics and security, has long favored state-building policies as the key to stability in the East Asia region, and since the early 1990s has rivaled the United States as the first or second largest national donor of official development assistance (ODA) in the world.

In the context of the war on terrorism, Japan is therefore presented with important questions about how it should respond to new global and regional security agendas. On the one hand, it is faced with demands to expand its military contribution to security via the mechanism of U.S.-inspired coalitions. On the other hand, Japan has been presented with new opportunities to use its economic power to support a political economy approach to security. This may involve contributions to U.S. reconstruction efforts in Iraq, but also support for the European powers' emphasis on state-building projects. Japan is presented with the need to reconcile military and economic approaches to security. In some areas these two approaches may prove compatible with each other and with both U.S. and European policy, but in others Japan may diverge toward either a military role that fits with that of the United States or a political economy approach that fits with that of the European powers. In any case, the war on terrorism carries fundamental implications for Japan's relative commitment to military and economic power in the overall makeup of its security policy.

The case of Japan, beyond demonstrating the effects that the new U.S. global security agenda can have on a particular state's economic approaches to security, also carries implications for other states worldwide. For if it can be divined that Japan, as one of the developed states most committed to the use of economic power for security ends, and as one of the largest aid donors in the world, has become less convinced of the efficacy of economic approaches to security, then this raises the question of how far the other developed states will persist with these approaches. In other words, if even Japan feels that it cannot make a difference to global and regional security through the use of economic power, this leads to the consideration that the future of the new security agenda may indeed be dominated by U.S. conceptions of the primacy of military power.

Japan's security policy evolution is thus an important test case to examine the impact of the war on terrorism on the political economy of security and related policy implications for a range of developed states. I begin by examining Japan's conceptions of the interconnections between economics and security both prior to and after September 11, and the means by which it has used economic power in the past in the service of its security policy. I then explore how these economic tools of security policy have fared under and been adapted to the post–Cold War and post–September 11 security environment, and examine Japan's policymaking commitments to the use of both economic power and military means in addressing security problems arising from the war on terrorism.

I seek to stress that Japan, in responding to the war on terrorism, has in some ways actually strengthened or least sharpened its usage of economic power. Japan has retained its strong conceptions of comprehensive security and been obliged to make a series of changes to its economic statecraft and ODA policies that in many instances have resulted in development of more sophisticated instruments for conflict prevention. However, I also argue that although Japan remains committed to political economy approaches to achieving security, it is simultaneously and increasingly entertaining a large military role for itself. The overall consequence is that Japan's military role is beginning to outstrip its economic role in international security. Hence, the greater likelihood is that Japan, over the longer term, may emerge as a bigger military actor more closely aligned to the United States, rather than as an important economic actor forging a role closer to that of the European powers.

Japanese Conceptions of the Political Economy of Security

Traditional Approaches in the Early Modern to Contemporary Eras

Japan's policy elites, prior to and since the emergence of the Japanese state in the modern international system, have been aware of the inextricable linkages between political economy and security. The Japanese term for "economy," *keizai,* formulated during the Tokugawa Shogunate (1603–1867), is an abbreviation of the phrase *keikoku seimin,* which can be translated literally as "administrating the nation and relieving the suffering of the people." This phrase is derived from Confucian thought, which stresses public ethics as the basis for the virtuous ruler. Japanese views of economics have thus been fundamentally bound up with questions of social justice and stability, and have often contrasted with Western-oriented and Newtonian-influenced views of economics as an objective science that can be disembedded from social contexts (Morris-Suzuki 1989, pp. 13–14).

This stress on the interrelationship between economic management and stability, both domestic and international, was carried through into the Meiji period (1868–1912), when Japan was first to emerge as a modern state. Japanese policymakers were aware that, in order to survive and avoid colonization as a late-starter in an international order dominated by the early-starter military and economic imperial powers of the West, it was necessary for their country to embark on an intensive program of nation and state building, a process encapsulated in the slogan of *fukoku kyôhei* (rich nation, strong army), which emphasized in equal measure the development of a strong domestic economy as well as technologies and complementary military capabilities (Samuels 1991). Japanese policymakers in the remainder of the Meiji period, and in the succeeding Taishô and Shôwa periods prior to the outbreak of the Pacific War in 1941, further came to the conclusion that their program of state building and national survival required access to natural resources and overseas markets, and thus the acquisition of their own empire in East Asia (Hook et al. 2001, p. 28).

Japan's catastrophic defeat at the hands of the Allied powers in World War II, and the failure of its regionalist imperial experiment in the shape of the Greater East Asia Co-Prosperity Sphere, greatly discredited in the eyes of many Japanese the role of military power as the primary, or necessarily sufficient, means to achieve security. Japan's demilitarization under the U.S.-led Allied Occupation, and the corresponding growth of antimilitaristic and antinuclear norms in Japanese society, further ensured that its future military role would be heavily circumscribed. Japanese policymakers certainly did not ignore altogether the role of military power in security affairs. Prime Minister Yoshida Shigeru's decision to seek and sign a security treaty with the United States in 1951 (revised in 1960), and to accept Japanese light rearmament through the eventual formation of its Self-Defense Forces in 1954, reflected a pragmatic perception that alignment with and security guarantees from the United States were essential to Japan's survival in the midst of intensifying Cold War pressures in East Asia. In turn, by the early 1980s, as U.S.-Japanese security cooperation increased, Japan's alignment with the United States gave way to a security relationship that could openly be termed an alliance. Moreover, Japan, encouraged by the United States, upgraded its national military capabilities and range of missions in support of U.S. power projection functions in the region.

Nevertheless, despite Japan's willingness to depend in large part on the United States for military security during the Cold War and since, it is arguable that the most distinct feature of Japanese security policy in the postwar period has been the continuing recognition of the interrelationship between economics and security. Prime Minister Yoshida's vision of postwar Japan's role in international society, often referred to as the Yoshida Doctrine, was one that, while not eschewing military power altogether, saw Japan as ultimately ensuring its national security through economic means. Yoshida and other influential Japanese policymakers in the early postwar period were aware that it had been domestic economic instability during the "Great Crisis" of the 1930s, and the subsequent failure of the state to provide economic benefits and redistribute economic costs, that had precipitated domestic social and political instability, and that had then fueled militarism and Japanese external military adventurism. Hence, even if the Japanese state had not entirely failed in this period, its prewar history had demonstrated the chain of linkages between domestic economic, societal, and political insecurity, and the generation of international conflicts.

Japanese policymakers were also aware that economic insecurity, and the incapacity of state structures to respond to the resulting challenges and concomitant risks of conflict, were not limited solely to their own example. From the Meiji period onward, Japan's elites looked on in apprehension at China's failure to emerge into modern statehood and to develop commensurate economic and military institutions, its internal disintegration, and then its consequent dismemberment by the imperial powers. Japan's decision, often haphazardly arrived at, to intervene in China and to seek its own further imperial aggrandizement, was seen at the time as a defensive act to prevent the Western domination of Japan's neighbor. Following Japan's eventual defeat in World War II, policymaking opinion remained divided over the justification and wisdom of Japanese actions. Nonetheless, Japanese policymakers were united in accepting that prewar China's travails represented an example of how failing states could produce conditions for internal conflict, external intervention, and regional destabilization, with the end result that Japan could be dragged into a disastrous conflict.

Japanese policymakers' historical experience in East Asia thus reinforced the long-held view of the intrinsic linkages between economic, social, political, and military security dynamics. In many ways, economic insecurity, and the inability of states to provide the conditions for economic prosperity and social stability, were seen as the root causes motivating conflict on Japan's part, and conflict centered on neighboring states. Japan's fundamental understanding of the political economy of security, derived from the Tokugawa period and running through the pre- and postwar eras, in turn fed into key security policy measures premised on the importance of economics.

Therefore, in addition to alignment with the United States and light rearmament, the Yoshida Doctrine's other major tenet was that Japan should concentrate on economic restructuring and the rebuilding of the state's economic functions, as only this could fully guarantee Japan's internal security and stabilize its external security behavior. In conjunction, Yoshida and successive policy elites emphasized the importance of restoring economic ties with East Asia and other regions in order promote the stability of Japan's international security environment. This task was thought to be especially important in East Asia because many of the newly independent sovereign states of the region were systemically weak. These states needed to be buttressed economically to cope with the internal stresses derived from the legacy of colonialism, such as ethnic divides and questions of regime legitimacy, and to cope with the harsh external pressures of the onset of the Cold War in the region. Japan's concentration on economic reconstruction and economic ties with East Asia without doubt contained a large element of mercantilism. Nonetheless, this mercantilism was benign to some extent, charged as it was with the Japanese belief that improved economic ties would certainly boost the economy back to a position of preeminence in East Asia, but that it would still benefit the other states of the region through enhancing their economic development and state-building processes.

Comprehensive Security Policy and ODA Policies

Japan's keen perception of the linkages between economics and security was further demonstrated in the Cold War period by its conceptualization of comprehensive security policy and its development of economic security policy tools. The concept of comprehensive security was first articulated during the administration of Prime Minister Ôhira Masayoshi (1978–1980), with the premier's commissioning of the National Institute for Research Advancement (NIRA) to produce a report on the matter. The successor administration of Prime Minister Suzuki Zenkô (1980–1982) then adopted elements of the report as national policy, and established the Comprehensive National Security Council in December 1980 (Chapman, Gow, and Drifte 1983). The concept of comprehensive security was set against a background of enhanced economic uncertainty and strategic fluidity in the international system, and was notable in stressing not only the interrelationship between economic insecurity and the generation of military conflict, but also that problems of access to economic resources and economic dislocation should be viewed as security threats to states and their citizens in their own right.

NIRA's emphasis on the political economy of security was matched by Japan's emerging aid policy in this period. Japan had been a modest ODA donor in East Asia since the 1950s and 1960s as part of its reparations and normalization program with former colonies. Japan rapidly increased its ODA disbursements in East Asia and globally from the mid-1970s onward. In part, its expansion of ODA provision was a device to counter hostile sentiment resulting from increased Japanese economic penetration of East Asian states, to secure energy resources in the Middle East, and Japan's growing image as an "economic animal" and purveyor of economic threats. Japan also significantly increased its aid provision in order to support U.S. Cold War strategy and those states in East Asia and other regions that were seen as crucial in playing a "frontline" role (or as described in the official Japanese parlance, "aid to countries bordering on areas of conflict") in countering the resurgence of Soviet power. Japan thus increased its "aid to U.S. aid" in the Horn of Africa, Pakistan, Thailand, the Philippines, Indonesia, and South Korea (Pharr 1993, p. 251).

Nonetheless, at the same time that Japan accepted the need and utility to provide aid to support key U.S. allies, it is also apparent that Japanese ODA policy in this period was motivated by a deep and genuine recognition of the links between economics and security, and a wider security agenda that went beyond the immediate exigencies of the Cold War. Japanese ODA in this period not only was designed to ensure the security of pro-U.S. regimes, but also had a very significant bent toward long-term developmentalism and state building. Japan's aid to "frontline" states in Northeast and Southeast Asia was concentrated in efforts to develop the industrial infrastructure to foster long-term economic growth and domestic political stabilization. Moreover, Japanese ODA was not allocated exclusively to overt U.S. allies. Japan directed increasing quantities of ODA toward China as a means to support its reform efforts and to assist in preserving its internal economic and political stability. For Japan's policymakers the prewar lessons held constant: there was only one threat greater to Japan than a strong China, and that was a weak one, with all its attendant problems of civil strife and unpredictable external relations (Hughes 2004, p. 155).

Japan's emergence as an ODA "great power" in the latter stages of the Cold War was clearly not without problems. ODA was often directed to serve Japanese private business interests as well as those of the recipient state; its strategic and security purpose was often poorly articulated and the implementation subject to interministerial rivalries; the emphasis was on large industrial infrastructure projects and immediate economic growth rather than human development; and it was often directed to support authoritarian regimes in the belief that these offered the most viable governing structures to support high-speed growth, and that they would then steadily evolve into more democratic forms as economic development produced manageable incremental social and political change (Watanabe 2001). Still, Japan's provision of ODA in this period represented a clear manifestation of the belief that economic growth held the key to state-building strategies, internal social and political stabilization, and thus ultimately the prevention of conflict domestically and internationally.

Japan's conviction in the interconnection between economics and security is further shown by the fact that in the post–Cold War period it has not only maintained but in certain ways strengthened its economic approaches to security policy. Its government-commissioned reports relating to the future of national security policy have continued to argue that Japan should adopt a comprehensive approach whereby it employs economic and military power in careful combination (Japanese Advisory Group on Defense Issues 1994, p. 7; Prime Minister's Commission on Japan's Goals in the Twenty-First Century 2000, p. 45). In addition, the onset of globalization pressures and the East Asian financial crisis of 1997–1998 have indicated anew the security threats associated with economic dislocation. Japanese policymakers have witnessed how in the case of Indonesia the financial crisis has plunged individuals into poverty, heightened societal insecurity, questioned the legitimacy of the ruling elites, enfeebled the central and local government apparatus of the state, undermined state-building agendas, and opened a Pandora's box of ethnic tensions and separatism, often leading to violent conflict.

The Japanese government's response to these security problems engendered by economic liberalization and globalization has been to continue to provide large-scale ODA to the states of East Asia. Japan's principal economic approach toward security in East Asia thus remains one of developmentalism in the belief that this will undergird state-building programs and eventual economic and political stability (Hughes 2000, pp. 232, 243, 250–251). However, Japan's ODA policy in the post–Cold War period and in dealing with the fallout from globalization has not been static and has shown new adaptability. Japan approved an ODA charter in 1992 that outlined for the first time the principles underlying its aid program, and emphasized that in future aid allocations Japan would take note of issues such as recipient states' record on the development of WMD, arms expenditure, democratization, and human rights. Japan then revised its ODA charter in mid-2003, giving its aid policy an increasingly heavy emphasis on conflict prevention (Japanese Ministry of Foreign Affairs 2003b).

Japan's record of strictly following these principles has been open to question, particularly its subordination of political issues to economic interests (Hook and Zhang 1998). It is fair to say, though, that the original and revised ODA charters have given Japan's aid programs a more explicit political- and security-oriented character in the post–Cold War period, and that this has then slowly fed into important changes in the sectoral direction of ODA provision. The majority of Japan's ODA is still directed toward economic infrastructure and production. But this share since the late 1980s has gradually decreased, whereas Japanese support for the less physical and material aspects of state building, such as education, health, administration, and civil society, has gradually increased (Hirono 2001, pp. 13–14). Japan has also begun to follow other developed states in promoting programs such as security sector reform; disarmament, demobilization, and reintegration; and improved governance. This type of approach was emphasized particularly by the Japanese government's Advisory Group on International Cooperation for Peace, which was established by Prime Minister Koizumi Junichirô to investigate ways to increase Japan's role in international efforts for the consolidation of peace and nation building (Kokusai Kyôryoku Kondaikai 2002).

Japan's increasingly targeted ODA policy has been further refined through articulation of the concept of human security. In 1998 the Japanese government established a United Nations trust fund to support UN human security–centered agencies, and in January 2001 formed the Commission on Human Security, charged with deepening understanding of the concept. Under the banner of human security Japan has mainly emphasized those threats to human life, livelihoods, and dignity generated by globalization and economic liberalization, including poverty and debt relief, environmental degradation, illicit drugs, transnational crime, infectious diseases, and the provision of health care. In May 2003 the Commission on Human Security issued its final report. The report again drew attention to the importance of ODA as a means to address the root economic sources of human security, conflict prevention, and postconflict recovery; and it stressed the interconnection between poverty, human security, and conflict generation, and the consequent need to use economic means to address this set of issues (Commission on Human Security 2003, pp. 72–90).

Japan's future ODA programs and emphasis on human security should once again not be seen as unproblematic. Because of economic difficulties, its ODA budget has been subject to cuts (10 percent a year since 2001). Renewed Sino-Japanese tensions have enhanced pressures inside Japan to use ODA as a means of leverage over China rather than a means to engage and build economic interdependence, and these principles may be applied to other contexts. ODA implementation and strategy is still subject to interministerial rivalry, and the bulk of ODA allocation is still focused on large economic infrastructure projects. Human security is also problematic in that Japan needs to iron out certain contradictions and inconsistencies. It needs to consider whether support for authoritarian regimes in East Asia is always consistent with individual human security, and why it chooses to "securitize" (Waever 1995) certain problems such as migration and hunger in certain parts of East Asia but refuses to treat similar issues in the same way in the case of North Korea (Hughes 2004, pp. 218–219).

Nevertheless, Japan's ODA policy and economic approaches to insecurity have had important applications in the East Asian region in the post–Cold War period. Its involvement in the Cambodian peace process was notable because it saw the first dispatch of Japanese self-defense forces on limited peacekeeping operations. But Japan's most important role was the use of economic assistance for postconflict reconstruction, and the offering of economic inducements to the governing parties to maintain the peace settlement following the abortive coup of 1997 (Hook et al. 2001, pp. 188–189). Japan has had a similar involvement in East Timor: dispatching its largest contingent of self-defense forces to date for peacekeeping and reconstruction duties, as well as providing targeted aid for state-building activities (in fact, underwriting Timor-Leste to the point of providing 25 percent of the total aid budget for the new state).

*   *   *

From the early modern through to the contemporary period, Japan has been consistently characterized by an emphasis on the economic roots of insecurity and, concomitantly, the importance of economic policy tools to tackling extant security problems. Japan has professed, and to a large degree practiced, a comprehensive view of security that seeks to use economic and military power in balanced combination, often with economic power as the foremost policy instrument.

Japan has sought to use ODA and the building of economic interdependence as a means to promote developmentalism, economic growth, and state-building agendas. In the post–Cold War era it has further complemented its conception of comprehensive security with one that seeks to address the economic causes of individual human security.

In many ways, then, Japan stands apart from other developed states in the consistent level of its commitment to, and prioritization of, political economy approaches to security. Japan would also seem to be well placed to respond to a range of contemporary security problems that are generated by economic globalization, or that require the application of economic power. It could be argued that Japan is also in a uniquely strong position to contribute to international security in the war on terrorism through support for state-building agendas and human security.

Japanese Comprehensive Security Policy and the War on Terrorism

Japan's security policy following the events of September 11, 2001, and initiation of the U.S. war on terrorism has been presented with some difficult choices, and subsequently divisions have emerged among its policymakers regarding the optimum response and the appropriate mix of military and economic policy tools. Japanese policymakers, on the one hand, have expressed their abhorrence at the terrorist attacks on the United States, recognized fully the threat of transnational terror networks to international security, and pledged backing for the efforts of the United States and international community, including military action, to eradicate terrorism. Japan's own experience of "hyper-terrorism"—the Aum Shinrikyô sarin nerve gas attacks on the Tokyo subway in 1995—has heightened its sense of the importance of countering transnational terrorism.

On the other hand, though, despite the shared recognition of the potential threat of terrorism and acceptance of the need for a measure of military response, Japan's policymakers have maintained serious reservations about the general wisdom and effectiveness of the U.S. policy approach. In particular, Japanese policymakers and the public have debated whether the application of overwhelming military power should be the primary means to combat terrorism, and how effective this approach will really prove over the longer term if it is not backed up with the application of appropriate and sufficient amounts of economic power (Terashima 2002). Japan's policy elites, above all, have argued that the root causes of domestic and transnational terrorist phenomena lie in economic dislocation, societal alienation, human insecurity, and the failure of state apparatus to provide for the security of their citizens. Japan has contended that the logical response to terrorism should be the application of economic power. This should address not only the humanitarian fallout from military action, but also the very roots causes of terrorism, by engaging in economic stabilization and state-building programs. Hence, Japan's policymakers in the immediate aftermath of the September 11 attacks often found themselves occupying a position closer to their counterparts in Europe than in the United States.

Japan's overall preference for political economy understandings and approaches toward terrorism was demonstrated by its response to the U.S.-led war in Afghanistan. Japanese policymakers soon after September 11 sensed that it would undoubtedly be necessary to provide support for U.S. military action against Al-Qaida in Afghanistan and were motivated in this belief by a variety of factors. Japan's political and bureaucratic leadership were certainly wary that there should be no repeat of the "Gulf War syndrome" of 1990–1991, when Japan had been subject to heavy U.S. and international criticism for its alleged reliance on "checkbook" diplomacy and provision of economic assistance to the coalition war effort, rather than making a "human" and military contribution. In addition, some Japanese policy elites were conscious that the response to the events of September 11 would form a major test of the political credibility of the U.S.-Japanese alliance relationship, and an opportunity for Japan to further expand incrementally the potential range of its support for U.S. global and regional military strategy. Just as important, though, and as indicated above, many Japanese policymakers were also convinced that an initial military response would be necessary to disrupt the Al-Qaida network in Afghanistan, even if this also involved the simultaneous destruction of the Taliban regime.

Japan was therefore prepared to offer a degree of heavily circumscribed military assistance to the U.S.-led coalition in the Afghanistan campaign.

Japan's antiterrorism special measures law enabled the dispatch of its self-defense forces to the Indian Ocean area in order to provide noncombat logistical support to U.S. and other forces. The antiterrorism law was drafted in such a way that Japanese support for the campaign was made possible only by the existence of relevant UN resolutions and was consequently limited to operations in Afghanistan. Japan has no obligation under its antiterrorism law to provide support in any other theater of operation, and support itself is limited to a two-year, although extendable, time frame. Thus Japan did take important new steps in its military policy in dispatching its self-defense forces overseas for the first time during ongoing combat operations, and the antiterrorism law has set important potential precedents for U.S.-Japanese cooperation in other contexts (Hughes 2002). But Japan's support for the Afghanistan campaign still represented only one more incremental step in the expansion of its military role in international security, and demonstrated its continued inherent caution in becoming embroiled in military conflicts.

Japan's principal contribution to attempts to eliminate terrorism in Afghanistan came instead through use of economic power. In the run-up to the Afghanistan campaign, Japan in certain ways reprised its Cold War role of providing ODA to "frontline" states in order to buttress U.S. military strategy. Japan provided a total of $300 million in bilateral assistance to Pakistan from September 2001 onward for education, health, and poverty reduction. From October 2001 onward it also discontinued its limited sanctions on India and Pakistan, imposed since May 1998 in response to their nuclear testing activities. Japan further pledged a total of $18 million in immediate assistance to Tajikistan and Uzbekistan. Japan's self-defense forces delivered a range of humanitarian assistance to Pakistan for Afghan refugees, and the government pledged $102 million via the UN and other agencies for refugee assistance.

However, Japan's approach in using economic power to contribute to the effort against Al-Qaida consisted of more than just immediate humanitarian aid and support for states friendly to U.S. war aims on the periphery of Afghanistan. Following the fall of the Taliban, Japan demonstrated that it was deeply committed to state-building efforts in Afghanistan as forming the most likely eventual solution to terrorist activity in the region. Japan hosted in Tokyo the International Conference on Reconstruction Assistance to Afghanistan on January 21–22, 2002. At the conference, Japan pledged up to $500 million for rebuilding the government and physical infrastructure of the country, and the conference itself raised a total of $4.5 billion. It then dispatched a fact-finding mission to Afghanistan in March 2002, which concluded that Japan should concentrate its ODA toward Afghanistan not simply in short-term humanitarian assistance but also in longer-term assistance in areas such as the rebuilding of media infrastructure, capacity building in administration, human resource development in education and health, and training for women for reintegration into public life. Japan also concluded that significant proportions of its ODA should be allocated to grassroots projects managed by nongovernmental organizations, including the drilling of water wells and training in heath and education. Japan from July 2002 onward announced its intention to support UN programs for the disarmament, demobilization, and reintegration of former combatants, the training of Afghan civilian police, drug control, and the resettlement of refugees. It then sponsored a further conference in Tokyo in February 2003 on consolidation of peace in Afghanistan, which reiterated these aims. Finally, Japan has seen the Afghanistan situation as a means to further expand its program of human security: providing assistance under its UN human security trust fund for programs relating to health, education, and the removal of antipersonnel land mines.

Japan has played a highly active role in attempting to combat the reemergence of terrorism in Afghanistan by nonmilitary means. Its approach has focused on the provision of aid for state-building and human security agendas. It has devoted funds not just to the rebuilding of physical infrastructure, but also to enable the new Afghan administration to attempt to effect economic and social restructuring. Japan has also shown that its commitment to Afghanistan's future is long term. All of these efforts indicate that Japan is very much concerned with the intricacies of state building, and in this sense it has certainly been able to stand upon its conceptions of comprehensive security and to make a distinct contribution to international security. Japan's stance has been closer to that of the European powers than to that of the United States. For while Japan's economic assistance has often complemented that of the United States, which has shown a significant commitment to the reconstruction of Afghanistan, the Bush administration's interest in Afghanistan as a whole, let alone state building, has been questioned since early on.

Japan's political economy approach to addressing security problems, especially the issue of terrorism, has extended also to its own region in East Asia. The U.S. response to the Abu Sayyaf Group's terrorism and insurgency in the Mindanao province of the Philippines has been to employ a mix of military and economic means reminiscent of the Cold War. Since late 2001 the United States has dispatched up to 1,200 special forces personnel to assist in training the Philippine armed forces in antiterrorism techniques. It has also provided $100 million in aid, but a significant proportion of this comprises military assistance in the form of weaponry transfers. Japan's approach has contrasted strongly with that of the United States. Japan's constitutional prohibitions clearly preclude it from any type of military option in the Philippines. But again, Japan has shown a distinctly different understanding of the root causes of terrorism and the optimum means to assist the Philippine government in dealing with it.

Japan has viewed intrastate separatist conflict and terrorism in Mindanao as partly caused by the relative failure to date of the Philippine state's developmental agenda and the resultant severe economic disparities imposed on the province. Consequently, the Japanese government in December 2002 unveiled a support package for peace and stability. It argued that strife in Mindanao had "aggravated the issue of poverty in the area, creating a hotbed of terrorism" (Japanese Ministry of Foreign Affairs 2002, p. 2). Moreover, it stressed that the conflict undermines opportunities for foreign direct investment in the region and the development of the Philippines as a whole, thus reinforcing the cycle of poverty and conflict. Japan's ODA package for Mindanao has aimed to break this cycle by improving the training of human resources in the region, and by providing basic human needs such as medical care, rural development, and infrastructure. In this way, Japan's declared aim has been to support the Philippine government's efforts to fight poverty and terrorism simultaneously.

Japanese policy in Indonesia has also taken a slightly different tack from that of the United States. As noted earlier, Japanese policymakers watched with apprehension the onset of the East Asian financial crisis from 1997 to 1998 and the strictures imposed by the International Monetary Fund and the United States on assistance to Indonesia, aware that these would undo many of the state-building efforts of the Indonesian regime and subsequently have major implications for political stability and internal security. Japanese predictions were borne out with the political turmoil at the center of Indonesia, which produced the collapse of successive governments, challenges to the territorial integrity of the Indonesian archipelago, and enhanced conditions for the operation of terrorism. Japan's preferred policy has been to maintain the territorial integrity of Indonesia, for which it has disbursed large sums of bilateral and multilateral ODA, and it only switched to support of Timorese independence when it became clear that international intervention made this a fait accompli. Japan also attempted to broker in 2002 what has ultimately turned out to be an unsuccessful cease-fire agreement in Aceh as another means to preserve the territorial integrity of Indonesia.

Japan's current political and economic support for Indonesia is clearly problematic in terms of bolstering what has become a democratic regime, but a regime that is also engaged in the repression of internal dissent in certain of its provinces. Japanese policymakers, however, see their support for the Indonesian state as the policy option least likely to result in insecurity for the bulk of the population, and also as a means of addressing the problem of terrorism. Japan again sees that the key to tackling terrorism in Indonesia lies in strengthening state capacities, improving economic conditions, and dealing with economic disparity, poverty, and injustice, factors that were termed in a 2003 joint Japan-Indonesia announcement on fighting international terrorism as the "root causes of terrorism" (Japanese Ministry of Foreign Affairs 2003a). Japan's approach to the war on terrorism in Indonesia, as in the Philippines, has contrasted with that of the United States due to its inability to project military power in the region or offer any form of military assistance.

But with its heavy emphasis on continued state building, development, and curbing the impact of economic liberalization, Japan's approach has had a stronger political economy edge than that of the United States.

Japan, the Political Economy of Security, and the "Axis of Evil"

Japan's reaction to the terrorist attacks of September 11, 2001, and to the U.S.-led campaign against Al-Qaida in Afghanistan, indicates that it has sought to further and incrementally expand its military role in international security, but that its prime response has been to emphasize approaches to security that utilize economic power. This political economy approach to security has to some extent complemented that of the United States by supporting key allies in the war on terrorism, but in other ways Japan has shown signs of diverging from the U.S. path due to its long-term commitment to state building and human security. Japan has continued to stand upon its principles of comprehensive security policy, and has indeed sharpened the focus of many of its tools of economic security.

However, as the U.S. war on terrorism has developed in scope and intensity, it is probable that Japan may find it increasingly difficult to adhere to the comprehensive security policy line, and that the overall balance in its security policy may begin to shift decisively toward the use of military power. President Bush's identification of the "axis of evil" in the 2002 State of the Union address, with its seeming translation of this into actual U.S. security strategy, has posed severe dilemmas for Japan. Japanese policymakers, while implacably opposed to terrorism and the proliferation of WMD, had long been skeptical about the real state of Iraq's WMD program and about any real link between Iraq and Al-Qaida. Just as important, they perceived few links between prewar Iraq, Iran, and North Korea. Japan is aware of the possible trade in ballistic missile technology between the latter two. Nevertheless, Japan's policy since the late 1970s has actually been to attempt to improve ties with Iran. Its motivations for this policy include a strong interest in energy security and oil supplies from Iran, but also a conviction, similar to that of many European Union states, that engagement with Iran is the approach most likely to moderate its security behavior and development of WMD. Even as late as February 2004, and as international pressure mounted on Iran to open its nuclear facilities to inspections, Japan concluded new oil concessions in Iran's Azadegan fields.

North Korea, in contrast, is perceived as a clear threat to Japanese security due to its previously clandestine and now openly declared nuclear weapons program and development of ballistic missiles. But again, Japan's optimum policy approach toward North Korea since the mid-1990s has been one of balanced military deterrence and economic engagement. Japan thus looked upon the "axis of evil" concept with a mixture of puzzlement and apprehension: puzzlement in that it could see no linkages between its component states; apprehension in that it saw the United States as possibly intending not only to eliminate the Iraqi regime and wage war in the Middle East, but also to engage North Korea, provoking an unnecessary conflict in East Asia with deep implications for Japan's own military security policy.

Japan has consequently reacted to the war in Iraq with considerable caution. It has felt obliged to express strong backing for U.S. military actions because of its shared concern over WMD proliferation, and because it has seen its public support for the United States as a test of the political solidarity of alliance ties. Moreover, while Japan has felt deep discomfort over the eventual sidelining of the UN by the United States in launching the Iraq War, it has adopted an approach that views limited cooperation with the United States as the best way to curb its unilateralist tendencies over the longer term. However, Japan has remained highly cautious about being drawn into the Iraq conflict militarily. Japan's antiterrorism special measures law, as noted above, premises dispatch of its self-defense forces on explicit UN resolutions related to the combating of terrorism, a condition clearly not met in the case of the Iraq War. Though in June 2003 Japan did pass a law concerning special measures on humanitarian assistance to enable the dispatch of its self-defense forces for logistical and reconstruction efforts, they have been tasked with a purely non-combat role—in Samawah, southwest of Basra, the most stable area that the Japanese government could find in the country and thus the area with the minimum risk of becoming involved in armed clashes.

Meanwhile, Japan has attempted to compensate for its inability to contribute militarily to the war in Iraq by again employing economic power. Japan has been a major donor of humanitarian aid to Iraq, and hinted strongly at its willingness to provide ODA for reconstruction efforts. Japan announced a plan in May 2003 to provide economic aid for rebuilding the physical infrastructure of Iraq in the areas of water and energy supplies, health, and education. At the International Donors Conference on Reconstruction of Iraq in October 2003, Japan pledged $5 billion ($1.5 billion in grants and $3.5 billion in ODA loans) to be disbursed bilaterally and multilaterally and in cooperation with nongovernmental organizations. However, Japan's ability to employ its economic power for security ends in Iraq has been hindered by the lack of stronger UN mandates supporting the U.S. and UK reconstruction efforts, its need to conform very much to a U.S.-dominated reconstruction agenda that has focused on physical infrastructure, and the seeming lack of a consistent plan on behalf of the occupying powers for the rebuilding of the Iraqi state.

The case of Iraq is one in which Japan's comprehensive security policy and application of tools of economic security policy have been very much blunted by the U.S. approach to its war on terrorism. Arguably, though, the case of North Korea, at the other end of the "axis of evil" and as another potential target of the U.S. war on terrorism and campaign against WMD proliferation, is one in which Japan may find that it has to radically transform the nature of its economic security tools or discard them altogether. As noted above, Japan's approach toward North Korea since the first revelations of its suspected plutonium-route nuclear program in the mid-1990s has been one of military deterrence combined with economic engagement. Japan's primary military role in responding to the potential North Korean nuclear threat has been to further augment its support for U.S. power projection capacity to deal with military contingencies on the Korean Peninsula and elsewhere in Northeast Asia. This has taken the form of the revised 1997 Guidelines for Japan-U.S. Defense Cooperation, which make clear for the first time the range of logistical support that Japan will provide to its ally in a military contingency. At the same time, Japan has supported U.S. efforts to engage North Korea via the framework agreement of 1994 and the establishment of the Korean Peninsula Energy Development Organization (KEDO). KEDO has sought to provide heavy fuel oil and funding for the construction of two light-water nuclear reactors in North Korea, in return for the North's freezing and eventual dismantlement of its nuclear program. Japan has pledged a total of $1 billion for the construction of the reactors. Japan additionally has supported South Korea's "Sunshine" engagement policy toward the North, and has periodically provided major quantities of food aid bilaterally and via multilateral agencies to North Korea.

Japanese economic engagement of North Korea since the mid-1990s has been hampered by the lack of normalized diplomatic relations between the two states, which precludes the full-scale provision of ODA. In turn, Japan–North Korea normalization talks, ongoing since the early 1990s, have been undermined by a range of bilateral disputes, including the fate of Japanese citizens abducted to North Korea since the 1970s, and North Korea's claims for compensation and apologies from Japan for its period of colonial rule on the Korean Peninsula. Japan has persisted with attempts to engage North Korea bilaterally, and to support U.S. and South Korean engagement strategies, in the realization that military conflict to resolve the nuclear problem is a highly costly option, and that in large part North Korea's external military brinkmanship is driven by its internal economic crisis and the need to extract economic concessions from the United States and its allies to ensure its survival (Hughes 1999). Moreover, if Japan were to finally engage with North Korea, it would mean that significant Japanese economic power could be brought to bear in seeking to resolve the root economic causes of North Korea's insecurity and its presence as a threat to regional security—Japan likely as it is to agree to provide up to $10 billion in ODA and what it terms "economic cooperation" in order to settle North Korea's claims for colonial compensation.

Japan's approach toward the North Korean security problem can be seen as one that understands the North's military behavior as being driven by economic insecurity, and is grounded on the belief that the North can to some degree be contained militarily, but that ultimately its security behavior can only be moderated through the application of military power. Japan's approach toward North Korea, though, has been thrown very much off balance since the advent of the Bush administration. North Korea's inclusion within the "axis of evil" confirmed for many Japanese policymakers the U.S. disenchantment with engagement policies toward the North, and raised fears that the United States might even consider military action against the North to halt its nuclear program, a policy line that had previously been thought of as a nonoption due to the likely devastation of the Korean Peninsula and the strong objections of China and U.S. allies.

Japan has been further unnerved by North Korea's defiant stance toward the United States since late 2002. In October 2002, North Korea revealed that it possessed a previously unknown uranium enrichment program, providing another possible route to nuclear weapons acquisition. Following this, in December 2002, North Korea announced that it would restart its plutonium reprocessing program, and in January 2003 its intention to withdraw from the Nuclear Nonproliferation Treaty. By 2003 both North Korea and the United States had declared the 1994 framework agreement as effectively void, throwing the future of KEDO into doubt.

Japan's own policy response has been to attempt to use diplomatic means to nudge both sides back into dialogue. Japanese prime minister Koizumi Junichirô made landmark visits to North Korea in September 2002 and May 2004 for direct talks with Kim Jong-Il. The purpose of these summits was to clear away many of the obstacles to the progress of Japan–North Korea normalization, to stress Japan's concerns to the North about its nuclear program and solidarity with the U.S. position on nonproliferation, and to demonstrate to the United States the importance of dialogue with the North. Japan's diplomacy experienced a number of successes and failures, which cannot be explored in depth here. But while Japan was not wholly successful in decoupling North Korea from the "axis of evil" in U.S. eyes, its diplomacy, together with that of South Korea, has at least succeeded in contributing to the restart of intermittent U.S.–North Korean dialogue and the holding of six-party talks on the North Korean issue from 2003 onward.

But Japan still faces a harsh dilemma over the North Korean issue. Its optimum policy is one that addresses the political economy of insecurity in North Korea through dialogue and economic engagement. However, the restart of the U.S.–North Korean dialogue has proved to be a fractious process, resulting in further North Korean threats toward the United States and its allies involving its nuclear program and other military capabilities. Meanwhile, Japan itself is unable to engage North Korea more vigorously because of its own bilateral difficulties in the normalization process, its concerns about North Korea's WMD and ballistic missile programs, and its desire not to be seen as breaking ranks with its U.S. ally. Japan is thus faced with a deteriorating security situation on the Korean Peninsula and has few policy tools that it can activate for its stabilization.

The outcome is that Japan may be faced with serious choices about how it will react if North Korea refuses to desist from its nuclear program. If the United States pushes for economic sanctions against the North, Japan will have to convert its tools of economic engagement from carrots to sticks. It is envisaged that Japan will cut remittances from the large North Korean community resident in Japan, and cooperate in the interdiction of North Korean shipping. Japan's National Diet in January 2004 passed legislation to enable the stoppage of remittances in the event of UN sanctions, and in October 2004 hosted exercises for the U.S.-led Proliferation Security Initiative.

Even more significant, if there is a repeat of the North Korean nuclear crisis of 1994, Japan will need to provide clear military support for the United States under the revised defense cooperation guidelines. Japan may be forced to consider other types of military action if North Korea continues to try to coerce its neighbors with its threatened nuclear program. Japan since December 2003 has agreed to purchase an off-the-shelf ballistic missile defense system from the United States, with all the attendant consequences for further accelerating North Korea's ballistic missile program and China's nuclear modernization. Hawkish Japanese policymakers, such as the current director-general of the Japan Defense Agency, Ishiba Shigeru, have also begun to moot the issue of what approximates preemptive strikes by Japan on North Korean missile sites—an interesting echo of the new U.S. national security strategy. Hence, the end result of the U.S. intention under the Bush administration to pressure North Korea more actively on its nuclear program as part of the "axis of evil" and campaign against WMD, could be for Japan to ultimately abandon its economic engagement approach toward the North, and to prod it into becoming a more assertive military actor in the region and to contravene many of its postwar concepts of comprehensive security.

Conclusion: Japan's Opportunities for Comprehensive Security Found and Lost?

Japan since September 11, 2001, has found itself caught in a chain of events that, like other developed states and U.S. allies, has obliged it to reconsider its stance vis-à-vis the United States, and to reconsider its overall security policy. For Japan, this challenge has been particularly acute, as the constraints upon its use of military power and high degree of military dependence on the United States have necessitated that it move with considerable caution in order not to alienate the United States. It is clear that Japan has experienced varying degrees of ambivalence toward the U.S. war on terrorism and the "axis of evil." It has agreed with the objectives of eliminating terrorism and WMD, but has often doubted whether the United States fully understands the underlying political economy causation of these threats, and whether the somewhat crude U.S. application of military and economic power really promises a long-term solution to these problems. Nonetheless, Japan has felt it necessary to offer a degree of support to the United States, and the war on terrorism and "axis of evil" have begun to effect important change in its security policy.

Japan's immediate response to the September 11 attacks and the war in Afghanistan, through the mechanism of its antiterrorism special measures law, has established important precedents for the expansion of its military role. However, the reconstruction of Afghanistan has also offered opportunities for Japan to refine its political economy approach to security and deploy economic assistance in state-building and human security projects, thus representing in many ways a continuation of its comprehensive security policy.

The "axis of evil," the Iraq War, and the new nuclear crisis brewing in North Korea, however, have not proved so conducive to the practice of comprehensive security policy. Japan has found it difficult to bring its economic power to bear in Iraq, and in a situation so heavily dominated by U.S. visions of state reconstruction. Meanwhile, in the case of North Korea, and possibly regardless of Japanese attempts to prevent the United States from extending its military approach to halting WMD proliferation to East Asia, Japan is now confronted with a looming military crisis. Japan finds itself unable to use economic approaches to resolving the crisis and, when push comes to shove, may choose enhanced military cooperation with the United States and the buildup of its own military capabilities in order to respond to the nuclear threat. The result will be to push the balance in Japan's security policy much more toward that of military power, so undermining its claims to comprehensiveness.

The U.S. war on terrorism and "axis of evil" are indeed generating fundamental changes in Japan's security policy, and these changes may take the form of Japan's declining emphasis on the political economy aspects of international security. Arguably, this is ironic, given that the onset of globalization and evidence from the post–September 11 security environment indicate that economic insecurity more than ever accounts for many sources of contemporary threats. Moreover, if it is asked where Japan is best equipped to make a difference regionally and globally in a post–September 11 world, the most likely response would be through a political economy approach to security rather than through military means. However, U.S. logic in its "axis of evil," and Japan's deepening alliance ties with the United States, are creating the circumstances that may push Japan away from comprehensive approaches to security.

PART 2

U.S. Policies and the Emerging Political Economy of Security

7

U.S. Statecraft in a Unipolar World

Lars S. Skålnes

To understand the vicissitudes of U.S. statecraft in the post–Cold War era, the international distribution of power is largely irrelevant. Because a preponderance of power translates into freedom of action, U.S. primacy implies that how policies play in Peoria will loom larger in the minds of policymakers than how they play in Paris. The lack of international constraints, in other words, translates into greater salience for domestic constraints.[1] No longer able to appeal to the necessity of responding to international pressures, policymakers fall prey to the clamor of domestic interest groups. If primacy implies that U.S. domestic politics will largely determine U.S. security and trade strategy, U.S. policymakers may not be able to integrate economics and security in statecraft, that is, adopt trade policies (and economic policies more broadly) that are "subordinated to and supportive of security concerns" (Mastanduno 1998, p. 827; see also Kapstein 1999, p. 468; and Mastanduno 1997, p. 85). Pressured by the different domestic interests in the trade and security policy realm, U.S. policymakers may be more prone to implement trade and security strategies that work at cross-purposes. This matters because disintegrated strategies run the risk of undermining national security (Posen 1984, pp. 16, 24–25). The main contrast is to the situation during the Cold War, when policymakers could appeal to strategic imperatives to overcome domestic pressures for protectionist trade policies that would have undermined the military alliances constructed to counter the Soviet threat. During the Cold War, the strategic imperative to strengthen military alliances integrated trade and security in U.S. statecraft: policymakers had at their disposal trade policies and economic policies more broadly that helped cement military alliances crucial to U.S. national security

In analyzing U.S. statecraft in the post–Cold War era, analysts have so far given pride of place to systemic factors.[2] One claim has been that unipolarity both motivates and makes it easier for policymakers in the dominant state to integrate economics and security in statecraft (Mastanduno 1998, pp. 827–828). The argument in this chapter differs by giving analytical primacy to domestic factors. Whether U.S. economics and security will be integrated in statecraft will be a function not of the international distribution of power but of U.S. domestic politics.

More specifically, I argue that U.S. hegemony in both the international military and trade arenas, and the freedom that this gives the United States, imply that the choice of security and trade strategies will be determined in large part by institutional features of U.S. domestic politics, particularly the number of domestic veto players in the national security and trade policy-making arenas. Moreover, these features will significantly influence the extent to which the security and trade elements of statecraft can be made to work in tandem. The degree of integration, that is, ultimately will depend on the characteristics of the domestic institutional environment facing U.S. policymakers in the national security and trade policy arenas.

Because the number of veto players is higher in the trade arena than in the security arena, we should expect more policy stability in the former than in the latter. That is, trade strategy is likelier to remain close to the status quo established during the Cold War. Accordingly, trade policy will remain largely multilateral—that is, based on "'generalized' principles of conduct . . . which specify appropriate conduct for a class of actions, without regard to the particular interests of the parties or the strategic exigencies that may exist in any specific occurrence" (Ruggie 1992, p. 571). Concretely, trade policy will focus on preserving and extending the reach of international rules and regulations embodied in the World Trade Organization (WTO).

The U.S. commitment to free trade and multilateralism, however, has been tempered by a simultaneous commitment to "fair" trade policies designed to protect domestic producers against foreign trade as well as policies of redistribution designed to cushion the blow of foreign competition (Goldstein 1988, p. 181). The liberalism of free trade in the post–World War II era was an "embedded liberalism" in which multilateralism would go hand in hand with domestic interventionism (Ruggie 1982, p. 393). Even during the Cold War, in other words, the U.S. commitment to multilateral free trade was never absolute. Deviations from the status quo in the post–Cold War era should therefore be looked for not so much in the occasional capitulations to the clamors for protection as in an abandonment of multilateralism in favor of bilateral and regional trade agreements.

The number of veto players in the security arena, in contrast, is small enough that the choice of strategy is likely to be determined by factors idiosyncratic to particular presidential administrations.[3] Security strategy is for this reason likelier to deviate from the status quo and thus exhibit relatively less stability than trade strategy. Specifically, abandoning the status quo in favor of a unilateral strategy would mean that the United States would exhibit a greater "tendency to *opt out* of a multilateral framework (whether existing or proposed) or to *act alone* in addressing the particular global or regional challenge rather than choosing to participate in collective action" than it did, say, during the Cold War (Malone and Khong 2003, p. 3, emphasis in original).[4] While the United States might appreciate political and military support from others, that is, it would not be willing to sacrifice much to acquire it, nor would a lack of support fundamentally change its policies. Prompted in large part by the war on terrorism and the perceived need to be able to launch preemptive or preventive attacks, U.S. unilateralism also manifests itself in a reluctance to abide by long-standing international norms such as sovereignty and self-defense (Ikenberry 2002, esp. pp. 51–54).[5]

As many have pointed out, one should not exaggerate the distinction between multilateral and unilateral policies. Strategies often combine both multilateral and unilateral elements, leading to such appellations as "ambivalent multilateralism" and "inconsistent multilateralism" (Malone and Khong 2003, p. 3; Patrick 2002, pp. 1, 13; see also Nye 2001–2002, p. 6; and Nye 2003, p. 64). Some deny that unilateral strategies are even possible, claiming that the choice is really between different kinds of multilateral strategies (Zelikow 2003, pp. 24–25). With these caveats in mind, the definitions of unilateralism and multilateralism are nevertheless useful in characterizing strategies as more or less unilateral, more or less multilateral.

The greatest obstacle to integrating economics and security in U.S. statecraft is the expected lack of stability in security affairs. If national security policies are likely to shift with changing presidential administrations, then integration will become more difficult. Nevertheless, although the loose international constraints and the differential domestic constraints facing U.S. policymakers in the trade and security arenas may lead one to expect disintegration, things are not so simple. Combining unilateral security policies with multilateral trade policies does not necessarily preclude the integration of trade and security in statecraft. Indeed, if, as U.S. defense secretary Donald Rumsfeld has argued, the mission determines the coalition, then a trade policy oriented toward strengthening the WTO—and thus implicitly emphasizing nondiscriminatory trade policies—would seem to be the trade policy best suited to keeping U.S. options open and coalition partners available as the nature of the mission changes.

I begin this chapter by making the case that the current international system is unipolar. Next I argue that unipolarity can be expected to last for decades—an important point, because the longer unipolarity can be expected to last, the greater the freedom afforded U.S. policymakers and the more important domestic institutional factors should be in shaping U.S. statecraft. I then take a closer look at the primacy of domestic political considerations in determining the foreign policies of the dominant power, maintaining that the war on terrorism has not restored structural constraints to the importance they had during the Cold War; outline the theory of veto players and discuss its implications for both security and trade strategies; and discuss U.S. security strategy and U.S. trade strategy and the extent to which they can be said to have deviated from the status quo established during the Cold War. I conclude the chapter by briefly considering theoretical and policy implications.

The Current International System Is Unipolar

Most scholars, it seems, agree that the post–Cold War international system should be characterized as unipolar, with the United States as the dominant power. As would be expected when the discussion turns to how to assess distributions of power, however, there are dissenters. Samuel Huntington believed as late as 1999 (pp. 36–37) that the current system is "uni-multipolar," by which he meant that the current system has one superpower with the capacity to project its power and interests globally and several major powers with the ability to project their power and interests regionally. Whereas the United States can veto international action, it is not able to settle key international issues without cooperation from others.[6] Kenneth Waltz argued in 1993 (p. 52) that "bipolarity endures but in an altered state,"[7] but he has since changed his mind, now believing that, "upon the demise of the Soviet Union, the international system became unipolar" (2000, p. 27).

John Mearsheimer offers perhaps the most carefully reasoned attack, not just on the notion of U.S. dominance, but also on the notion of dominance or hegemony generally. Mearsheimer argues that the "stopping power of water" makes it impossible for any state to achieve global hegemony.[8] By limiting the ability to project military power, oceans constitute the main barrier to any state seeking to achieve global hegemony. Regional hegemony, however, though not easy to achieve, is possible. The United States provides the only example of a regional hegemon in modern history, indicating how difficult even regional hegemony is (Mearsheimer 2001, pp. 41, 83–84). Still, while the oceans and distance more generally may limit the ability of the United States to project power, it does not therefore follow that the United States is not a hegemon and the current system not unipolar. Evolution in technology may already have made distance as well as oceans largely irrelevant, opening the possibility of a global hegemony that rests on conventional and not just nuclear weapons. It would seem preferable to allow for this possibility than simply to rule it out more or less by definition as Mearsheimer does.

Denying that power is (completely) fungible, others have argued that it makes no sense to speak of U.S. hegemony except in military affairs. In economic affairs such as international trade and "antitrust matters," they maintain, the distribution of power is multipolar. We know this because in economic affairs, the United States cannot achieve the outcome it wants without cooperation from the European Union (EU) and, perhaps to a lesser extent, Japan (Nye 2002, pp. xiii, 4–5, 30–31, 38–39; Nye 2003, p. 65). But this is only true if we assume that the United States will continue to prefer a multilateral trading system organized around the WTO. Were the United States to choose to focus its energies on bilateral or regional strategies such as the development of a free trade area of the Americas, it is much less clear that it would need the cooperation of the EU and Japan.

In any case, to avoid tautology, we need some measures of relative economic capabilities. Unsurprisingly, the picture here is somewhat mixed, making firm conclusions about the nature of polarity difficult. Add to this the inevitable arbitrariness regarding how dominant the United States would have to be for the economic realm to be characterized as unipolar, and it is no wonder analysts disagree.

The United States in 1999 had a gross domestic product (GDP) almost equal to that of Japan, Germany, France, Britain, Russia, China, and India combined (Nye 2002, p. 37, tab. 1.2).[9] As a proportion of world product, the U.S. share in 1997 was approximately 21 percent. Since 1970, this percentage has slowly declined, from 23.8 percent in 1970, to 22.3 percent in 1980, to 22 percent in 1990. In comparison, China's share in 1997 was 11.7 percent, Japan's 8.1 percent, Germany's 4.8 percent, India's 4.1 percent, France's 3.5 percent, the United Kingdom's 3.3 percent, and Russia's 1.7 percent (Central Intelligence Agency 1998, tab. 1).

If we consider the proportion of world trade—exports plus imports—accounted for by the United States, the picture is again mixed.[10] A lot depends on whether we treat the European Union as an actor or instead consider individually the great power members of this union, namely France, Germany, and the United Kingdom. As Table 7.1 shows, if the EU is a relevant actor, then by this measure the EU is the hegemon, accounting for approximately 35–37 percent of world trade, more than twice that of the United States and far more than even the United Kingdom at its peak in the nineteenth century.[11] In other words, we don't have multipolarity in economic affairs; we have unipolarity, albeit with the EU as the dominant power. This means that those who argue that in international trade the world is multipolar do not in the end believe that the EU should be treated as an actor (at least not on a par with nation-states).[12] If the EU is not the relevant actor, in contrast, then the United States either is the hegemonic power or comes close to being so. Its 15 percent of world trade is almost twice that of number two, Germany.[13] Moreover, the 6.7 percent difference between number one and number two is greater today than it was in 1960, when the United States accounted for 15.3 percent of world trade and the United Kingdom, the number two, accounted for 9.6 percent, a difference of 5.7 percent.[14] In short, it seems reasonable to argue that, at least with respect to international trade, the structure is unipolar with the United States as the hegemon.

Table 7.1   Proportion of World Trade, 2001 (percentage)

Country	Proportion[a]	Proportion[b]
China (excluding Hong Kong and Macao)	5.1	3.7
China (including Hong Kong and Macao)	7.0	6.9
India	0.8	0.8
Japan	5.8	6.0
Russia	1.3	1.0
United States	15.1	15.3
France	5.0	5.2
Germany	8.4	8.5
United Kingdom	4.8	4.7
European Union	35.4	37.0

Source: International Monetary Fund 2003.
Notes: a. Calculated using exports and imports of the world to and from the respective countries.
   b. Calculated using exports and imports of the respective countries to and from the world.

Despite the somewhat mixed and ambiguous data on relative economic strength and size, then, in the end it seems difficult to disagree with Stephen Brooks and William Wohlforth (2002, p. 21) when they argue that "If today's American primacy does not constitute unipolarity, then nothing ever will."[15] Besides being the dominant military power, the United States is also the dominant power in technology, in economic affairs, and geopolitically, and with the exceptions noted above, its dominance in this regard is unprecedented in modern international history (Wohlforth 1999, esp. pp. 7, 13).[16]

The issue of how long unipolarity will last becomes important here, because if unipolarity is but a fleeting moment in history and policymakers realize this, they would presumably immediately start preparing for unipolarity's aftermath, thus blunting its effects on policy. Put differently, if unipolarity is here today but gone tomorrow, the United States would remain constrained by the international system. This would undermine my argument that to understand U.S. grand strategy, we need to pay close attention to domestic institutional constraints instead.

How Long Will Unipolarity Last?

While most scholars agree that the current system is unipolar, there is less consensus on how long unipolarity will last. Moreover, to some analysts, the duration of unipolarity is largely structurally determined, whereas to others, duration depends in part on the policies the dominant power, in this case the United States, will adopt. For these latter analysts, the dominant power can preserve its dominance by adopting policies designed to reassure and engage potential claimants to the position as hegemon.

Some believe that unipolarity will last but a moment. Huntington (1999, p. 37), for instance, maintains that unipolarity was but a flash in the pan, briefly discernible during the first Gulf War before giving way to a uni-multipolar system expected to last one or two decades (see also Joffe 1995). Christopher Layne predicted in 1993 (p. 7) that the unipolar moment would quickly fade away and give way to multipolarity between 2000 and 2010.[17] Uneven growth rates have made it possible for other powers to catch up with the United States. In a unipolar system, Layne argues, there is "overwhelming" pressure on "eligible" states—Germany and Japan, in the current system—to increase their relative capabilities to avoid being taken advantage of by the hegemon. All that seems to remain before the era of unipolarity can be declared over is for Germany and Japan to emulate the United States and "acquire the full spectrum of great power capabilities, including nuclear weapons" (Layne 1993, pp. 11, 37). So far, the evidence that Germany and Japan are acting in the way Layne predicted seems thin, however (Mastanduno 1997, p. 58).[18] On the whole, one gets the impression that scholars such as Huntington, Layne, and Waltz move too quickly from the claim that states should want to change unipolarity to the conclusion that they either have acquired or will quickly acquire the ability to do so (Wohlforth 1999, p. 34). As the old saying reminds us, "wishing it were so does not make it so."

Others predict that unipolarity will last much longer. In the absence of a precipitous economic decline on the part of the United States, Charles Krauthammer (1991, pp. 24, 26; also Krauthammer 2002–2003, p. 17) argues, the unipolar moment is expected to last three or four decades. William Wohlforth agrees, arguing that only differential growth in power or the emergence of the European Union as a state can end the era of unipolarity.[19] Other realists, focusing on threat rather than power, reach similar, albeit more contingent, conclusions. How long unipolarity will last, they argue, will be a function of the particulars of U.S. policy and the cleverness of its diplomacy. The United States, if it plays its cards right and pursues policies designed to engage and reassure other powers, can transform the unipolar moment into a unipolar era (see, in particular, Mastanduno 1997, esp. pp. 86–88; and Krauthammer 2002–2003, p. 17).

On balance, the evidence would seem to favor those who argue that unipolarity can be expected to be more than a fleeting moment (Posen 2003, pp. 5–6). How long it will last, no one can say. This is particularly so if its durability is contingent on the acumen of U.S. policymakers. It should also be noted that the discussion over how long unipolarity will last ignores U.S. domestic politics. As the dominant power in a unipolar system, the United States is essentially unconstrained by the international system. Thus, whether the

United States will play its cards right and transform the moment into an era will depend to a significant extent on U.S. domestic politics.

Unipolarity and the Lack of International Constraints

The power disparities between the hegemon and the other states give the hegemon great freedom to pursue its most preferred policies (Mastanduno 1997, p. 55). Wohlforth (1999, p. 8) contends that U.S. preponderance of power means that "the United States is freer than most states to disregard the international system and its incentives" (see also Brooks and Wohlforth 2002, pp. 30–31). Michael Mastanduno (1997, p. 88) argues that "In a unipolar setting the dominant state, less constrained by other great powers, must constrain itself." Josef Joffe (1995, pp. 99, 101), although he agrees with Huntington that the international system is "uni-multipolar," likewise maintains that the strategic environment in which the United States finds itself is "ultra-permissive."

The emergence of terrorism as a strategic threat in the wake of September 11, 2001, has not fundamentally changed this environment. Whereas the threat is serious enough, its emergence has not changed the unipolar structure of the international system nor will it undermine continued U.S. hegemony (Walt 2001–2002, p. 64). Because the underlying structure has not changed, the war on terrorism has not fundamentally altered U.S. statecraft. If anything, "the war on terrorism has confirmed American primacy in an altogether compelling manner" (Tucker 2002, p. 7; see also Joffe 2002, p. 17) and reinforced the unilateralist aspects of U.S. foreign policy (Kupchan 2002, pp. 27–29). The empirical record so far seems to bear out this argument.

Coalitions to fight terrorism may be needed, but they will not be allowed to constrain U.S. policy. Supporting this interpretation is U.S. defense secretary Donald Rumsfeld's oft-quoted statement, made in a television interview with Larry King, that the "mission determines the coalition." In that interview, broadcast on December 5, 2001, Rumsfeld observed that "dozens and dozens of countries are helping with overflight rights, with landing rights, with intelligence gathering, with law enforcement, with freezing bank accounts, with supplying troops in some cases and supplying aircraft and ships in other places." But when asked "whether it was very important that the coalition [against Al-Qaida] hold," he replied, perhaps somewhat cavalierly, "No." He went on to elaborate:

> First of all, there is no coalition. There are multiple coalitions. . . . Countries do what they can do. Countries help in the way they want to help. . . . And that's the way it ought to work. I'll tell you why. The worst thing you can do is to allow a coalition to determine what your mission is. The mission has to be to root out the terrorists. It's the mission that determines the coalition. So

it's what element of that task do countries want to help with, and that then is the coalition. (Rumsfeld 2001)

This view was echoed in U.S. secretary of state Colin Powell's observation in an interview in June 2002 that "we knew [the coalition against terrorism] would be a fluid coalition. It would have three pieces to it . . . or it might be a floating coalition. Or as Don Rumsfeld said on a number of occasion [*sic*], it might be a coalition of coalitions that are constantly shifting and, shifting and changing as the needs shifted and changed" (Powell 2002; see also Tucker 2002, p. 5). In short, U.S. policymakers seem to have concluded that the requirement of floating coalitions to fight terrorism implies that "no particular ally is an indispensable element of any coalition" (Goodin 2003, p. 123; see also Mandelbaum 2002, p. 68).

If the mission determines the coalition, then efforts to build more permanent and lasting coalitions are counterproductive. This is a completely different assessment from that prevalent during the Cold War and it is therefore no wonder that a return to postwar liberal multilateralism in security affairs has not (yet) taken place. Nor, as long as U.S. policymakers continue to emphasize fluid coalitions, would we expect to see trade discrimination in favor of allies become an important strategic instrument in the war on terrorism the way it did during the Cold War. Indeed, to the extent that trade is a useful strategic instrument, the emphasis on shifting coalitions should lead us to a continued move away from discriminatory trade. This is because preferential trade concessions typically come at the expense of other countries, thus creating tension with those countries and making more difficult the establishment of the shifting coalitions needed to fight terrorism.

One consequence of the unprecedented freedom enjoyed by the United States is indeterminacy of policy. Even some of those who agree that the United States has considerable freedom in formulating foreign policy still have not fully come to terms with the implications of their analysis. If it is true that for the United States "anything goes" (Joffe 1995, p. 99), then an explanation of U.S. foreign policy that relies exclusively on systemic-level theories such as balance-of-power theory or balance-of-threat theory will necessarily be indeterminate.[20]

U.S. security strategy after the Cold War has been largely consistent with balance-of-threat theory, Mastanduno argues, whereas its economic strategy is more consistent with balance-of-power theory. The loose constraints of unipolarity explain why the two strategies have diverged. He also observes that "taken together, [the two theories] point to an important tension within overall U.S. strategy" (1997, p. 85). But because both theories in the end rely on the level of threat (structural constraints) to derive propositions about state behavior, neither theory has much to say about behavior when the constraints are as loose as they currently are for the United States. It is thus no surprise that neither theory can explain the alleged tension in U.S. statecraft, or, for that matter, the opposite, namely a lack of tension in U.S. statecraft.[21]

It should be noted that Mastanduno (1998, p. 827) has also argued in an apparent contradiction that because a unipolar structure "tempts" the dominant state to try to stay top dog, the dominant state is "motivated" to integrate economic and security strategies. If no potential challenges to hegemony loom on the horizon, however, only dominant powers with very long time horizons would seem to have the proper motivation to integrate economics and security. In the absence of looming challengers, it is unclear whether the dominant state will adopt a long time horizon and focus on a distant payoff or adopt a short time horizon and focus on more immediate gratification. This is a question of which decision criterion states will adopt, and on this question, structural theory is indeterminate. When structure is ambiguous, domestic politics will in the end determine the criterion (Stein 1990, p. 202 and passim). To get a handle on U.S. security strategy in a unipolar world, therefore, we need to come to terms with the main implication of the freedom of maneuver afforded by unipolarity, namely the increased importance of domestic politics.[22]

Unipolarity and Domestic Politics

Given the loose constraints of the international system, systemic imperatives will be of little help in explaining U.S. statecraft. Understanding unipolar statecraft requires that we pay attention to domestic politics, particularly the domestic politics of the dominant power, the United States. Toward that end, I rely on some simple insights derived from the theory of veto players (see, in particular, Tsebelis 1995; Shugart and Haggard 2001; Cox and McCubbins 2001; and Tsebelis 2002).[23] For my purposes, the main advantage of the theory of veto players is that it allows us to derive predictions about the degree to which policies will remain stable in both the security and trade arenas and thus to say something about the overall integration of economics and security in U.S. statecraft. Other theories of domestic politics either focus on security or trade policy, typically having little to say about policymaking in other policy areas. Consequently they have little to say about how policymaking might differ in the two issue areas (see, e.g., Snyder 1991).[24]

The theory of veto players is designed to explain policy stability, defined as the "impossibility for significant departures from the status quo" (Tsebelis 2002, p. 2).[25] A veto player "is a person, group, or faction who, through their control of an office, post, or branch of government, can reject any proposed changes to existing policy" (Haggard and McCubbins 2001, p. 5, n. 10). The greater the number of veto players, the greater is policy stability, that is, the more difficult it is to change existing policy (the status quo). The reason is that a large number of veto players makes it more difficult to agree on a policy that offers enough value to the each of the players (Cox and McCubbins 2001, p. 27).

In cases where decisionmaking is delegated to one individual player, policy will reflect this player's preferences or ideal point. When the decisionmaker's preferences change, or when that person is replaced by another decisionmaker with different preferences, so too does policy change (Tsebelis 1995, p. 295). This has an important consequence: in a situation with more than one veto player, if the veto players share the same preferences, the *effective* number of vetoes is reduced to one (Cox and McCubbins 2001, p. 26). Accordingly, the more preferences differ among veto players, the greater policy stability will be (Tsebelis 2002, p. 2).

There are two kinds of veto players, institutional and partisan. The former are defined as such by the constitution, the latter by the political system (the party system and government coalitions). In the United States, there are, generally speaking, three institutional veto players—the president, the House, and the Senate.[26] Examples of partisan veto players are the members of a government coalition in Western Europe (Tsebelis 2002, p. 2; Tsebelis 1995, pp. 302, 304–305). For an actor to count as a veto player, minimally two conditions must be satisfied: first, the actor must be an actor capable of collective action, and second, the actor must have a veto.[27]

The number of veto players can, however, vary by issue (Tsebelis 1995, pp. 306–307). As Randall Ripley and James Lindsay (1993, p. 19) argue, foreign and defense policy is "not a single, undifferentiated area." They propose that foreign policies fall into three general categories—crisis, strategic, and structural—and that the relative power of Congress, and by extension the number of veto players, varies across these policy types. Presidential power, they argue, is at a maximum in crisis situations. The president retains substantial power in strategic policy, that is, the specification of the "goals and tactics of defense and foreign policy,"[28] although this influence is not as great as in crisis situations. The president is weakest in structural policy, or policies governing how resources are used (Ripley and Lindsay 1993, pp. 19–20). Such policies require appropriations, giving Congress relatively great influence (Ripley and Lindsay 1993, pp. 21–22). Ripley and Lindsay (1993, p. 21) also note that many policies fall into more than one category. For instance, trade policy involves both a strategic element (preference for free trade or protectionism) and a structural element (maintaining quotas on various goods). Defense policy, they argue, is similar.

Because, as I argue, the number of veto players in the trade policy arena is greater than in the security policy arena, trade policy will generally be more stable than security policy. That is, we should see greater changes in security policy (shifts in the status quo) after the end of Cold War than in trade policy. In other words, unipolarity indirectly—by increasing the importance of domestic institutional factors—decreases policy stability in the security arena but not in the trade arena.

Unipolarity and Security Policy

The U.S. Constitution designates the president as the commander in chief of the armed forces, but Congress alone has the power to "declare war," to "raise and support Armies," and to "provide and maintain a Navy." Nevertheless, in foreign affairs, despite occasional congressional attempts to rein in the executive branch, decisionmaking today is typically formally delegated to the president and the executive branch.[29] Since the presidency of Harry Truman, there has been a broad expansion of executive prerogative in foreign affairs through a reinterpretation of the Constitution. According to this interpretation, "in foreign affairs the president alone has final authority, and when the national security was imperiled (a judgment left to the executive) the president was legitimately entitled to override constitutional constraints to preserve and protect that security" (Silverstein 1997, p. 9). As Gordon Silverstein (1997, p. 214) argues, this reinterpretation "increasingly has been accepted by Congress and the Supreme Court" and "been adopted in law and enshrined in precedent." True, Congress and others may continue to informally influence foreign policy and there may even be evidence that such informal influence has increased in recent years. Nevertheless, executive prerogative means that the president is more likely to prevail in disputes between the two branches over policymaking authority (Silverstein 1997, pp. 14–16).[30]

With the increasing acceptance in the courts of the executive prerogative doctrine, it seems reasonable to argue that in crisis and strategic decisionmaking, only the executive possesses a veto. It should be noted, however, that because treaties require the consent of the Senate, the number of veto players in this context is two. Moreover, on trade policy, the president still needs the approval of Congress, making the number of veto players in trade policy three rather than one. Matters are also different in structural policy, where Congress can use its power of appropriations to veto executive proposals.

Nevertheless, this discussion implies that U.S. strategic policy will largely reflect the president's preferences. The end of the Cold War and the emergence of a unipolar world did not change this state of affairs, although U.S. military dominance may have shifted the president's preferred policies. The absence of a threat *and* the absence of domestic constraints mean that the president is free to choose between, broadly speaking, unilateral and multilateral security strategies.[31] Equally important, in the absence of an international threat, the general direction as well as the particulars of strategic policy are likely to change when the president is replaced. The status quo, in other words, will reflect the new president's preferences. In the absence of either systemic or domestic constraints, security policy will likely reflect largely idiosyncratic factors such as ideology, bureaucratic politics, and the particular mix of personalities in the administration.[32] In short, as long as we find ourselves in a unipolar system, shifts in U.S. security policy will take place both within and particularly across administrations to reflect differences in the president's preferences.

George W. Bush's foreign policy has been consistently unilateral, marking a shift from the largely multilateral foreign policies pursued during Bill Clinton's two terms in office. Bush's foreign policy has shown a greater tendency to opt out of multilateral frameworks and a greater willingness to act alone than was the case during the Clinton administration.[33] Moreover, this tendency characterized Bush's foreign policy both before and after September 11, 2001.

Nevertheless, analysts have pointed to unilateral elements in Clinton's foreign policy (Schlesinger 1998–1999, p. 38), some going as far as to argue that the "defining essence" of Clinton's foreign policy was the unilateral exercise of power (Walt 2000, p. 77). Others have failed to see any essence at all, complaining that Clinton's foreign policy lacked an "overall perspective" and therefore "degenerate[d] into tactical manipulations" (Hyland 1999, p. 203). One assessment of the "evolving" grand strategy of the Clinton administration, as found in the 1996 document *A National Security Strategy of Engagement and Enlargement,* found an "uneasy amalgam" of no less than three strategies, namely selective engagement, cooperative security, and primacy." The "dash of primacy" giving unilateralist piquancy to the strategy was discernible above all in the many references to the need for U.S. leadership and in the emphasis on maintaining an ability to deal with threats not just multilaterally, but also unilaterally. In other respects, however, the document called for strengthening international institutions and relying on multilateral solutions in areas such as arms control (Posen and Ross 1996–1997, pp. 5, 44–45).[34]

Several commentators have also noted policy differences between the first and second Clinton administration. Whereas the doctrine of "democratic enlargement"—with its emphasis on spreading democracy and free markets—that was developed in the first Clinton administration marked an essential continuity with policies pursued during the Cold War (Maynes 1993–1994), U.S. foreign policy in the second administration, it is argued, had a more unilateralist bent (Dumbrell 2002b, pp. 48–49; Dumbrell 2002a, p. 282). The conventional view is that this bent reflected Clinton's inability to overcome opposition from a Republican and nationalist Congress after the 1994 elections (Dumbrell 2002b, p. 53; Dumbrell 2002a, p. 282). The Senate's constitutional right to ratify treaties, in particular, stymied Clinton's efforts to commit the United States to multilateral solutions in a number of policy areas. Since these solutions typically required signing new treaties, it gave the Senate veto power over these efforts, and preserved the status quo or policy stability.

Even commentators who claim to notice a more unilateralist thrust to the second Clinton administration's foreign policy nevertheless see a clear move in the direction of unilateralism with the coming to power of George W. Bush in 2001 (Dumbrell 2002b, p. 53). While pointing to the increasing emphasis on military power in the last years of the Clinton administration, they also note that Clinton's foreign policy during this period was "more multilateral and liberal, and more concerned with international legitimacy" than the strategy adopted by President George W. Bush (Posen 2003, p. 6; see also Kupchan 2003b). There is a difference between the Clinton administration's "assertive multilateralism"—and even the later, more pragmatic internationalism embodied in the slogan "multilateral when we can, unilateral when we must"—and the Bush administration's "à la carte" embrace of multilateralism, an embrace that from the very beginning was tempered by Condoleezza Rice, Bush's foreign policy adviser, in her denial that "the support of many states—or, even better, of institutions like the United Nations—is essential to the legitimate exercise of power." U.S. interests, she argued in 2000, should not play second fiddle to the interests of an "illusory international community" (quoted in Patrick 2002, pp. 13–14).

In short, whereas analysts have found considerable ambivalence in the U.S. support of multilateral approaches during the Clinton presidency—encapsulated in the phrase "ambivalent engagement"—they nevertheless see in this ambivalence a contrast to the "growing unilateral disengagement" characterizing the Bush administration's foreign policies (Patrick 2002; Malone and Khong 2003, p. 4).[35] The contrast between Clinton's ambivalent engagement and Bush's unilateral disengagement is evident in a number of policy arenas.

The Clinton administration decided in September 2000 to delay deploying so-called national missile defense in part because they needed more time to consult with Russia as well as U.S. allies in Europe. In announcing the decision, President Clinton argued that "it would be far better to move forward in the context of the [1972] ABM [Anti-Ballistic Missile] Treaty and allied support." The Bush administration felt differently, simply abandoning the ABM Treaty and formally notifying Russia that it would abrogate the treaty in December 2001.

Similarly, whereas the Clinton administration signed the 1997 Kyoto Protocol to the 1992 United Nations Framework Convention on Climate Change, and attempted to renegotiate some aspects of the protocol to make it more palatable to a firmly opposed Congress, the Bush administration in March 2001 announced that the United States would retreat from the protocol (Steurer 2003). Bush's alternative, embodied in the so-called Clear Skies and Global Climate Change Initiatives, announced in February 2002, was purely domestic in scope, involving no further multilateral initiatives on the part of the United States to control greenhouse gas emissions (Steurer 2003, p. 351).

In July 2001 the Bush administration announced that it would not support a legally binding protocol intended to "promote compliance with" the 1972

Biological Weapons Convention. Once it became clear that the United States would withdraw its support, efforts to negotiate such a protocol, which had started in 1995, were quickly abandoned by the other parties to the negotiations. In contrast, President Clinton strongly supported these efforts, although he did not give the negotiations the kind of attention they needed, and the U.S. contribution was consequently limited by bureaucratic infighting (Rosenberg 2001).

Finally, both the Clinton and George W. Bush administrations had misgivings about the International Criminal Court (ICC), worrying that it would facilitate politically motivated prosecutions of U.S. nationals for alleged war crimes. Despite misgivings, President Clinton nevertheless signed the Rome Statute that would create the ICC, on December 31, 2000, the deadline for signing. Clinton argued that signing would put the United States "in a position to influence the evolution of the Court," while not signing would give the United States no influence. "The United States," Clinton continued, "should have the chance to observe and assess the functioning of the Court, over time, before choosing to become subject to its jurisdiction." Accordingly, he recommended that his successor not submit the treaty to the Senate for ratification "until our fundamental concerns are satisfied."[36] In contrast, in May 2002, a month after the Rome Statute had received the number of ratifications needed to bring it into force, the Bush administration decided to "unsign" it. Whereas the Clinton administration sought to minimize the risk to U.S. nationals, the Bush administration seems simply to have assumed that this was not possible (Orentlicher 2004, pp. 422–423).

In short, whereas the Clinton administration tried to amend these various multilateral frameworks to accord with U.S. interests, the Bush administration walked away from them (Jervis 2003b, 374). The evidence, then, supports the claim that the Bush administration has moved U.S. foreign policy much closer to the unilateral end of the continuum than was the case during the Clinton administration. Moreover, as evidenced in the decisions to abandon the Kyoto Protocol and the efforts to promote compliance with the Biological Weapons Convention, this shift in policy preceded September 11 and the war on terrorism.

In trade policy, in contrast, there has been no such shift; instead, trade policy has remained close to the status quo. The main reason is that the number of veto players is greater in the trade than in the security policy arena.

Unipolarity and Trade Policy

There are three institutional veto players in the trade policy–making arena: the House, the Senate, and the president. These actors are capable of collective action, and they can veto trade policy. The U.S. Constitution grants to Congress the "power to regulate Commerce with foreign Nations." The president, in contrast, is given no trade-specific power in the Constitution. He can veto trade bills passed by Congress, which in turn can override his veto by a two-thirds majority in both houses.

With the passage of the 1934 Reciprocal Trade Agreements Act, Congress delegated tariff-making authority to the president. The 1974 Trade Reform Act instituted a set of so-called fast-track procedures for implementing the trade treaties negotiated by the executive branch. While the fast track limits debate and precludes congressional amendment to trade agreements, fast-track procedures still give Congress a veto over executive actions (O'Halloran 1993, p. 288; see also Nivola 1997, p. 247). Thus, even if granted fast-track negotiating authority, the president must notify both the Senate Finance Committee and the House Ways and Means Committee of the intention to begin negotiations. Either committee can at that point and within sixty days pass a resolution disapproving the negotiations, in which case fast-track procedures no longer apply. The 1974 act also requires the president, through the U.S. trade representative, to consult with private sector advisory committees prior to the negotiations, and it allows members of Congress to participate in the negotiations as official delegates. The 1988 Omnibus Trade and Competitiveness Act further strengthened the hand of Congress. Congress can decide to repeal fast-track procedures if it decides that the president has not met the requirements for consultation with Congress. If both chambers pass a disapproval resolution within any sixty-day period, the negotiations are terminated (O'Halloran 1993, pp. 290–294). Once a trade agreement is signed, it needs to be approved by both the House and the Senate by a simple majority. The bill implementing the trade agreement then goes to the president for signature. In short, despite the changes in tariff-making authority since 1934, both houses of Congress still play the role of veto players, and the number of such players remains three: the House, the Senate, and the president.

As noted above, in situations with more than one veto player, if the veto players share the same preferences, the *effective* number of vetoes is reduced to one. So while we have established that in trade policy, the number of institutional veto players is three, this says nothing about the effective number of players. Determining the effective number requires a discussion of the preferences of the representatives, the senators, and the president.[37]

Because these three bodies respond to different constituencies, generally their preferences regarding trade policy are likely to differ. Scholars have argued that the size of a representative's electoral district determines his or her preferences over trade policy. The smaller the electoral district, the greater the influence of special interests is likely to be, and thus the more protectionist representatives will be (Rogowski 1987, pp. 208–209; Milner 1999, p. 101; Frieden and Martin 2002, p. 133).[38] In the U.S. case, this implies that the House of Representatives will be more protectionist than the Senate, which in turn will be more protectionist that the president.[39]

The president's trade policy preferences may also be derived from strategic considerations. By delegating trade policy–making authority to the executive branch, Stephan Haggard (1988) has argued, the 1934 Reciprocal Trade Agreements Act made it possible for the president to place trade policy in the service, at least in part, of broader international economic and political considerations. Although strategic imperatives lead one to expect that the president will favor discriminatory trade policies in which military allies receive preferential access to the U.S. markets, the strategic imperatives of the Cold War facilitated the push toward freer trade (albeit on a discriminatory basis).[40] With the Cold War threat gone, and the U.S. ability to go it alone in military affairs, strategic considerations may be expected to play a much reduced role in determining the president's preferences on trade policy. Still, in representing a national constituency, the president should continue to favor freer trade.

In sum, because the preferences of the House, Senate, and the president are likely to differ, the effective number of veto players in the trade policy–making area is three, making it likely that U.S. trade policy will hew closer to the Cold War status quo than has security policy.

The U.S. Commitment to a Multilateral Trading System

Although the evidence at this point is somewhat ambiguous, U.S. trade policy before and after the Cold War is characterized by stability. Despite the war on terrorism and the shifts in security strategy, with respect to trade policy, trade policy as it was defined during the Cold War has remained essentially unchanged, that is, policy has remained committed to preserving and strengthening a multilateral trading system centered on the WTO (Nivola 1997).[41] This is so despite the many bilateral and regional trade agreements concluded since the end of the Cold War, which some have interpreted as evidence that the United States is ready to abandon a multilateral trading system. At least if U.S. policymakers are to be believed, this interpretation is wrong. The agreements should be regarded not as attempts to undermine the WTO but rather as efforts to widen its scope.

Scholars who have focused in particular on the first Clinton administration's emphasis on improving U.S. international economic competitiveness, however, have seen a departure from the Cold War status quo (Mastanduno 1997; Nau 1995). Indicative of this departure are policies such as U.S. demands that allies share in the burden of foreign policy commitments; aggressive promotion of U.S. firms in international competition; demands for market access; and a waning commitment to multilateral free trade. Driving these policies was the fear that the economic position of the United States was declining relative to its main economic partners (see Mastanduno 1997, pp. 75–80).

In contrast, others fail to see a departure from the status quo. There are exact parallels between commercial disputes with the Japanese in the mid-

1990s, for instance, and attempts by the Nixon administration to establish "a more equitable relationship" with Japan. Moreover, the Super 301 and antidumping measures embodied in the 1974 Trade Reform Act and the moves in a more protectionist direction during the Reagan administration in the 1980s were arguably more severe than anything contemplated by the Clinton administration and Congress during the 1990s (Nivola 1997, pp. 235–239). From this perspective, the Clinton administration's emphasis on improving U.S. international competitiveness represents a continuation and not a departure from the status quo (Nivola 1997, pp. 241–242).[42] Some policymakers have seen departures from the status quo where continuity exists. Consider, for instance, U.S. trade representative Charlene Barshefsky's comment in 1996 that "with the Cold War over, trade agreements must stand or fall on their merits. They no longer have a security component. If we do not get reciprocity, we will not get freer trade" (quoted in Mastanduno 1997, p. 80).[43] This may sound like a departure from the status quo until one recalls similar statements by one of Nixon's aides in 1971: "In the past, economic interests were sacrificed when they came into conflict with diplomatic interests." In the future, other countries would discover that, in the words of a cabinet officer, "Santa Claus is dead" (quoted in Nivola 1997, p. 235).

It is also important to put in perspective the efforts by various administrations to improve U.S. competitiveness. While these efforts are in many ways protectionist and lead to conflicts with allies, they remain islands of conflict in the sea of cooperation constituted by the multilateral trading system. Were the U.S. commitment to a multilateral trading system truly to weaken, the case for a departure from the Cold War status quo would be much stronger. There is little evidence that the commitment is weakening, however.

Two essential elements in the status quo are support for freer trade and support for multilateral negotiations through the General Agreement on Tariffs and Trade (GATT)/WTO to promote free trade. Continued strong U.S. support for freer trade during the rounds of multilateral trade negotiations under the auspices of the GATT/WTO shows that the United States has remained committed to the status quo in trade policy in the post–Cold War era. Although the Uruguay Round negotiations started in 1986 during the Cold War, they were completed only in 1993, that is, after the end of the Cold War. The support for another round of trade negotiations at Doha in 2001 is perhaps the best example of the continuity of the commitment to free trade.

The simultaneous U.S. push to conclude bilateral or regional free trade agreements (FTAs) with other countries means, however, that the evidence for continuity is not conclusive. Many see in the increasing U.S. emphasis on concluding bilateral and regional trade agreements a waning commitment to multilateral free trade.[44] FTAs, involving as they do discrimination against nonsignatories and trade diversion, are perceived as incompatible with a commitment to continued liberalization of international trade. For this reason, bilateral and regional trade agreements, instead of paving the way for nondiscriminatory multilateral agreements, are viewed by many as obstacles to such agreements (see, e.g., Gordon 2001, 2003).[45]

In assessing U.S. trade policy, however, much depends on whether we conceive of these FTAs as ends in their own right or, as U.S. policymakers insist, simply as steppingstones on the road to a global multilateral agreement under the auspices of the WTO. If they are regarded as ways for the United States to increase its bargaining power in multilateral trade negotiations, they signify not a waning commitment to multilateral trade agreements but rather a shift in bargaining tactics.[46] At least publicly, U.S. officials both in the Clinton and George W. Bush administrations have insisted that bilateral and regional efforts will help pave the way for global multilateral trade agreements.

For instance, Jeffrey Garten, who served as U.S. undersecretary of commerce for international trade in the Clinton administration from 1993 until October 1995, argues that unilateral and bilateral means have a multilateral end—the ultimate purpose is to achieve stronger and more enforceable multilateral agreements. When the United States acts bilaterally, as in the case of putting pressure on Japan to open its automotive markets, it does so largely because the issues at stake are beyond the purview of the WTO (Garten 1995, pp. 55–57, 59, 61). Moreover, the bilateral agreement between the United States and Japan that resulted applied to other nations as well.

During the George W. Bush administration, the United States has continued this strategy, evidently seeking to use regional and bilateral trade agreements to put pressure on the Europeans and the Japanese in particular to complete the Doha Round of trade talks (Gordon 2003, p. 105). Thus, in late 2001, U.S. trade representative Robert Zoellick wrote:

> I believe a strategy of trade liberalization on multiple fronts—globally, regionally, and bilaterally—enhances our leverage and best promotes open markets. As Europeans have pointed out to me, it took the completion of NAFTA [North American Free Trade Agreement] and the first APEC [Asia Pacific Economic Cooperation] Summit in 1993–94 to persuade the EU to close out the Uruguay Round. I favor a "competition in liberalization" with the U.S. at the center of the network. (quoted in Gordon 2003, p. 105)[47]

In a different context the following year, Zoellick elaborated on this so-called competitive liberalization strategy: "While I appreciate those economists that are fully committed to the multilateral system, most of them have never had to negotiate anything. And so I firmly believe that a process of trying to have competitive liberalization will enhance our ability to get Doha done" (quoted in Blustein 2002c, p. E3).

The strategy of using bilateral and regional means for multilateral ends thus shows an essential continuity between the Clinton and the George W. Bush administration. Had the United States abandoned its multilateral trade policy developed during the Cold War, it is not clear why it should have remained committed to global trade negotiations. This commitment preceded September 11, 2001, as evidenced in President Clinton's call for a new round of global trade negotiations in his 1999 State of the Union address. The Bush administration as well pushed for a new round of global trade talks before September 11 (see, e.g., Lamy and Zoellick 2001), an effort that was crowned with success in November 2001 with the launching of the Doha Round of the WTO. These efforts seem to indicate that the United States remains committed not only to preserving the multilateral trading system but indeed to strengthening it.[48] As the support for a new global trade round suggests, the war on terrorism has done nothing to break the essential continuity of U.S. trade strategy.

The War on Terrorism and U.S. Trade Strategy

The war on terrorism has not appreciably changed U.S. trade strategy. True, Zoellick explicitly linked trade policy and the fight against terrorism in the immediate aftermath of September 11, 2001, when he argued that "we need an economic strategy that complements our security strategy" (quoted in Mufson 2001, p. A9; see also Bacevich 2002, pp. 232–233). In that regard, he urged congressional approval of trade promotion authority (TPA) to help the United States gain support from other countries in its fight against terrorism (Zoellick 2001; Dionne 2001). Still, the underlying strategy has not changed. While the United States has continued its pursuit of bilateral and regional trade treaties, its efforts regarding the launch of the Doha Round suggest that it is still committed to multilateralism. That the terrorist threat has changed trade strategy little is perhaps even more evident with respect to Congress.

Less convinced than Zoellick that combating terrorism required Congress to cede control over trade policy, the House of Representatives barely approved TPA in December 2001 on a vote of 215–214.[49] Of crucial importance in ensuring passage of TPA were signals from the Bush administration that the steel and lumber industries would receive protection (Blustein 2002a). The administration kept its promise in March 2002 when it imposed safeguard tariffs ranging from 8 percent to 30 percent on various steel products for three years from countries such as Russia, an important ally in the fight against terrorism.[50]

The administration's action in this regard is open to at least two interpretations. The first interpretation, especially popular in Europe, regards the administration's decision as motivated by electoral considerations. It was believed that steel tariffs would improve President Bush's electoral prospects in swing states such as Pennsylvania, West Virginia, and Ohio. Add to that the fact that Dick Cheney during the 2000 election campaign promised West Virginia's steel workers that Bush would not leave them in the lurch the way Bill

Clinton had and the argument for an electoral motivation seems strong. The second interpretation is that the promise to impose tariffs on steel and softwood lumber was necessary in order to ensure passage of TPA. The lumber tariff, for instance, was motivated by the need to appeal to important senators such as Democrat Max Baucus, chairman of the finance committee under whose jurisdiction trade legislation belongs, and Senate Minority Leader Trent Lott. According to this interpretation, steel and lumber tariffs made possible TPA, which in turn was necessary to ensure that the United States could conclude agreements that in the future would lead to freer trade (Blustein 2002a; "Romancing Big Steel" 2002).

The 2002 U.S. farm bill has likewise been regarded as a major blow to those who want to push for free trade on a multilateral basis. The bill increased federal subsidies by over 80 percent, nullifying the progress made in the 1996 farm bill in moving toward a removal of subsidies in favor of income support (which is less trade-distorting). Although the 2002 farm bill originated in Congress, and although Secretary of Agriculture Ann Veneman proposed unlinking subsidies from production, President Bush still signed it ("Dangerous Activities" 2002). Some in the Bush administration argue that both the steel tariffs and agricultural subsidies will force other nations to the bargaining table and thus pave the way for future trade liberalization.[51] Consistent with this argument is the fact that the Bush administration followed its acquiescence to an increase in farm subsidies with commitments to sweeping cuts in both farm subsidies and agricultural tariffs if Europe and Japan would follow suit. "We're ready to cut if others step up to the plate, too," Zoellick claimed (quoted in Blustein 2002b, p. E1).[52]

Another explanation for the Bush administration's position is again electoral politics: the farm subsidies were passed with the November 2002 congressional elections in mind. Senate races in farm states such as Iowa, South Dakota, and Missouri were expected to be close, and farm subsidies would help Republicans in those states ("Bush the Anti-Globaliser" 2002).

Whereas the war on terrorism has done nothing to prevent the passage of protectionist measures, commentators have seen in the bilateral negotiations over free trade areas a clear attempt by the United States to favor its coalition partners, particularly those, such as Australia and Singapore, that have supported the United States in the war against Iraq. That is, the war on terrorism has changed the motives underlying the FTAs: these FTAs were concluded not (just) to strengthen the U.S. negotiating position in the Doha Round but (also) to cement the political and military ties linking the United States and Australia and Singapore.

In support of the latter interpretation, agricultural interest groups in the United States moderated their opposition to negotiating a free trade agreement with Australia once it became clear to them that such an agreement had become a top priority of a Bush administration eager to round up support for its war in Iraq. Other evidence, however, suggests that rounding up support for the war in Iraq had little to do with the agreements with either Singapore or Australia. Thus, Zoellick, in response to Australian pressure for an FTA, had indicated that he personally supported such an agreement well in advance of the war with Iraq (Colebatch 2003; Rushe and Kemeny 2003).

The timing is also wrong in the case of Singapore: the trade talks that led to the signing of the free trade agreement in May 2003 started in late 2000—well before September 11, 2001—and concluded in November 2002, four months before the start of the war with Iraq. In an April 2003 speech at the launch of the U.S. Asia Pacific Council—an organization backed by the State Department and made up of distinguished U.S. citizens—C. Fred Bergsten of the Institute for International Studies in Washington, D.C., predicted that the United States was likely to use trade agreements to favor those who supported the U.S. position in Iraq. Thus, "Singapore, a member of the coalition, will see its free-trade agreement proceed on schedule. Chile, which did not cooperate, will not." Yet only a month separated the signing of the two agreements: the agreement with Singapore was signed in May 2003, that with Chile in June 2003 (Mitton 2003).[53]

Moreover, apart from an unwillingness to include New Zealand—highly critical of the U.S. invasion of Iraq—in the trade negotiations with Australia (Armstrong 2003),[54] there is some evidence that U.S. trade officials have sought to use trade policy not to differentiate between supporters and opponents but instead to repair relations with opponents of the United States. This is particularly so in its relations with the EU, where U.S. policymakers seem to have responded to pressure from U.S. companies to avoid economic retaliation (Alden and de Jonquieres 2003).[55] True, the timing of the U.S. decision in May 2003 to bring a case before the WTO challenging the EU's de facto moratorium on authorizing the import of genetically modified food struck EU officials as "eccentric," as the moratorium was due to be lifted at the end of 2003.[56] The United States had threatened a challenge to the moratorium since October 2002, but the White House, hoping to drum up European support for a war against Iraq, put the challenge on hold in January 2003. While the timing thus might seem peculiar, the decision to bring the case before the WTO seems wholly unrelated to any desire to punish opponents of the invasion of Iraq. Instead, the United States seemed eager to head off similar moratoriums in other countries, as well as EU plans for restrictions on trade in chemicals that could pose safety risks (Alden, Buck, and de Jonquieres 2003).

Perhaps the best support for the argument that the war on terrorism (but not the war against Iraq) has had an effect on U.S. trade strategy is to be found in U.S. trade policy toward the Middle East and other Islamic countries. The plan for a Middle East free trade area, proposed by President Bush in a speech in May 2003, envisioned signing free trade agreements with Egypt and Bahrain as stepping-stones on the way to a more encompassing free trade area to be completed by 2013.[57] Trade negotiations with Morocco, announced in April 2002, were expected to be concluded by the end of 2003. Both Egypt and Morocco were critical of the U.S. invasion of Iraq. Egypt has since fallen into disfavor, in part because in the U.S. view it has been dilatory in its implementation of economic reforms, particularly modernization of its customs laws, and in part because it purportedly reneged on its promise to support the United States in its case at the WTO challenging the EU moratorium on genetically modified foods (Khalaf 2003; Alden 2003).

Reflecting in part the perceived need for allies in the fight against terrorism and perhaps in part the notion that trade liberalization can alleviate poverty, analysts have advocated opening the U.S. market to Pakistani exports and the general lowering of trade barriers to exports from the developing world (Walt 2001–2002, pp. 66–67). Whereas the United States pledged $600 million in economic aid to Pakistan two months after the September 11 attacks and lifted the economic sanctions imposed in 1998 and 1999, the United States dragged its feet regarding reductions in the tariffs on and increase in the quotas for Pakistan's textiles.[58] This was in sharp contrast to the European Union, which moved promptly to ease the way for Pakistani textile exports to the EU. Not until February 2003 did the United States act, offering Pakistan a three-year package of trade bonuses, including the increase of some textile quotas. The economic benefits to Pakistan have been insignificant in part because some of the increases affected products that Pakistan produces in very limited quantities. The Trade and Investment Framework Agreement, signed with Pakistan in June 2003, is also consistent with a trade policy status quo. While the agreement commits the U.S. president to ask Congress for $3 billion in aid to Pakistan, it offers Pakistan no concessions on textiles. All the agreement does is to set up annual talks between the two countries. According to a U.S. trade official, "Pakistan is a friend of the U.S. So are many other countries that are textile exporters. I think it would be very unlikely that we would offer special benefits to Pakistan that we would not be prepared to offer other countries" (quoted in Altman 2003, p. C11). Besides, even if the United States would have wanted to discriminate in favor of Pakistani textiles, textile quotas for members of the WTO are due to disappear in 2005 (although tariffs are not). Any concession on quotas offered to Pakistan would therefore have been of very limited duration. Although the U.S. trade official quoted above mentions the interests of the domestic textile producers as another obstacle to textile concessions, electoral considerations probably play much less of a role here than they might in the steel sector. Bush's support in both North and South Carolina, important textile-producing states, is so solid that any action on Pakistani textile quotas would probably have little impact on his electoral prospects (Altman 2003).

In short, the commitment to a multilateral trading system was evident before September 11, 2001, and represented an essential continuity with the trade policy developed during the Cold War. Whereas the war on terrorism may have served to deepen this commitment, it has not fundamentally altered it.

Conclusion

Will the United States, as the dominant power in a unipolar system, remain wedded to the security and trade strategies that it developed during the Cold War? I have argued that an answer to this question requires that we consider U.S. domestic institutions, specifically the number of veto players in the foreign economic and security policy–making arenas. In this regard, the analysis differs from the largely systemic analysis that has hitherto dominated the analysis of U.S. statecraft in the post–Cold War world. Such analysis, relying in large part on structural factors such as the distribution of power, fails to come to grips with perhaps the most salient fact of unipolar systems: that the dominant power is essentially unconstrained and that we can therefore not rely on structural constraints to derive expectations about the foreign policies such powers are likely to pursue. This is particularly so if, as argued above, the era of unipolarity can be expected to last beyond a decade or so. My argument should not be understood, however, as a general plea for granting domestic variables analytical primacy over systemic variables. Somewhat paradoxically, the salience of domestic political factors in shaping U.S. statecraft is at least in part a function of unipolarity, that is, of a particular distribution of power.

Some may grant this much, but object that domestic political factors are only important in security affairs. In international economic affairs, even a power as dominant as the United States is still so constrained by international regimes and institutions that domestic political factors lose much of their explanatory power. In support of their view, they might point to the recent decision by the Bush administration to lift the steel tariffs imposed in 2002 after the WTO had declared the tariffs illegal. It seems hard to avoid the conclusion that the WTO made the price of protecting the steel industry too high (Sanger 2003). If so, this implies that stability in trade policy may be better explained by focusing on the constraining effects of international regimes than on domestic variables such as the number of veto players.

Veto player theory still seems relevant, however. The theory predicts that the United States will remain committed to a multilateral trading system. For the theory to be correct, the bilateral and regional trade deals being pursued must be intended as stepping-stones toward multilateral agreements. The WTO does not force the United States to choose to remain committed to multilateralism; bilateral and regional deals are generally allowed under WTO rules, implying that the choice to remain committed to strengthening the WTO is a function of domestic politics and thus within the scope of veto player theory.

The decision to rescind the steel tariffs may be taken as a sign not that the United States has no other choice but to abide by the rulings of the WTO, but that the United States remains committed to a multilateral trading order and seeks to strengthen it.

The salience of domestic political constraints in the dominant power and the likelihood that those constraints will differ in different policy arenas mean that policymakers in the dominant power generally will face difficulties integrating economics and security in statecraft. Nevertheless, the present combination of a largely unilateral security strategy with a largely multilateral trade strategy does not imply that economic and security strategies pull in different directions and that U.S. statecraft is therefore disintegrated; on the contrary, the attempt to extend the reach of the WTO in the current Doha Round would seem compatible with the flexibility required by a security strategy in which the mission determines the coalition. Whereas discriminatory policies risk closing doors to potential coalition partners, nondiscriminatory policies help keep them open.

Perhaps the most controversial claim made in this chapter has been that the war on terrorism has not restored structural constraints to the importance they had during the Cold War. U.S. security and trade strategies continue to reflect domestic political factors, not systemic imperatives. The United States is still the dominant power in both the security and economic realms, and this dominance can be expected to last for decades. The terrorist threat does not alter this situation. U.S. dominance makes possible the belief that permanent coalitions are not necessary to win the war on terrorism, and that the coalitions that are needed can be cobbled together on an ad hoc basis. Should this belief turn out to be wrong or should a strategy based on it be deemed too risky, the war on terrorism may alter U.S. statecraft more fundamentally in the future than it has so far, and push the United States back toward a more multilateral security strategy. It also remains to be seen whether a multilateral foreign economic policy is sustainable in an environment of unilateral security policies.

In the short to medium term, however, one might think that the main threat to integrating economics and security in statecraft is found not in U.S. unilateralism in national security policy but in the moves away from multilateralism in trade policy. Were the current Doha Round of the WTO to fail and were the United States to continue its pursuit of discriminatory free trade arrangements, international trade could become increasingly regionalized, constituting a threat to the continued viability of a strategy that relies on fluidity in international coalition building. This is because bilateral and regional trade arrangements run the risk of increasing conflict with those not party to these arrangements, thus undermining a security strategy based on missions determining coalitions. The theory of veto players suggests that such a departure from the multilateralism of the Cold War is unlikely to happen. The presence of three institutional veto players in the trade policy arena implies that the United States will be able to stay the trade policy course staked out during the Cold War and avoid the conflicts and tensions inherent in an increasingly regional world economy.

Notes

I thank Eugene Gholz, Steven Hook, and the other contributors to this volume for suggestions that greatly improved this chapter.

1. See, for example, Stein 1990, p. 202; Wohlforth 1999, p. 40; Kapstein 1999, p. 468; Bender 2003, p. 155; and Kissinger 2001, pp. 287–288. These authors all argue that loose international or structural constraints imply that domestic political constraints will play a significant role in determining foreign policy. This is also one of the implications of the literature on hegemonic stability theory. Thus, Arthur Stein (1984, p. 384) argued that the economic hegemon faces a dilemma in that it has a choice between maximizing its own economic returns and maximizing its relative positions. It has to choose, that is, between economic openness and closure. Similarly, scholars debated whether the hegemon should pursue free trade policies or instead exploit its size and consequent market power to impose optimal tariffs on imports (Conybeare 1984; Gowa 1989; Mansfield and Busch 1995; Lake 1993, esp. pp. 473–474). In other words, structural constraints—in this case the international distribution of economic power—are indeterminate regarding which trade strategy the hegemon will choose. The indeterminacy of structural constraints provided a major justification for why scholars in international political economy turned their attention to domestic political factors such as interest-group pressures, electoral politics, and political institutions. For an early statement of the problem, see Krasner 1976.

2. See, for example, Mastanduno 1997, 1998; Mastanduno and Kapstein 1999; Kapstein 1999; Ikenberry 2003b; Jervis 2003a, 2003b; and Kupchan 2003a. These authors rely on systemic theories ranging from balance-of-power and balance-of-threat theory to hegemonic stability theory to international institutionalist theories to aid in the analysis of U.S. grand strategy. To the extent that they discuss domestic variables, these appear largely to explain the residuals. See, for example, Kapstein 1999, p. 468.

3. John Ikenberry (2003a, pp. 539, 548 n. 36) makes a similar point.

4. The debate over the direction of U.S. security policy has focused on two different strategies, unilateral and multilateral. Isolationism has received scant attention from policymakers. For this reason, I do not discuss isolationism in this chapter. For a discussion of what an isolationist policy might look like, see Gholz, Press, and Sapolsky 1997.

5. Ikenberry (2002) provides an excellent discussion of the various elements in the new U.S. grand strategy. See also Ikenberry 2001, 2003a.

6. The basis for Huntington's claim that the system is not unipolar is twofold. First, a unipolar system "would have one superpower, no significant major powers, and many minor powers." Second, the United States "cannot effectively resolve important international issues alone" (1999, p. 35). Referring to the notion that the dominant power must be able to resolve important issues alone, Stephen Brooks and William Wohlforth (2002, p. 23) point out that "in no previous international system would it ever have occurred to anyone to apply such a yardstick." Charles Krauthammer (2002–2003, p. 6) adds that "this is a standard not for unipolarity but for divinity."

7. According to Waltz (1993, p. 53), nuclear weapons changed the way system polarity was to be assessed by altering the link between economic capability and military power.

8. Global hegemony would only be possible in the unlikely event that a great power achieves nuclear superiority (Mearsheimer 2001, p. 128).

9. According to Nye's figures (2002, p. 37, tab. 1.2), in 1999 U.S. GDP adjusted for purchasing power parity was $9,225 billion compared to $9,902 billion for the other seven major powers combined. The United States, in other words, has a 48.4 percent share of the total product of the eight major powers.

10. This was a popular measure among the proponents of hegemonic stability theory. For a discussion, see Lake 1988, esp. pp. 29–40. Nye (2002, p. 55) questions the relevance of this measure in today's world economy, arguing that it provides "a very incomplete picture of global economic linkages."

11. In 1870 the United Kingdom accounted for 24 percent of world trade, a figure that declined to 14.1 percent in 1913 (Lake 1984, p. 160, tab. 1).

12. Whereas the EU represents its individual members in the WTO's current Doha Round, there is no agreement among countries such as the United Kingdom, Germany, and France on trade policy. For an illustration, see the discussion in Gordon 2001, pp. 54–55, regarding in particular differences over the desirability of a Transatlantic Free Trade Area that would merge the signatories of North American Free Trade Agreement and the EU in a free trade area. The idea was originally Germany's (Gordon 2001, p. 50).

13. According to David Lake (1984, p. 160, tab. 1), at 15 percent of world trade a country is either an imperial or hegemonic leader. In comparison, the United States in 1950 accounted for 18.4 percent of world trade.

14. The 1960 figures are from Lake 1984, p. 164, tab. 2.

15. Obviously, it is possible that nothing ever will. Wohlforth (1999, esp. p. 7) offers an extensive discussion of quantitative indicators showing that the United States is the dominant power. See also Krauthammer 1991; Mastanduno and Kapstein 1999, p. 14; Ikenberry 2000, p. 10; Kennedy 2002; Kupchan 2003a, p. 28; and Brooks and Wohlforth 2002, pp. 21–23.

16. Ikenberry (2000, p. 10; also p. 233 n. 59, pp. 277–281 [app. 2]) agrees that the United States is dominant in both the economic and military spheres. Kapstein (1999, p. 472), while concurring that the United States is the dominant power in economic affairs, notes that President Bill Clinton in 1993 apparently believed that in economic affairs "we now live in a tripolar world, driven by the Americas, by Europe, and by Asia." U.S. trade dominance, of course, is not unprecedented. Indeed, the United Kingdom was far more dominant in the nineteenth century than the United States is today.

17. Waltz (1993, p. 50) expected unipolarity to end within ten to twenty years.

18. See also the evidence presented in Layne 1993, pp. 37–39, and the discussion in Waltz 1993, pp. 61–70.

19. See the discussion in Wohlforth 1999, pp. 28–37.

20. Whether balance-of-threat theory is a systemic-level theory is a topic I do not discuss here.

21. Andrew Bacevich (2002, p. 227; also p. 232) argues in contrast that the United States throughout the 1990s pursued an integrated grand strategy designed to create an open and economically integrated world that would preserve the U.S. empire. The degree of integration is so tight that even the war on terrorism after September 11, 2001, is a "war to preserve and to advance the strategy of openness" (p. 227).

22. Barry Posen and Andrew Ross (1996–1997, p. 50) suggest as much when they argue that "one likely source of a major change in U.S. grand strategy is change in U.S. domestic politics." They also argue that an ad hoc approach to U.S. strategy is likely to continue "until a crisis impels a choice" (p. 53).

23. See Kastner and Rector 2003 for an application of George Tsebelis's theory to explaining the regulation of international capital movements. These authors argue that international regimes will mute the effect of domestic variables (p. 6).

24. Jack Snyder (1991) provides an explanation for why foreign policy making in democracies is likely to differ from those in cartelized states. His explanation is that power in democracies is more widely dispersed among interest groups, thus leading to less expansionary foreign policies. He does not address the question of whether the different elements of democratic statecraft may be subject to varying domestic pressures, however.

25. Tsebelis (1995, pp. 292–293) defined policy stability as the absence of the "potential for policy change."

26. It should be noted that whereas there may be many different interest groups trying to influence both the security and economic elements of U.S. statecraft, these groups do not have a veto over policy, and thus do not count as institutional veto players.

27. Gary Cox and Mathew McCubbins (2001, pp. 24–26) provide a more extensive discussion of these two criteria.

28. According to Randall Ripley and James Lindsay (1993, p. 19), strategic policy "encompasses much of what is commonly called foreign policy as well as those aspects of defense policy that specify the basic mix and mission of military forces."

29. "In foreign policy the president is allotted extraordinary discretion and even prerogative authority" (Silverstein 1997, p. 7). See also the discussion in Whittington and Carpenter 2003, pp. 504–507; and Peterson 1994.

30. Some may object that, although the military is not an institutional veto player, this analysis of security policy making nevertheless ignores the important role played by the military, and that civil-military relations are much more important in understanding U.S. security policy than are relations between the executive branch and Congress. While scholars have found significant differences of opinion between the military and civilians regarding the use of force, and have found that civilians with a military background are much less likely to initiate militarized disputes than are civilians without such a background (Feaver and Gelpi 2003), it does not therefore follow that the military can veto the use of force.

31. International threats increase the likelihood that the preferences of various presidents will overlap, so that policy remains stable. A constant level of threat, in other words, has the same effect on security policy as does a large number of effective veto players.

32. Compare the discussion in Tsebelis 1995, p. 295. We cannot conclude, however, that the new policy will therefore be far away from the status quo. It might be, but it need not be. See Tsebelis 2002, p. 32, for a discussion.

33. Although veto player theory does not predict this shift for the reasons noted, it is nevertheless consistent with the theory's emphasis on the importance of idiosyncratic factors when there is only one veto player.

34. A subsequent assessment dubbed the strategy of the last years of the Clinton administration "selective (but cooperative) primacy," whereas the strategy of the second Bush administration is labeled "primacy" (Posen 2003, p. 6).

35. Ivo Daalder and James Lindsay (2003) argue that George W. Bush is responsible for a revolution in U.S. foreign policy, supporting the notion of a shift away from the status quo in security policy.

36. For the full text of Clinton's statement, see http://clinton4.nara.gov/textonly/library/hot_releases/december_31_2000.html.

37. There are generally three ways to determine actor preferences: by assumption, through empirical investigation, or by deduction from prior theoretical principles (Frieden 1999).

38. Susanne Lohmann and Sharyn O'Halloran (1994, pp. 598–599) spell out a somewhat different logic: legislators are assumed to care only about the costs and benefits to their individual districts. Thus, each legislator will ignore the negative externalities that protectionist policies impose on other districts and focus only on the benefits and costs of protectionism to his or her own district. The president, in representing a national constituency, cannot ignore these externalities and will therefore be more likely to oppose protectionist policies.

39. For a skeptical view, see Hiscox 1999, p. 677. The author points out that before 1950, Republican presidents supported protectionist policies. Since 1950 both Democratic and Republican presidents have generally supported free trade. The reason might be that only with the delegation of trade policy–making authority to the president in 1934 did it become possible for the president to use trade policy as a strategic instrument to serve broader international economic and political considerations. This fact in turn may have changed the president's preferences on trade policy.

40. For elaborations of this argument, see, for example, Gowa 1994; and Mansfield 1994. See Mastanduno 1998 for a discussion of arguments linking trade policy and security considerations.

41. The continuity in U.S. trade policy, Pietro Nivola (1997, p. 236) argues, is best explained by the need "to continue reconciling economic wants with wider strategic interests." Other factors deemed important are the legacy of the Smoot-Hawley Act, the U.S. Constitution and the power it gives Congress over trade policy, and global economic integration (pp. 246–247).

42. Nivola (1997, esp. p. 254) argues that while commercial considerations dominated the Clinton administration's trade policy in its first three years, broader foreign policy considerations played an increasingly important role. The end result was a reduced emphasis on opening foreign markets to U.S. goods and thus a less confrontational trade policy.

43. See also Jeffrey Garten's claim that, whereas during the Cold War the United States championed multilateralism largely because it would strengthen political alliances, it now "supports multilateralism because it is in its commercial interest" (1995, p. 51).

44. Recently, bilateral free trade agreements were signed with Jordan (October 2000), Singapore (May 2003), and Chile (June 2003). Negotiations for free trade areas are currently under way with Australia, the five members of the Central American Common Market, Morocco, and the South African Customs Union. In response to pressure from several Middle Eastern governments, free trade agreements with Bahrain and Egypt, conceived of as the first step toward a U.S.–Middle East free trade area by 2013, have also been proposed. U.S. officials have also indicated a willingness to negotiate free trade areas with the other nine members—besides Singapore—of the Association of South East Asian Nations. Finally, the United States has long been committed to extending the North American Free Trade Agreement to involve all of Latin America (except Cuba) in a "Free Trade Area of the Americas."

45. The theoretical literature reaches contradictory conclusions regarding the question whether discriminatory preferential trading arrangements promote or retard multilateral liberalization (Mansfield and Milner 1999, pp. 603–604).

46. Edward Mansfield and Eric Reinhardt (2003) argue that states conclude preferential trade arrangements to increase their bargaining power, and they find evidence

that states are more likely to enter such arrangements during multilateral trading rounds.

47. The quote is from a letter Zoellick wrote to Bernard Gordon.

48. In response to demands from the developing countries and at U.S. insistence, a major objective of the Doha Round negotiations is to liberalize trade in agriculture. Freer trade in textiles—again demanded by the developing countries—is another major aim of the negotiations.

49. TPA finally passed both houses of Congress when the Senate voted in August 2002 to grant it to the president.

50. Brazil and Russia were treated more leniently than was the European Union ("Romancing Big Steel" 2002). Nevertheless, in retaliation, Russia imposed quotas on meat imports from the United States and temporarily banned chicken imports from the United States, the latter being the top U.S. export to Russia. Protectionist measures designed to safeguard the steel and lumber industries are recurring features of U.S. domestic trade policy battles and thus nothing new (Nivola 1997, p. 238).

51. Thus, the steel tariffs, for instance, are seen as a way to induce Brazil to support negotiations for a "Free Trade Area of the Americas" (Blustein 2002a).

52. This was followed in November 2002 by a proposal to eliminate tariffs on industrial and consumer goods by 2015.

53. The official reason for the delay, according to the Chilean ambassador to the United States, was difficulties in translating the agreement into Spanish ("War Allies Win Praise" 2003), although he also admitted that the signing of the agreement had been influenced by Chile's refusal to vote for a UN resolution authorizing the use of force against Iraq (Armstrong 2003). Whatever the reason, President Bush signed both agreements into law on September 3, 2003, after they had passed both the House and the Senate by nearly identical margins.

54. There may of course be other reasons why New Zealand was not included.

55. The difficulty of using trade policy to differentiate between friend and foe is particularly obvious in the case of the EU, whose members consist of both supporters and opponents of the U.S. war against Iraq.

56. The moratorium was imposed in October 1998.

57. Underlying the proposal is the hope that an FTA will encourage trade, foreign investment, and economic development, which will build a middle class that has elsewhere supported political and social reforms, thus creating stability in the Middle East (Deans 2003).

58. The textile industry is Pakistan's main industry and accounts for the majority of its exports to the United States.

8

New Rationales and Old Concerns About U.S. Arms-Export Policy

Steven W. Hook and David B. Rothstein

Issues concerning the global arms industry are of vital concern at the intersection of the global political economy and international security. Arms transfers, whether on cash terms or as a form of foreign aid, play crucial and overlapping roles in the defense and foreign economic policies of suppliers and recipients alike.[1] The calculations of exporting states are further complicated by growing commercial pressures in the arms industry that often overshadow the security dangers associated with the spread of military technology.

These pressures have intensified amid a general contraction in the global arms market. The value of new agreements fell from their post–Cold War peak of nearly $38 billion in 2000 to $25.6 billion in 2003, a decline of nearly one-third (Grimmett 2004, p. 75). Primary causes of the downturn include the protracted economic recession in the developing world, the primary destination of most transfers; the continuing need of many recipients to "absorb" large-scale arms deliveries from the 1990s; and the desire of many industrialized states to promote domestic arms production as a precursor to entering the export market on a more competitive basis.

This chapter explores these trends in the arms industry. Of particular interest is the increased market share of the United States, which grew from 34 percent in the late 1990s to 57 percent in 2003 (Grimmett 2004, p. 77). As in the case of military spending, the U.S. government not only signed arms agreements of higher aggregate value than any other supplier in 2003, but its agreements were more valuable than those of all other supplier states *combined.*

The United States, which has dominated this market since the Cold War, openly justifies arms exports as an adjunct of trade policy. Overcapacity within U.S. defense firms after the Cold War elevated the importance of exports in sustaining the nation's military-industrial base, whose shift toward defense conversion in the early 1990s was halfhearted and short-lived (see

Clarke and O'Connor 1997). Bill Clinton's embrace of arms transfers as agents of U.S. foreign economic policy coincided in the mid-1990s with a government-guided consolidation of defense firms and expanded federal subsidies for the surviving contractors. While both measures created efficiencies in the defense industry, they further discouraged the conversion by these firms to civilian product lines (Oden 1999).

The September 2001 terrorist attacks provided George W. Bush, already an advocate of expanded weapons production, the political support he needed to increase research and development (R&D) subsidies to defense firms and to accelerate arms exports. In addition to meeting the needs of existing U.S. customers, Bush targeted new aid packages to "frontline states" in the war on terrorism, often waiving embargoes that were previously imposed due to the recipients' repressive rule or destabilizing security policies. Overall, the United States approved $12.8 billion in government-to-government sales in 2003 while providing $6 billion worth of security assistance (U.S. Defense Security Cooperation Agency 2004). Government officials reviewed hundreds of licenses for commercial weapons sales in 2002 and 2003 while accelerating U.S. military training programs, which served 117 countries in 2003.[2]

As we argue in this chapter, despite the aggregate drop in new arms agreements, a permissive environment exists today that encourages the trafficking of weapons despite its potential to create new proliferation risks, inflame regional and domestic tensions, exacerbate patron-client relations, and divert public resources from developmental needs. Even before September 11, arms transfers were sufficiently entrenched in the international political economy that efforts to restrain them were consistently frustrated. "A supposedly addictive process greatly complicates efforts to control the global spread of weapons or convert from defense to other forms of manufacturing," Frederic Pearson observed more than a decade ago. "No matter the form of government, it will have a keen interest in the type, amount, and destination of arms produced within its borders" (1994, p. 40).

We begin our analysis by placing these trends in the context of complementary internal and external pressures that enable interstate arms transfers. The impact of this bilevel pressure on policymaking is noteworthy given its contrast to the *contradictory* domestic and external pressures most often associated with "two-level games" (Putnam 1988). We then focus on arm transfers from the U.S. government, in which preexisting industry pressure for increased market share melded after September 11 with new imperatives stemming from the war on terrorism. Next we describe the detrimental effects of unrestrained arms trafficking, and then highlight the normative issues raised by U.S. government transfers in the war on terrorism to regimes overseas that violate the human rights of their citizens. We conclude by anticipating future developments in the global "arms bazaar" and considering the prospects for curbing these dangers in the years to come.

A Permissive Environment for Future Arms Transfers

The recent contraction in the volume of arms agreements does not suggest a permanent downsizing of the global arms market. None of the constraints noted above, particularly the economic recession in recipient states, will persist indefinitely. In place of these constraints, changes in the post–September 11, 2001, security environment are likely to stimulate greater demand in light of the systemic, regional, and domestic uncertainties prompted by the war on terrorism. Rapid advances in weapons technology will create additional incentives for governments to modernize their forces. As in the past, these recipients will use potential import agreements to gain leverage from suppliers in other sectors of bilateral trade.

In this permissive environment, global arms transfers in the next decade can be expected to return to their levels of the late Cold War, when U.S.-Soviet competition extended to military sales and subsidized transfers to most countries in the interstate system. This militarization of domestic politics and regional relations carried over into the 1990s as the United States assumed primacy in arms exports upon the Soviet Union's collapse. Several post-Soviet states in Eastern Europe became customers of U.S. weapons exports and beneficiaries of its military training programs, while long-term U.S. commitments to existing customers continued to be honored (see Klare and Volman 1996). Having consolidated its position in the reshaped arms market, the United States accounted for nearly half of all arms deliveries between 1996 and 2003 (see Figure 8.1).

The aggregate value of arms agreements reached a post–Cold War peak in 2000 before falling steadily in the following three years (see Figure 8.2). The U.S. government, whose $19.4 billion in 2000 arms agreements also represented a high-water mark after the Cold War, experienced a steep drop to $12.5 billion 2001 before rebounding in 2002 and 2003.[3] These totals, when combined with the sizable arms agreements signed by the Russian government during these years, provided the two leading arms suppliers with two-thirds of the worldwide arms market in the new millennium. The rest of the export market belonged primarily to European suppliers, whose energies were divided between refining domestic products and forming partnerships across the European Union to gain long-term competitive advantage over the United States and Russia.

Upward pressure on global arms transfers in the next decade will derive from a convergence of systemic and domestic factors (see Figure 8.3). At the systemic level, security dilemmas inherent to the interstate system create fears and uncertainties that policymakers will continually seek to overcome through several means, including defense modernization. Their recourse to arms transfers is further enabled by a lack of institutional constraints on arms trafficking and proliferation (see Keller and Nolan 2001; and Pierre 1997).

Figure 8.1   Global Arms Agreements, 1996–2003

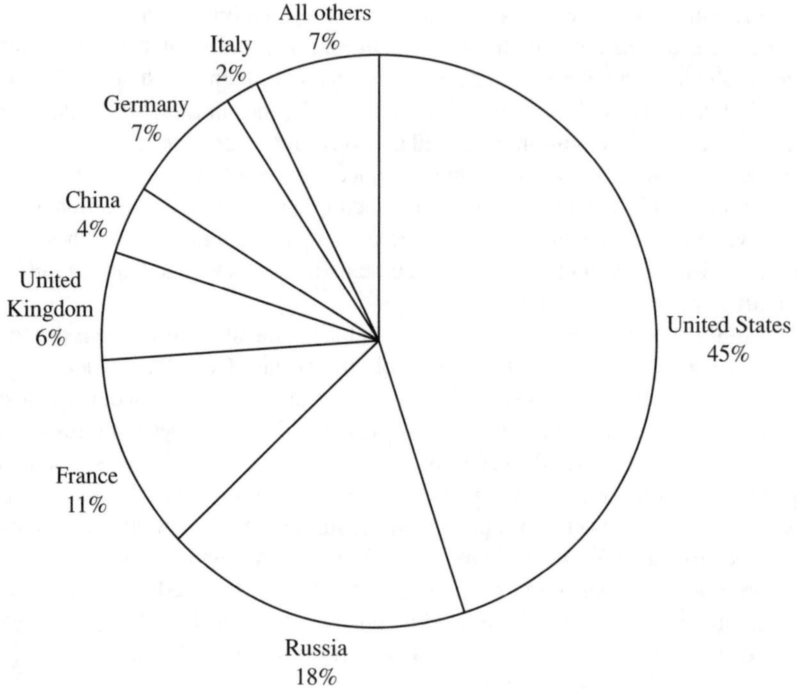

All others 7%
Italy 2%
Germany 7%
China 4%
United Kingdom 6%
United States 45%
France 11%
Russia 18%

Source: Grimmett 2004, p. 76.

While multilateral measures such as the Missile Technology Control Regime and the Wassanaar Arrangements have enhanced transparency, both remain vulnerable to conflicting interpretations and a lack of enforcement.

Heightened tensions following September 11 have created new sources of demand for military supplies that are not likely to abate. States such as Brazil, Indonesia, Japan, Pakistan, and the Philippines justified post–September 11 requests for U.S. security assistance on the basis of countering terrorist groups within their borders. Such requests from these governments were common during the Cold War, although anticommunism rather than counterterrorism provided the rationales that resulted in large military aid packages from the United States. Governments in the Middle East, among the top recipients of weapons transfers prior to September 11, responded to the terrorist attacks by gaining "fast-track" access to new weapons systems from the United States and other suppliers.

Demand from many European arms importers, meanwhile, also increased in 2002 and 2003, although their rationales extended beyond counterterrorism to the deployment of interoperable weapons systems following their entry into

Figure 8.2   Global Arms Agreements by Supplier, 1996–2003 (millions of constant 2003 U.S. dollars)

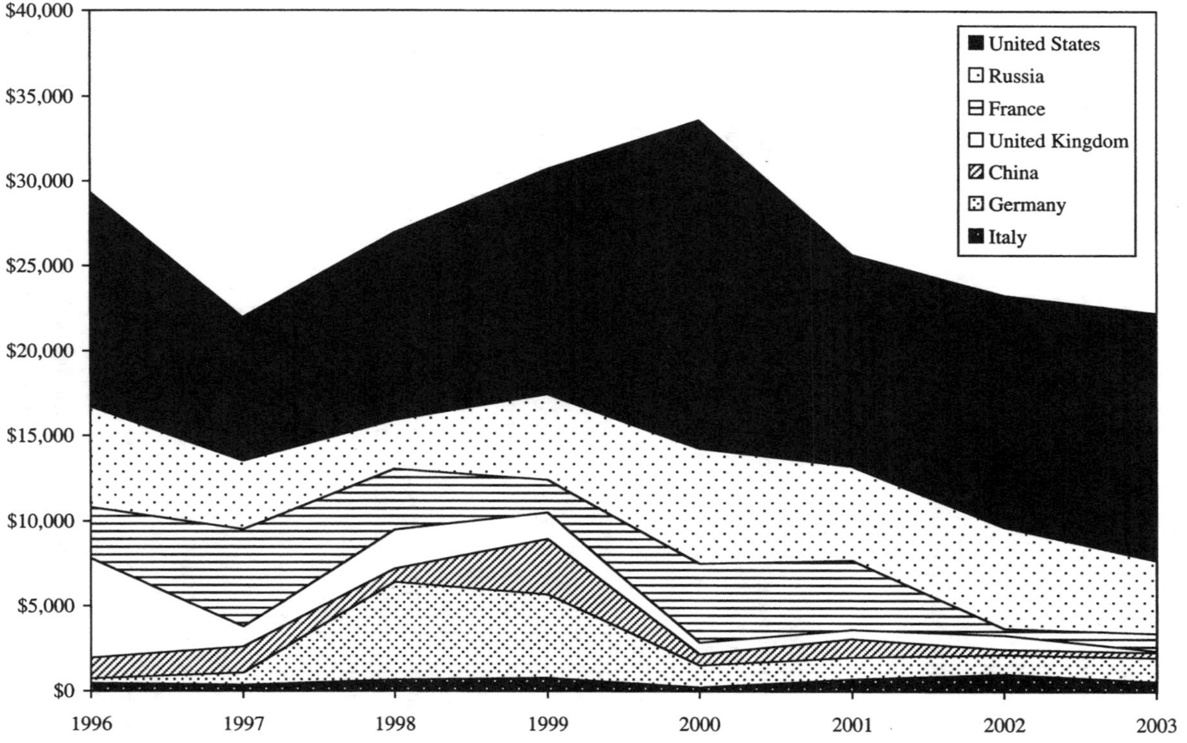

Figure 8.3   Bilevel Sources of Arms Transfers

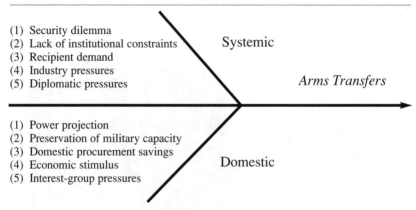

(1) Security dilemma
(2) Lack of institutional constraints
(3) Recipient demand
(4) Industry pressures
(5) Diplomatic pressures

Systemic

Arms Transfers

(1) Power projection
(2) Preservation of military capacity
(3) Domestic procurement savings
(4) Economic stimulus
(5) Interest-group pressures

Domestic

the North Atlantic Treaty Organization (NATO).[4] While the U.S. government approved military aid packages to most Eastern European and post-Soviet states, in April 2003 the United States signed a $3.5 billion deal with Poland for the delivery of forty-eight F-16 fighter jets over ten years. The Bush administration lent Poland the entire financial package at low interest. Along with other U.S. firms, Lockheed Martin, the winning contractor, offered Polish officials an even greater volume of offset agreements to invest elsewhere in the Polish economy.

Taken together, these weapons recipients form an importer market that, in contrast to the concentrated range of suppliers, is highly diversified. Countries in the developing world, which accounted for two-thirds of global export agreements between 1996 and 2003, often qualify for grants or low-interest loans from supplier governments.[5] Increased demand from these states can be expected in the early stages of economic recovery as well as from industrialized states in Europe given the need to integrate the defense forces of the enlarged NATO. Additional demand comes from East Asian and Pacific states such as Australia, Japan, and Taiwan, which placed orders with the U.S. government valued at $1.6 billion in 2003 alone (U.S. Defense Security Cooperation Agency 2004).

In conjunction with these demand-side pressures, the weapons industry imposes supply-side pressures that are especially acute in two respects. First, globalizing trends in the industry facilitate the diffusion of technology along with closer cooperation among supplier states and firms. Second, the *marketization* of the defense sector legitimates the effort by political leaders to pursue arms exports as a means of improving trade balances, securing foreign investments through offset agreements, and in some cases, gaining access to badly needed hard currency. Globalizing and commercializing defense industries exacerbate a collective-action problem among suppliers and recipients that rewards porous export controls and punishes self-restraint in the arms market. Free-riding is always an option under these conditions, creating disincentives for restraint.

Competition among suppliers is likely to stiffen in response to developments in the global defense industry. Russia reemerged as a leading arms supplier a decade after the Soviet Union's collapse, prompting President Vladimir Putin to declare in December 2001, "Today we have only begun to recover lost opportunities" (quoted in Meyer 2001). Like President Clinton, Putin identified arms exports as a vital source of revenue and a boost for domestic manufacturing interests and employment. The Russian arms industry, previously devoted to domestic or bloc procurement, increasingly turned to overseas markets for revenue (see Anthony 1998; and Pierre and Trenin 1997). Following in line with U.S. defense consolidation, Putin merged Russia's two largest defense firms and concentrated government supports within the surviving giant, Rosoboronexport.[6] The September 11 terrorist attacks were of particular interest to Russian leaders, who for years had depicted their struggle with Chechen rebels as a theater of combat in the global fight against terrorism.

European suppliers, meanwhile, hope to increase their market share through consolidation and regional cooperation. Emerging heavyweights such as BAE Systems, the Thales Group, and EADS routinely collaborate with other defense firms (see Vlachos-Dengler 2002). The Western European Armaments Group, created in 1993 under the direction of the Western European Union, seeks to open internal markets, decrease regional dependence on the United States for weapons, and strengthen the region's technological and industrial base.[7] Although new NATO member states from Eastern Europe have relied primarily on U.S. security assistance for defense modernization, these European suppliers are determined to serve this market more extensively in the future. Recent strains between the United States and many European governments relating to the war on terrorism, particularly the U.S.-led preventive invasion and subsequent occupation of Iraq, provide additional impetus for a European defense "identity."[8]

The globalization of the defense industry extends to all aspects of the production process, inviting firms from many countries to contribute specialized components of single weapons systems. The design, parts production, and assembly of U.S. systems, for example, are commonly outsourced among overseas firms. A wave of cross-national mergers and alliances among weapons contractors, along with expanded trade in dual-use technology, further contributes to the rise of "world weapons" (Markusen and Costigan 1999; see also Keller 1995).

This permissive environment extends beyond systemic and industry-level factors to include five domestic pressures within supplier states. The first two of these may be considered *strategic,* the second two *economic,* and the third *political.* Of the strategic pressures, arms transfers first and foremost serve as extensions of the supplier's military power, which is enhanced through the strengthening of friends and allies. Such arrangements are also beneficial to recipients given the greater autonomy they gain from arms imports rather than relying on security guarantees or the granting of base rights to the dominant state. The second strategic incentive for arms exports involves the preservation of military-industrial capacity in peacetime for use in possible future military conflicts. Political leaders fear that demilitarization will force defense firms out of business and impair military readiness. Keeping production lines "hot" through the export of weapons is thus viewed as essential to prevent the emasculation of defense capacities.

This strategic incentive relates to the primary economic pressure for arms transfers, reducing domestic procurement costs. The economies of scale in the defense sector are especially high given its emphasis on long-range research, large-scale weapons programs, and technological sophistication. In permitting these weapons systems to be transferred overseas, in the form of either sales or security assistance, governments reduce the unit costs borne by their taxpayers. More broadly, arms transfers provide a stimulus to the economies of supplier states that is relatively immune from cycles in national or global economic growth. Advanced weapons systems further contribute to economic growth by introducing technological innovations with spin-off applications in civilian sectors.

Finally, domestic political pressures come into play that encourage arms transfers. Especially in liberal states with vibrant civil societies and significantly privatized defense industries, arms manufacturers and trade associations form powerful interest groups that exercise enormous influence within their governments.[9] The benefits these groups seek—profitable contracts with foreign customers—combine with the groups' considerable financial resources to create a formidable lobbying presence. The political clout of these groups is further strengthened when retired military leaders with close ties to government decisionmakers join their ranks. Opponents of arms exports, in contrast, tend to be more diffused, less well endowed financially, and thus less able to mobilize effectively against the proponents of arms transfers. All of these pressures reinforce a political bias favoring arms exports.

The Political Economy of U.S. Weapons Exports

Each of these pressures revealed themselves in the United States as it captured the lion's share of the global arms market in the 1990s and compounded these gains after September 11. While the security rationales for U.S. arms exports persisted after the Cold War, even in the absence of a compelling international rival, economic rationales became more prevalent. It is now customary for U.S. leaders to cite commercial benefits in promoting arms exports. Among the reasons commonly cited for export licenses and military aid packages are the gains they bring to domestic producers, manufacturing employment, and the U.S. balance of trade, which suffers chronic deficits in most other sectors.[10] Political pressures have also intensified in recent years as U.S.-based firms and trade associations pursue, with considerable success, a loosening of restrictions against arms exports, particularly direct commercial sales.

The U.S. government's heightened interest in commercial exports reflects an ongoing shift "from military aid to military markets" (Klare and Volman 1996). Overseas U.S. sales expanded significantly after September 11, reaching dozens of industrialized countries as well as many developing countries (Stohl 2003). South Korea was the largest single customer after September 11, purchasing F-15 jet fighters and other high-end weapons systems at a cost of more than $6 billion. The Turkish and Polish governments each spent about $4 billion on U.S.-made aircraft and missile systems. Arms packages exceeding $1 billion were also approved for Australia, Austria, Brazil, Kuwait, Malaysia, Oman, Poland, and Taiwan in 2002 and 2003.

Given these developments, a closer look at the political economy of U.S. arms transfers is warranted. Military equipment represented nearly 5 percent of total U.S. exports in the 1990s, a higher level than for all other exporters and nearly three times the world average. The U.S. defense-industrial sector, therefore, is not only much larger than that of other supplier states in absolute terms, but also relatively more important to U.S. competitiveness in the world economy. Its technological supremacy in this sector, combined with the economic and political clout of the U.S. government, makes the nation's defense-industrial model a tempting one for other states to emulate. Unrestrained U.S. arms exports, therefore, are likely to discourage restraint elsewhere, especially as military technology and the production of weapons systems become more disbursed. This prospect makes greater scrutiny of U.S. arms-export policies more essential. The United States maintains a complex system of transferring arms to its recipients (see Table 8.1). Four programs are of particular importance. First, U.S. officials facilitate government-to-government transactions through foreign military sales (FMS), which accounted for more than two-thirds of U.S. transfers in recent years.[11] Second, the United States promotes direct commercial sales (DCS), which are negotiated by individual weapons manufacturers before export licenses are reviewed by the State Department.[12] Third, the U.S. government supports many recipients with foreign military financing (FMF), a program that uses public funds to subsidize the provision of military goods and services to developing countries.[13] Given the scale of the U.S. economy and its defense-industrial sector, security assistance is relatively more affordable to the United States than to other weapons suppliers, which gives the U.S. government a further comparative advantage in the export market. Finally, the United States provides training to defense forces and civilian personnel overseas through the International Military Education and Training (IMET) program.[14]

Table 8.1   U.S. Programs for Arms Transfers and Security Assistance

Program	Description	Total Value 1992–2003 (current U.S.$)	Percentage of Total Arms Transfers and Security Assistance
Foreign military sales	Government-to-government sales of defense equipment, services, and training	151 billion	69
Foreign military financing	Financing through grants and loans in order to purchase U.S. military articles, services, and training	48 billion	21
Direct commercial sales	Commercial export sales licensed under the Arms Export Control Act	24 billion	10
International Military Education and Training	Provides training on a grant basis to students from allied and friendly nations	574 million	Less than 1

Source: U.S. Department of Defense, Defense Security Cooperation Agency (various years).
Notes: The Military Assistance Program ended in 1989 and grant and loan assistance was channeled to foreign military financing. The data for direct commercial sales are often incomplete and underestimated due to the nature of commercial sales (see Grimmett 2004).

The issue of arms transfers is largely an *apolitical* one in the United States, not a matter of significant political contention in Congress or the executive branch. While individual transfer agreements may be debated among legislatures or bureaucrats within the executive branch, the principle of large-scale arms transfers to friendly governments overseas, on market or concessional terms, is uncontroversial. This consensus also applies to the public, which displays little interest in this issue. As a result, arms sales and security assistance programs are driven by domestic interest groups with a tangible stake in weapons transfers and with finely tuned political connections to their representatives in Congress and the White House.

Key Developments in Arms-Export Policy

Arms transfers first played a vital role in U.S. foreign policy in the early days of World War II, when military equipment provided to Great Britain under the lend-lease program marked the first phase of U.S. military involvement in that struggle. Economic and military aid figured prominently in the containment policy that spanned nine presidential administrations during the Cold War (see Klare 1984). The Nixon Doctrine, proclaimed late in the Vietnam War, called for replacing U.S. troops with security assistance, thereby forcing U.S. allies to "take responsibility" for their own defense. After a brief lull during the Carter administration, the levels of arms exports soared in the 1980s. Ronald Reagan favored such exports as a means to counter perceived Soviet advances in developing regions. The increases in arms exports under Reagan's watch also resulted from new obligations to Israel and Egypt under the Camp David Accords and to higher funding to base-rights nations such as Turkey, Spain, and the Philippines.

After the Cold War, the U.S. government encouraged and guided the consolidation of defense firms. The emerging giants—Lockheed Martin, Boeing, Raytheon, General Dynamics, and Northrop Grumman—retained many of their domestic procurement contracts and R&D subsidies (Markusen and Costigan 1999). Reduced domestic demand, however, forced these contractors to shift their emphasis toward the export market.[15] Along with globalization, or the melding of national markets, came a stronger interest by the U.S. government in collaborating with other suppliers, particularly those in Europe, to create interoperable weapons systems deemed essential in coalition warfare.[16] This outward shift in U.S. arms-export policy reflected broader changes in the defense industry. A 1999 report by the Defense Science Board concluded that the U.S. defense-industrial base "no longer exists in its Cold War form. Today, DoD is supported by a broader industrial base that includes both defense-intensive and commercial sectors and which is increasingly international in character" (p. 7).

Despite their dominant position in many defense industrial sectors, domestic suppliers claimed they were being penalized in the global arms market by burdensome domestic regulations and restrictions.[17] In response to pressure from the Aerospace Industries Association and other trade groups, President Clinton adopted the Defense Trade Security Initiative in May 2000, which met many of the industry's demands: a streamlined process of reviewing export licenses, possible reductions in the U.S. munitions list that identifies non-exportable military equipment, and the elimination of export barriers to the "NATO Plus Three" states (Japan, Australia, and New Zealand).

George W. Bush came to office in January 2001 promising to ease these restrictions further. The terrorist attacks of September 11 added new urgency to this initiative, as Bush identified arms exports as a major element in his counterterrorism strategy. "If governments are willing to cooperate against terrorism," State Department spokesman Richard Boucher (2001) stated three weeks after the attacks, "that will result in a change in the level of our ability to cooperate with them." In November 2002, Bush launched a formal review of defense trade export policy and national security that explored further reforms in U.S. policy that would expedite arms transfers to governments overseas.[18] Even as the review was under way, security considerations compelled government officials to hasten the shipment of U.S. weapons overseas.

Institutional Actors in the Policy Process

Clinton and Bush carried enormous weight in meeting the needs of the U.S. defense industry. As in other foreign policy areas, the president has a variety of inherent advantages in governing arms exports: direct ties to foreign governments, an ability to set the agenda, and a presumed disposition to be "above politics" and speak for the national interest rather than parochial concerns.[19]

The president's administrative control of the federal bureaucracy is especially vital given the many agencies involved in arms-export policy. Within the executive branch, the State Department negotiates FMF packages with foreign governments, reviews export-license applications, and conducts annual reviews of the human rights conduct of foreign countries that are to be used in evaluating their fitness for future weapons deliveries. The Department of Defense (DoD) oversees weapons production and conducts military training programs, while the Commerce Department promotes commercial arms sales through routine contacts based in U.S. embassies and by hosting trade shows overseas. Intergovernmental consensus favoring arms exports generally minimizes internal conflict in this area. Institutional tensions exist, however, between functional bureaus of the State Department, between State and DoD on security assistance programs, and between State and Commerce over the pace of export-license reviews.

Although Congress's role in this process is vital (see Lindsay 1994), the legislative branch generally reinforces the White House's disposition favoring arms exports. The power of the purse gives Congress considerable institutional leverage in shaping the direction, volume, and terms of U.S. security assistance. The foreign operations bill, the only regularly scheduled foreign policy debate on the congressional calendar, gives legislators their "most visible and important mechanism for affecting foreign policy" (Clarke and O'Connor 1997, p. 215). Amendments to the Foreign Operations Appropriations Act, such as those added by Senator Patrick Leahy of Vermont involving human rights concerns, provide further restrictions on U.S. arms transfers. Congress also plays an oversight role and is authorized under the Arms Export Control Act of 1976 to review major arms deals proposed by the executive branch.[20]

These restrictions are prone to manipulation and abuse, however, and they tend to be eased in times of crisis. The Reagan administration's secret arms transfers to Iran and the Nicaraguan contras in the mid-1980s directly violated existing laws and oversight provisions. Following September 11, and especially after the midterm elections of November 2002, which restored a Republican majority in both chambers, Congress generally deferred to the White House on matters relating to the war on terrorism. In addition to approving nearly all weapons transfers proposed by the Bush administration, Congress permitted the Defense Security Cooperation Agency to "fast-track" the implementation of security-assistance programs (see Docherty 2002).

Domestic political pressure on Congress and the president originates primarily from interest groups rather than the general public. While elected officials are aware of the public's low regard for foreign aid programs, particularly involving military equipment, such opposition does not resonate deeply and has little effect on voting behavior. In contrast, presidents and members of Congress are highly sensitive to interest-group pressure. Defense-related firms and trade associations maintain a high profile in the arms-transfer policy process, lobbying elected officials on behalf of security assistance packages, the approval of commercial export licenses, R&D subsidies, and looser restrictions on technology transfers.[21] The activities of these groups are weakly counterbalanced by opposing groups and citizens.

The Dangers of Unrestrained Arms Transfers

The multiple national interests that are presumably served by U.S. arms exports cannot be viewed in isolation. As critics have long argued (see Klare 1984; and Pierre 1982), attention must also be paid to the dangers and potentially destabilizing consequences of unrestrained transfers from arms exporters in general and the United States in particular. This section first identifies four dangers that apply broadly to arms transfers from all producers. These dangers include accelerated weapons proliferation, regional instability, dependency relationships, and opportunity costs. Four additional dangers are then described—political "backfire," technological diffusion, iron triangles, and the promotion of repressive regimes—that apply particularly to the United States given its predominant world role and arms industry and the distinctive features of its political system.

We begin by considering problems relating to arms transfers that apply to all transfers, not only those from the United States. The most serious of these problems relates to the inherent dangers of weapons proliferation to the internal security of states along with regional and global security. As William Keller and Janne Nolan (2001, p. 178) observed, these proliferation risks are becoming more grave as "the arms business is rapidly becoming an adjunct of private enterprise." Globalizing and commercializing arms industries provide an impetus for arms transfers that may not otherwise be consistent with the security interests of supplier states.

A second concern common to all arms transfers is their potential to increase the risk of large-scale political violence in volatile regions. The security dilemma noted previously that provides a pretext for arms transfers becomes self-fulfilling as acquisitions are viewed as menacing by neighboring states. Regional arms races in these cases are likely to disrupt power balances and tempt states to take preemptive action in the face of perceived declines in relative capabilities. A prominent example of this is South Asia, where Indian and Pakistani leaders routinely cite arms imports by the other state in appealing for, and often gaining, a continuous flow of weapons from a variety of exporters.[22] In other cases, such as the protracted Iran-Iraq War in the 1980s, previous weapons deliveries from the United States and other suppliers greatly increased the scale of death and destruction in that conflict. Civil wars, such as those fought in the former Yugoslavia, are far more destructive when their combatants gain access to weapons not otherwise available.

Arms transfers create a third set of problems by creating or intensifying patron-client relations that restrict the autonomy, and in some cases the de facto sovereignty, of recipients (see Kinsella 1998). These transfers do not occur in a vacuum and are routinely tied to other political, economic, and military aspects of asymmetric bilateral relationships. This was clearly the case during the Cold War, when the United States and Soviet Union used the "carrot" of security assistance to draw dozens of developing countries into their respective spheres of influence (Catrina 1988). France, meanwhile, used offers of economic and military aid to its former colonies in francophone Africa to preserve its regional influence, while Great Britain pursued the same strategy in anglophone Africa. In the 1980s, Japan became a leading aid donor by using its offers as leverage in gaining access to the trade and investment markets of its recipients (Hook 1995).

The concentration of military transfers to the developing world continues today, as does the origin of most weapons transfers in Moscow and Washington. Frontline states in the U.S.-led war on terrorism, nearly all of which are located in developing areas, are among the most attractive destinations of U.S. weapons exports. As in the past, the U.S. government hopes to use these transfers to retain influence within recipient states. Some recipients, including President Pervez Musharraf of Pakistan, took enormous personal as well as political risks by accepting U.S. financial assistance in return for their embrace of U.S. interests.

It is appropriate to view most relationships between the sources and recipients of arms as ones of *mutual dependence.* As noted earlier, arms exports serve a variety of important functions for exporters in terms of projecting their own military power, stimulating national economic output, and preserving production capacity that may be needed in the future to support the nation's military operations. Furthermore, arms transfers take place in a broader context of bilateral relations that include base rights to the supplier, diplomatic cooperation in regional and global negotiations, access to the recipient's strategically important raw materials, and market access to the recipient state in nonmilitary goods and services. Each of these provides some element of leverage to potential recipients of arms transfers, suggesting a relationship of mutual rather than unitary dependence.

A fourth and related systemic concern involves the potential opportunity costs of North-South arms transfers. It is widely agreed within the foreign aid regime that official development assistance (ODA) is a higher "quality" form of financial support than security assistance and that arms transfers may divert or impair the flow of economic assistance to developing countries (Wood 1986).[23] The Organization for Economic Cooperation and Development (OECD) established this and other standards of aid quality in the 1970s in order to encourage aid flows that responded to the needs of developing countries rather than the self-interests of donors. Other standards, such as a designated minimum level of ODA as a percentage of gross national product, grants rather than loans, and significant shares of aid directed toward least-developed states, were also adopted by the OECD and remain explicit criteria for the evaluation of its members' aid programs. As in the past, military aid commitments may limit available ODA funding along with the organizational capacity of recipient states to implement and manage nonmilitary programs (see Sadowski 1993).

Arms transfers from the United States, whether in the form of security assistance or commercial sales, raise a set of distinctive concerns. The first involves their tendency to backfire when placed in the wrong hands. While weapons systems may be operational for long periods of time, the political leadership overseeing them frequently changes hands, sometimes abruptly. Political allegiances toward the weapons suppliers shift in response to these developments, leading in some cases to the coming to power of adversarial regimes that enjoy access to the military hardware provided by their newly declared enemy. The U.S. government experienced this type of backfire twice in 1979—in Iran after the Shah's overthrow, and in Nicaragua following the Sandinista revolution.[24] In subsequent military interventions in Panama (1989), Somalia (1992–1993), and Haiti (1994), U.S. troops confronted adversaries largely equipped with U.S.-made weapons.

The backfire of U.S. arms transfers to Iraq is the most troubling given current circumstances. Among other military equipment, Saddam Hussein's regime received materials from the United States that were used to develop chemical and biological weapons (see Jentleson 1994).[25] These same weapons of mass destruction (WMD), which were used against Iran and Saddam's own citizens, were later viewed as threatening to the United States after Saddam renounced his former patron in 1990 and invaded Kuwait. In the aftermath of the first Gulf War, Saddam's WMD capabilities become the object of a protracted and costly UN-sponsored inspection regime that ended in 1998. In its aftermath, the perceived continuing threat to the United States formed the basis of the Bush administration's preventive invasion and subsequent occupation of the country in 2003. In this and other cases, exported U.S. military equipment was transformed from an *extension* of U.S. power into a *threat* to that power.

A second problem of particular concern to the United States involves the prospects for the technological diffusion of weapons systems that results from

U.S. military transfers. Recipient states increasingly demand and receive concessions from the United States regarding licensed production and coproduction of weapons systems. An early example of this was the 1991 deal with South Korea that included the delivery of twelve fighter jets along with thirty-six aircraft "kits" for assembly in South Korea. The government in Seoul also bought the rights to produce seventy-two more F-16s in South Korea, a measure clearly designed to advance its own arms industry. While such arrangements may be justified in isolation, taken together they threaten to erode U.S. technological superiority while placing sensitive military technologies in the hands of potentially unstable or unreliable regimes. The prospect of diffusion is particularly troublesome given the vital role of technological primacy in the Bush administration's post–September 11 national security strategy (White House 2002).

Third, one must consider the iron triangle of military contractors, past and present government officials, and influential members of Congress who share private interests in arms transfers that may not be consistent with the nation's security (see Hartung 1994; Mayer 1991; and Adams 1982). The dangers inherent in such a network were first raised in 1961 by President Dwight Eisenhower, who warned that the military-industrial complex encouraged weapons production that exceeded the nation's defense needs while compromising the democratic conduct of foreign policy. His warning had little effect on future policy, however, and the resulting dangers are especially salient today (Singer 2003). As military exports increasingly become accepted in Washington as a matter of economic as well as security policy, weapons producers gain unprecedented access to decisionmakers and receive increasingly favorable treatment with regard to individual arms transfers, R&D subsidies, tax breaks, and regulatory relief.

Some simple statistics illustrate the pervasive influence of U.S. military suppliers (see Table 8.2). The top five defense contractors spent more than $33 million in 2000 on lobbying efforts while contributing $8 million to candidates in federal elections. Lobbyists for Lockheed Martin, the leading U.S. defense manufacturer in 2000 with nearly $15 billion in sales, contributed nearly $3 million to candidates that year.[26] The war on terrorism provided an economic windfall to U.S. defense contractors. Lockheed Martin received $17 billion in defense contracts in 2002, an increase of more than $2 billion from the year before (Donnelley and Hartung 2003). Boeing, meanwhile, reported a $3 billion increase in defense contracts, to $16.6 billion. The U.S.-led war against Iraq and subsequent occupation of the country yielded benefits to other companies, some of which maintained close ties with senior members of the Bush administration. The Halliburton Company, for which Vice President Dick Cheney formerly served as chief executive officer, gained up to $7 billion in contracts to rebuild Iraq's oil wells, awarded by the U.S. Army in December 2001 without competitive bidding.

Table 8.2   Top Defense Contractors and Political Contributors, 2000

Company	Department of Defense Contract Value (U.S.$ billions)	Lobbying Budget (U.S.$ millions)	Total Political Contributions (U.S.$ millions)	Percentage to Democrats	Percentage to Republicans
Lockheed Martin	15.1	11.2	2.8	39	61
Boeing	12.0	7.8	1.9	44	56
Raytheon	6.3	2.7	1.1	39	60
General Dynamics	4.2	4.7	1.4	41	59
Northrop Grumman	3.1	6.9	0.8	38	61

Sources: Center for Responsive Politics 2003, "Opensecrets.org: Your Guide to Money in U.S. Elections," available at http://www.opensecrets.org; U.S. Department of Defense 2003.

Finally, arms transfers from the United States are problematic when they are provided to "non-democratic, repressive, or aggressive governments, often in apparent violation of U.S. law" (Lumpe 1999, p. 290). This pattern was evident throughout the Cold War, when the U.S. government supported dozens of authoritarian regimes in Iran, the Philippines, Nicaragua, Chile, and elsewhere, solely on the basis of their anticommunist credentials and statements of support for U.S. foreign policy goals. Efforts by some presidents, particularly Jimmy Carter, to curb arms exports to human rights violators ultimately succumbed to security considerations. While President Bill Clinton embraced arms transfers as a means to promote democratic reforms in recipient states, he continued the U.S. government's practice of allowing large-scale transfers to repressive regimes considered strategically vital to the United States (see Amnesty International 1995). This pattern continues today.

"Dangerous Dealings" in the War on Terrorism

A central problem associated with recent U.S. arms transfers is their provision in many instances to governments that violate standards of human rights that are widely accepted by the international community and the U.S. government itself. Section 502(b) of the 1961 Foreign Assistance Act prohibits the provision of security assistance to any government that "engages in a consistent pattern of gross violations of internationally recognized human rights."[27] Although generally observed, this and subsequent restrictions are routinely overridden by U.S. officials on national security grounds. Their selective observance of human rights concerns, previously identified with Cold War transfers to dozens of authoritarian regimes, raises renewed concerns about arms transfers in the war on terrorism.[28]

In the aftermath of September 11, the Bush administration waived sanctions against six countries—Armenia, Azerbaijan, India, Pakistan, Tajikistan, and the former Federal Republic of Yugoslavia—in return for their pledges of cooperation in the war on terrorism. Many other repressive countries also receive U.S. security assistance and gain access to advanced weapons systems as commercial sales on a regular basis. Beyond their human rights abuses, acknowledged by the State Department in its annual reports, many of these regimes confront domestic and interstate challenges that threaten their hold on power. Arms transfers to these regimes not only contradicted the Bush's administration's pledge to promote a global order that "favors human freedom," a recurring theme in its 2002 national security strategy (White House 2002), but also introduced new dangers to regional and international security.

Consideration of this dilemma must start with Israel and Egypt, by far the largest recipients of U.S. security and economic assistance. The war on terrorism provided new impetus for the United States to maintain its massive military aid flows to both countries. Israel, the primary U.S. ally in the Middle East, received a total of $4.1 billion in military aid in 2002 and 2003. Egypt, long viewed by U.S. leaders as a moderating influence among Arabs, Muslims, and developing nations, received $2.6 billion (see Mark 2003a, 2003b). This financial support, a by-product of the 1978 Camp David Accords, continues despite reports of chronic human rights abuses by both governments. According to the U.S. Department of State (2003b), Israeli leaders "did little to reduce institutional, legal, and societal discrimination against the country's Arab citizens." Egyptian forces, meanwhile, violently repressed the political opponents of President Hosni Mubarek, whose National Democratic Party "dominated the political scene to such an extent that citizens did not have a meaningful ability to change their government."

These "dangerous dealings" (Human Rights Watch 2002) involve many other countries considered vital in the war on terrorism. The U.S. government after September 11 renewed its military ties to the government of the Philippines, which faced an attempted secession by Islamic militants associated with the Abu Sayyaf terrorist organization. Military assistance and sales to Turkey also increased as the United States sought access to its territory and defense facilities. Military transfers and training were provided to both governments despite their known records of violating human rights.

India and Pakistan

After staging tit-for-tat underground nuclear weapons tests in 1998, both South Asian countries were barred from receiving U.S. arms transfers and development assistance.[29] These restrictions were lifted immediately after the September 11 attacks, as President Bush anticipated help from India and Pakistan in the imminent war on terrorism. Pakistan, the target of U.S. sanctions years earlier for proceeding with nuclear weapons development, was especially vital given its large Islamic population, proximity to Afghanistan, and known links to Al-Qaida (see Rennack 2003). For its part, India also pledged to support the United States and to discourage political violence against Pakistan that nearly escalated into open warfare in 1999 and 2000. Despite the poor human rights records of both governments (see U.S. Department of State 2003b; Freedom House 2002; and Human Rights Watch 2002), India and Pakistan each received $50 million in FMF assistance in 2003 and received dozens of other packages of military equipment in the form of commercial sales.

Saudi Arabia

The United States has maintained close economic and security relations with the Saudi monarchy since September 2001, despite the fact that fifteen of the nineteen hijackers on September 11, along with Osama bin Laden, were citizens of the country. The two governments signed arms agreements in 2002 and 2003 amounting to $879 million and $693 million, respectively (U.S. Defense Security Cooperation Agency 2004, p. 5). U.S. arms exports to Saudi Arabia, paid on a cash basis, often include the most sophisticated weapons systems in the U.S. arsenal, including advanced fighter jets and surface-to-air missiles. Many of these agreements elicit protests from Saudi Arabia's regional neighbors, including Israel, which insist on countervailing arms transfers from the United States or turn to other suppliers to compete against Saudi modernization efforts. Large-scale arms sales continue despite the U.S. Department of State's (2003b) repeated findings of human rights abuses by the Saudi government, including a lack of government legitimacy, unfair trials, the routine use of torture, violence against women and children, press censorship, and discrimination against ethnic minorities.

Armenia and Azerbaijan

Both governments in the Caucasus Mountain region were denied U.S. weapons from 1993 until 2002, when the Bush administration identified them as vital frontline states in the war on terrorism. The U.S. government subsequently approved $7 million in security assistance to both governments in 2002 and 2003, along with funding for U.S.-sponsored military training. In approving this financial support, the Bush administration determined that security concerns outweighed the consistent pattern of human rights abuses that had led to the imposition of sanctions against both countries. According to the U.S. Department of State (2003b), the governments of Armenia and Azerbaijan continued to violate human rights after U.S. security assistance was renewed, denying their citizens basic freedoms of speech, press, religion, and association. Most abuses by security forces stemmed from the conflict between the two countries in the disputed territory of Nagorno-Karabakh.

Tajikistan and Uzbekistan

The United States also offered security assistance and training to several post-Soviet states in central Asian countries in exchange for military access and political support in the war on terrorism. The governments of Tajikistan and Uzbekistan, both of which faced serious internal challenges from Islamic fundamentalists, accepted these arrangements and offered the U.S. government access to former Soviet military bases and training facilities. In January 2002 the State Department waived restrictions on Tajikistan's eligibility for U.S. arms imports and approved more than $4 million in U.S. aid in 2002 and 2003 (U.S. Defense Security Cooperation Agency 2003). Uzbekistan, meanwhile, received more than $62 million in U.S. security assistance during these two years. Closer ties to the United States, however, did not prevent either government from violating the human rights of its citizens. Widespread mistreatment of political prisoners was reported by the U.S. Department of State (2003b) along with ethnic persecution, denial of political freedoms, and the trafficking of women and children for prostitution and forced labor.

Indonesia

Following the terrorist attacks of September 11, Indonesian president Megawati Sukarnoputri was the first head of state to visit the White House and openly declared common cause with the United States in waging the war on terror. Like other developing countries with historically close ties to the United States, Indonesia faced a variety of military challenges from domestic groups, some of which sought to overthrow the government or gain regional autonomy. In branding these groups terrorists and pledging to support the U.S. counteroffensive against Al-Qaida, Sukarnoputri received $1 million in IMET funds for fiscal years 2003 and 2004 (see U.S. Department of State 2003a) along with an $8 million DoD grant to "vet, train, and equip" a counterterrorism unit (Garcia 2002). The U.S. government also approved a $50 million economic aid package to Jakarta for unspecified uses. This support was granted despite the U.S. Department of State's finding that Indonesia routinely engaged in the "shooting of civilians, torture, rape, beatings and other abuses" (2003b).

Colombia

Since the late 1980s, Colombia has received large volumes of U.S. security assistance to support its effort to curb the production of illegal drugs and trafficking into the United States. The Bush administration linked this effort after September 11 with the war on terrorism, providing $98 million in FMF support to Colombia in 2003. Colombia is also a primary recipient of IMET funds; Bush's fiscal year 2004 request called for more than $1.5 million for the training and education of Colombian troops. The nation's record on human rights remains poor, however, with widespread abuses by Colombian police and paramilitary forces, corruption in the legal system, and mistreatment of prisoners (see Berrigan 2002). "Impunity remained at the heart of the country's human rights problems" (U.S. Department of State 2003b).

*   *   *

A consistent pattern in these cases is the role of security forces in committing the most egregious human rights violations, including torture, rape, and murder. Military organizations such as Indonesia's TNI (Tentara Nasional Indonesia) operate with considerable autonomy, gaining resources and political support from elected leaders often through intimidation. The abuses by TNI during the government's 1999 crackdown on East Timor, tolerated by the government in Jakarta, prompted an array of economic sanctions from the United States and other weapons exporters. The U.S. government eased these sanctions after September 11, allowing exports of "nonlethal" military equipment and an expanded military training program. The terrorist attacks in Bali late in 2002 affirmed the Bush administration's view of Indonesia as a pivotal state in the war on terrorism. Despite the validity of this claim, it diminishes the past role of TNI as an agent of state terror and the possibility that renewed assistance from the United States will be taken as a sign that TNI forces can commit abuses in other trouble spots such as Aceh and Moluccas.

This pattern of U.S. assistance to repressive security forces not only raises normative questions about U.S. foreign policy but also increases the risk of backfire, either by newly empowered regimes such as that in postrevolutionary Iran or by marginalized dissidents that remain out of power and turn to terrorism. External support for abusive military forces threatens to deepen rather than resolve the internal schisms in these countries that stimulated the rise of the dissidents and their resort to political violence. "The modifications in the U.S. foreign military assistance program make it easier for known violators to acquire the tools of abuse, thus implicating the United States in abuses that result," Human Rights Watch observed. "The loosening of restrictions on military assistance also sets a dangerous example for arms exporting nations around the world" (2002, p. 2).

Conclusion

Arms trafficking represents a slight fraction—less than 1 percent—of world trade, and the recession of the global economy since the late 1990s limits the capacity of importers to satisfy their appetites for new military equipment. Nonetheless, interstate arms transfers remain an entrenched aspect of the international political economy. To a growing number of supplier states, arms transfers promote national interests that extend beyond their security concerns. Importers, meanwhile, look to arms transfers not simply for near-term security enhancements but also as a basis for long-term defense modernization. The development of indigenous arms industries in many recipient countries, spurred in large measure by previous technology transfers, creates new sources of supply on commercial markets. The Cold War demonstrated the debilitating effects of rampant arms transfers, felt long after its conclusion. After a decade of reduced global tensions and declining arms exports, this pattern may soon reappear in the war on terrorism.

Future trends are difficult to forecast given the volatility of the international security environment and persistent strains in the world economy. It is virtually certain, however, that the current U.S. dominance of global arms markets will continue for at least the next decade as an interactive combination of domestic (supply-side) and international (demand-side) factors propel future arms sales, security assistance programs, follow-on maintenance and munitions contracts, government subsidies, and regulatory relief. The adoption of U.S. arms exports as a matter of economic as well as security policy is unlikely to be reversed given the interests of public and private actors that are permanently mobilized on behalf of these transactions. Robust U.S. arms exports will be further enabled by a general public that has registered little concern about this issue while generally favoring the aggressive steps taken by the government in waging the war on terrorism since September 2001.

Given the likely persistence of U.S. primacy in the global arms market, dangers are posed by large-scale transfers to foreign governments on the singular basis of counterterrorism. The experience of the Cold War provides ample evidence of the catastrophic human costs that result when entire regions are viewed by U.S. policymakers simply as battlefields of global conflicts. The U.S. government distorted the societal roots of domestic and regional political conflicts during this period, ignoring underlying tensions that had little to do with ideological concerns. Not only did the United States play a lead role in militarizing these regions, but its support of authoritarian regimes fueled populist uprisings and coups that ultimately weakened the U.S. government's position in many areas.

As dysfunctional patterns from the Cold War reemerge in the war on terrorism, one must return to basic assumptions regarding the merits and potential pitfalls of global arms exports. In carefully selected cases, such transfers may strengthen vulnerable states along with their arms suppliers while deterring the outbreak of political violence. In other cases, however, arms transfers divert the limited resources of importing states, ignite new cycles of arms competition, and increase the prospects for war. Although hardly the direct cause of political violence, the availability of weapons may intensify such conflicts and lead to greater levels of death and destruction. "Halting or denying deliveries may not prevent or stop the fighting, but more weapons clearly tend to make conflicts longer and bloodier" (Pearson 1994, pp. 65–66).

Prospects for restraint are limited in the permissive environment that currently exists. Multilateral agreements such as the Missile Technology Control Regime and the Wassenaar Arrangement have established norms regarding the most dangerous and destabilizing weapons systems. Other multilateral treaties, including a convention on the transfer of small arms, which are weapons of choice in the developing world, also set important standards that encourage multilateral cooperation. Compliance with these agreements is far from universal, however, due to a lack of enforcement mechanisms and the nonsupport of some major suppliers, especially the United States in the case of small arms.[30]

Weak institutional barriers to arms transfers also account for the continuing cascade of black market weapons to conflict zones in the developing world (see Lumpe 2000). As in the case of legally sanctioned arms transfers, substantial demand exists for illicit weapons, primarily by private groups and paramilitary forces that do not otherwise have access to military equipment. This demand is satisfied by multiple sources of supply, including arms dealers in the former Soviet bloc who maintain massive stockpiles of weapons no longer under government control. Efforts to restrain this black market are especially difficult given the limited cooperation by the major arms-supplying countries and a lack of consensus on what is considered "illegal" in the arms market. Unfortunately, the U.S. government has little leverage on this issue given its unwillingness to restrain its arms transfers on open markets and its opposition to multilateral restraints on small-arms trafficking.

Other measures, such as arms embargoes, have reduced the flow of arms into several war-torn countries. But widespread violations of these embargoes prevent them from having significant impact. In Pakistan, for example, the U.S. sanctions imposed in the early 1990s merely invited other arms suppliers to fill the void. For the same reason, national and international codes of conduct have proven ineffective in regulating arms transfers given the willingness of nonsignatories to serve the needs of importers. Such codes, furthermore, are notoriously prone to disregard by their own sponsors. Congress's passage of the International Code of Conduct Act of 1999 hardly stopped the Clinton administration from transferring weapons to repressive regimes. Finally, steps to promote transparency in arms transfers shed much-needed light on the arms trade. The growing prevalence of commercial sales as opposed to government-to-government agreements, however, creates new barriers to public reporting.

All these preventive measures face an uphill battle in overcoming the bilevel pressures that propel global arms transfers. For real reform to take place, the underlying systemic factors must be confronted: unmitigated security dilemmas and collective-action problems, inadequate institutional constraints, and market incentives on both the supply and demand side. Supplier governments, particularly the United States, must also confront domestic pressures from interest groups and government agencies that benefit from arms exports. Most important, the U.S. government must rethink its adoption of arms exports as an instrument of foreign economic policy. This position, based on narrow measures of economic advantage, neglects broader dangers that result from the free flow of weapons systems across national borders. The potentially destabilizing effects of such transfers, along with past transactions that backfired against the United States, must be added to the balance sheet. Thus, the example U.S. policy sets for other active or potential military exporters should be weighed against the merits of arms exports in advancing U.S. and global security interests.

Notes

1. An "arms transfer" in this analysis is defined as the contracted movement of military goods and services between nation-states on a cash or subsidized basis. Although most weapons suppliers selectively offer security assistance to recipients in the form of grants, low-interest loans, trade concessions, or other benefits, cash sales have become more common in recent years.

2. These figures are drawn from the databases provided by the Federation of American Scientists (http://www.fas.org) and the Center for Defense Information (http://www.cdi.org). For other sources of recent data and analysis, see *Arms Control Today* and *Defense News*. While data regarding U.S. security assistance are widely available from government sources, most notably the Defense Security Cooperation Agency, details on commercial sales are more difficult to obtain beyond the government's annual "Section 655" report. See Lumpe and Donarski 1998 for a useful guide to research in this area.

3. The largest of these agreements included advanced reconnaissance aircraft and attack helicopters to Turkey, attack helicopters to Kuwait, and jet fighters to South Korea, Malaysia, and Oman.

4. The European case demonstrates how weapons importers maintain the upper hand in the global market for military equipment. Heightened competition among suppliers provides customers with considerable leverage in negotiating discounts, technology transfers, licensed production, and other forms of "offsets."

5. The array of weapons systems exported by the United States to developing nations between 2000 and 2003 included 2,953 surface-to-air missiles, 308 antiship missiles, 46 supersonic combat aircraft, 200 tanks, and 120 helicopters (Grimmett 2004, p. 67).

6. This firm, whose name translates roughly to "Russian Weapons Exports," seeks customers on its corporate website (see http://www.rusarm.ru), which promotes "famous brands of Russian armaments, classed among the world's best . . . with high-skilled workforce and time-tested traditions."

7. For more information on this organization, see http://www.weu.int/weag.

8. Progress toward an integrated European defense industry is likely to be slowed, however, by the disproportionate output of France, Germany, and Great Britain (see Freedman and Navias 1997).

9. The political influence of military industrialists is not limited to democratic states. Arms manufacturers in autocratic states may have even greater clout by maintaining closer but less transparent and regulated ties to political leaders.

10. In 1995 these economic interests were acknowledged formally by Clinton in Presidential Decision Directive 34. The document also endorsed arms transfers on the more familiar grounds that, by strengthening U.S. allies overseas and stabilizing regional power imbalances, they enhanced U.S. security at home.

11. The FMS program provided more than $125 billion worth of arms from 1992 until 2001. Saudi Arabia received more than 15 percent of those transfers while Israel and Egypt received nearly 9 percent each.

12. The Bush administration notified Congress of nearly 300 pending commercial sales in 2002 and 2003 (http://www.fas.org).

13. Under the FMF program, the United States exported nearly $40 billion worth of arms between 1992 and 2001, primarily to Israel and Egypt (U.S. Defense Security Cooperation Agency 2003). In addition to these allocations of public funds, the U.S. government further subsidizes arms exports by providing economic aid to developing countries to use for the purchase of U.S.-made military equipment. Although a precise measurement is elusive, it is widely accepted that the U.S. government provides $1 in defense-industrial subsidies, including security assistance, for every $2 in arms exports.

14. Although the financial cost of IMET to U.S. taxpayers—about $80 million in fiscal year 2003—is modest compared to the cost of subsidized arms exports, the pervasive reach of IMET to more than 10,000 students in most foreign countries makes it a vital component of U.S. security assistance.

15. Many weapons systems continue almost entirely with this market in mind, including the F-15E Strike Eagle fighter bomber, the M1A2 Abrams main battle tank, the AH-64A Apache attack helicopter, and the MIM-23 Hawk air defense missile (Lumpe and Donarski 1998, chap. 2).

16. The primary example of this is the Joint Strike Fighter, a massive multiservice weapons program that involves several U.S. and foreign defense contractors. The financial investments of European participants in the project determine their status as "full patrons" (Great Britain), "associate partners" (Denmark, the Netherlands, and Norway), "informed partners" (Canada and Italy), and "major participants" (Israel, Singapore, and Turkey).

17. The Arms Export Control Act of 1976 established a precedent by stating that arms transfers contributed to regional conflicts. Other pertinent legislation includes the Foreign Assistance Act of 1961, which created the current system of security as well as economic assistance, and the Export Administration Act of 2001, which regulated the transfer of sensitive technology.

18. These efforts to expedite U.S. arms transfers gave new meaning to the word "reform" in this context. The term is most often associated with restricting weapons exports.

19. The classic statement in this regard is still Wildavsky 1966.

20. The rejection of such proposed exports is rare, however, especially given the hurdles that must be surmounted for "resolutions of disapproval" to be passed: the review and release of such resolutions by the armed services committees of both chambers and their passage by the full membership of each chamber by veto-proof majorities, all within fifteen to thirty days.

21. Ethnic groups also have interests in U.S. arms transfers that pertain to their countries of origin (see Ambrosio 2002). These preferences are especially noted in House districts with substantial blocs of ethnic voters. In these cases, congressional activity is driven by electoral as well as financial concerns.

22. Of the 270 commercial sales proposed by the Bush administration between 2002 and November 2003, for example, one-third were with India and Pakistan. This flood of arms to the two nuclear powers, if fully achieved, would almost certainly compound the lethality of a direct confrontation between them.

23. Levels of U.S. development aid dropped steadily in the late 1990s due to opposition from Republicans in Congress, who gained majority status in the November 1994 midterm elections. Although these levels have increased in recent years, the United States consistently ranks lowest among aid donors in the proportion of its economic output directed toward development assistance.

24. The Soviet invasion of Afghanistan late in 1979 prompted the U.S. government to provide covert military assistance to the mujahidin, who ultimately defeated the Soviet Union, gained power through the Taliban, and targeted the United States as a key enemy. This case further illustrates the enduring consequences of backfire.

25. Iraq imported a wide variety of conventional weapons from the United States and other suppliers during the 1980s, ranking first among arms importers during the decade.

26. For detailed summaries of campaign contributions from defense firms, see the website of the Center for Responsive Politics, http://www.opensecrets.org.

27. This measure does not prevent the U.S. government from selling weapons on commercial markets to repressive regimes such as Saudi Arabia.

28. This more lenient arms-export policy revived the Cold War pattern in which U.S. aid often flowed to egregious violators of human rights (Schoultz 1981). Empirical studies of these transactions found that while human rights concerns had a modest impact on the U.S. government's initial decision to provide security assistance, there was little linkage among recipients between their receipt of U.S. aid and their respect for human rights (see Poe and Meernik 1995; Poe 1991; and Cingranelli and Pasquarello 1985). The same pattern was evident in a subsequent study by Shannon Blanton (2000), whose coverage beyond the Cold War suggested that the U.S. government's selective observance of human rights criteria had deeper roots.

29. Arms transfers to both countries were largely limited to nonlethal equipment such as radar and surveillance systems, technical data, and spare parts for existing weapons systems. It is widely known, however, that both governments desire more sophisticated medium- and long-range missile systems to complement their nuclear forces. Restraint by other suppliers in this area may be less likely given the U.S. government's reentry in the Indian and Pakistani arms markets.

30. Opposition by the U.S. government also weakened a regional convention approved in 1997 by the Organization of American States to restrict the trafficking of small arms in the region.

9

Protecting Critical Infrastructure: The Role of the Private Sector

Sue E. Eckert

More than any other event in recent memory, September 11, 2001, underscored the vulnerability of the United States to new types of security threats. At stake is not just the security of innocent civilians going about their daily business, but also the physical and cyber infrastructures upon which U.S. economic prosperity and well-being are based. In particular, the events of September 11 brought to the fore the need for new thinking regarding the private sector role in a new security environment. Unfortunately, as time passes since the attacks, the urgency behind this effort has diminished, putting U.S. national success and economic well-being at risk.

With approximately 85 percent of U.S. key infrastructures privately owned or operated, the private sector is an increasingly important actor in the new security issues associated with homeland security (U.S. Department of Homeland Security 2002). While an integral part of national security, homeland security differs in that it is a shared responsibility that cannot be met by the federal government alone. It requires coordinated action on the part of government (federal, state, and local) *and the private sector.* New forms of public-private partnerships are essential to meet the challenges posed by new technologies and nontraditional threats.

Prior to September 11, independent advisory groups and government agencies warned of possible attacks on U.S. soil and the need for the public and private sectors to work together to address such risks.[1] Progress in establishing a sustained effort in the late 1990s, however, was slowed by the lack of perceived threat, especially within the private sector. The tragic events of September 11, however, changed this, at least temporarily. The attacks prompted renewed attention to the issue and motivated both government and industry to pursue cooperative mechanisms that had previously languished. One of the most significant of these initiatives is the Information Sharing and Analysis

Centers (ISACs). ISACs are intended to promote collaboration and information sharing both between government and industry and within key industries with respect to threats. They are the primary means of partnering for the protection of critical infrastructure, although little public attention or analysis has been focused on them.

This chapter explores a topic at the intersection of emerging political economy and security issues—government's increasing reliance on the private sector to help secure the homeland.[2] It surveys the record of U.S. public-private partnerships to date in addressing critical infrastructure protection, examines impediments faced by industry collaboration through the ISACs, and offers analysis and recommendations for enhancing such partnerships so as to provide greater security in the future.

Changed Conceptions of Security

September 11, 2001, marked an important turning point in how Americans perceive security. Until then, security was generally viewed in traditional terms—military efforts to defend U.S. interests against external threats, principally from states. With the nightmare of fuel-laden commercial planes being flown into key buildings and the resulting catastrophic loss of life and economic disruption, however, came the realization that a new, more comprehensive security paradigm is required—one broad enough to encompass protection of both Americans at home and also key areas of the economy vulnerable to attack—that is, "critical infrastructure." In the aftermath of September 11, protection of the homeland, or homeland security, has become an integral part of U.S. security, this in a way that the indiscriminate threat of nuclear devastation never required.[3]

Prior to September 11, few in the U.S. worried about threats against domestic facilities. The attacks changed this by vividly demonstrating U.S. vulnerability. Subsequent information found in Afghanistan—diagrams of U.S. nuclear plants and water supplies—underscored the nature of these new threats against commercial targets (Clarke 2002). Furthermore, recent communications of Al-Qaida specifically focus on the U.S. economy as a target, or in Osama bin Laden's words, on "this policy in bleeding America to the point of bankruptcy" (bin Laden 2004). The Federal Bureau of Investigation (FBI) and Department of Homeland Security (DHS) have issued repeated warnings of possible targeting by terrorists of nuclear utilities, chemical facilities, and modes of transportation, especially aviation and rail. In August 2004, financial institutions in the New York and Washington areas became the first sector publicly warned of specific terrorist threats, with the DHS issuing an elevated threat advisory (Lichtblau 2004). Thus "the front lines of defense in this new type of battle have moved into our communities and the individual institutions that make up our critical infrastructure sectors" (White House 2003b).

The U.S. government owns and controls very few of these national assets—estimates of private sector critical infrastructure ownership range from 80 to 85 percent.[4] Because of technological developments, especially increased reliance on interconnected computer and telecommunications networks, a broad range of modern economic activity is now more vulnerable to exploitation. Global financial systems, power plants and electrical grids, gas and oil distribution pipelines, water treatment systems, oil and chemical refineries, transportation systems, and even essential military communications—all rely on an interdependent network of information systems that continuously connect and increasingly control the operations of other critical infrastructures. These systems are attractive and viable targets for terrorists, or other adversaries, through either physical bombing or cyber attacks (Tenet 2002). The August 2003 power blackouts of much of the East Coast further underscored the susceptibility of interconnected networks not only to terrorist attacks, but also to severe disruption.

In this new security environment, the boundary between the private and public sector has blurred. Whereas security as traditionally defined has been the province of the federal government, homeland security is a shared responsibility of government at all levels as well as the private sector.[5] "Just as winning this war [on terrorism] requires international coalitions, intelligence sharing, and law enforcement cooperation, so too does it require finding a new division of labor between the public and private sectors" (Rothkopf 2002).

Defining Critical Infrastructure

Critical infrastructure has been defined in various ways over time, but generally consists of "those physical or cyber-based systems essential to the minimum operations of the economy and government" (White House 1998).[6] Since the events of September 11, 2001, and passage of the Patriot Act, the definition has been expanded by adding, "the incapacity or destruction of which . . . would have a debilitating impact on the security, national economic security, and national public health or safety."[7]

In 1996 the Clinton administration defined eight sectors as critical: telecommunications, electric power systems, oil and gas storage and transportation, banking and finance, transportation, water supply systems, emergency services, and continuity of government (White House 1996). In 2003, other sectors were added or reorganized to form fourteen critical sectors, including food, public health, and the chemical industry and hazardous materials.[8] While all have a basis for being considered "critical," the expansive definition covers a broad cross section of economic and governmental activity.[9]

To get a sense of magnitude, the U.S. Department of Homeland Security (2004) characterizes the nation's critical infrastructures and key assets as including 68,000 public water systems, 300,000 oil and natural gas production facilities, 4,000 offshore platforms, 278,000 miles of natural gas pipelines, 361 seaports, 104 nuclear power plants, 80,000 dams, and tens of thousands of other potentially critical targets across fourteen diverse critical infrastructure sectors. While several policy documents and Congress have mandated the development of a uniform methodology to identify and catalogue critical facilities and systems, a comprehensive list has proven problematic.[10]

The Clinton Administration's Critical Infrastructure Policies

A concerted effort by the U.S. government to address critical infrastructure issues systematically is relatively recent. The Reagan administration considered aspects of national security challenges posed by new telecommunications technology, especially as they related to encryption and the government's ability to wiretap. An advisory committee of U.S. companies was formed, but ad hoc interactions between the government (primarily the National Security Agency) and affected companies were the norm. Rather, it was during the Clinton administration that the first comprehensive effort was made to address national infrastructure issues.

The concept and lexicon of critical infrastructure, and the focus on public-private partnerships to address such concerns, first emerged in the mid-1990s when the Clinton administration initiated a dialogue with computer and telecommunications companies. Partially in response to growing concern for computer vulnerabilities and the need to protect information systems from attack, President Clinton issued Executive Order 13010 on July 15, 1996, establishing the President's Commission on Critical Infrastructure Protection (PCCIP), a governmental body formed to recommend a national policy and strategy to protect critical and increasingly vulnerable and interconnected infrastructures from physical and cyber threats (White House 1996). As part of its tasks, the PCCIP was charged with identifying and working with private sector entities that conduct, support, or contribute to infrastructure assurance. In October 1997 the commission issued its report, urging greater cooperation and communication between the private sector and government, since critical infrastructure protection was deemed a shared responsibility (President's Commission on Critical Infrastructure Protection 1997).

Building on the recommendations of the commission, Presidential Decision Directive (PDD) 63 was promulgated in 1998 as the first comprehensive attempt to protect physical and cyber-based systems essential to the economy and government (White House 1998). PDD 63 established critical infrastructure protection as a national goal and articulated a strategy for cooperative government–private sector initiatives to accomplish it. The policy emphasized that government would, to the extent feasible, focus on market-based incentives for addressing critical infrastructure protection and avoid increased government regulation. The government was to consult with owners and operators of critical infrastructures to encourage the voluntary creation of private sector ISACs.

PDD 63 also established the National Infrastructure Protection Center (NIPC) within the FBI to serve as the principal body to facilitate the U.S. government's infrastructure threat assessment, encompassing aspects such as early warning, vulnerability, law enforcement investigation, and response. The NIPC was designated to serve as the conduit for information sharing with the private sector through the ISACs. The Critical Infrastructure Assurance Office (CIAO) within the Department of Commerce was also created under PDD 63, to coordinate the federal government's initiatives on critical infrastructure assurance efforts and to support the ISACs. To provide overall direction to the policy, President Clinton designated Richard Clarke, a seasoned career bureaucrat, as national coordinator for security, infrastructure protection, and counterterrorism.[11]

Because of increasing incidents of cyber attacks on both government facilities and private companies, infrastructure protection initially focused primarily on cyber security.[12] The run-up to Y2K and denial-of-service attacks in 2000 highlighted this vulnerability and heightened awareness, especially among the information industries. The Clinton administration actively encouraged the formation of sector-specific ISACs to begin sharing information among companies, and between the government and the private sector. While the effort got off to a slow start, four ISACs were established in 1999–2001, in the financial services, telecommunications, electronics, and information technology sectors. With varying degrees of industry participation and differing operational methods, ISACs have evolved into the primary mechanisms for government-industry interaction on critical infrastructure issues.

Post–September 11 Critical Infrastructure Initiatives

In early 2001 the George W. Bush administration allowed most infrastructure protection activities initiated under President Clinton to continue while it conducted an internal review of policies. There was little public attention to the issue in the first nine months of Bush's presidency, and apparently little private sector initiative. As a result, the momentum behind the creation of the first ISACs diminished. The events of September 11 intervened, however, and critical infrastructure issues became a priority unlike at any time in the past.

In response to the attacks, President Bush signed two relevant executive orders. The first, Executive Order 13228 on October 9, 2001, established the new Office of Homeland Security within the National Security Council (NSC), headed by an assistant to the president for homeland security. Its mission was to develop and coordinate the implementation of a comprehensive national strategy to secure the United States from terrorist threats, and to protect U.S. critical infrastructure from terrorist attacks (White House 2001a). In July 2002 a national strategy for homeland security was released, detailing the range of governmental initiatives to protect the U.S. homeland, including efforts to work with the private sector. Specifically, the strategy identified protection of U.S. critical infrastructure and key assets as one of six critical mission areas (U.S. Department of Homeland Security 2002).

Increasing congressional pressure for a more permanent institution dedicated to homeland security, however, ultimately gave way to the administration's decision to eliminate the homeland security office within the NSC and to create a homeland security department. On November 22, 2002, Congress approved creation of the Department of Homeland Security—the largest government reorganization since the Truman administration's creation of the Department of Defense and the National Security Council. With a mission that specifically included the protection of critical infrastructure, the DHS consolidated responsibility for cyber and physical protection efforts, including functions formerly of the NIPC at the Federal Bureau of Investigation and the CIAO at the Department of Commerce.

The second executive order, issued concomitantly with the creation of the Office of Homeland Security, established infrastructure protection policy and its organizational structure. Building on PDD 63, President Bush issued Executive Order 13231 on October 18, 2001, which laid out establishment of such bodies as the President's Critical Infrastructure Protection Board and the National Infrastructure Advisory Council:

> It is the policy of the United States to protect against disruption of the operation of information systems for critical infrastructure and thereby help to protect the people, economy, essential human and government services, and national security of the United States, and to ensure that any disruptions that occur are infrequent, of minimal duration, and manageable, and cause the least damage possible. The implementation of this policy shall include a voluntary public-private partnership, involving corporate and nongovernmental organizations. (White House 2001b)

In February 2003 the administration elaborated its critical infrastructure objectives in two policy documents—a national strategy for the physical protection of critical infrastructures and key assets, and a national strategy for the securing of cyberspace (White House 2003b, 2003c). Both documents emphasize the importance of developing effective mechanisms between the public and private sectors to exchange information regarding threats, vulnerabilities, and incidents. On December 17, 2003, President Bush codified the policy in Homeland Security Presidential Directive (HSPD) 7, which super-seded PDD 63 and requires federal departments and agencies to identify, pri-oritize, and protect U.S. critical infrastructures from attack (White House 2003a).

In its most important aspects, the Bush administration's stated policy concerning critical infrastructure protection has essentially been the same as that of the Clinton administration.[13] While bureaucratic structures differ, both administrations emphasized the importance of working with the private sec-tor, not regulating it. Indeed, the national strategy for the physical protection of infrastructures called for "a new paradigm of cooperation and partnership . . . that requires a culture of trust and ongoing collaboration among relevant public and private stakeholders, rather than more traditional systems of com-mand and control [of the Cold War]" (White House 2003b).

Private Sector Role in Security

A private sector role in the national security realm is certainly not new—ei-ther in practice or in treatment of the issue by academics. For as long as there have been wars, governments have hired mercenaries and purchased arma-ments produced by private industry. Traditionally, scholars have tended to concentrate on topics related to weapons production and arms trade, and more broadly, defense-industrial concerns, when addressing issues at the intersec-tion of national security and political economy.[14] More recently, academic in-terest has focused on issues surrounding the "privatization of security" in warn-torn regions and the increasing private sector support of logistical ser-vices, as seen in Iraq (see Singer 2001–2002).

Aaron Friedberg's *In the Shadow of the Garrison State: America's Anti-Statism and Its Cold War Grand Strategy* (2000) detailed the reasons behind the privatization of arms production in the United States following World War II, the result of which placed primary reliance on the private sector to produce the nation's arms. Reflecting an antistatist political tradition, the United States established a mechanism to procure arms from privately owned firms instead of adopting a more onerous industrial policy. According to Friedberg (2000), this represents the success of the national security state in harnessing the pri-vate sector and private resources for national purposes, largely through the government's near-monopoly over military acquisition. However, at the same time, the government created a system with heavy dependence on privately owned institutions.[15]

In the post–September 11 world, the security threat is not one that can be successfully managed through the purchasing power of the government. Rather, the risks are now more specifically shared. At issue is no longer whether or not the private sector can be replied upon to manufacture high-quality weaponry at a reasonable cost, but whether or not the private sector will invest the necessary resources to defend itself, short of direct government intervention. Unwilling, or unable, to compel such a response, the federal government under both the Clinton and Bush administrations has opted to encourage action through cooperative measures. Questions remain, however, as to whether such a voluntary approach can produce the necessary outcome (see, in particular, Flynn 2004, p. 56).

Information Sharing and Analysis Centers

A variety of government-industry initiatives have evolved to address critical infrastructure protection issues. The Partnership for Critical Infrastructure Security (PCIS), formed in 1999, provided an overall forum for dialogue on infrastructure security issues across sectors.[16] InfraGard, a pilot program started in 1996, is a partnership between companies and the government—the FBI originally and the DHS now—to provide for the secure exchange of information on cyber intrusions, vulnerabilities, and infrastructure threats.[17]

The Computer Emergency Response Team (CERT), administered by Carnegie Mellon in cooperation with the DHS, provides a coordination center to direct the U.S. response to possible cyber attacks, ensuring that all necessary information to repel an attack is distributed across all critical infrastructure sectors during an attack or heightened level of alert. In addition, the DHS's Information Analysis and Infrastructure Protection division provides a range of bulletins and advisories of interest to professionals involved in protecting public and private infrastructures.[18]

Yet the Information Sharing and Analysis Centers remain the primary vehicle to address infrastructure protection concerns. As envisioned in PDD 63, ISACs were to facilitate on a sectoral basis the voluntary gathering, analyzing, and dissemination of information to and from industry sectors and the federal government. Activities were to focus on infrastructure vulnerabilities, threats, and best practices for private sector organizations in designated sectors.

The policies of both the Clinton and Bush administrations emphasized that ISACs were not to interfere with direct information exchanges between companies and the government. Although ultimately designed by members, ISACs were modeled on mechanisms, such as the Centers for Disease Control and Prevention, that have proven effective, particularly in extensive interchanges with the private and nonfederal sectors. As such, ISACs were to possess a large degree of technical focus and expertise, primarily on nonregulatory and non–law enforcement missions. The expectation was that they would establish baseline statistics and patterns on various sectors, become a clearinghouse for information within and among members and sectors, and provide a library of historical data to be used by the private sector and, as deemed appropriate by the ISACs, the government (White House 1998). Of particular importance to the government, ISACs were to provide it with information on security incidents experienced by companies.

From the private sector perspective, ISACs were envisioned as a means to deal with concerns that detailed security incident reports to the government might otherwise reveal. Public disclosures of vulnerabilities can have a negative impact on corporate reputations and impinge on business proprietary information, in particular due to the Freedom of Information Act (FOIA) and open-record requirements of federal agencies. Both PDD 63 and the Homeland Security Act contain provisions intended to enable ISACs to share security information outside of the burdens of open-record laws—if the information relates to security vulnerabilities, threats, and incidents. However, ongoing industry concerns for the confidentiality of shared information have proven to be a significant factor affecting greater exchange.

Evolution of ISACs

Initially, ISACs got off to a slow start after PDD 63, both because they were breaking new ground and because of the natural reluctance of market competitors to share information. ISACs originally focused on cyber security issues, with the basic structure in place in related sectors when cyber attacks escalated to unprecedented levels in February 2000. Such events provided momentum, especially for the Telecommunications ISAC and the Information ISAC, to intensify their efforts. The events of September 11, 2001, served to broaden further the scope of ISAC responsibilities, to deal with physical protection against terrorist risks and incidents.

In October 1999, banking, finance, and security organizations formed the Financial Services ISAC (FS-ISAC), and hired Global Integrity, a subsidiary of Scientific Applications International Corporation, to design and operate it. The FS-ISAC maintains a database to which members voluntarily report information (on either an anonymous or attributed basis) regarding security threats, vulnerabilities, incidents, and solutions. Security specialists analyze the input and, depending on the seriousness of the case, the FS-ISAC will distribute an alert to members. While the exact number of incidents submitted is confidential, there have been over 2,000 entries related to general threats, vulnerabilities, and solutions impacting the critical information infrastructure at large (see http://www.fsisac.com/faq.cfm). The database cannot be accessed by the government. Instead, it is used to share incident information among members and to develop trending and benchmarking information for the benefit of FS-ISAC members. Likewise, ISACs have been established in the telecommunications, information technology, electric power, energy (oil and natural gas), food, chemical, water, transportation, and emergency fire service sectors (see Table 9.1 for an overview).[19]

Table 9.1 Overview of Current ISACs

Component/ Sector	Financial Services	Tele-communications	Electricity	Information Technology	Energy (Oil and Gas)
Formation Date	Oct. 1999	Jan. 2000	Oct. 2000	Dec. 2000	Nov. 2001
ISAC Operator	Science Applications International Corporation (SAIC)	National Communications System (NCS)	North American Electric Reliability Council (NERC)	Internet Security Systems Inc.	SAIC
Lead Agency (Federal)	Department of Treasury	Department of Homeland Security (DHS)	Department of Energy/ DHS	Department of Homeland Security	Department of Energy
Private Sector Partner	American Bankers Association, Securities Industry Association	NCS	NERC	Computer Emergency Response Team (CERT)	National Petroleum Council
Structure of ISAC	501C(6) nonprofit corporation	National Coordinating Center (NCC)	Nonprofit corporation	Nonprofit, limited liability corporation (LLC)	LLC
Membership	Banks, savings and loans, credit unions, securities firms, insurance companies, credit card companies, mortgage banking companies, industry associations	Thirty individual tele-communications companies providing tele-communications or network services, equipment, or software; and three associations	Entities in electricity sector: American Public Power Association, Canadian Electricity Association, National Rural Electric Cooperative Association, NERC regions, etc.	Vendor, manufacturer, or provider of information technology (including Internet and e-commerce) products (hardware and software), solutions, or services	Licensed energy industry companies—oil or natural gas, pipeline, energy trading, or industry service and support companies

continues

Table 9.1 continued

Component/ Sector	Food	Chemical	Transportation (Surface)	Transportation (Public)	Water
Formation Date	Feb. 2002	Apr. 2002	May 2002	Jan. 2003	Dec. 2002
ISAC Operator	Food Marketing Institute (FMI)	American Chemical Council's Chemical Transportation Emergency Center (CHEMTREC)	EWA Information & Infrastructure Technologies Inc.	EWA Information & Infrastructure Technologies Inc.	Association of Metropolitan Water Agencies
Lead Agency (Federal)	DHS, Department of Agriculture (meat/poultry), Department of Health and Human Services (all other foods)	Department of Homeland Security	Department of Homeland Security	Department of Transportation	Environmental Protection Agency
Private Sector Partner	FMI	American Chemistry Council (ACC)	Association of American Railroads (AAR)	American Public Transport Association (APTA)	Association of Metropolitan Water Agencies
Structure of ISAC	Individual subscriptions overseen by FMI	ACC members and individual subscribers	AAR members	APTA— nonprofit association	Nonprofit organization with board of managers of water utility leaders appointed by eight U.S. drinking water and wastewater organizations
Membership	Over forty food industry trade associations and members	Companies or organizations involved in the manufacture, storage, transportation, or distribution of chemical products	Major North American freight railroads and Amtrak	Public and private transit systems and commuter rail operators, transit associations, and state departments of transportation	U.S. drinking water and wastewater systems, regardless of size or type of ownership

continues

Table 9.1   continued

Component/ Sector	Financial Services	Tele- communications	Electricity	Information Technology	Energy (Oil and Gas)
Website	www.fsisac .com Detailed information: operating rules, presentations, testimony, press releases, frequently asked questions (FAQs)	www.ncs.gov/ ncc/main/html Members list, capabilities, and initiatives	www.esisac .com Information on security standards, guidelines and workshops, board members, testimony, FAQs	www.it-isac .org Detailed information: by-laws, articles of incorporation, alerts and advisories, corporate members, FAQs	www.energyisac .com Detailed information, operating rules, FAQs
Funding	Tiered membership fees based on level of service: free up to $10,000; Treasury grant	NCS; agencies bear costs of personnel	NERC	Tiered membership fees based on level of service: free up to $40,000	Department of Energy grant; $150 login fees beyond two free
Scope of ISAC Coverage	Represents 90 percent of sector—more than 800 members; 8,500 firms receive alerts	95 percent of infrastructure— 95 percent wireless providers and vendors, 90 percent Internet service networks	90 percent of NERC members	70 percent of information technology globally; 85 percent cross-sector	85 percent of oil and gas sector
Sharing Mechanisms	Text-based alerts, biweekly conference calls with DHS	Critical Infrastructure Warning Information Network (CWIN)	Secure telephone and website	CWIN, secure website, Government Emergency Tele- communications Service (GETS)	Secure website

continues

Reflecting the unique characteristics of individual sectors, each ISAC operates independently. Each determines its own structure, operational procedures, business model, and funding mechanisms. Most ISACs are managed or operated by private entities as nonprofit, limited liability corporations, owned by members, for the processing and sharing of information; others are managed as parts of existing industry trade associations. Articles of corporation and by-laws have been established, as well as boards of directors responsible for approving members through an application process open to U.S. firms in the designated sector. Differing funding mechanisms are used, with many ISACs financed largely through membership fees. Some ISACs offer tiered member-

Table 9.1 continued

Component/ Sector	Food	Chemical	Transportation (Surface)	Transportation (Public)	Water
Website	www.fmi.org/ isac Business plan news releases, security alerts, food and disease infor- mation, FAQs	www. chemicalisac. chemtrec.com FAQs about CHEMTREC	www.surface transportation isac.org FAQs, virus alerts, news	www.surface transportation isac.org FAQs, virus alerts, news	www.waterisac .org Information on board, services, FAQs
Funding	No current funding; volunteer labor contributed by FMI; no charge to participants	CHEMTREC	Membership fees and grant from Federal Transit Administra- tion	Federally funded	EPA grant; subscription fees
Scope of ISAC Coverage	More than forty industry trade associations	CHEMTREC	95 percent of freight railroad industry, and Amtrak	100 major transit organizations	275–300 water utilities, more than 1,000 individuals at drinking water and wastewater systems
Sharing Mechanisms	Watch Commander List	Biweekly conference call with DHS; secure communications network	Secure telephone	Secure e-mail	Secure portal and e-mail

Sources: Derived from ISAC websites; ISAC Council White Paper "Reach of Major ISACs," January 31, 2004; and U.S. Government Accounting Office Report no. 04-780, "Critical Infrastructure Protection: Establishing Effective In-formation Sharing with Infrastructure Sectors," April 21, 2004.

ships with fees based on the level of service (see https://www.it-isac.org/ faq.php). The Financial Services ISAC provides five levels of service, ranging from free basic service, to $750 for limited access to websites and reports, up to $10,000, $25,000, and $50,000 for commensurate access and benefits (see http://www.fsisac.com/join.cfm). Other ISACs have partnered with federal agencies, with some having received federal grants or contracts.[20]

Benefits of membership include early notification of threats, anonymous information sharing, subject matter expertise, and access to trending and other benchmark data. Membership is voluntary. Since membership lists are confidential, it is difficult to confirm the degree of industry participation, although indications are that most ISACs have good corporate participation. The ISAC Council, a group of eleven ISACs created to improve cross-sectoral coordination and effectiveness, estimated that as of January 2004, ISAC membership and outreach extended to approximately 65 percent of U.S. private critical infrastructure.[21] Table 9.1 includes the estimated scope of industry coverage by each ISAC.

Assessment of ISACs

The relative novelty of most ISACs, and especially the lack of transparency common to them, makes anything more than a preliminary assessment difficult. Progress has been made in establishing ISACs and beginning the process of information sharing. The DHS has organized numerous briefings with industry sectors, exercises, and cross-sectoral ISAC meetings. In October 2004, for example, more than 200 security executives from a wide variety of industries and ISAC members met with government representatives for ISAC Congress tabletop exercises to improve detection and response to threats and vulnerabilities facing infrastructure (FS-ISAC 2004). In addition, as noted previously, some government funding of ISAC operations has been provided.

However, much more needs to be done. To begin with, only a few critical infrastructure sectors have more than rudimentary ISACs. Moreover, the record of those that do varies considerably, especially in terms of sector participation and also in terms of the actual information being shared (see Darcey 2003, p 25).

Less broadly, there are several important practical stumbling blocks hindering the effectiveness of ISACs:

1. A uniform methodology for identifying facilities, systems, and functions with national-level criticality has been difficult to establish, thereby impeding prioritization and resource allocation. Members of Congress who have been briefed on the work in progress have been critical of the list, characterized as consisting of more than 30,000 potential targets (Starks and Anderson 2004).[22]

2. Follow-through has been poor on implementing the government's touted partnerships with industry to address security issues (Krim 2004). Beyond meetings and recommendations, there has been little in the way of concrete actions. As the U.S. General Accounting Office (GAO) has noted, the DHS has not developed a plan to address the challenges in building public-private information-sharing partnerships (2004, p. 11).

3. The Department of Homeland Security—the lead agency responsible for ISACs and critical infrastructure protection—has been preoccupied with

its own internal startup and organization, thereby weakening government leadership in public-private partnering. Industry, Congress, the GAO, and the DHS's inspector-general have been critical of various aspects of the DHS's overall effort, citing a lack of coordination, poor communication, and a failure to set priorities (Krim 2004). A sense that "not enough is happening" pervades the issue.

Challenges to Public-Private Cooperation

Provided these impediments can be overcome, several serious challenges remain that are likely to hinder effective ISAC partnerships between government and the private sector.

Information Sharing

Information sharing has been identified consistently as the key element of government and private sector efforts to protect critical infrastructure. While all embrace the concept, developing effective information-sharing mechanisms has proven difficult. Overcoming long-standing cultural differences between the two communities and establishing trusted relationships and information-sharing mechanisms necessary to support such coordination are not a simple or quick matter. Information sharing is evolving slowly, and according to a 2003 report by the National Academy of Sciences, "most information sharing still occurs through informal channels. Fundamental questions persist about who should share what information, when, how, why, and with whom" (Personick and Patterson 2003).

From the outset, industry raised concerns about the protection of proprietary information shared among members and with the government. Specifically, many industry representatives believe that confidential information provided to the government may be disclosed to third parties under the Freedom of Information Act. To address the issue, Section 204 of the Homeland Security Act provides that information voluntarily provided by nonfederal parties to the Department of Homeland Security that relates to infrastructure vulnerabilities or other vulnerabilities to terrorism is not subject to public disclosure under the FOIA.[23] While some cite the FOIA exemption as substantial progress in removing legal obstacles to the sharing of information between the government and the private sector, public interest groups have criticized the provision and proposed legislation to restore FOIA provisions, potentially reversing the information-sharing improvements.

In February 2004 the DHS attempted to resolve the issue through the launch of the Protected Critical Infrastructure Information Program (PCII). The PCII is intended to encourage industry to voluntarily share confidential, proprietary, and business-sensitive information about critical infrastructure with the government by establishing a specific process to exempt from disclosure to the public any critical infrastructure information voluntarily submitted to the department ("DHS Launches" 2004). Based on the reaction from public interest groups, however, it appears that the issue is still not entirely settled, reducing the certainty that government hoped to provide and fueling continued private sector reluctance to move forward with information sharing (Block 2004; and Mintz 2004).

An additional private sector concern relates to the risk of prosecution under antitrust regulations for sharing information with other companies.[24] Like the FOIA issue, the new antitrust exemptions called for by business raise a host of serious questions, and persistent perception problems related to what is permissible or illegal under existing law appear to serve as a disincentive for firms to share information (Personick and Patterson 2003, pp. 30–34).

As information sharing is a two-way street, it appears that problems also exist with the information provided by the government to the private sector. Historically, the government has been reluctant to share information that could compromise intelligence sources or investigations. According to the Business Roundtable, "Improving the flow of information will depend in part on improving the ability of the government to communicate relevant and sensitive information—including pertinent, but often classified, threat intelligence—in a timely manner without violating security classification protocols" (Business Roundtable 2003, p. 27). Moreover, the quality of information provided has been cited as a problem. Chemical companies indicate that they do not receive enough specific threat information and that it frequently comes from multiple sources. This represents a significant problem, since industry officials have stated that they need more specific information about potential threats in order to design their security systems and protocols (Darcey 2003, p. 29).

Liability

A related issue of concern revolves around broad questions of liability.[25] What are companies' downstream or third-party liabilities for the effects of attacks on infrastructure? What responsibility do owners and operators of infrastructure facilities have for managing risk? To what degree must utilities and service providers protect customers, including upgrading physical security and infrastructure? Since legal liability often depends on which actors are best positioned to prevent harmful activities, answering such concerns is extremely complicated.

One of the reasons for the lack of progress in information sharing on infrastructure protection relates to the confusion regarding liabilities in sharing information within and between industry sectors and the government. This concern specifically affects industry's willingness to participate in ISACs.

Companies fear liability if they provide flawed information to the ISAC, or if the ISAC prepares flawed analysis. What happens if ISAC members fail to share or disclose information that could have averted an attack? Is membership in the ISAC a mitigating factor if losses occur and the company is sued? The host of unanswered questions and uncertainty represent important issues that need to be addressed. Many analysts believe, however, that industry's questions will be answered in court before long, perhaps leading the private sector to advocate liability protection for participation in ISACs.

Incentives for Infrastructure Protection

Beyond sharing information as to threats, the critical question remaining is how to ensure that industry takes the necessary actions to protect privately owned critical infrastructure. Firms clearly have inherent incentives to protect their assets, not the least of which are profitability and reputational concerns. Even prior to September 11, 2001, private sector costs for security were reported to exceed $40 billion annually, with the cyber security market alone reaching $10 billion.[26] As a result of September 11, costs are estimated to have increased as much as 100 percent, even without factoring in increased insurance costs. While difficult to measure precisely, security-related expenses are considerable.

Business groups, however, note that shareholders have little financial incentive to invest in security beyond their stake in the corporation, and so shareholders support security investments only to the extent that to do so would be profitable (Business Roundtable 2003, p. 19). Thus, private markets themselves would not normally generate sufficient incentives to secure infrastructure vulnerabilities. "Relying on best practices and industry self-policing was acceptable for meeting our pre-9/11 regulatory needs, but they are simply inadequate in the post-9/11 world" (Flynn 2004, p. 130). Hence there is a need for new types of incentives to encourage infrastructure protection.

But the question of who appropriately bears the cost for enhanced security is a significant one. Some have proposed that the starting point for determining responsibility for business and government should focus on the costs of the security program and its beneficiaries, but even this is not a simple task (see Business Roundtable 2003, pp. 45–48). Innovative solutions, such as the cost recovery program instituted by the Federal Energy Regulatory Commission after September 11, or Environmental Protection Agency grants of $51 million provided to assist water utilities prepare vulnerability assessments and security plans, provide models to encourage greater private sector investment in infrastructure protection (see U.S. GAO 2003a, p. 57). Yet even with government funding of additional ISAC activities, questions arise as to government access to the information shared in the ISAC (Anderson and Starks 2004).

Improving the security of the U.S. homeland requires substantial new investments by both the public and private sectors. The Bush administration's fiscal year 2005 Homeland Security budget proposed $865 million for the Information Analysis and Infrastructure Protection Directorate, an increase of $31 million from fiscal year 2004.[27] While this includes a broad spectrum of measures, some beyond critical infrastructure protection, the figure is clearly dwarfed by the financial costs of securing the vast privately owned and operated critical infrastructure. As noted by the 9/11 Commission, "private sector preparedness is not a luxury; it is a cost of doing business in the post 9/11 world" (National Commission on Terrorist Attacks upon the United States 2004, p. 398). Because little new money has been provided to state and local authorities for infrastructure protection, let alone to the private sector, questions concerning who pays for security will remain problematic.

Consistently, U.S. policy has emphasized the voluntary nature of private sector efforts to protect critical infrastructure. The power outages in August 2003, however, and recent attention to vulnerabilities of chemical and nuclear plants, beg the question of whether voluntary efforts on industry's part alone are sufficient, or whether regulation is necessary to compel the adoption of safeguards. While a 2003 GAO report praised the chemical industry's voluntary security efforts to date, it also raised serious questions as to the adequacy of such efforts (U.S. GAO 2003b). In such high-risk sectors, legislation has been introduced in Congress to establish uniform standards for securing chemical sites and to provide the DHS with authority to enforce such standards.[28] These efforts have so far failed, however, largely due to industry opposition and the administration's continued reliance on voluntary and self-regulatory approaches.

Enhanced regulation of critical infrastructure raises serious questions regarding the desirability, feasibility, and cost of such an approach. Legislation and regulations relevant to infrastructure protection are a patchwork, making efforts to develop a comprehensive regulatory framework, let alone enforce it, complicated.

The Bush administration has vigorously pursued self-regulatory approaches, leaving it to private industry to determine whether, how, and to what degree to protect itself. Government officials cite initiatives such as that of the Self-Storage Association (SSA) as an example of how business can effectively take the lead in setting standards. Concerned that the federal government would impose new requirements following September 11, the SSA put into place new checks to verify customers' identities and ascertain any criminal records; the new procedures were funded through a $7.50 charge per renter for the security check. This "know your customer" system has not been widely utilized yet, but is expected to grow as companies try to preclude mandatory regulation (Uchitelle and Markoff 2004).

Yet a purely voluntary approach by industry alone is not the answer. Public safety demands some minimal degree of standards, and serious questions remain as to the adequacy of existing requirements developed for purposes other than security or protection against terrorism. The 2004 presidential campaign addressed the issue, with Senator John Kerry criticizing the Bush administration's laissez-faire approach to infrastructure protection, arguing for mandatory measures to improve security at high-risk targets such as chemical and nuclear facilities. And while most industry groups favor market-based incentives to increasing security, a recent study by the National Infrastructure Advisory Council indicated that some industry representatives acknowledge that regulation may be needed for certain sectors (Wodele 2004).

Notwithstanding progress within certain industry sectors in adopting voluntary standards, the imperative of securing critical infrastructure requires a more concerted approach—one involving both established standards and increased incentives for investments in security. "Unfortunately, without standards, or even the threat of standards, the private sector will not secure itself."[29]

When the next attack comes, the likely result will be enhanced government regulation. The threat of regulation, therefore, should serve to motivate industry to pursue aggressively self-regulatory efforts. This is an appropriate initial step while the effectiveness of such measures and the need for mandatory requirements in certain sectors are being evaluated and new incentives created. Indeed, increased participation in ISACs is viewed as one indicator that the private sector is moving toward greater self-regulation in critical infrastructure areas (Personick and Patterson 2003, pp. 56–60).

Conclusion

> One of the most dangerous shortcomings in the Administration's homeland security activities to date has been the general absence of measures to strengthen private-market incentives. (Orszag 2003, p. 1)

Prior to the events of September 11, 2001, incremental advancements were achieved in addressing threats to critical infrastructure protection. Since then, some genuine progress has been made to foster public-private cooperation. Frankly, however, much of what has been accomplished amounts to lip service to the idea, without adequate or effective efforts to realize the objective. As was a common theme in the presidential 2004 campaign, the question is not whether Americans are safer, but whether Americans are safe enough. The gap between the rhetoric of creating public-private partnerships to address these security issues, and reality of action to support such efforts, is significant. Much more needs to be done to meet the challenges the United States faces.

There are a number of legitimate reasons for the slow progress—the general inability of government to utilize effectively the private sector, traditional government-industry concerns regarding information sharing, the distraction resulting from the bureaucratic reorganization to create the Department of Homeland Security, and most important, the lack of appropriate incentives to motivate the private sector to embrace critical infrastructure protection. Ironically, the apparent success of the United States in thwarting additional attacks on the homeland may have served to decrease the urgency to act perceived by the private sector. It would be nice if the threat had indeed receded, but terrorism will be a fixture well into the twenty-first century.

Thus a more concerted strategy is needed to encourage the private sector to put into place adequate security measures. A system of public policy incentives—for example, tax incentives, loan programs or grants for investment in protection, cost-recovery measures, government underwriting of insurance—should be developed to harness market forces to provide infrastructure protection.[30] The U.S. government should use its purchasing power to encourage enhanced security, requiring vendors to take steps to make products more secure. Given the enormity of the task, new and creative ideas to promote public-private partnerships must be explored, including new mechanisms and funding.[31]

The national strategy for homeland security acknowledges the need to use "all available policy tools," including legislation, and in some cases regulation, to create incentives for the private sector. But the sense of urgency has diminished, and creative leadership on new approaches is lacking. Now is the time to redouble efforts and devise new approaches. Minimal security standards, with appropriate incentives to reward companies investing in security and partnering with the government, are more likely to be successful than attempting to regulate compliance.

In addition, the government needs to make critical infrastructure protection a higher priority. Understandably, the effort to erect the Department of Homeland Security was an enormous task, but appropriate attention to and leadership on these issues within the DHS has not been forthcoming. Frustration among industry and Congress has mounted, threatening the credibility of current initiatives. Moreover, greater effort needs to be devoted to defining what is "critical." An overly broad understanding of critical infrastructure will actually serve to weaken protection by diffusing efforts and funding.

In short, the government and the private sector both need to work together more effectively. Increased attention to and support of the ISACs, successfully demonstrating how legitimate concerns can be addressed, will promote cooperation and encourage new modes of partnership. New challenges require new thinking, not business as usual. Nothing less than the continued national success and economic well-being of the United States depend on it.

Notes

My views on this issue were informed by my role as assistant secretary of commerce from 1993 to 1997, when I was involved with early efforts by the Clinton administration to engage the private sector on critical infrastructure issues.

1. See, in particular, warnings by the U.S. Commission on National Security in the Twenty-First Century (the Hart-Rudman Commission), two years prior to September 11, 2001, of the likelihood of attacks against U.S. citizens on U.S. soil with heavy casualties; the commission recommended the creation of a national homeland security agency (available at http://www.nssg.gov/reports/reports.htm.).

2. This chapter focuses on U.S. experiences with critical infrastructure protection, as the United States is a forerunner in the field, but the trend of relying on the private sector to secure infrastructure is not limited to the United States. See Dunn and Wigert 2004. My ongoing work includes comparative analysis of other countries' efforts to address critical infrastructure protection issues.

3. It is important to distinguish between homeland security and homeland defense. Homeland security is the concerted national effort to prevent terrorist attacks within the United States, with primary responsibility resting with the Department of Homeland Security. Homeland defense is defined as the military protection of U.S. territory, the domestic population, and critical defense infrastructure against external threats and aggression. The Department of Defense (DoD), through a new assistant secretary of homeland defense, is primarily responsible for homeland defense, as following the September 11 attacks, defense of the homeland was restored as a primary mission of the DoD. See Bowman 2003. Also of note is that most European efforts analogous to homeland security in the U.S. context are referred to as "internal security."

4. Approximately 85 percent of critical infrastructures and key assets were owned and operated by private industry in February 2003 (White House 2003b). While subsequent executive branch documents have not always characterized the amount of critical infrastructure in private hands the same, the figure of 85 percent of critical infrastructure and key assets owned and operated by private industry has become widely quoted and broadly accepted, although no data appear to be available to assess the number. An industry group places private sector ownership and control at "over eighty percent of our critical infrastructure, including various networks, services, and physical facilities that provide us necessities like electronic power, agriculture, and water services" (Business Roundtable 2003).

5. The issue of an effective response to terrorist threats against the homeland raises numerous questions of federalism, and the appropriate role for the state and local levels of government, as well as the private sector. While an important topic that has been the subject of considerable study of late, the state and local issues will not be addressed in this chapter, since the focus is on the private role in protecting infrastructure and the partnership necessary primarily with the U.S. government to achieve this objective.

6. For a discussion of the varying definitions of critical infrastructure, see Moteff, Copeland, and Fischer 2003; and Moteff and Parfomak 2004.

7. The USA Patriot Act (U.S. Public Law no. 107-56, Section 1016(e)) defines critical infrastructure as those "systems and assets, whether physical or virtual, so vital to the United States that the incapacity or destruction of such systems and assets would have a debilitating impact on security, national economic security, national public health or safety, or any combination of those matters."

8. In the most recent listing of critical infrastructure sectors, the oil and gas storage and transportation area was combined with the electric power systems to form an overall energy sector. In addition, information was added to telecommunications to

form a combined information and telecommunications sector. New sectors include agriculture, food, public health, defense-industrial base, chemical industry and hazardous materials, and postal and shipping. See White House 2003b.

9. The broad characterization of critical infrastructure has led some to question whether too expansive a definition may have the effect of actually diluting protection efforts. See Lewis 2003. Because of the preliminary stage that critical infrastructure efforts are currently at, it is not possible to determine if this is in fact the case. Based on other governmental experiences, however, especially in the area of export controls, I believe that it is important to try to identify as precisely as possible which infrastructures and which parts are "truly critical."

10. The Department of Homeland Security has developed a framework to identify vulnerabilities, but it is still in its infancy. Members of Congress who have been briefed on the effort have been critical of the effort, with more than 30,000 potential targets identified. Such a study is an essential first step in helping to prioritize protection efforts, and help decide where available resources should be spent. See Belopotosky (2004).

11. Richard Clarke details the administration's deliberations in developing PDD 63 and related critical infrastructure initiatives in his book *Against All Enemies* (2004, pp. 167–171).

12. According to Carnegie Mellon University's CERT Coordination Center, the number of cyber security incidents has been increasing at an alarming rate—from 20,000 in 2000 to 52,000 in 2001, to 82,000 in 2002, to more than 76,000 in the first six months of 2003 See: http://www.cert.org/annual_rpts/cert_rpt_02.html#intro.

13. See Moteff 2002, p. 10, for a comparison of the two administrations' approaches to critical infrastructure protection.

14. For an overview of issues traditionally addressed by scholars in this context, see Kapstein 1992.

15. See also Friedberg 1992 for a discussion of the history of military-industrial interactions.

16. The PCIS was a private sector initiative to share information and strategies across sectoral lines, and although the federal government is not officially part of the partnership, it liaises (first through CIAO and subsequently DHS) with the group and provides administrative support. The PCIS was incorporated as a nonprofit in 2001, and is operated by companies and associations in each of the critical infrastructure sectors. See http://www.pcis.org/index.cfm.

17. See "About InfraGard" at http://www.infragard.net/about.htm. InfraGard has expanded membership substantially, from 277 in October 2000 to more than 16,409 in April 2005, with members including industry and other government agencies and the academic community. Darcey 2003, p 24.

18. An example of the type of unclassified information disseminated by the government is the DHS's "Information Analysis and Infrastructure Protection Daily Open-Source Infrastructure Report," which is a daily summary and assessment of open source published information concerning critical infrastructure issues, located at http://www.nipc.gov.

19. As of April 2003 the Department of Homeland Security reported that there were sixteen ISACs, including some established for sectors not identified as critical infrastructure. See U.S. General Accounting Office (GAO) 2003a, p. 25. In July 2004 the GAO reported on nine ISACs in critical infrastructure sectors, as well as others (real estate and research and education) and continuing efforts to establish ISACs in agriculture and health care. See U.S. General GAO 2004, pp. 6–7.

20. The FS-ISAC received a $2 million contract from the Treasury Department to enhance security awareness and protect critical infrastructure. FS-ISAC 2003. The Environmental Protection Agency issued a $2 million grant in March 2004 to the Water ISAC to fund operations and increase ISAC membership. U.S. GAO 2004, p. 8.

21. The ISAC Council released a series of white papers in early 2004. See ISAC Council 2004.

22. There appears to be some confusion as to how critical assets are identified, as the DHS's Information Analysis and Infrastructure Directorate reported in April 2004 on its list of 1,700 assets deemed "nationally" critical, which was derived from a database of 33,000 assets considered regionally or locally critical. See Moteff and Parfomak 2004, p. 13.

23. The purpose of the FOIA is to ensure U.S. citizens access to government information. The issue of FOIA exemption for sharing of critical infrastructure information has been an extremely thorny and confused one, with public interest groups opposed to industry for what they view as an overly broad exception to the FOIA that could allow a wider range of information to be protected, and possibly shield owners and operators from liability under environmental, health, tax, or other laws. Critical infrastructure operators, however, contend that current law does not provide certain protection and have advocated in favor of additional clarity. Legislation on both sides of the issue has been introduced in Congress that could have a substantial effect on companies' willingness to provide information to the government. For a thorough discussion of the issues, see Moteff 2003.

24. Officials of the Energy ISAC stated to the General Accounting Office that they have not reported incidents because of the Freedom of Information Act and antitrust concerns. Darcey 2003, p. 26.

25. For a discussion of liability issues and industry concerns, see Personick and Patterson 2003, chap. 3, "Liability for Unsecured Systems and Networks," pp. 35–60.

26. Limited information is available on private sector spending in the United States, but even before September 11, 2001, it was placed at $40–55 billion annually. See Lenain, Bonturi, and Koen 2002, p. 31; and White House 2002, p. 65. See also "Picking the Locks" 2001, which estimated the cyber security market prior to September 11 at $10 billion in products and services, which does include physical security measures.

27. The directorate is the focal point for infrastructure protection efforts within the DHS. See U.S. Department of Homeland Security 2004, pp. 46–47.

28. See legislation introduced by Senator Jon Corzine (D–N.J.) mandating security requirements at certain chemical plants, which died at the end of 2004 as a result of strong industry opposition. The issue was raised as part of the 2004 presidential campaign, with Senator John Kerry criticizing the Bush administration's voluntary approach to chemical and nuclear safety issues.

29. See Flynn 2004, p. 54, for a discussion of how the absence of clearly defined standards actually places companies that invest in protective measures for infrastructure at a competitive disadvantage due to "tragedy of the commons" dilemma. See also pp. 130–131.

30. Peter Orszag (2003, p. 5) describes such measures as antiterrorism subsidies.

31. See, in particular, Flynn 2004, pp. 145–155, for discussion of the merits of the creative idea of a Federal Reserve–like system for homeland security.

PART 3

A Window on the Future

10

Understanding Security Through the Eyes of the Young

Mark A. Boyer, Scott W. Brown,
Michael Butler, Natalie Hudson,
Paula R. Johnson, and Clarisse O. Lima

It has become a truism that conceptions of security have changed over the past several decades and that they continue to evolve in our current world system. Even during the overt militarization of the Cold War, policymakers around the world began to focus attention on the transnational impact of macroeconomic policies. The creation of the European Economic Community and its follow-on organizations was prompted at least partly by a need to provide economic security for the rebuilding European economies. In stark fashion, the first and second oil shocks in the 1970s were catalysts for thinking about new views of security and the policy changes necessary for us to remain secure. Most striking, the terrorist attacks of September 11, 2001, have forced the world community (and especially people in the insular United States) to grapple with threats to security that were once remote geographically and temporally. Nonetheless, a more diverse and open-ended security dialogue has developed across global political entities and across issues traditionally divided into a high- and low-politics dichotomy. Diversity in the security dialogue is possibly best exemplified by the rise of discussions of "human security" throughout the scholarly and policymaking realms, even though much of the recent policy dialogue itself has centered on countering the terrorist threat.

The changing discourse of security also highlights the notion that security, or at least the ways that each of us perceive it, is a construct of our socialization processes and the security environment in which we live. Individuals in war-torn regions are more likely to list physical safety as a higher priority than economic prosperity. Those in developing societies are more likely to emphasize basic human needs; and citizens of developed countries may emphasize "luxury" conceptions of security, such as economic prosperity, in their own views of what is important for feeling secure. In all instances, people's perceptions of security are conditioned by the physical, social, economic, and even emotional setting of the world around them.

Our examination focuses on understanding whether or not the evolving security discourse in our field reflects the reality of security perceptions held by people within U.S. society. We begin by briefly reviewing some of the scholarly literature on evolving conceptions of security and then turn to an examination of conceptions of security held by today's youth (and tomorrow's leaders).

Security in an Evolving Global Context

Much has been written over the past several decades about changing conceptions of security. But little consensus exists about the nature of security today. Edward Newman argues that "whilst our basic human needs—at least in biological terms—have changed little, our conceptualizations of security, and our approaches to achieving and maintaining security, have" (2001, p. 239). Similarly, Michael Klare and Yogesh Chandrani argue that "we have seen the emergence of entire new *categories* of security challenges: environmental degradation, resource scarcities, transnational criminal activities, mass human migrations, and so on" (1998, p. vii, emphasis in original). James Rosenau suggests in the broadest terms that the complexity and interdependency of human affairs have demanded an understanding of security that goes beyond the "simple matter of maintaining military readiness and effective international alliances" (1994, p. 255). The one common theme throughout these eclectic studies of security is the notion that we must go beyond military and territorial conceptions of security if we are to apply the concept accurately to contemporary problems from the global to the local. To do this as scholars and ultimately to incorporate these notions into policy are not a simple task, however, because of the entrenched frameworks—theoretical, conceptual, and political—that surround the term "security." As James Der Derian states, it is no surprise that security is the "preeminent concept of international relations. . . . No other concept in international relations packs the metaphysical punch, or commands the disciplinary power, of 'security'" (1995, pp. 24–25).

The voices of these new conceptions of security are even more prominent when we account for the variety of dichotomies that exist within contemporary world politics—for example, male/female and North/South. Looking at one of these dichotomies—gender—provides us with some insight into the diversity of security perceptions and their socially constructed bases. Many voices have been heard on the importance of understanding gendered perspectives in global politics and the role women can play in widening the security debate. For instance, Angela King, Assistant Secretary-General in the

UN, argues that the introduction of gender as an important variable in the security debate:

> has led to the assumption that if women were involved in a sufficient number in peace, security and conflict resolutions, these definitions would be transformed and so would all related policies, activities, and institutional arrangements. Broadening both these concepts and participation in conflict resolution would open new opportunities for dialogue. It would replace the traditional model of negotiations aimed at ceasefire or crisis management by a real conflict resolution model, where the root causes of conflict are addressed, all aspects of human security are taken into consideration, and the process of negotiation is inclusive involving representatives of civil society, including women's organizations. (2001, p. vii)

Moreover, a recent interview-based study by Sally Reis (1998) suggests that women involved in the security policymaking process ask different questions and thus force different issues to the policy foreground than their male counterparts. This broadly implies that as participation in the policymaking and knowledge-building processes is broadened across gender, socioeconomic, or other lines, conceptions of security will also broaden, becoming more diverse and less centered on traditional political-military concepts.

In many ways, the term "complex insecurity" can help center our understanding of the security challenges facing the world system today. Davis Bobrow (1996) argues that as enemy-based security challenges have declined in the post–Cold War world, the complexity of the threats remains high and policy structures possessed by states may not be well-suited (at least not yet) for coping with those challenges.[1] In today's transnational policy environment, this centers policy concerns on threats, such as terrorism, environmental degradation, disease, and resource scarcity, that do not emerge solely from a geopolitical entity in the traditional sense. Threats thus seem to have different and even multiple sources compared to those of the past.

Building on the concept of security introduced in the United Nations Development Programme's *Human Development Report* (1994), Newman and many others assert that human security "seeks to place the individual—or people collectively—as the referent of security rather than, although not necessarily in opposition to, institutions such as territory and state sovereignty." This concept "reflects the impact of values and norms in international relations" and "embraces a range of alliances, actors and agendas that have taken us beyond the traditional scope of international politics and diplomacy" (Newman 2001, pp. 239–240).[2] Caroline Thomas echoes these concerns by arguing that security is achieved only when basic human needs are met and "meaningful participation in the life of the community" and human dignity are realized (1999, p. 3). Bruce Russett also makes this normative argument, but also broadens its institutional setting, by stating that "the focus of the post–Cold War United Nations . . . should be on *human security*—not just the security of states . . . but the security of populations within states" (1995, xi, emphasis in original). The question that remains to be answered (and that our analysis partly addresses below) is whether Newman (2001, p. 241) is correct in stating that shifts in attitudes, and ultimately longer-term shifts in behavior, are placing increasing value on human rights and human needs within the "model of human security."

In short, security remains a contested concept. As Terry Terriff and colleagues (1999, p. 2) argue, "what is in dispute is not so much the concept of security *per se* as the sorts of specification that are made about security." The following analysis focuses on these divergent concepts by examining perceptions of security held by young people and how those perceptions might translate into concepts and policy in later years.

The GlobalEd Project Research Environment

To provide a context for our data collection and analysis, it is important to discuss briefly the experimental environment in which we collected our data. The GlobalEd Project is a research project examining gender differences in knowledge, attitudes, and behaviors (KABs) related to international studies, the use of technology, and student learning. GlobalEd research is based on the premise that observed gender differences are socially constructed and not biologically driven.[3] Thus we concur with J. S. Goldstein's distinction (2001) between "sex" as the biological distinction and "gender" as the culturally driven difference. We accordingly focus on and use the term "gender" in our analyses. As a result, the sample that we examine in this study—middle school social studies students ranging in age from twelve to fourteen—should, in theory, provide a rich sample for examination that it is relatively uncorrupted in terms of the gender differences that are often masked by women decisionmakers who have been socialized into male structures through their later educational and career processes. However, given space constraints, the data examined in this chapter are not broken down by gender, but the reader is welcome to contact the authors for more information about the gender aspects of the project.

The GlobalEd Project has its roots in the work of Project ICONS, developed at the University of Maryland in the early 1980s for college-level political science students. The middle school simulation component was launched in 1998 at the University of Connecticut and has been more fully developed under the auspices of the GlobalEd Project (Florea et al. 2003; Brown et al. 2003).

Students involved in GlobalEd are assigned their country six to eight weeks before the simulation begins and are given concrete analytical tasks related to five broad topical areas (human rights, global environment, conflict and cooperation, international economics, and world health) presented in the simulation scenario. Students are told that their country has to "stay in character" (e.g., remain consistent with the policy positions and core national and cultural value systems of their assigned country), while attempting to develop comprehensive policy responses to particular problems within these five issue areas. The scenario for the simulation is set six months into the future.[4]

Students are instructed to learn about the values and customs of their respective countries prior to the simulation, so that they are prepared to make appropriate "in-character" responses. Most simulations include ten to fifteen country-teams, and students are assigned by their teachers to become "experts" on a particular issue group. Within the GlobalEd Project context, the issue groups are organized along gender lines, with all-female, all-male, and mixed-gender issue groups formed within each simulation. Thus, within a particular simulation issue, GlobalEd has sought to obtain a relative balance of all three gender groupings; at the very least, in a given simulation, there should be at least one all-female human rights group, one all-male human rights group, and one mixed-gender group. Students do not know the "gender" of the other groups with whom they are negotiating.

A simulation lasts a total of five weeks and students participate each school day in the simulation, whether through online conferences, e-mails to other countries, searching the Web for information, or preparing diplomatic documents and responses. Additionally, students are able to use their own computers from home or other public access points to draft messages, review data, and collaborate within their own country or with other countries. There are no student names exchanged between countries, nor are any references made to the gender of specific student negotiators. Only names such as "Canada (human rights committee)" are used to communicate with, for example, "Nigeria (human rights committee)." Since the simulation software provides all e-mail and conferencing access, the anonymity of the participants is maintained between countries. Students are restricted to the use of the simulation software for interclass/intercountry communications. During the game, students must interact with participants from other schools using the technology tools within the simulation in order to discuss, debate, and negotiate real international issues.

As mentioned above, the GlobalEd research environment allows us to collect data from online surveys (before and after the simulation experience) on a variety of KAB indicators. One of these sets of measures is the focus of our analysis below. In addition, the issue-based gender groupings allow project staff to analyze negotiating strategies through a coding scheme first published in "Negotiating from Mars to Venus" (Florea et al. 2003). For more information about all the facets of the project, the reader is encouraged to visit http://www.globaled.uconn.edu.

Why the Ideas of Young People Matter

One of the primary themes of this volume is the changing nature of security in recent decades and most particularly since September 11, 2001. Implied in this endeavor is the next step in our thinking: a possible forecast for evolving conceptions of security in the coming years. Unfortunately for scholars and policymakers, we are rarely in a position to forecast political phenomena in accurate ways, though the topic continues to be of major interest in our field.[5] We do, however, possess what is arguably a hazy window on the future of security conceptions, provided to us by the attitudes of adolescents regarding security and international relations. We argue that an examination of these attitudes is relevant and less hazy than some might expect and is thus worthy of close examination. We hold this view for two primary reasons.

The first reason centers on the reality that today's adolescents are tomorrow's voters and decisionmakers. Democratic theory is instructive in this regard, as it reminds us that the assumption and discharge of responsibility in the public arena in the long and short term can only be conducted successfully with the participation of informed citizens and leaders, who as a whole provide what Jurgen Habermas (1996) characterizes as an unimpeded deliberative sphere. Ian Shapiro's interpretation is even more to the point: "democrats are committed to rule by the people . . . the people are sovereign; in all matters of collective life they rule over themselves" (1996, p. 224). Though democratic practice often does not measure up to democratic ideals, this deviation hardly obviates the need for systematic analysis of individual political views and preferences in democratic societies.

This need is no less great with respect to *future* generations of citizens and leaders, and perhaps may be greater, given the relative paucity of explorations of this kind; after all, it is precisely the age cohort studied here who will soon inherit the burdens of democratic citizenship and political and economic leadership in U.S. society (whether we like it or not). As is clear from all of the selections in this volume, security is evolving in complex directions and those who are "only kids" will in fact determine society's security tomorrow.

But this generational evolutionary rationale is incomplete if there is little relationship between the attitudes they hold today and the ones they will espouse tomorrow. As the following brief discussion will show, this relationship is quite robust and indicates that their current attitudes will be relatively good predictors of the trajectory of security perceptions in the future. Along these lines, an extensive and interdisciplinary body of literature dealing with attitude formation and change in the area of political socialization has chronicled the viability of this connection, frequently referred to as the "impressionable years hypothesis" (Krosnick and Alwin 1989). Notably, many of the seminal studies exploring this hypothesis have explicitly targeted school-age children, largely because of an interest in better understanding the attitudes of those members of society who had previously been assumed to represent a "blank slate" with regard to political attitudes (Greenberg 1970).

The emergence of a modern political socialization "school" has been attributed to the publication of sociologist Herbert Hyman's *Political Socialization* (1959). Other contributions to this field focused on the role of political socialization in adolescence as serving a crucial, system-maintaining function in the U.S. political system (see Key 1961; Mitchell 1962; and Lane 1962). Perhaps colored by the era of good-feelings during the Eisenhower years, early researchers of political socialization sought to explore the underlying reasons behind the exceedingly high degrees of loyalty to nation and the near-absence of any attitudes exemplary of "fragmentation politics" in the United States. A great deal of attention during this period was paid to attitudes among U.S. schoolchildren about the nation and its symbols and institutions (see especially Lane 1962).

Building on this work, Fred Greenstein (1965) produced a more comprehensive study of the origins of childhood attitudes and orientations toward politics and political authority. Greenstein's findings demonstrated the strong emotional or affective appeal of the content of political socialization upon children, an appeal making the associated (favorable) messages relating to authority figures and the political system extremely durable and resistant to change. His work suggests that the affective component of political socialization lingers well into adulthood, remaining robust even in the face of the introduction of contradictory stimuli with respect to political figures and political life. Greenstein's findings were further confirmed by Robert Hess and Judith Torney (1967), who found what they called a "bond" on perceptions of particular figures and institutions of government rather than the more generic concepts of "authority figures" and "system."

David Easton and Jack Dennis (1967, 1969) were among the first to examine political efficacy as not only a norm within democratic societies, but also a socialized disposition among school-age children. In the process, they attempted to elaborate upon the linkage stretching from early political socialization through basic political orientations to adolescent and adult orientations, and the role of socialization processes in contributing to system "persistence."[6] In an important distinction from some of their predecessors, they found that this linkage was two-way and multidimensional rather than passive and monolithic.

Easton and Dennis's findings also indicate that the process of acquiring one's political worldview is not simply a matter of accepting a preceding generation's orientations outright, or what they called the "transmission belt" model (1969, p. 11). Independent learning, direct experience, and modeling the attitudes of other nonadults are also important mechanisms throughout childhood and adolescence, helping define the acquisition of political attitudes and explaining their resilience into adulthood. This rejection of the "transmission belt" model was further supported by extensive studies of political attitudes and values demonstrating large shifts in young-aged cohorts and negligible shifts in middle-aged and older cohorts, indicating both the importance of independent learning and experience as well as the fertile attitudinal ground that childhood and adolescence represent within the parameters of the "impressionable years" hypothesis (Converse 1976; Markus 1979; Glenn 1980).

More recent studies have further confirmed the viability, as well as extended the scope, of the "impressionable years" hypothesis. These studies demonstrated not only the stability of political attitudes acquired during youth upon transition to adulthood (Krosnick and Alwin 1989), but also the degree that attitudes acquired during childhood and adolescence are functionally related to relevant action during both youth and adulthood. Though the introduction of social and contextual variables during adulthood can and do modify and in limited cases may sever the linkage between attitudes and attitude-relevant behavior (Krosnick 1988; Krosnick et al. 1993), attitude-behavior consistency has been shown to be robust in cases where the attitude in question pertains to a "vested interest," that is, an object of great perceived personal consequence (Crano 1997). Given this finding, it is relatively safe to assume that *security* (whether at the individual, state, or global level) registers as a vested interest for most individuals, lending further credence to our rationale for why the knowledge and attitudes of children toward security deserve attention.

This portrayal of political socialization as a process with significant effects lasting well into adulthood raises three important implications for those concerned with the origins and transmission of political attitudes. First, the key to the effectiveness of political socialization (at least within the U.S. context) lies in the fact that it offers many points of access to the political system and process. These access points help to generate in childhood the diffuse support essential for generating nonspecific feelings of loyalty and obligation to system and process that carry over into adulthood and serve as critical linchpins for any democratic society.[7] Second, cognitive as well as affective images play an important role in the connection between school-aged children and their orientations toward the political system and political issues in later life. The findings of Easton and Dennis, in particular, concerning the cognitive dimension of political learning, underscore the third implication; namely, their rejection of the "concentric circles" model (1969, p. 103) once dominant in the literature and in school curricula. Whereas children were once presumed to broaden their range of political awareness, knowledge, and interest outward from the concerns of their immediate neighborhood and school in tedious and sequentially ordered stages, more recent research has demonstrated greater variability in the absorption of ideas and expression of views on political matters, suggesting that there is no linear connection from close to distant objects, or from simple to complex ideas, and hence no rationale for limiting exposure along either dimension. It also lends further credence to the notion that individuals construct their own unique knowledge base and identity.

Each of these implications, in turn, bears striking relevance for testing our own preconceived notions as academicians about the changing nature of security in the wider populace. If political socialization does in fact imprint relatively early in life, then the political culture (and the security perceptions it generates) that sustains democracy and citizenship among current and future generations is an important set of concepts to study. We turn now to our findings about these perceptions and what implications they may have for future perceptions and policies in the security realm.

Data and Analysis

This portion of the chapter examines data from surveys taken from a sample of U.S. middle school students during winter 2002–2003. The surveys were administered before and after the students participated in the GlobalEd simulation. Drawing on the analytical approach employed by Scott Brown and Frederick King (2000) and Scott Brown and colleagues (2003), our analysis focuses on the knowledge, attitudes, and behaviors of the students involved in the simulation program. Based on the pioneering work of B. S. Bloom and colleagues (1956), the KAB evaluation approach focuses the researcher's attention on three dimensions of learning: cognitive (what does the person know?); affective (attitudes; how does the person feel about the topic?); and behavior (performance; what can the person do related to the topic?). The three survey questions we examine in this chapter focus on student interpretations of what is perceived as important in attaining a desirable level of personal, national, and global security. The total sample size was n = 349.

This chapter's appendix displays the exact wording of the three questions, focusing on personal security (question 1), national security (question 2), and global security (question 3). Participants were asked to rank order the three items (from a set of choices) they perceived to be most important for attaining security in each sense. For each question, we have generated two graphs displaying the responses to the question. The first graph shows data for respondents' first choice selections for the most important concept for security, while the second shows the total number of respondents choosing a concept as either a first, second, or third choice (thus the sum of all three possible choices for a particular security concept). Each graph also displays two horizontal bars for each concept. The first bar represents the presurvey responses and the second bar represents the postsurvey responses. Displaying the two bars allows us to speculate on the impact of the simulation experience on student attitudes about security. In addition, chi-square results are included for each graph to determine if the differences between pre- and postsurvey responses are statistically significant.

Perceptions of Personal Security

Figures 10.1A and 10.1B display the responses to our personal security question, with 10.1A showing the first choice selections and 10.1B showing the summed choices across all three possible rankings. Figure 10.1A shows the dominance of basic human-need concerns for personal security. Shelter ranked the highest among the choices, while education, control of one's future (in the presurvey), and the two personal safety choices (freedom from physical abuse and ability to defend oneself) also received relatively higher levels of support than other responses. These results are echoed, and even amplified, in Figure 10.1B, with money, adequate food, and available medical attention showing higher numbers of responses when shown in aggregate across all three ranking choices.

Also in Figure 10.1A, we see that only shelter and freedom from mental abuse showed statistically significant increases from pre- to postsurvey, while control over one's future showed a significant decrease. The results of the chi-square analyses for the different response patterns from pre- to postsurvey, when rankings were collapsed across the top three ranks (Figure 10.1B), did not reveal any statistically significant differences.

These personal security results, then, demonstrate a heavy emphasis on basic needs among this sample of students, even though we would expect that most of our respondents have few worries about the basic daily needs in their own lives. While the demographics of our sample are quite reflective of the overall U.S. population, U.S. middle school students as a whole should be less concerned about basic human needs than students from many other countries. It would be interesting to administer this same set of surveys among developing-world youth to see if the basic human-needs emphasis is even more dramatic in that setting.

Perceptions of National Security

Turning to perceptions of national security needs, Figures 10.2A and 10.2B display the responses for that question. Most striking and certainly in line with the overarching themes in this volume, a strong national economy is far and away the dominant first choice selection in Figure 10.2A, with over 30 percent of the respondents selecting it as the most important factor for national security. Only good diplomatic relations with other countries, freedom from attack, and a strong military received more than 10 percent of the first choice selections.

The patterns from the first choice data are echoed in the aggregate results shown in Figure 10.2B. The choice for a strong national economy was selected

Figure 10.1A   Most Important for Personal Security

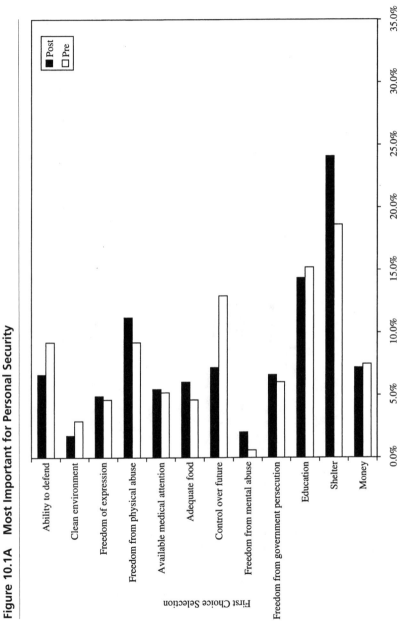

Figure 10.1B   Aggregate of Top Three Choices for Personal Security

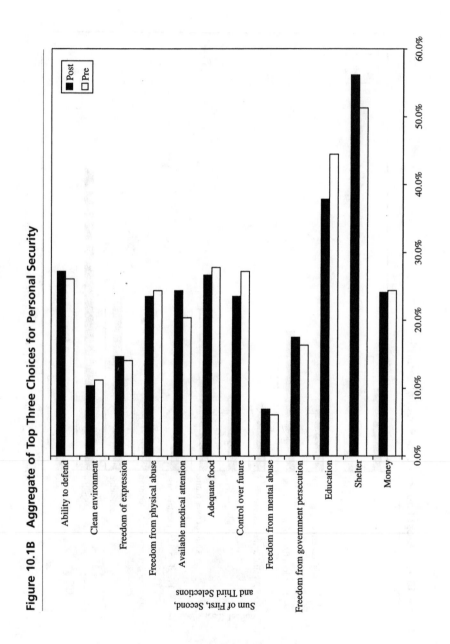

by 57 percent of respondents as one of the three most important factors for national security. Adequate health care (in the presurvey), freedom from attack, and a strong military all showed top-three support above 30 percent, with good diplomatic relations close to that threshold at 29.5 percent in both the pre- and postsurveys.

Regarding the changes from pre- to postsurvey results, only the choice for a quality educational system showed a significant increase, while the choice for a strong military showed a significant decrease. Intuitively, throughout the simulation experience, the students are continually sensitized to the need for research and data gathering as essential for successful negotiations. Thus it is not surprising that they come out of the experience placing a higher value on education as an element of security, even if it still registers lower relative to other security choices. In addition, diplomacy and peaceful conflict resolution are the primary focus on the GlobalEd simulation experience, so it is not surprising that the need for a strong military is somewhat less emphasized in the postsurvey than in the presurvey. The chi-square analyses for the aggregate rankings in Figure 10.2B revealed four significant differences: increases for a quality educational system ($p < 0.001$) and adequate food supplies ($p < 0.001$), and decreases for democratic government ($p < 0.05$) and adequate health care ($p < 0.01$).

In sum, the results for our national security question clearly show the dominance of economics in security conceptions for our sample. But they also show the duality that continues to exist in present-day national and world affairs about the value of the military as an essential tool for security maintenance. It is also worth noting that these surveys were administered in December 2002 (presurvey) and February 2003 (postsurvey) during the workup to the Bush administration's intervention in Iraq. So even though the students were being sensitized through their research into contemporary international affairs in the popular press, they still held the national economy at a distinctly higher level than the military and even showed a significant decline placed on the value of democratic government as important for security.[8] This lends some credence to the notion that economic drivers for security have become more entrenched over the past several decades.

Perceptions of Global Security

Moving to perceptions of global security, a number of different ideas emerge than seen in the previous two sets of figures. Figure 10.3A parallels the national security responses quite clearly, especially with the dominance of the responses for a strong global economy. Not surprisingly in the post–September 11, 2001, context and in the midst of the pre–Iraq War press attention, eliminating weapons of mass destruction (WMD) ranked second in importance to the economy, even if at much lower levels as a first choice selection.

Figure 10.2A   Most Important for National Security

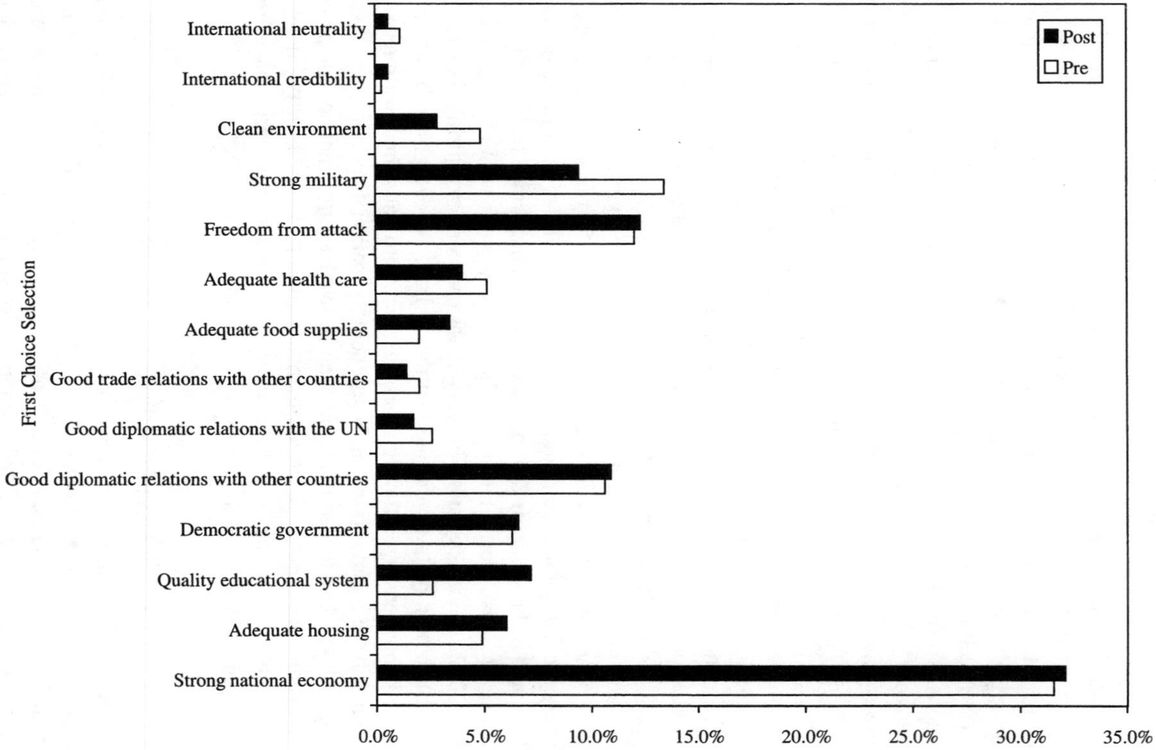

Figure 10.2B   Aggregate of Top Three Choices for National Security

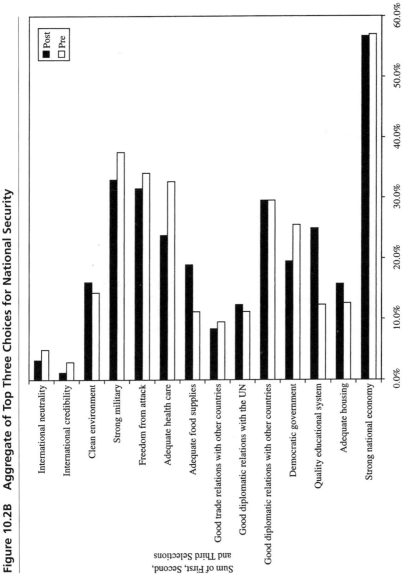

It is also worth noting the relatively high first choice responses for education (in the postsurvey), democratic global governance (in the presurvey), and a strong and effective UN.

The picture changes somewhat, as shown in Figure 10.3B, when the responses are aggregated across the three levels of importance. A strong global economy is now rivaled by eliminating WMD. Put simply, this means that while fewer students saw WMD as a top priority item in contrast to a strong global economy, WMD ranked very strongly as a second and third choice among our sample. Interestingly enough, it is also worth noting that the number of responses that might be interpreted as "traditional realist" values ranked relatively low on this scale. In particular, a strong United States and strong major world powers ranked rather low compared to the other choices available. This might suggest that even though WMD was at the forefront of our respondents' concerns for global security, they also perceived unilateral efforts to deal with security as less important than other strategies for combating the threat.

A number of other interesting issues emerge from Figure 10.3B, especially as we examine the changes that occurred for the question from pre- to postsurvey. Again, increases are shown for education ($p < 0.001$), adequate food supplies ($p < 0.05$), and a strong and effective international military force ($p < 0.001$) as first choice selections, while a smaller increase is found for a strong and effective UN, though this change was not statistically significant. Noticeable decreases were found for democratic global governance ($p < 0.001$), a strong United States ($p < 0.01$), adequate health care ($p < 0.001$), a clean natural environment ($p < 0.05$), and positive trade relations between countries ($p < 0.05$). These results suggest some continued support for what might be considered "nontraditional" aspects of security even when we move beyond the personal or national levels. Implicitly, there also seems to be greater support for multilateral approaches to global problems than there is for unilateral ones. These results are roughly echoed in the aggregate results, with significant increases shown for education ($p < 0.001$), a strong and effective UN ($p < 0.05$), adequate food supplies ($p < 0.001$), and strong major world powers ($p < 0.05$), and with decreases shown for democratic global governance ($p < 0.001$) and adequate health care ($p < 0.001$).

Conclusion

All of the chapters in this volume have highlighted the changing nature of security in the contemporary world system. Clearly, economic concerns have become more important relative to other, more traditional conceptions of security, even if traditional conceptions remain prominent in the ways that many view the world and their place within it. Taking these conceptions at face

Figure 10.3A   Most Important for Global Security

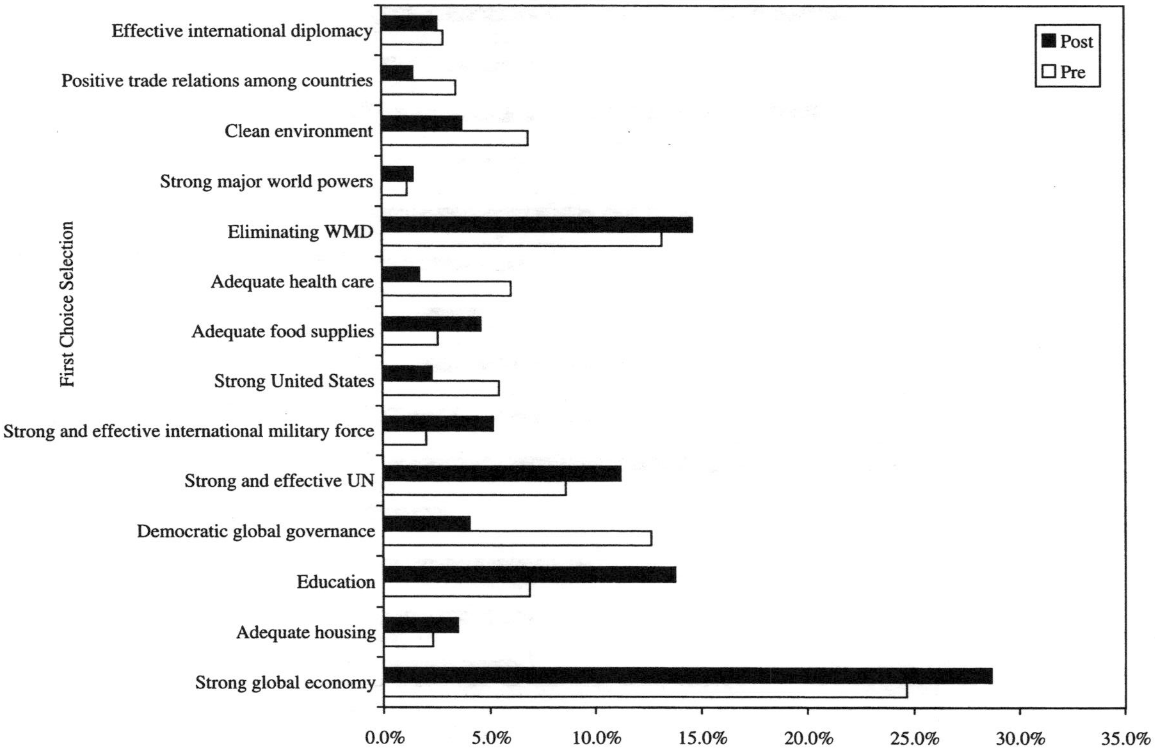

Figure 10.3B   Aggregate of Top Three Choices for Global Security

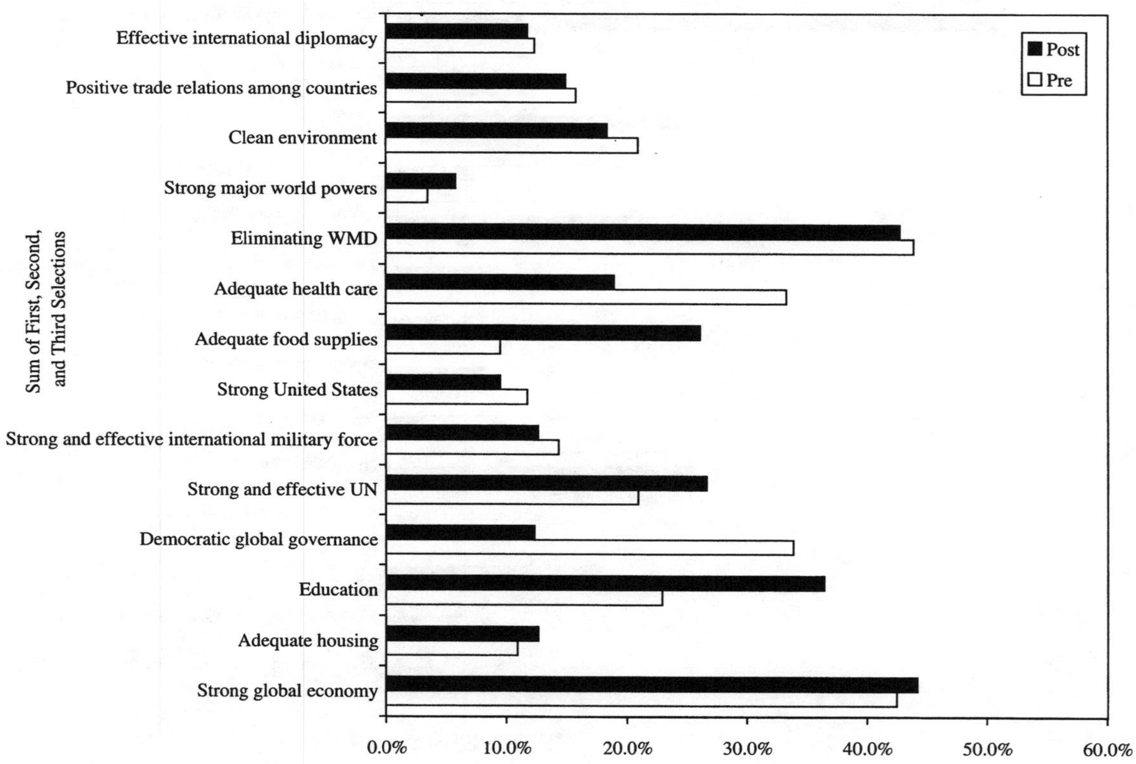

value thus means that states in the contemporary system must continue to adapt to the changing security environment in which they operate and to the changing perceptions held by their citizens. But policy adaptation becomes problematic if our decisionmakers have little guidance about the trajectory of future policy concerns and citizen demands.

The survey data discussed in this chapter provide a window on the future of security perceptions. Research in the political socialization field tells us that a link exists between attitudes held in adolescence and attitudes held in adulthood. In addition, because the students of today will become the citizens and leaders of tomorrow, what they think matters if our current cadre of policymakers are to develop long-term approaches to the complex national and global problems that face the United States in the coming years. So along these lines, what do the data tell us about the future of security?

First, the security perceptions that our sample identified suggest that students value human-centered security quite highly. This is clear from both the personal security question and the global security question, even if somewhat less so for the national security question. Second, the importance of economic security is clear throughout our data. In fact, economic security received by far the highest frequency of responses on both the national and global security questions. This indicates that the students in our sample may indeed be internalizing the new security discourse that emphasizes economic issues and, more broadly, concerns about human needs.

Third, military conceptions of security are still important, even if apparently secondary to other factors in student evaluations. This may be an artifact of the reality that students in the United States live in a relatively safe national security environment compared to what similar-aged students experience in countries like Israel, Kosovo, or East Timor. Still, given the timing of our surveys during the media-charged months prior to the 2003 war in Iraq, it is quite striking that military factors did not rank higher in importance. Nonetheless, the threat of WMD for global security showed a continued prominence of military threats to security, even if they are from a somewhat nontraditional source.

It is also worth briefly examining some roughly comparative data from adult samples to put the student results into context with historical attitudes on similar topics. Tables 10.1A and 10.1B display the results from two questions asked from 1978 to 2002 as part of the Chicago Council on Foreign Relations studies: identification of the two or three biggest problems facing the United States at that time, and identification of the two or three biggest *foreign policy* problems facing the United States at that time. We have condensed the survey results by only showing items that were selected by at least 10 percent of the respondents in a single year during the series. As these tables show, economic issues dominate the identified "problems," with other issues such as crime (on the domestic front), dealings with Russia, and the Middle East situation also gaining and losing importance. Notably, Iraq only appears to have

Table 10.1A   "What do you feel are the two or three biggest problems facing the country today?"

Issues	1978[a] (%)	1982 (%)	1986 (%)	1990 (%)	1994 (%)	1998 (%)	2002 (%)	Change in % Points (1998–2002)
Terrorism	n.a.	n.a.	n.a.	n.a.	n.a.	n.a.	36	+36
Economy (unspecified)	n.a.	18	10	16	10	11	22	+11
Education (improving our schools)	4	2	5	8	12	15	11	–4
Defense (national security)	5	3	2	1	*	1	10	+9
Unemployment (low wages/ recession)	19	64	26	10	20	9	9	0
Immorality (ethics in society, moral decline, decline in religion, pornography)	2	6	7	7	8	11	8	–3
Drug abuse	1	3	27	30	18	21	7	–14
Health care/insurance (high medical costs, Medicare increase)	5	1	2	5	19	8	7	–1
Crime (violence, hate crimes, killings in schools)	9	16	10	15	42	26	6	–20
Poverty (hunger, homelessness)	3	2	10	13	15	11	6	–5
Dissatisfaction with government (unqualified politicians, corruption in government, lack of leadership)	8	7	5	18	9	8	6	–2
Middle East situation (unspecified)	1	2	1	11	*	1	4	+3

continues

been important during the early 1990s, and by the late 1990s and into 2002 was of little importance to the average respondent. What this comparison highlights, though, is that our findings for middle school students are roughly similar to those for the adult population today, and both samples appear to be in line with the broadening security discourse discussed above. Either this, or

Table 10.1A continued

Issues	1978[a] (%)	1982 (%)	1986 (%)	1990 (%)	1994 (%)	1998 (%)	2002 (%)	Change in % Points (1998–2002)
Taxes (high taxes, tax reform)	18	6	6	10	5	6	2	−4
Budget deficit (failure to balance budget, national debt, excessive government spending)	9	5	12	30	9	4	2	−2
Inflation (high prices, value of the dollar, decline in purchase power)	67	35	8	6	2	2	1	−1
Nuclear war (nuclear threat, freeze, fallout)	n.a.	9	12	1	*	*	1	+1
The president (poor leadership, isn't doing his job, impeachment)	n.a.	n.a.	n.a.	n.a.	n.a.	12	1	−11
Oil crisis (cost of oil, energy crisis)	11	3	1	8	*	n.a.	1	+1
Other domestic problems	15	18	18	3	2	*	3	+3
Other foreign problems								
Policy/international problems	1	2	12	*	1	2	2	0
Total	217	237	235	242	243	205	204	

Source: Worldviews 2002, U.S. 9/11 Key Findings Topline Data; project by Chicago Council on Foreign Relations in coordination with the German Marshall Fund of the United States, pp. 5–9 (http://www.worldviews.org).

Notes: Totals exceed 100 percent due to multiple responses. Only problems that received at least 10 percent support (or more) at any given time are shown (n = 1,106).

a. The 1978 question differed slightly. It read the same as the current question but also included the phrase "that you would like to see the Federal government do something about."

n.a. = not available

* = less than 0.5%

the security discourse was never really as narrow as Cold War policymakers and analysts have led us to believe.

Last, as educators, one of our goals is to help our students to begin thinking about the challenges that confront them as they move into adulthood and take on roles as citizens and policymakers. Our data suggest that the development of global studies programs that allow students to engage in complex dis-

Table 10.1B   "What do you feel are the two or three biggest foreign policy problems facing the country today?"

Issues	1978[a] (%)	1982 (%)	1986 (%)	1990 (%)	1994 (%)	1998 (%)	2002 (%)	Change in % Points (1998–2002)
Terrorism	n.a.	n.a.	20	2	1	12	33	+21
Middle East situation (unspecified)	20	19	7	21	3	8	12	+4
Foreign aid (too much sent to other countries, don't pay us back, help our own first)	18	16	9	18	16	7	8	+1
Stay out of affairs of other countries	11	8	5	6	19	7	7	0
Immigration (illegal aliens)	*	3	3	1	12	3	7	+4
Arms control (nuclear weapons, too much military equipment sold or given to other countries)	7	13	16	2	3	7	5	−2
War (threat of war, threat of nuclear war)	n.a.	11	8	8	3	4	4	0
Oil problems (relations with OPEC nations, dependency on oil-producing countries, need to develop energy resources)	11	6	2	14	1	*	4	+4

continues

cussions of the issues that face the world today can indeed have an impact on the way they perceive the world around them. The differences between our pre- and postsurvey results show that students' minds are not entirely made up about the issues of the day, though the basic outlines seem quite stable across the issues. We are thus faced with a normative choice about what we should be teaching our students about the world. They are certainly still constructing their worldviews, and what they learn and how they think about world affairs will have manifest results in the ways of war and peace in the coming generations. And the views they form and hold today will be quite similar to the ones they use to make decisions a generation from now.

Table 10.1B continued

Issues	1978[a] (%)	1982 (%)	1986 (%)	1990 (%)	1994 (%)	1998 (%)	2002 (%)	Change in % Points (1998–2002)
Iraq (Saddam Hussein, invasion of Kuwait)	n.a.	n.a.	n.a.	18	11	4	3	−1
World economy	2	2	1	3	2	11	3	−8
Balance of payments (trade deficit, too much money going out of country, import of foreign products)	12	13	15	14	6	10	2	−8
Dealings with Russia	13	15	22	3	3	4	1	−3
Latin/South/ Central America	2	5	10	2	*	*	*	0
Our relationship with Haiti	n.a.	n.a.	n.a.	n.a.	10	n.a.	0	0
Don't know	21	16	16	13	14	21	11	−10
Miscellaneous	7	10	7	3	9	14	5	−9
Total	165	173	181	178	184	157	174	

Source: Worldviews 2002, U.S. 9/11 Key Findings Topline Data; project by Chicago Council on Foreign Relations in coordination with the German Marshall Fund of the United States, pp. 9–11 (http://www.world-views.org/).

Notes: Totals exceed 100 percent due to multiple responses. Only problems that received at least 10 percent support (or more) at any given time are shown (n = 1,116).

a. The 1978 question differed slightly. It read the same as the current question but also included the phrase "that you would like to see the Federal government do something about."

n.a. = not available

* = less than 0.5%

Appendix

Global Security Survey Questions

In international relations, the term "security" refers to a feeling of safety or freedom from harm. In the next three questions, you are asked to choose which three items are most important for your security, for the security of a country, and for the security of the whole world. Please choose three items from the list, ranking what you think is the most important as #1, the second most important as #2, and the third most important as #3.

1. Which of the following items do you think are important in making you feel *personally* secure and safe? (place a #1 next to the most important, #2 next to the second most important, and #3 next to the third most important)

___ Money	___ Adequate food
___ Shelter (housing)	___ Available medical attention
___ Education	___ Freedom from physical abuse or attack
___ Freedom from government persecution	___ Freedom of expression
___ Freedom from mental abuse	___ A clean natural environment
___ Control over your future	___ The ability to defend yourself

OTHER: _____

2. Which of the following items do you think are important to the security and safety of the *country* you live in? (place a #1 next to the most important, #2 next to the second most important, and #3 next to the third most important)

___ A strong economy	___ Adequate food supplies
___ Adequate housing	___ Adequate health care
___ A quality educational system	___ Freedom from attack
___ A democratic government	___ A strong military
___ Good diplomatic relations with other countries	___ A clean natural environment
___ Good diplomatic relations with the UN	___ International credibility
___ Good trade relations with other countries	___ International neutrality

OTHER: _____

3. Which of the following items do you think are important to the security and safety of the *world* as a whole? (place a #1 next to the most important, #2 next to the second most important, and #3 next to the third most important)

___ A strong global economy	___ Adequate food supplies
___ Adequate housing	___ Adequate health care
___ Education	___ Eliminating weapons of mass destruction
___ Democratic global governance	___ Strong major world powers
___ A strong and effective UN	___ A clean natural environment
___ A strong and effective international military force	___ Positive trade relations between countries
___ A strong United States	___ Effective international diplomacy

OTHER: _____

Notes

All authors are members of the GlobalEd Project staff. The project (fully titled *The GlobalEd Project: An Experimental Web-Based Study of Gender Differences in Group Decision Making and Negotiation Skills*) was funded by a three-year grant from the U.S. Department of Education, Office of Educational Research and Improvement (OERI) (the OERI was recently renamed the Institute for Educational Sciences [IES]), OERI Project no. ED-ERI-84.30ST. More information about GlobalEd can be obtained at http://www.globaled.uconn.edu. The opinions and positions expressed here are those of the authors and do not necessarily represent the position of the U.S. Department of Education. Correspondence should be sent to Mark Boyer at mark.boyer@uconn.edu.

1. James Hamill (1998) has since used the phrase "threats without enemies" to discuss similar ideas.

2. Newman does recognize that traditional security—the military defense of territory—is a necessary but not a sufficient condition to human welfare.

3. For a good discussion of the differences between constructivist and essentialist understandings of gender, see Smith 2001.

4. The objective of this future orientation to the simulation scenario is that it allows students to develop creative and innovative solutions to the problems presented to them, rather than simply regurgitating headlines or public statements of world leaders gleaned from the news media on a daily basis during the simulation.

5. One recent effort in forecasting the future of international relations is seen in the Summer 1999 issue of *International Studies Review,* guest edited by Davis B. Bobrow.

6. Easton and Dennis found that these attitudes were formed by the time of entry into middle school (see also Alvik 1968). They also explicitly replace the more common language of system "maintenance" or system "stability" with "persistence," which they argue more effectively captures the ultimate concern of political socialization research—how socialization keeps the system's broad parameters in place and functioning. This distinction is important, they contend, because it helps transcend the conservative bias of early political socialization research, which underemphasized possibilities for alternative discourses within the system (and ignored the socialization processes and agents fueling them).

7. These feelings are of course critical to the evolution and persistence of a democracy-sustaining and enhancing "civic culture" (Almond and Verba 1963).

8. The reader should note that much of the background work that GlobalEd students do in researching their country's foreign policy on the simulation issues is Web-based and generally relies heavily on access to websites such as CNN.com and those of other major news outlets. Thus it is safe to expect that students during winter 2002–2003 were well sensitized to issues of military intervention.

11

The New Security Environment: Policy Implications

Peter Dombrowski

From the contributions to this volume, it might seem logical to conclude that the old trope that security and economics are separate areas of inquiry has been put to rest once again. But at least in the United States, this view is largely inconsistent with public ideologies. From a political-economic perspective, classical liberalism seeks to separate the economic from the political and security spheres. State involvement in economic affairs is viewed as a detriment to peace and order even when national security is at stake. From a policy perspective, the strictures have historically been even stronger. Even in times of duress, when the U.S. government has relied enormously on private firms, it has usually attempted to limit restrictions on private enterprise, even when there is evidence of inefficiency, corruption, and policy failures (Friedberg 2000; Koistinen 1987).[1]

For other countries, international organizations, and nongovernmental organizations, separating the economic matters from strategic objectives in international affairs has rarely been a priority. Historically, most empires explicitly integrated economic and security strategies or failed to distinguish between the two. Indeed, one potentially efficient way to maximize synergies is to ensure that private greed would complement the government imperialists. Who can separate out the political from the economic in the emergence of the British Raj, not to mention all Great Britain's geoeconomic maneuverings to stave off imperial decline at the turn of the twentieth century? In the first half of the twentieth century, Germany also made few pretenses about marshaling economic interests to support state ends (Hirschman 1945). The lack of squeamishness remains in the contemporary world. Expansion of the European Union can be viewed from the economic lens of creating a larger "single market," as well as from the security lens of building strategic depth against the troubled lands of the post-Soviet empire.

The scholarly community often reinforces artificial distinctions that keep security affairs separate from economic issues, even though, as Norrin Ripsman argues in Chapter 2, this amounts to a misreading of the intellectual traditions of the international relations discipline. Yet each of the authors in this volume is committed to linking empirically and theoretically the study and practice of political economy and security. They may use different theoretic standpoints, empirical approaches, and methodologies for examining the intersection across a variety of issues, but they share an interest in both economics and security. The common denominator is an interest in breaking the artificial boundaries.

The conclusions of these authors are driven in part by the issues under consideration. We should revisit the parameters of international change and continuity introduced in Chapter 1 to assess the impact of U.S. actions and the consequent responses of both allies and adversaries.

Sovereignty

Sovereignty in the classical, ideal-type sense that flourishes only in academic texts is an unaffordable luxury for all but the most powerful and successful states. For the less powerful and less well situated members of the interstate system, outside intrusions and internal challenges are pervasive. Internally, many are plagued with terrorists, separatist groups, and ethnic insurgencies. Externally, threats to state autonomy, both formal and informal, are many. Numerous less advantaged countries are barely able to battle the resources of multinational corporations that by design seek to exploit resources, labor surpluses, and relatively lax regulatory and enforcement institutions. In return for financial and technical assistance, both international organizations and wealthy states of the Organization for Economic Cooperation and Development impose conditionalities that limit the policy choices available to weaker states. Refusing conditional assistance and even publicly opposing the "Washington consensus" is a recipe for ostracism—international financial institutions, private firms, and even governments will be much less likely to conduct business with the recalcitrant country.

Governance

Numerous policy challenges facing the global community require either the strong leadership of a powerful state or small group of states, or institutionalized cooperation among larger groups of states. Even the George W. Bush administration has actively courted the United Nations and the world international financial institutions to bear some of the burdens of reconstructing Afghanistan and Iraq. The policy challenges presented by these unfortunate countries require solutions that outstrip the resources of individual donors. Hegemonic stability theory has argued that hegemons, including the United States, provide public goods and distribute the costs of providing public goods among other members of the interstate system. But for many contemporary problems, other states are not willing to contribute sufficient resources without the legitimacy conferred by international institutions, nor are they as susceptible to coercive pressure by the United States to contribute resources and agree to specific institutional arrangements and outcomes as they were in previous decades.

Public-Private Partnerships

In many cases sovereignty has eroded involuntarily due to forces beyond the control of states; in other cases, however, states have voluntarily ceded aspects of their sovereignty by contracting for key services with the private sector. As domestic political constraints retrain state spending and the sensitivities of client states limit their willingness to host military personnel, technicians, or advisers from donor states, many countries have resorted to private firms. Sovereignty is ceded because there are limits to the control that can be exercised over private subcontractors. In the Iraq War, for one evocative example, some military contractors refused to perform their duties when conditions became too dangerous. In the postwar reconstruction period, the differing interests of private contractors and their state clients have been a major source of disagreement and a major impediment to moving rapidly to reconstruct Iraqi infrastructure damaged by fighting and years of sanctions.

Limiting the autonomy of private firms or even attempting to shape corporate behavior in the interest of national security remains controversial in most advanced capitalist societies. Government intrusions into the affairs of private enterprises, even for the best of purposes, constrain property rights and profits, thus generating opposition from commercial interests.[2] Although the chapters in this volume that deal with these phenomena largely focus on U.S. cases, the dilemmas of public-private cooperation are not unique.

U.S. Hegemony

Wishing away the extraordinary wealth and military power of the United States will not make them disappear. The rest of the world will have to cope with U.S. predominance, often unwillingly, because the United States government often acts to maintain predominance, and because other countries, as of yet, lack effective tools for challenging U.S. military supremacy. The failure of the United States to win the support of the United Nations Security

Council or attract substantial military force from other nations did not affect, in a material way, its ability to wage war against Iraq.

From a strategic perspective, this means that opponents of U.S. hegemony must accommodate to the realities of U.S. power without undermining their own policy preferences, much less their core values. In Chapter 6, on Japan's emerging post–September 11, 2001, approach to national security, Christopher Hughes describes one such effort: the Japanese government adapted its long-standing emphasis on human security to support the U.S. global war on terror and the major campaigns against Afghanistan and Iraq.

In some circumstances, it may also mean a return to linkage politics as a means of shifting conflicts into areas where other nations can operate on a more equal playing field. The European Union, for example, is increasingly able to match and even exceed the economic leverage of the United States. China, with its enormous trade surplus, may constitute another example; witness, for example, the numerous failures of long-standing attempts to force China to revalue the yuan to redress growing trade imbalances.

For the United States, hegemony could mean exercising power in ways that are effective, unifying, and not in and of themselves divisive. The Bush administration has chosen to act and speak in a more unilateralist and militarist fashion. Much of the foreign policy and national security disputes in the 2004 presidential election involved, in one form or another, differences over how and why the United States should exercise power.

Mission Creep

First, the United States has adopted a more expansive definition of its security interests both geographically and functionally. Geographically, it has staked claims everywhere and anywhere that terrorists flourish. States like Russia and India that are dealing with their own insurgencies and indigenous terrorists are treated as partners in the global war on terror despite long-standing and unresolved disagreements. Military bases are being established in new areas of the globe closer to the Middle East and other potential hotspots such as Africa.

This new U.S. interest can be a mixed blessing for targeted countries. On the one hand, it promises new resources, both military and economic, in return for greater cooperation with the war on terror, Iraqi reconstruction, and other security objectives. On the other hand, it also threatens to draw coalition partners into disputes that might otherwise be avoided and stimulates domestic anti-U.S. and antiregime resistance.

Economic Statecraft

The United States has also pledged new resources to engage the global community in the name of combating terrorism. Both the Millennium Challenge

Account and the AIDS Prevention Fund, for example, cannot be understood without reference to the Bush administration's recognition that a dysfunctional global economy may exacerbate trends toward terrorist solutions. The United States has extended its security perimeter to most transportation hubs that facilitate international commerce—from airports to container ports—in an effort to prevent terrorist attacks and the smuggling of dangerous goods and materials. Although the costs of such activities have yet to be analyzed in a satisfactory fashion, it is possible that globalization may finally have met serious obstacles.[3] Such initiatives, especially when combined with new and more comprehensive restrictions on the movements of people and ideas across national borders, attempt to limit, contain, and perhaps even reverse economic globalization, again with little regard as to whether the long-term costs of such actions outweigh the immediate, and highly contested, security benefits. In any case, in this volume in Chapter 7, Lars Skålnes reminds us of the difficulty of engaging in economic statecraft in a time when there is not a single overarching state-based threat in the international security environment.

Multilateralism à la Carte

Rhetorically the Bush administration has veered between aggressive unilateralism and pleading for the validation of multilateral support for its policies and programs. Much has been made of the rejection of international agreements—ranging from the Kyoto Protocols to the new International Criminal Court—in the months between assuming office and the September 11, 2001, attacks. Since September 11 the administration has, on occasion, resorted to strong-arm tactics, as it did by withdrawing from the Anti-Ballistic Missile Treaty. With trade, the United States resorted to a clearly illegal steel tariff to placate domestic constituencies in key states, but then backed down in the face of a strong ruling by the World Trade Organization.

The pattern has been no less clear with regard to issues spanning the economic and security spheres. The United States unilaterally punished states that opposed its push for war against Iraq by denying them the opportunity to bid on reconstruction contracts. It also sought bilateral and multilateral concessions on Iraqi debts by arguing that debt reduction and forgiveness were necessary to give the new Iraqi government an opportunity to rebuild and recover from ten years of sanctions. Meanwhile, the United Nations, after having its principles and decisionmaking processes scorned in the prelude to the Iraq War, has been asked to assume an ever-increasing role of providing legitimacy and technical expertise for the process of rebuilding a functioning Iraq.

Perhaps the most coherent conceptual framing of these phenomena is that the Bush administration has adopted a strategy of à la carte multilateralism in both the security and economic spheres. When it serves the instrumental, often short-term interests of the United States, the Bush administration is willing to work within multilateral frameworks. When multilateral arrangements get in the way of specific policy preferences or threaten to slow down an initiative, they are abandoned with little ceremony.

The implications of this approach for world politics are now becoming clear. First, there is the serious danger that the cavalier treatment of established multilateral norms and formal international institutions will erode the already fragile support for the United Nations, the World Bank, and the International Monetary Fund, not to mention alliances such as the North Atlantic Treaty Organization. In short, other nations might demonstrate similar instrumental instincts as well. Second, the United States risks its own legitimacy as a superpower, but more importantly as an exemplar of rules- and norms-based international behavior. Finally, there remains the distinct possibility that other countries will, in effect, resist U.S. high-handedness, both publicly and privately.

Final Observations

International and national resistance to U.S. policies is possible, but costly and difficult for those who choose this path. The United States is able to marshal military, economic, and political resources that far exceed those of most other individual countries, and even those of most combinations of countries working in concert. Given its predominance, the freedom of action afforded the United States by its economic strength and military dominance forces other countries to respond to U.S. initiatives regardless of whether they support or oppose specific proposals. Of course, this freedom of action may come at a price expressed in both economic and security terms.

Notes

1. See especially Paul Koistinen's discussion (1987) of the House Select Committee on Expenditures in the War Department, the War Policies Commission, and the Senate Special Committee Investigating the Munitions Industry.

2. "When the Bush administration came into office, I wanted to raise the profile of efforts to combat terrorist financing, but found little interest. The new President's economic advisor, Larry Lindsey, had long argued for weakening U.S. money laundering laws in a way that would undercut international standards. The new Secretary of the Treasury Paul O'Neill, was lukewarm toward the multilateral efforts to 'name and shame' foreign money laundering havens" (Clarke 2004, p. 196).

3. For a comprehensive account of the relationship between globalization and U.S. foreign and security policies, see Kugler and Frost 2001, vols. 1–2.

References

Abdelal, Rawi, and Jonathan Kirshner. 1999. "Strategy, Economic Relations, and the Definition of National Interests." In Jean-Marc F. Blanchard, Edward D. Mansfield, and Norrin M. Ripsman, eds., *Power and the Purse: The Political Economy of National Security.* London: Frank Cass.

Adams, Gordon. 1982. *The Politics of Defense Contracting: The Iron Triangle.* New Brunswick: Transaction.

Ahlburg, Dennis. 1994. "Population Growth and Poverty." In Robert Cassen, ed., *Population and Development: Old Debates, New Conclusions.* New Brunswick: Transaction.

————. 1998. "Julian Simon and the Population Growth Debate." *Population and Development Review* 24 (2): 317–328.

Alberts, David S., John J. Garstka, and Frederick P. Stein. 1999. *Network Centric Warfare: Developing and Leveraging Information Superiority.* Washington, D.C.: C4ISR Cooperative Research Program (CCRP) Publication Series.

Alden, Edward. 2003. "U.S. Beats Egypt with Trade Stick." *Financial Times,* June 30, p. 8.

Alden, Edward, Tobias Buck, and Guy de Jonquieres. 2003. "Sowing Discord: After Iraq, the U.S. and Europe Head for a Showdown over Genetically Modified Crops." *Financial Times,* May 14, p. 11.

Alden, Edward, and Guy de Jonquieres. 2003. "U.S. Trade Envoys in Europe Seek to Heal War Wounds." *Financial Times,* May 5, p. 18.

Alexander, Dean C. 2004. *Business Confronts Terrorism: Risks and Responses.* Madison: University of Wisconsin Press/Terrace Books.

Allen, Kenneth W. 2000. "PLA Air Force Operations and Modernization." In Susan M. Puska, ed., *People's Liberation Army After Next.* Carlisle Barracks, Pa.: Strategic Studies Institute.

Almond, Gabriel A., and Stanley Verba. 1963. *The Civic Culture.* Princeton: Princeton University Press.

Altman, Daniel. 2003. "Trade Pact with Pakistan Reflects Politics, Not Economics, Critics Say." *New York Times,* July 2, p. C1.

Alvik, Trond. 1968. "The Development of Views on Conflict, War, and Peace Among School Children." *Journal of Peace Research* 5 (2): 171–195.

Ambrosio, Thomas, ed. 2002. *Ethnic Identity Groups and U.S. Foreign Policy.* Westport: Praeger.

Amnesty International. 1995. *Human Rights and U.S. Security Assistance.* New York: Amnesty International.

Anderson, Martin Edwin, and Tim Starks. 2004. "Three Years After 9/11, U.S. Security 'Partnerships' with Industry Are a Work in Progress." *Congressional Quarterly's Homeland Security.* Available at http://www.ewa-iit.com/content.asp?sectionid= 47&contentid=139.

Anderson, Mary B., and Luc Zandvliet. 2001. *Corporate Options for Breaking Cycles of Conflict.* Cambridge, Mass.: Collaborative for Development Action.

Angell, Norman. 1933. *The Great Illusion.* London: William Heinemann.

Anthony, Ian, ed. 1998. *Russia and the Arms Trade.* New York: Oxford University Press.

Areieli, Gil. 2003. "Knowledge: The Thermonuclear Weapons for Terrorists in the Information Age." Institute for Counterterrorism, March 6. Available at http://www.ict.org.il/articles/articledet.cfm?articleid=465.

Arkin, William. 2001. "Operation Allied Force: 'The Most Precise Application of Air Power in History.'" In Andrew J. Bacevich and Eliot A. Cohen, eds., *War over Kosovo: Politics and Strategy in a Global Age.* New York: Columbia University Press.

Armstrong, David. 2003. "Aftermath of War." *San Francisco Chronicle,* May 11, p. 11.

Arquilla, John, and David Ronfeldt. 2001. "The Advent of Netwar (Revisited)." In John Arquilla and David Ronfeldt, eds., *Networks and Netwars: The Future of Terror, Crime, and Militancy.* Santa Monica: Rand.

Arreguin-Toft, Ivan. 2001. "How the Weak Win Wars: A Theory of Asymmetric Conflict." *International Security* 26 (1): 93–128.

Art, Robert J. 2003. *Grand Strategy for America.* Ithaca: Cornell University Press.

Auty, Richard M. 1998a. "Julian Simon and the Population Growth Debate." *Population and Development Review* 24 (2): 317–327.

———. 1998b. "Resource Abundance and Economic Development: Improving the Performance of Resource-Rich Countries." Research for Action no. 44. Helsinki, Finland. World Institute for Development Economics and Research.

———. 2001. "The Political Economy of Resource-Driven Growth." *European Economic Review* 45 (4–6): 839–846.

Avant, Deborah. 2000. "From Mercenary to Citizen Armies: Explaining Change in the Practice of War." *International Organization* 54 (1): 41–72.

Ayoob, Mohammed. 1997. "Defining Security: A Subaltern Realist Perspective." In Keith Krause and Michael C. Williams, eds., *Critical Security Studies.* Minneapolis: University of Minnesota Press.

Bacevich, Andrew J. 2002. *American Empire: The Realities and Consequences of U.S. Diplomacy.* Cambridge: Harvard University Press.

Baechler, Günther, Volker Böge, Stefan Klötzli, Stepan Libiszewski, and Kurt R. Spillmann. 1996. *Environmental Degradation as a Cause of War: Environmental Conflicts in the Third World and Ways for Their Peaceful Resolution.* Vol. 1. Berne: Swiss Peace Foundation/Swiss Federal Institute of Technology.

Baechler, Günther, and Kurt R. Spillman, eds. 1996. *Environmental Degradation as a Cause of War: Regional and Country Studies.* Vols. 2–3. Berne: Swiss Peace Foundation/Swiss Federal Institute of Technology.

Baldwin, David A. 1971. "The Power of Positive Sanctions." *World Politics* 24 (1): 19–39.

———. 1980. "Interdependence and Power: A Conceptual Analysis." *International Organization* 34 (4): 471–506.

———. 1985. *Economic Statecraft*. Princeton: Princeton University Press.

———. 1989. *Paradoxes of Power*. Oxford: Basil Blackwell.

Ballentine, Karen, and Jake Sherman. 2003. *The Political Economy of Armed Conflict: Beyond Greed and Grievance*. Boulder: Lynne Rienner.

Banfield, Jessica, Virginia Haufler, and Damian Lilly. 2003. *Transnational Corporations in Conflict Zones: Mapping Policy Responses and a Framework for Action*. London: International Alert.

Baocun, Wang. 2001. "China and the Revolution in Military Affairs." *China Military Science* 4 (1): 148.

Barbieri, Katherine. 1996. "Economic Interdependence: A Path Toward Peace or Source of Interstate Conflict." *Journal of Peace Research* 33 (1): 29–49.

Barbieri, Katherine, and Jack S. Levy. 1999. "Sleeping with the Enemy: The Impact of War on Trade." *Journal of Peace Research* 36 (4): 1–17.

Barnett, Michael N. 1992. *Confronting the Costs of War*. Princeton: Princeton University Press.

Barnhart, Michael A. 1987. *Japan Prepares for Total War: The Search for Economic Security, 1919–1941*. Ithaca: Cornell University Press.

Batschelet, Allen W. 2002. "Effects-Based Operations: A New Operational Model?" Strategy Research Project. Carlisle Barracks, Pa.: U.S. Army War College.

Beagle, T. W. 2001. "Effects-Based Targeting: Another Empty Promise?" Unpublished manuscript. School of Advanced Airpower Studies, Maxwell Air Force Base, Ala.

Bean, Richard. 1973. "War and the Birth of the Nation State." *Journal of Economic History* 33 (1): 203–221.

Belopotosky, Danielle. 2004. "Homeland Security Identifies Potential Infrastructure Targets." *National Journal's Technology Daily*. Available at http://www.govexec.com/dailyfed1004/101404tdpml.htm.

Bendell, Jem. 2004. *Barricades and Boardrooms: A Contemporary History of the Corporate Accountability Movement*. Geneva: United Nations Research Institute for Social Development.

Bender, Peter. 2003. "America: The New Roman Empire?" *Orbis* 47 (1): 145–159.

Benjamin, Daniel, and Steven Simon. 2003. *The Age of Sacred Terror: Radical Islam's War Against America*. New York: Random House.

Bennett, Juliette. 2001. *Public Private Initiatives in Preventing Conflict: An Examination of Revenue Sharing Provisions in the Extractive Industry*. New York: United Nations Global Compact.

Berdal, Mats, and David M. Malone, eds. 2000. *Greed and Grievance: Economic Agendas in Civil Wars*. Boulder: Lynne Rienner.

Berejikian, Jeffrey, and John S. Dryzek. 2000. "Reflexive Action in International Politics." *British Journal of Political Science* 193 (4): 193–216.

Berman, Jonathan. 2000. "Boardrooms and Bombs: Strategies of Multinational Corporations in Conflict Areas." *Harvard International Review* 22 (3). Available at http://hir.harvard.edu/articles/index.html?id=853.

Bernauer, Thomas, and Dieter Ruloff, eds. 1999. *The Politics of Positive Incentives in Arms Control*. Columbia: University of South Carolina Press.

Berrigan, Frida. 2002. "War on Terror Expands at Expense of Human Rights, Future Stability." *Foreign Policy in Focus*. Available at http://www.fpif.org/commentary/2002/0204hr.html.

Betts, Richard K. 2002. "The Soft Underbelly of American Primacy: Tactical Advantages of Terror." *Political Science Quarterly* 117 (1): 19–36.

Biersteker, Thomas J., and Cynthia Weber, eds. 1996. *State Sovereignty as Social Construct.* Cambridge: Cambridge University Press.

"Big Oil's Dirty Secrets." 2003. *The Economist,* May 8, p. 55.

bin Laden, Osama. 2004. "Transcript: Translation of Bin Laden's Videotaped Message." Translation of Osama bin Laden's videotaped message aired on the Al-Jazeera satellite television network on November 1, provided by the U.S. government. Available at: http://washingtonpost.com/ac2/wp-dyn/a16990-2004nov1?language+printer.

Birdsall, Nancy, and Steven W. Sinding. 2001. "How and Why Population Matters." In Nancy Birdsall, Allen C. Kelley, and Steven W. Sinding, eds., *Population Matters: Demographic Change, Economic Growth, and Poverty in Developing Countries.* Oxford: Oxford University Press.

Bishop, Matt, and Emily O. Goldman. 2003. "The Strategic Logic of Information Warfare." *Contemporary Security Policy* 24 (1):113–139.

Bitzinger, Richard A., and Bates Gill. 1996. *Gearing Up for High-Tech Warfare? Chinese and Taiwanese Defense Modernization and Implications for Military Confrontation Across the Taiwan Strait, 1995–2005.* Washington, D.C.: Center for Strategic and Budgetary Assessments.

Blainey, Geoffrey. 1988. *The Causes of War.* 3rd ed. New York: Free Press.

Blanchard, Jean-Marc F., Edward D. Mansfield, and Norrin M. Ripsman. 1999. "The Political Economy of National Security: Economic Statecraft, Interdependence, and International Conflict." In Jean-Marc F. Blanchard, Edward D. Mansfield, and Norrin M. Ripsman, eds., *Power and the Purse: The Political Economy of National Security.* London: Frank Cass.

Blanchard, Jean-Marc F., and Norrin M. Ripsman. 1996. "Measuring Vulnerability Interdependence: A Geopolitical Perspective." *Geopolitics* 1 (3): 225–246.

———. 1999. "Asking the Right Question: When Do Economic Sanctions Work Best?" *Security Studies* 9 (1): 228–264.

———. 2001. "Rethinking Sensitivity Interdependence: Assessing Trade, Financial, and Monetary Linkages Between States." *International Interactions* 27 (2): 95–127.

Blanton, Shannon L. 2000. "Promoting Human Rights and Democracy in the Developing World: U.S. Rhetoric Versus U.S. Arms Exports." *American Journal of Political Science* 44 (1): 123–131.

Block, Robert. 2004. "U.S. Law Shields Company Data Tied to Security." *Wall Street Journal,* February 18, p. B1.

Bloom, B. S., M. D. Englehart, E. J. Frost, W. H. Hill, and D. R. Krathwol. 1956. *Taxonomy of Educational Objectives.* Handbook 1, *Cognitive Domain.* New York: David McKay.

Blustein, Paul. 2002a. "A Free-Trade Gamble by the U.S." *Washington Post,* March 29, p. E1.

———. 2002b. "U.S. Proposes Global Cut in Farm Subsidies, Tariffs." *Washington Post,* July 26, p. E1.

———. 2002c. "U.S., Singapore Near Pact on Trade." *Washington Post,* November 20, p. E3.

Bobrow, Davis B. 1996. "Complex Insecurity: Implications of a Sobering Metaphor." *International Studies Quarterly* 40 (4): 435–450.

Böge, Volker. 1992. *Bougainville: A "Classical" Environmental Conflict?* Environment and Conflicts Project Occasional Paper no. 3. Berne: Swiss Peace Foundation and Center for Security Studies and Conflict Research.

Bomann-Larsen, Lene. 2003. *Corporate Actors in Zones of Conflicts: Responsible Engagement*. Oslo: Confederation of Norwegian Business and Industry (NHO) and Research Institute of Oslo.

Boserup, Ester. 1965. *The Conditions of Agricultural Growth*. Chicago: Aldine.

Boucher, Richard. 2001. "U.S. Department of State Daily Press Briefing." October 2.

Bowman, Steve. 2003. *Homeland Security: The Department of Defense's Role*. Washington, D.C.: Congressional Research Service, May 14.

Broad, Robin, and John Cavanagh. 1998. *The Corporate Accountability Movement: Lessons and Opportunities*. Washington, D.C.: World Resources Institute.

Brodie, Bernard. 1959. *Strategy in the Missile Age*. Princeton: Princeton University Press.

Brooks, Stephen G., and William C. Wohlforth. 2002. "American Primacy in Perspective." *Foreign Affairs* 81 (4): 20–33.

Brown, Scott W., Mark A. Boyer, Hayley J. Mayall, Paula R. Johnson, Lin Meng, Michael J. Butler, Natalie Florea, Magnolia Hernandez, and Sally Reis. 2003. "The GlobalEd Project: Gender Differences in a Problem-Based Learning Environment of International Negotiations." *Instructional Science* 31 (4–5): 255–276.

Brown, Scott W., and Frederick King. 2000. "Constructivist Pedagogy and How We Learn: Educational Psychology Meets International Studies." *International Studies Perspectives* 1 (3): 245–254.

Bryant, Raymond L., and Sinead Bailey. 1997. *Third World Political Ecology*. London: Routledge.

Bunker, Robert J. 1995. "The Tofflerian Paradox." *Military Review* 85 (3): 99–102.

"Bush the Anti-Globaliser." 2002. *The Economist,* May 9, pp. 14–15.

Business Roundtable. 2003. "Terrorism: Real Threats, Real Costs, Joint Solutions." June. Available at http://www.businessroundtable.org.

Byman, Daniel, and Matthew Waxman. 1999. "Defeating U.S. Coercion." *Survival* 41 (2): 107–120.

Carr, Edward Hallett. 1946. *The Twenty Years' Crisis 1919–1939: An Introduction to the Study of International Relations*. New York: Harper and Row.

Castel, Albert. 2003. "Liddell Hart's *Sherman:* Propaganda as History." *Journal of Military History* 67 (2): 405–426.

Castells, Manuel. 2000. *The Information Age: Economy Society and Culture*. Vol. 1, *The Rise of the Network Society*. London: Blackwell.

———. 2002. *The Information Age: Economy Society and Culture*. Vol. 3, *End of Millennium*. London: Blackwell Publishers.

Catrina, Christian. 1988. *Arms Transfers and Dependence*. New York: Taylor and Francis.

Central Intelligence Agency. 1998. *The Handbook of International Economic Statistics, 1998*. Langley: Central Intelligence Agency.

Cerny, Philip G. 1995. "Globalization and the Changing Logic of Collective Action." *International Organization* 49 (4): 595–625.

———. 2005. "Terrorism and the New Security Dilemma." *Naval War College Review* 58 (1): 11–33.

Cha, Victor. 1999. "Globalization and the Study of International Security." *Journal of Peace Research* 37 (3): 391–403.

Chapman, John M. W., Ian T. M. Gow, and Reinhard Drifte. 1983. *Japan's Quest for Comprehensive Security: Defence, Diplomacy, Dependence*. London: Pinter.

Christiansen, Alte Christer. 2002. *Beyond Petroleum: Can BP Deliver?* Lysaker: Fridtjof Nansen Institute.

Cincotta, Richard P., Robert Engelman, and Daniele Anastasion. 2003. *The Security Demographic: Population and Civil Conflict After the Cold War.* Washington, D.C.: Population Action International.

Cingranelli, David L., and Thomas E. Pasquarello. 1985. "Human Rights Practices and the Distribution of U.S. Foreign Aid to Latin American Countries." *American Journal of Political Science* 29 (3): 539–563.

Clarke, Duncan L., and Daniel O'Connor. 1997. "Security Assistance Policy After the Cold War." In Randall B. Ripley and James M. Lindsay, eds., *U.S. Foreign Policy After the Cold War.* Pittsburgh: University of Pittsburgh Press.

Clarke, Richard A. 2002. "Administrative Oversight: Are We Ready for a Cyber Terror Attack?" Testimony before the Senate Committee on the Judiciary, Subcommittee on Administrative Oversight and the Courts, by Richard A. Clarke, special adviser to the president for cyberspace security and chairman of the President's Critical Infrastructure Protection Board. February 13.

———. 2004. *Against All Enemies: Inside America's War on Terror.* New York: Free Press.

Cliff, Roger. 2001. *The Military Potential of China's Commercial Technology.* Santa Monica: Rand.

Cohen, Joel E. 1995. *How Many People Can the Earth Support?* New York: W. W. Norton.

Colebatch, Tim. 2003. "A Favour for an Ally: The Americans Come to Town to Talk Trade." *The Age,* March 18, p. 15.

Collier, Paul. 2000. *Economic Causes of Civil Conflict and Their Implications for Policy.* Washington, D.C.: World Bank, June 15.

Collier, Paul, Lani Elliot, Havard Hegre, Anke Hoeffler, Marta Reynal-Querol, and Nicholas Sambanis. 2003. *Breaking the Conflict Trap: Civil War and Development Policy.* Washington, D.C.: World Bank and Oxford University Press.

Collier, Paul, and Anke Hoeffler. 2001. *Greed and Grievance in Civil War.* Rev. ed. Washington, D.C.: World Bank, October 21.

Commission on Human Security. 2003. *Human Security Now.* New York: Commission on Human Security.

Conca, Ken. 2002. "The Case for Environmental Peacemaking." In Ken Conca and Geoffery Dabelko, eds., *Environmental Peacemaking.* Washington, D.C.: Woodrow Wilson Center Press and Johns Hopkins University Press.

Converse, P. E. 1976. *The Dynamics of Party Support: Cohort-Analyzing Party Identification.* Beverly Hills: Sage.

Conybeare, John A. C. 1984. "Public Goods, Prisoners' Dilemmas, and the International Political Economy." *International Studies Quarterly* 28 (1): 5–22.

Copeland, Dale C. 1995. "Economic Interdependence and War: A Theory of Trade Expectations." *International Security* 20 (4): 5–41.

Cordesman, Anthony H., and Arleigh A. Burke. 2003. *Understanding the New "Effects-Based" Air War in Iraq.* Washington, D.C.: Center for Strategic and International Studies.

Cortright, David, and George A. Lopez, eds. 2002. *Smart Sanctions: Targeting Economic Sanctions.* Lanham: Rowan & Littlefield.

Cortright, David, George A. Lopez, and Linda Gerber. 2002. *Sanctions and the Search for Security: Challenges to UN Action.* Boulder: Lynne Rienner.

Cox, Gary W., and Mathew D. McCubbins. 2001. "The Institutional Determinants of Economic Policy Outcomes." In Stephan Haggard and Mathew D. McCubbins, eds., *Presidents, Parliaments, and Policy.* Cambridge: Cambridge University Press.

Crano, William D. 1997. "Vested Interest, Symbolic Politics, and Attitude-Behavior Consistency." *Journal of Personality and Social Psychology* 72 (3): 485–491.

Crenshaw, Martha. 1990. "The Causes of Terrorism." In Charles W. Kegley Jr., ed. *International Terrorism: Characteristics, Causes, Controls.* New York: St. Martin's.

Crocker, Chester, Fen Hampson, and Pamela Aall, eds. 2001. *Turbulent Peace.* Washington, D.C.: U.S. Institute of Peace Press.

Cronin, Audrey Kurth. 2002–2003. "Behind the Curve: Globalization and International Terrorism." *International Security* 27 (3): 30–58.

Crumm, Eileen. 1995. "The Value of Economic Incentives in International Politics." *Journal of Peace Research* 32 (3): 313–330.

Culbertson, William S. 1924. *Raw Materials and Foodstuffs in the Commercial Policies of Nations.* Philadelphia: Annals of the American Academy of Political and Social Science.

Cutler, A. Claire, Virginia Haufler, and Tony Porter, eds. 1999. *Private Authority and International Affairs.* Albany: State University of New York University Press.

Daalder, Ivo H., and James M. Lindsay. 2003. *America Unbound: The Bush Revolution in Foreign Policy.* Washington, D.C.: Brookings Institution Press.

Dalby, Simon. 2002. *Environmental Security.* Minneapolis: University of Minnesota Press.

"Dangerous Activities." 2002. *The Economist,* May 9, pp. 69–72.

Daoudi, M. S., and M. S. Dajani. 1983. *Economic Sanctions: Ideals and Experience.* London: Routledge and Kegan Paul.

Darcey, Robert F. 2003. "Homeland Security: Information Sharing Responsibilities, Challenges and Key Management Issues." Statement before the Subcommittee on Cyberspace, Science, and Research and Development of the Subcommittee on Infrastructure and Border Security, Select Committee on Homeland Security, House of Representatives. September 17.

Dawson, William Harbutt. 1926. *Richard Cobden and Foreign Policy.* London: Allen and Unwin.

de Soysa, Indra. 2000a. "Natural Resources and Civil Conflict: Shrinking Pie or Honey Pot?" Unpublished manuscript.

————. 2000b. "The Resource Curse: Are Civil Wars Driven by Rapacity or Paucity?" In Mats Berdal and David M. Malone, eds., *Greed and Grievance: Economic Agendas in Civil Wars.* Boulder: Lynne Rienner.

de Vries, Michael S. 1990. "Interdependence, Cooperation, and Conflict: An Empirical Analysis." *Journal of Peace Research* 27 (4): 429–444.

Deans, Bob. 2003. "Bush to Urge Free Trade Pact Across Mideast." *Atlanta Journal and Constitution,* May 9, p. 15A.

Defense Science Board. 1999. *Final Report of the Defense Science Board Task Force on Globalization and Security.* Washington, D.C.: U.S. Department of Defense. Available at http://www.acq.osd.mil/dsb.

Demchak, Chris C. 2000. "Revolution in Military Affairs in Developing States: Botswana, Chile, and Thailand—Dilemmas of Image, Operations and Democracy." *National Security Studies Quarterly* 6 (4): 1–45.

Der Derian, James. 1995. "The Value of Security: Hobbes, Marx, Nietzsche, and Baudrillard." In Ronnie D. Lipschutz, ed., *On Security.* New York: Columbia University Press.

Derber, Charles. 1998. *Corporation Nation: How Corporations Are Taking Over Our Lives and What We Can Do About It.* New York: St. Martin's.

"DHS Launches Protected Critical Infrastructure Information Program to Enhance Homeland Security, Facilitate Information Sharing." 2004. Department of Homeland Security, February 18. Available at http://www.dhs.gov/dhspublic.

Dionne, E. J. 2001. "Trade and Terror." *Washington Post,* October 2, p. A25.

Dixon, Thomas F. Homer. 1994. "Environmental Scarcities and Violent Conflict: Evidence from Cases." *International Security* 19 (1): 5–40.

Docherty, Bonnie. 2002. "U.S. Military Aid After 9/11 Threatens Human Rights." Human Rights Watch, February. Available at http://www.hrw.org/press/2002/02/usmil0215.htm.

Dombrowski, Peter. 1996. *Policy Responses to the Globalization of American Banking.* Pittsburgh: University of Pittsburgh Press.

Dombrowski, Peter, Eugene Gholz, and Andrew Ross. 2002. "Selling Transformation: The Defense Industrial Sources of Sustaining and Disruptive Innovation." *Orbis* 46 (3): 523–536.

Domke, William. 1988. *War and the Changing World System.* New Haven: Yale University Press.

Donnelley, Ceara, and William D. Hartung. 2003. "New Numbers: The Price of Freedom in Iraq and Power in Washington." Arms Trade Resource Center, August. Available at http://www.worldpolicy.org/projects/arms/updates/081203.html.

Dorn, Walter L. 1963. *Competition for Empire, 1740–1763.* New York: Harper and Row.

Doxey, Margaret P. 1987. *International Sanctions in Contemporary Perspective.* New York: St. Martin's.

Drezner, Daniel. 1999. "Transaction Costs, Conflict Expectations, and Economic Inducements." In Jean-Marc F. Blanchard, Edward D. Mansfield, and Norrin M. Ripsman, eds., *Power and the Purse: The Political Economy of National Security.* London: Frank Cass.

Duffield, Mark. 2000. "Globalization, Transborder Trade, and War Economies." In M. Berdal and D. M. Malone, eds. *Greed and Grievance: Economic Agendas in Civil War.* Boulder: Lynne Rienner.

———. 2001. *Global Governance and the New Wars: The Merging of Development and Security.* London: Zed Books.

Dumbrell, John. 2002a. "Unilateralism and 'America First'? President George W. Bush's Foreign Policy." *Political Quarterly* 73 (3): 279–287.

———. 2002b. "Was There a Clinton Doctrine? President Clinton's Foreign Policy Reconsidered." *Diplomacy and Statecraft* 13 (2): 43–56.

Dunn, M., and I. Wigert. 2004. *International CIIP Handbook 2004: An Inventory and Analysis of Protection Policies in Fourteen Countries.* Zurich: Swiss Federal Institute of Technology, Center for Security Studies. Available at http://www.isn.ethz.ch/pubs/ph/details.cfm?r_oid=454&sid=ae7eb4e71753e9948a2ae4421d766ebd.

Earle, Edward Mead. 1986. "Adam Smith, Alexander Hamilton, Friedrich List: The Economic Foundations of Military Power." In Peter Paret, ed., *Makers of Modern Strategy.* Oxford: Clarendon.

Easton, David, and Jack Dennis. 1967. "The Child's Acquisition of Regime Norms: Political Efficacy." *American Political Science Review* 61 (1): 25–38.

———. 1969. *Children in the Political System: Origins of Political Legitimacy.* Chicago: University of Chicago Press.

Ehrlich, Paul R., and Anne H. Ehrlich. 1990. *The Population Explosion.* New York: Simon and Schuster.

Emeny, Brooks. 1936. *The Strategy of Raw Materials.* New York: Macmillan.

Feaver, Peter D., and Christopher Gelpi. 2003. *Choosing Your Battles: American Civil-Military Relations and the Use of Force.* Princeton: Princeton University Press.

Ferguson, Yale H., and Richard W. Mansbach. 1996. *Polities: Authority, Identities, and Change.* Columbia: University of South Carolina Press.

Financial Services Information Sharing and Analysis Center (FS-ISAC). 2003. "Financial Services Information Sharing and Analysis Center Funded to Protect America's Financial Infrastructure with Next-Generation Services." Press release, December 19. Available at http://www.fsisac.com.

———. 2004. "Private Sector Security Leaders Join Forces Against Terrorism." Press release, October 14. Available at http://www.fsisac.com.

Finnemore, Martha, and Kathryn Sikkink. 1998. "International Norm Dynamics and Political Change." *International Organization* 52 (4): 887–917.

Florea, Natalie, Mark A. Boyer, Scott W. Brown, Michael J. Butler, Magnolia Hernandez, Kimberly Weir, Paula Johnson, Lin Meng, Hayley Mayall, and Clarisse Lima. 2003. "Negotiating from Mars to Venus: Some Findings on Gender's Impact in Simulated International Negotiations." *Simulation and Games* 34 (2): 226–248.

Florini, Ann. 1996. "The Evolution of International Norms." *International Studies Quarterly* 40 (3): 363–389.

———, ed. 2000. *The Third Force: The Rise of Transnational Civil Society.* Washington, D.C.: Carnegie Endowment for International Peace.

———. 2003. *The Coming Democracy: New Rules for Running a New World.* Washington, D.C.: Island Press.

Flynn, Stephen E. 2002. "America the Vulnerable." *Foreign Affairs* 81 (1): 60–74.

———. 2004. *America the Vulnerable: How Our Government Is Failing to Protect Us from Terrorism.* New York: HarperCollins.

Fordham, Benjamin O. 1998. *Building the Cold War Consensus: The Political Economy of U.S. National Security Policy, 1949–1951.* Ann Arbor: University of Michigan Press.

Foster, William, and Seymour E. Goodman. 2000. *The Diffusion of the Internet in China.* Available at http://www.public.asu.edu/~wfoste1/chinainternet.pdf.

Freedman, Lawrence, and Martin Navias. 1997. "Western Europe." In Andrew J. Pierre, ed., *Cascade of Arms: Managing Conventional Weapons Proliferation.* Washington, D.C.: Brookings Institution Press.

Freedom House. 2002. *Freedom in the World, 2001–2002.* Piscataway, NJ: Transaction.

Freeman, Bennett. 2000. "Globalization, Human Rights and the Extractive Industries." Paper prepared for delivery by the U.S. deputy assistant secretary of state, read at the third Warwick Corporate Citizenship Conference, July 10, University of Warwick.

Fridtjof Nansen Institute. 2000. *Petro-States: Predatory or Developmental? Final Report.* Lysaker, Norway: Fridtjof Nansen Institute.

Friedberg, Aaron L. 1988. *The Weary Titan: Britain and the Experience of Relative Decline, 1895–1905.* Princeton: Princeton University Press.

———. 1992. "Why Didn't the United States Become a Garrison State?" *International Security* 16, no. 4 (Spring 1992): 136–141.

———. 2000. *In the Shadow of the Garrison State.* Princeton: Princeton University Press.

Frieden, Jeffry. 1999. "Actors and Preferences in International Relations." In David A. Lake and Robert Powell, eds., *Strategic Choice and International Relations.* Princeton: Princeton University Press.

Frieden, Jeffry, and Lisa L. Martin. 2002. "International Political Economy: Global and Domestic Interaction." In Ira Katznelson and Helen V. Milner, eds., *Political Science: The State of the Discipline*. New York: W. W. Norton.

Frieden, Jeffry, and Ronald Rogowski. 1996. "The Impact of the International Economy on National Policies: An Analytic Overview." In Robert O. Keohane and Helen V. Milner, eds., *Internationalization and Domestic Politics*. New York: Cambridge University Press.

Gaddis, John Lewis. 2002. "A Grand Strategy of Transformation." *Foreign Policy* (November–December): 50–57.

Galtung, Johan. 1967. "On the Effects of International Economic Sanctions: With Examples from the Case of Rhodesia." *World Politics* 19 (3): 378–416.

Garcia, Victoria. 2002. "U.S. Foreign Military Training: A Shift in Focus." Center for Defense Information. Available at http://www.cdi.org/terrorism/miltraining.cfm.

Garten, Jeffrey E. 1995. "Is America Abandoning Multilateral Trade?" *Foreign Affairs* 74 (6): 50–62.

Gasiorowski, Mark J. 1986. "Economic Interdependence and International Conflict: Some Cross-National Evidence." *International Studies Quarterly* 26 (1): 709–729.

Gasiorowski, Mark J., and Solomon Polachek. 1986. "Conflict and Interdependence: East-West Trade and Linkages in the Era of Détente." *International Studies Quarterly* 30 (1): 23–28.

Gellman, Barton. 2002. "The Cyber-Terror Threat." *Washington Post Weekly Edition*. July 1–14.

Geyer, Michael. 1986. "German Strategy in the Age of Machine Warfare." In Peter Paret, ed., *Makers of Modern Strategy: from Machiavelli to the Nuclear Age*. Princeton: Princeton University Press.

Gholz, Eugene, and Daryl G. Press. 2001. "The Effects of Wars on Neutral Countries: Why It Doesn't Pay to Preserve the Peace." *Security Studies* 13 (4): 1–57.

Gholz, Eugene, Daryl G. Press, and Harvey M. Sapolsky. 1997. "Come Home, America: The Strategy of Restraint in the Face of Temptation." *International Security* 21 (4): 5–48.

Gilpin, Robert. 1975. *U.S. Power and the Multinational Corporation: The Political Economy of Foreign Direct Investment*. New York: Basic Books.

———. 1981. *War and Change in International Politics*. Princeton: Princeton University Press.

Gleditsch, Nils Petter. 1998. "Armed Conflict and the Environment: A Critique of the Literature." *Journal of Peace Research* 35 (3): 381–400.

Glenn, N. D. 1980. "Values, Attitudes, and Beliefs." In O. G. Brim and J. Agan, eds., *Constancy and Change in Human Development*. Cambridge: Harvard University Press.

Global Witness. 1998. *Rough Trade: The Role of Companies and Governments in the Angolan Conflict*. London: Global Witness.

———. 1999. *A Crude Awakening: The Role of Oil and Banking Industries in Angolan Civil War and the Plunder of State Assets*. London: Global Witness.

Goldblatt, David, David Held, Anthony McGrew, and Jonathan Perraton. 1997. "Economic Globalization and the Nation-State: Shifting Balances of Power." *Alternatives* 22 (3): 269–285.

Goldman, Emily O. 2004. "Military Diffusion and Transformation." In Emily O. Goldman and Thomas G. Mahnken, eds., *The Information Revolution in Military Affairs in Asia*. New York: Palgrave.

Goldman, Emily O., and Leslie C. Eliason, eds. 2003. *The Diffusion of Military Technology and Ideas*. Stanford: Stanford University Press.

Goldstein, J. S. 2001. *War and Gender*. Cambridge: Cambridge University Press.

Goldstein, Judith. 1988. "Ideas, Institutions, and American Trade Policy." *International Organization* 42 (1): 179–217.

Goldstone, Jack A. 1991. *Revolution and Rebellion in the Early Modern World.* Berkeley: University of California Press.

———. 1997. "Population Growth and Revolutionary Crises." In John Foran, ed., *Theorizing Revolutions.* London: Routledge.

———. 2002. "How Demographic Change Can Lead to Violent Conflict." *Journal of International Affairs* 56 (1): 3–24.

Goldstone, Jack A., et al. 2000. *State Failure Task Force Report: Phase III Findings.* McLean, Va.: Science Applications International Corporation, September 30.

Goodin, Robert E. 2003. "How Amoral Is Hegemon?" *Perspectives on Politics* 1 (1): 123–126.

Goodwin, Crauford D. 1991. "National Security in Classical Political Economy." In Crauford D. Goodwin, ed., *Economics and National Security. A History of Their Interaction.* Durham: Duke University Press.

Gordon, Bernard K. 2001. *America's Trade Follies: Turning Economic Leadership into Strategic Weakness.* London: Routledge.

———. 2003. "A High-Risk Trade Policy." *Foreign Affairs* 82 (4): 105–118.

Gowa, Joanne. 1989. "Rational Hegemons, Excludable Goods, and Small Groups: An Epitaph for Hegemonic Stability Theory?" *World Politics* 41 (3): 307–325.

———. 1994. *Allies, Adversaries, and International Trade.* Princeton: Princeton University Press.

Grebler, Leo, and William Winkler. 1940. *The Cost of the World War to Germany and to Austria-Hungary.* New Haven: Yale University Press.

Greenberg, Edward S., ed. 1970. *Political Socialization.* New York: Atherton Press.

Greenstein, Fred I. 1965. *Children in Politics.* New Haven: Yale University Press.

Greider, William. 1997. *One World, Ready or Not: The Manic Logic of Global Capitalism.* New York: Touchstone/Simon and Schuster.

Gretton, Sir Peter. 1977. "The U-Boat Campaign in Two World Wars." In Gerald Jordan, ed., *Naval Warfare in the Twentieth Century, 1900–1945: Essays in Honour of Arthur Marder.* New York: Crane Russak.

Grieco, Joseph M. 1988. "Anarchy and the Limits of Cooperation: A Realist Critique of the Newest Liberal Institutionalism." *International Organization* 42 (3): 485–507.

Grimmett, Richard F. 2004. *Conventional Arms Transfers to Developing Nations, 1996–2003.* Washington, D.C.: Congressional Research Service.

Guaqeta, Alexandra. 2002. *Economic Agendas in Armed Conflict: Defining and Developing the Role of the UN.* New York: International Peace Academy and Fafo.

Haas, Peter M. 1990. *Saving the Mediterranean.* New York: Columbia University Press.

Haass, Richard N. 1997. "Sanctioning Madness." *Foreign Affairs* 76 (6): 74–85.

Habermas, Jurgen. 1996. *Between Facts and Norms.* Cambridge: MIT Press.

Haggard, Stephan. 1988. "The Institutional Foundations of Hegemony: Explaining the Reciprocal Trade Agreements Act of 1934." *International Organization* 42 (1): 91–119.

———. 1990. *Pathways from the Periphery: The Politics of Growth in the Newly Industrializing Countries.* Ithaca: Cornell University Press.

Haggard, Stephan, and Mathew D. McCubbins. 2001. "Introduction: Political Institutions and the Determinants of Public Policy." In Stephan Haggard and Mathew D. McCubbins, eds., *Presidents, Parliaments, and Policy.* Cambridge: Cambridge University Press.

Haglund, David G. 1986. "The New Geopolitics of Minerals: An Inquiry into the Changing International Significance of Strategic Minerals." *Political Geography Quarterly* 5 (3): 221–240.

Hamill, James. 1998. "From Realism to Complex Interdependence? South Africa, Southern Africa, and the Question of Security." *International Relations* 14 (3): 1–30.

Harknett, Richard J. 2003. "Integrated Security: A Strategic Response to Anonymity and the Problem of the Few." *Contemporary Security Policy* 24 (1): 13–45.

Hart, B. H. Liddell. 1967. *Strategy*. New York: Praeger.

Hartley, Keith, and Todd Sandler, eds. 1995. *Handbook of Defense Economics*. New York: Elsevier.

Hartung, William D. 1994. *And Weapons for All*. New York: HarperCollins.

Haufler, Virginia. 2001a. "Is There a Role for Business in Conflict Management?" In Chester Crocker, Fen Osler Hampson, and Pamela Aall, eds., *Turbulent Peace: The Challenges of Managing International Conflict*. Washington, D.C.: U.S. Institute of Peace Press.

———. 2001b. *A Public Role for the Private Sector: Industry Self-Regulation in a Global Economy*. Washington, D.C.: Carnegie Endowment for International Peace.

———. 2003. *Unexpected Expectations: Corporations and Intervention in Domestic Politics*. Oslo: Fridtjof Nansen Institute.

Hauge, Wenche, and Tanja Ellingsen. 1998. "Beyond Environmental Scarcity: Causal Pathways to Conflict." *Journal of Peace Research* 35 (3): 299–317.

Heckscher, Eli F. 1936. "Revisions in Economic History: V. Mercantilism." *Economic History Review* 7 (1): 44–54.

Herrera, Geoffrey. 2004. "Technology and International Systems." *Millennium Journal of International Studies* 32 (3): 559–593.

Hess, Robert D., and Judith V. Torney. 1967. *The Development of Political Attitudes in Children*. Chicago: Aldine.

Hessel, M. S., W. J. Murphy, and F. A. Hessel. 1942. *Strategic Materials*. New York: Hastings House.

Hirono, Ryôkichi. 2001. "Japan's International Development and Conflict Prevention Strategy: Building a Common Vision for the Future." Unpublished paper from the conference "Japanese-British Relations in the New Millennium: Prospects for International Cooperation," Royal United Services Institute, June 20–21.

Hirschman, Albert O. 1945. *National Power and the Structure of Foreign Trade*. Berkeley: University of California Press.

Hirst, Paul, and Grahame Thompson. 1995. *Globalisation in Question: The International Economy and the Possibilities of Governance*. Cambridge, UK: Polity Press.

Hiscox, Michael J. 1999. "The Magic Bullet? The RTAA, Institutional Reform, and Trade Liberalization." *International Organization* 53 (4): 669–698.

Ho, Joshua. 2004. "Economic Power, Maritime Power, and Maritime Challenges in East Asia." *Pointers: Journal of the Singapore Armed Forces* 30 (1). Available at http://www.mindef.gov.sg/safti/pointer/back/journals/2004/vol30_1/3.htm.

Holsti, Kalevi J. 1996. *The State, War, and the State of War*. New York: Cambridge University Press.

Homer-Dixon, Thomas F. 1991. "On the Threshold: Environmental Changes as Causes of Acute Conflict." *International Security* 16 (2): 76–116.

———. 1994. "Environmental Scarcities and Violent Conflict: Evidence from Cases." *International Security* 19 (1): 4–40.

———. 1995. "The Ingenuity Gap: Can Poor Countries Adapt to Resource Scarcity?" *Population and Development Review* 21 (3): 587–612.

———. 1999. *Environment, Scarcity, and Violence*. Princeton: Princeton University Press.

Homer-Dixon, Thomas F., and Jessica Blitt, eds. 1998. *Ecoviolence: Links Among Environment, Population, and Security*. Lanham: Rowan and Littlefield.

Hook, Glenn D., Julie Gilson, Christopher W. Hughes, and Hugo Dobson. 2001. *Japan's International Relations: Politics, Economics, and Security*. London: Routledge.

Hook, Steven W. 1995. *National Interest and Foreign Aid*. Boulder: Lynne Rienner.

Hook, Steven W., and Guang Zhang. 1998. "Japan's Aid Policy Since the Cold War: Rhetoric and Reality." *Asian Survey* 38 (11): 1051–1066.

Hufbauer, Gary Clyde, Jeffrey J. Schott, and Kimberly Ann Elliott. 1990. *Economic Sanctions Reconsidered*. 2nd ed. 2 vols. Washington, D.C.: Institute for International Economics.

Hughes, Christopher W. 1999. *Japan's Economic Power and Security: Japan and North Korea*. London: Routledge.

———. 2000. "Japanese Policy and the East Asian Currency Crisis: Abject Defeat or Quiet Victory?" *Review of International Political Economy* 7 (2): 219–253.

———. 2002. *Japan's Security Policy and the War on Terror: Steady Incrementalism or Radical Leap?* CSGR working paper, August. Available at http://www.warwick.ac.uk/fac/soc/csgr/wpapers/wp10402.pdf.

———. 2004. *Japan's Security Agenda: Military, Economic, and Environmental Dimensions*. Boulder: Lynne Rienner.

Hülsemeyer, Axel. 2003. Introduction to Axel Hülsemeyer, ed., *Globalization in the Twenty-First Century: Convergence or Divergence?* London: Palgrave Macmillan.

Human Rights Watch. 2002. "Dangerous Dealings: Changes in U.S. Military Assistance After September 11." *Human Rights Watch* 14 (1). Available at http://www.hrw.org/reports/2002/usmil.

Huntington, Samuel P. 1999. "The Lonely Superpower." *International Security* 78 (2): 35–49.

Huxley, Tim. 2004. "Singapore and the Revolution in Military Affairs." In Emily O. Goldman and Thomas G. Mahnken, eds., *The Information Revolution in Military Affairs in Asia*. New York: Palgrave.

Hyland, William G. 1999. *Clinton's World: Remaking American Foreign Policy*. Westport: Praeger.

Hyman, Herbert H. 1959. *Political Socialization*. Glencoe, Ill.: Free Press.

Ikenberry, G. John. 2000. *After Victory: Institutions, Strategic Restraint, and the Rebuilding of Order After Major Wars*. Princeton: Princeton University Press.

———. 2001. "American Grand Strategy in the Age of Terror." *Survival* 43 (4): 19–34.

———. 2002. "America's Imperial Ambition." *Foreign Affairs* 81 (5): 44–60.

———. 2003a. "Is American Multilateralism in Decline?" *Perspectives on Politics* 1 (3): 533–550.

———. 2003b. "State Power and the Institutional Bargain: America's Ambivalent Economic and Security Multilateralism." In Rosemary Foot, S. Neil MacFarlane, and Michael Mastanduno, eds., *U.S. Hegemony and International Organizations*. Oxford: Oxford University Press.

Information Sharing and Analysis Centers (ISAC) Council. 2004. "Reach of the Major ISACs" and "A Functional Model for Critical Infrastructure Information Sharing and Analysis: Maturing and Expanding Efforts." White paper, January 31. Available at http://www.isaccouncil.com.

International Commission on Intervention and State Sovereignty. 2001. *The Responsibility to Protect.* Ottawa: International Development Research Centre.

International Monetary Fund. 2003. *Direction of Trade Statistics Yearbook, 2002.* Washington, D.C.: International Monetary Fund.

International Peace Academy. 2001. *Private Sector Actors in Zones of Conflict: Research Challenges and Policy Responses.* New York: Fafo Institute for Applied Social Sciences, Programme for International Cooperation and Conflict Resolution; and International Peace Academy, Economic Agendas in Civil Wars Project.

ISIS Asset Management. 2003. News release. May 19.

Jackson, Robert. 2000. *The Global Covenant: Human Conduct in a World of States.* Cambridge: Cambridge University Press.

Japanese Advisory Group on Defense Issues. 1994. *The Modality of the Security and Defense Capability of Japan: The Outlook for the Twenty-First Century.* Tokyo: Ôkurashô Insatsukyoku.

Japanese Ministry of Foreign Affairs. 2002. "Support Package for Peace and Stability in Mindanao." Available at http://www.mofa.go.jp/region/asia-paci/philippine/pv0212/mindanao.html.

———. 2003a. "Japan-Indonesia Joint Announcement on Fighting International Terrorism." Available at http://www.mofa.go.jp/region/asia-paci/indonesia/pv0306/terro.pdf.

———. 2003b. "Revision of Japan's Official Development Assistance Charter." Available at http://www.mofa.go.jp/policy/oda/reform/revision0308.pdf.

Jentleson, Bruce W. 1994. *With Friends Like These: Reagan, Bush, and Saddam, 1982–1990.* New York: W. W. Norton.

Jervis, Robert. 2003a. "The Compulsive Empire." *Foreign Policy* 137: 83–87.

———. 2003b. "Understanding the Bush Doctrine." *Political Science Quarterly* 118 (3): 365–388.

Joffe, Josef. 1995. "'Bismarck' or 'Britain'? Toward an American Grand Strategy After Bipolarity." *International Security* 19 (4): 94–117.

———. 2002. "Of Hubs, Spokes, and Public Goods." *National Interest* 69: 17–20.

Jones, R. J. Barry. 1984. "The Definition and Identification of Interdependence." In R. J. Barry Jones and Peter Willetts, *Interdependence on Trial.* New York: St. Martin's.

Jones, Stephen B. 1971. "The Power Inventory and National Strategy." In W. A. Douglas Jackson and Marwyn S. Samuels, eds., *Politics and Geographic Relationships,* 2nd ed. Englewood Cliffs: Prentice-Hall.

Jonge Oudraat, Chantal de. 2000a. *Intervention in Internal Conflicts: Legal and Political Conundrums.* Washington, D.C.: Carnegie Endowment for International Peace.

———. 2000b. "Making Economic Sanctions Work." *Survival* 42 (3): 105–127.

Kahl, Colin H. 1998. "Population Growth, Environmental Degradation, and State-Sponsored Violence: The Case of Kenya, 1991–93." *International Security* 23 (2): 80–119.

———. 2000. *States, Scarcity, and Civil Strife in the Developing World.* PhD diss., Columbia University, New York.

———. 2002. "Review of *Violent Environments.*" *Environmental Change and Security Project Report* 8: 135–143.

Kaplan, Robert D. 1994. "The Coming Anarchy." *Atlantic Monthly* 273 (2): 44–76.

————. 1996. *The Ends of the Earth: A Journey at the Dawn of the 21st Century.* New York: Random House.

Kapstein, Ethan Barnaby. 1992. *The Political Economy of National Security.* New York: McGraw-Hill.

————. 1998–1999. "A Global Third Way: Social Justice and the World Economy." *World Policy Journal* 15 (4): 23–35.

————. 1999. "Does Unipolarity Have a Future?" In Ethan B. Kapstein and Michael Mastanduno, eds., *Unipolar Politics: Realism and State Strategies After the Cold War.* New York: Columbia University Press.

Kapstein, Ethan Barnaby, and Michael Mastanduno, eds. 1999. *Unipolar Politics.* New York: Columbia University Press.

Karl, Terry Lynn. 1997. *The Paradox of Plenty: Oil Booms and Petro-States.* Berkeley: University of California Press.

Kastner, Scott L., and Chad Rector. 2003. "International Regimes, Domestic Veto-Players, and Capital Controls Policy Stability." *International Studies Quarterly* 47 (1): 1–22.

Katzenstein, Peter. 1996. Introduction to Peter Katzenstein, ed., *The Culture of National Security: Norms and Identity in World Politics.* New York: Columbia University Press.

Keck, Margaret E., and Kathryn Sikkink. 1998. *Activists Beyond Borders: Advocacy Networks in International Politics.* Ithaca: Cornell University Press.

Keller, William W. 1995. *Arm in Arm: The Political Economy of the Global Arms Trade.* New York: Basic Books.

Keller, William W., and Janne E. Nolan. 2001. "Mortgaging Security for Economic Gain: U.S. Arms Policy in an Insecure World." *International Studies Perspectives* 2 (2): 177–193.

Kelley, Allen C. 1988. "Economic Consequences of Population Change in the Third World." *Journal of Economic Literature* 26 (4): 1685–1728.

————. 2001. "The Population Debate in Historical Perspective: Revisionism Revisited." In Nancy Birdsall, Allen C. Kelley, and Steven W. Sinding, eds., *Population Matters: Demographic Change, Economic Growth, and Poverty in Developing Countries.* Oxford: Oxford University Press.

Kelley, Allen C., and William P. McGreevey. 1994. "Population and Development in Historical Perspective." In Robert H. Cassen, ed., *Population and Development: Old Debates, New Conclusions.* Washington, D.C.: Overseas Development Council.

Kelley, Allen C., and Robert M. Schmidt. 2001. "Economic and Demographic Change: A Synthesis of Models, Findings, and Perspectives." In Nancy Birdsall, Allen C. Kelley, and Steven W. Sinding, eds., *Population Matters: Demographic Change, Economic Growth, and Poverty in Developing Countries.* Oxford: Oxford University Press.

Kennedy, Gavin. 1983. *Defense Economics.* London: Duckworth.

Kennedy, Paul. 1987. *The Rise and Fall of the Great Powers: Economic Change and Military Conflict from 1500–2000.* New York: Random House.

————. 2002. "The Eagle Has Landed." *Financial Times,* February 2, p. 1.

Keohane, Robert O. 1990. "International Liberalism Revisited." In John Dunn, ed., *The Economic Limits to Modern Politics.* Cambridge: Cambridge University Press.

Keohane, Robert O., and Joseph S. Nye Jr., eds. 1973. *Transnational Relations and World Politics.* Cambridge: Harvard University Press.

————. 1998. "Power and Interdependence in the Information Age." *Foreign Affairs* 77 (5): 81–94.

————. 2000. "Globalization: What's New? What's Not? (And So What?)" *Foreign Policy* 118: 105–119.

————. 2001. *Power and Interdependence.* New York: Addison, Wesley, Longman.

Key, V. O. 1961. *Public Opinion and American Democracy.* New York: Knopf.

Khalaf, Roula. 2003. "Zoellick Criticism Sets Back Egypt Hopes on a Free Trade Deal." *Financial Times,* June 24, p. 11.

King, Angela E. V. 2001. Foreword to Inger Skjelsbaek and Dan Smith, eds., *Gender, Peace and Conflict.* London: Sage.

Kinsella, David. 1998. "Arms Transfer Dependence and Foreign Policy Conflict." *Journal of Peace Research* 35 (1): 7–23.

Kirshner, Jonathan. 1997. "The Microfoundations of Economic Sanctions." *Security Studies* 6 (3): 32–64.

————. 1998. "Political Economy in Security Studies After the Cold War." *Review of International Political Economy* 5 (1): 64–91.

Kissinger, Henry. 2001. *Does America Need a Foreign Policy? Toward a Diplomacy for the 21st Century.* New York: Simon and Schuster.

Klare, Michael T. 1984. *American Arms Supermarket.* Austin: University of Texas Press.

————. 2001. *Resource Wars: The New Landscape of Global Conflict.* New York: Metropolitan Books.

Klare, Michael T., and Yogesh Chandrani, eds. 1998. *World Security: Challenges for a New Century.* 3rd ed. New York: St. Martin's.

Klare, Michael T., and Daniel C. Thomas, eds. 1994. *World Security: Challenges for a New Century.* New York: St. Martin's.

Klare, Michael T., and Daniel Volman. 1996. "From Military Aid to Military Markets." In Steven W. Hook, ed., *Foreign Aid Toward the Millennium.* Boulder: Lynne Rienner.

Kline, John. 1985. *International Codes and Multinational Business: Setting Guidelines for International Business Operations.* Westport: Quorum.

Knorr, Klaus. 1957. "The Concept of Economic Potential for War." *World Politics* 10 (1): 49–62.

————. 1970. *The War Potential of Nations.* Lanham: Lexington Books.

————. 1973. *Power and Wealth: The Political Economy of National Power.* London: Macmillan.

————. 1977a. "International Economic Leverage and Its Uses." In Klaus Knorr and Frank N. Trager, eds., *Economic Issues and National Security.* Lawrence: Regents Press of Kansas.

————. 1977b. "Military Strength: Economic and Non-Economic Bases." In Klaus Knorr and Frank N. Trager, eds., *Economic Issues and National Security.* Lawrence: Regents Press of Kansas.

————, ed. 1978. *Economic Issues and National Security.* Lawrence: University Press of Kansas.

Koistinen, Paul A. C. 1987. *Planning War, Pursuing Peace: The Political Economy of American Warfare, 1920–1939.* Lawrence: University Press of Kansas.

Kokusai Kyôryoku Kondankai. 2002. *Kokusai Kyôryoku Kondankai Hôkokusho.* Available at http://www.kantei.go.jp/jp/singi/kokusai/kettei/021218houkoku.html.

Korten, David C. 1995. *When Corporations Rule the World.* West Hartford: Kumarian Press.

Krasner, Stephen D. 1976. "State Power and the Structure of Foreign Trade." *World Politics* 28 (3): 317–347.

————, ed. 1983. *International Regimes.* Ithaca: Cornell University Press.

————. 1999. *Sovereignty: Organized Hypocrisy?* Princeton: Princeton University Press.

————, ed. 2001. *Problematic Sovereignty: Contested Rules and Political Possibilities.* New York: Columbia University Press.

Krauthammer, Charles. 1991. "The Unipolar Moment." *Foreign Affairs* 70 (1): 23–33.

————. 2002–2003. "The Unipolar Moment Revisited." *National Interest* 70: 5–17.

Krepinevich, Andrew F. 1994. "Cavalry to Computer: The Pattern of Military Revolutions." *National Interest* 37: 30–42.

Krim, Jonathan. 2004. "Report Faults Cyber-Security." *Washington Post,* July 23, p. E01.

Krosnick, Jon A. 1988. "The Role of Attitude Importance in Social Evaluation: A Study of Policy Preferences, Presidential Candidate Evaluations, and Voting Behavior." *Journal of Personality and Social Psychology* 55 (2): 196–210.

Krosnick, Jon A., and Duane F. Alwin. 1989. "Aging and Susceptibility to Attitude Change." *Journal of Personality and Social Psychology* 57 (3): 416–425.

Krosnick, Jon A., D. S. Boninger, Y. C. Chuang, M. K. Berent, and C. G. Carnot. 1993. "Attitude Strength: One Construct or Many Related Constructs?" *Journal of Personality and Social Psychology* 65 (6): 1132–1151.

Kugler, Richard, and Ellen L. Frost, eds. 2001. *The Global Century: Globalization and National Security.* Washington, D.C.: National Defense University Press.

Kupchan, Charles A. 2002. "Misreading September 11th." *National Interest* 69: 26–30.

————. 2003a. *The End of the American Era: U.S. Foreign Policy and the Geopolitics of the Twenty-First Century.* New York: Alfred A. Knopf.

————. 2003b. "The Rise of Europe, America's Changing Internationalism, and the End of U.S. Primacy." *Political Science Quarterly* 118 (2): 205–231.

Lake, Anthony. 2000. *6 Nightmares.* Boston: Little, Brown.

Lake, David A. 1984. "Beneath the Commerce of Nations: A Theory of International Economic Structures." *International Studies Quarterly* 28 (2): 143–170.

————. 1988. *Power, Protection, and Free Trade: International Sources of U.S. Commercial Strategy, 1887–1939.* Ithaca: Cornell University Press.

————. 1992. "Powerful Pacifists: Democratic States and War." *American Political Science Review* 86 (1): 24–37.

————. 1993. "Leadership, Hegemony, and the International Economy: Naked Emperor or Tattered Monarch with Potential?" *International Studies Quarterly* 37 (4): 459–489.

Lamy, Pascal, and Robert B. Zoellick. 2001. "In the Next Round." *Washington Post,* July 17, p. A17.

Lane, Robert. 1962. *Political Ideology.* New York: Free Press.

Layne, Christopher. 1993. "The Unipolar Illusion: Why New Great Powers Will Rise." *International Security* 17 (4): 5–51.

le Billon, Philippe. 2001. "The Political Ecology of War: Natural Resources and Armed Conflicts." *Political Geography* 20 (5): 561–584.

Lee, Ronald D., Andrew Mason, and Time Miller. 2001. "Savings, Wealth, and Population." In Nancy Birdsall, Allen C. Kelley, and Steven W. Sinding, eds., *Population Matters: Demographic Change, Economic Growth, and Poverty in Developing Countries.* Oxford: Oxford University Press.

Leitenberg, Milton. 2003. "Deaths in Wars and Conflicts Between 1945 and 2000." Peace Studies Program Occasional Paper no. 29. Ithaca: Cornell University Press.

Lenain, Patrick, Marcos Bonturi, and Vincent Koen. 2002. "Economic Consequences of Terrorism." Paris: Organization for Economic Cooperation and Development, July 17.

Lewis, James A. 2003. "Critical Infrastructure Protection: With All Deliberate Speed." *CIP Report* 2 (6). Available at http://gmu.edu/archives/cipp-report.html.

Lewis, Jim. 2002. *Assessing the Risks of Cyberterrorism, Cyber War, and Other Cyber Threats*. Washington, D.C.: Center for Strategic and International Studies.

Liberman, Peter. 1996. *Does Conquest Pay? The Exploitation of Occupied Industrial Societies*. Princeton: Princeton University Press.

Lichbach, Mark. 2002. "Global Collective Action." Unpublished manuscript.

Lichtblau, Eric. 2004. "U.S. Warns of High Risk of Qaeda Attack." *New York Times*, August 2, p. 1.

Lindsay, James M. 1986. "Trade Sanctions as Policy Instruments: A Reexamination." *International Studies Quarterly* 30 (2): 153–173.

———. 1994. *Congress and the Politics of U.S. Foreign Policy*. Baltimore: Johns Hopkins University Press.

Lipschutz, Ronnie D. 2000. *After Authority: War, Peace, and Global Politics in the 21st Century*. Albany: State University of New York Press.

Livingstone, Neil C. 1989. "A New U.S. Antiterrorism Strategy." In Loren B. Thompson, ed., *Low-Intensity Conflict: The Pattern of Warfare in the Modern World*. Lexington: Lexington Books.

Lobell, Steven E. 2003. *The Challenge of Hegemony: Grand Strategy, Trade, and Domestic Politics*. Ann Arbor: University of Michigan Press.

Lohmann, Susanne, and Sharyn O'Halloran. 1994. "Divided Government and U.S. Trade Policy: Theory and Evidence." *International Organization* 48 (4): 595–632.

Long, William J. 1996. "Trade and Technology Incentives and Bilateral Cooperation." *International Studies Quarterly* 40 (1): 77–106.

Losman, Donald. 1979. *International Economic Sanctions: The Cases of Cuba, Israel, and Rhodesia*. Albuquerque: University of New Mexico Press.

Lumpe, Lora. 1999. "A Framework for Limiting the Negative Consequences of Surplus U.S. Arms Production and Trading." In Ann R. Markusen and Sean S. Costigan, eds., *Arming the Future: A Defense Industry for the 21st Century*. New York: Council on Foreign Relations.

———. 2000. *Running Guns: The Global Black Market in Small Arms*. London: Zed Books.

Lumpe, Lora, and Jeff Donarski. 1998. *The Arms Trade Revealed: A Guide for Investigators and Activists*. Washington, D.C.: Federation of American Scientists.

Macgregor, Douglas A. 2003. *Transformation Under Fire: Revolutionizing How America Fights*. Westport: Praeger.

MacIsaac, David. 1976. *Strategic Bombing in World War Two*. New York: Garland.

Mahan, Alfred Thayer. 1941. *On Naval Warfare*. Boston: Little, Brown.

Malone, David M., and Yuen Foong Khong. 2003. "Unilateralism and U.S. Foreign Policy: International Perspectives." In David M. Malone and Yuen Foong Khong, eds., *Unilateralism in U.S. Foreign Policy: International Perspectives*. Boulder: Lynne Rienner.

Mandel, Robert. 1994. *The Changing Face of National Security*. Westport: Greenwood.

———. 1999. *Deadly Transfers and the Global Playground*. New York: Praeger.

Mandel, Robert, and Jon C. Pevehouse. 2000. "Trade Blocs, Trade Flows, and International Conflict." *International Organization* 54 (4): 775–808.

Mandelbaum, Michael. 2002. "The Inadequacy of American Power." *Foreign Affairs* 81 (5): 61–73.

Mansfield, Edward D. 1994. *Power, Trade, and War.* Princeton: Princeton University Press.

Mansfield, Edward D., and Rachel Bronson. 1997. "Alliances, Preferential Trading Arrangements, and International Trade." *American Political Science Review* 91 (1): 94–107.

Mansfield, Edward D., and Marc L. Busch. 1995. "The Political Economy of Nontariff Barriers: A Cross-National Analysis." *International Organization* 49 (4): 723–749.

Mansfield, Edward D., and Helen V. Milner. 1999. "The New Wave of Regionalism." *International Organization* 53 (3): 589–627.

Mansfield, Edward D., Jon C. Pevehouse, and David H. Bearce. 2000. "Preferential Trading Arrangements and Military Disputes." In Jean-Marc F. Blanchard, Edward D. Mansfield, and Norrin M. Ripsman, eds., *Power and the Purse: The Political Economy of National Security.* London: Frank Cass.

Mansfield, Edward M., and Brian Pollins, eds. 2003. *Economic Interdependence and International Conflict: New Perspectives on an Enduring Debate.* Ann Arbor: University of Michigan Press.

Mansfield, Edward D., and Eric Reinhardt. 2003. "Multilateral Determinants of Regionalism: The Effects of GATT/WTO on the Formation of Preferential Trading Arrangements." *International Organization* 57 (4): 829–862.

Marder, Arthur. 1940. *The Anatomy of British Sea Power: A History of British Naval Policy in the Pre-Dreadnought Era, 1880–1905.* New York: Octagon Books.

Mark, Clyde R. 2003a. *Egypt–United States Relations.* Washington, D.C.: Congressional Research Service.

———. 2003b. *Israel: U.S. Foreign Assistance.* Washington, D.C.: Congressional Research Service.

Markus, G. B. 1979. "The Political Environment and the Dynamics of Public Attitudes: A Panel Study." *American Journal of Political Science* 23 (2): 338–359.

Markusen, Ann R., and Sean S. Costigan, eds. 1999. *Arming the Future: A Defense Industry for the 21st Century.* New York: Council on Foreign Relations.

Marshall, Monty G., and Ted Robert Gurr. 2003. *Peace and Conflict 2003.* College Park, Md.: Center for International Development and Conflict Management.

Mastanduno, Michael. 1997. "Preserving the Unipolar Moment: Realist Theories and U.S. Grand Strategy After the Cold War." *International Security* 21 (4): 49–88.

———. 1998. "Economics and Security in Statecraft and Scholarship." *International Organization* 52 (4): 825–854.

Mastanduno, Michael, and Ethan B. Kapstein. 1999. "Realism and State Strategies After the Cold War." In Michael Mastanduno and Ethan B. Kapstein, eds., *Unipolar Politics: Realism and State Strategies After the Cold War.* New York: Columbia University Press.

Matthews, Jessica Tuchman. 1989. "Redefining Security." *Foreign Affairs* 68 (2): 162–177.

Mayer, Kenneth R. 1991. *The Political Economy of Defense Contracting.* New Haven: Yale University Press.

Maynes, Charles William. 1993–1994. "A Workable Clinton Doctrine." *Foreign Policy* 93: 3–21.

McAdam, Doug, Sidney Arrow, and Charles Tilly, eds. 2001. *Dynamics of Contention.* Cambridge: Cambridge University Press.

McKibben, Bill. 1998. "A Special Moment in History." *Atlantic Monthly,* May, pp. 55–78.

McPhail, Kathryn. 2002. "The Revenue Dimension of Oil, Gas and Mining Projects: Issues and Practices." Paper read at the SPE International Conference on Health, Safety, and Environment in Oil and Gas Exploration and Production, Kuala Lumpur, Malaysia, March 20–22.

Mearsheimer, John J. 1994–1995. "The False Promise of International Institutions." *International Security* 19 (3): 10–11.

———. 2001. *The Tragedy of Great Power Politics.* New York: W. W. Norton.

Merrick, Thomas. 2001. "Population and Poverty in Households: A Review of Reviews." In Nancy Birdsall, Allen C. Kelley, and Steven W. Sinding, eds., *Population Matters: Demographic Change, Economic Growth, and Poverty in Developing Countries.* Oxford: Oxford University Press.

———. 2002. "Population and Poverty: New Views on an Old Controversy." *International Family Planning Perspectives* 28 (1): 41–46.

Meyer, Henry. 2001. "Russian Arms Sales Hit Record $4.4 Billion Dollars in 2001." *Space Daily,* December 26. Available at www.spacedaily.com.

Miller, Benjamin. 2001. "The Concept of Security: Should It Be Redefined?" *Journal of Strategic Studies* 24 (2): 13–42.

Milner, Helen V. 1999. "The Political Economy of International Trade." *Annual Review of Political Science* 2: 91–114.

Milward, Alan S. 1965. *The German Economy at War.* London: Athlone Press.

———. 1977. *War, Economy, and Society.* Berkeley: University of California Press.

Mintz, John. 2004. "U.S. to Keep Key Data on Infrastructure Secret." *Washington Post,* February 19, p. A21.

Mitchell, William C. 1962. *The American Polity.* Glencoe, Ill.: Free Press.

Mitton, Roger. 2003. "U.S. Draws Sword of Trade Retribution." *Straits Times,* April 26. Available at www.persia2.asia1.com.

Molander, Roger C., Andrew S. Riddile, and Peter A. Wilson. 1996. *Strategic Information Warfare: A New Face of War.* Santa Monica: Rand.

Morgenthau, Hans J. 1985. *Politics Among Nations.* 6th ed. New York: McGraw-Hill.

Morris-Suzuki, Tessa. 1989. *A History of Japanese Economic Thought.* London: Routledge.

Moteff, John. 2002. *Critical Infrastructures: Background, Policy, and Implementation.* Washington, D.C.: Congressional Research Service, December 17.

———. 2003. "Critical Infrastructure Information Disclosure and Homeland Security." Report for Congress, RL31547. Washington, D.C.: Congressional Research Service, January 29.

Moteff, John, Claudia Copeland, and John Fischer. 2003. *Critical Infrastructure: What Makes an Infrastructure Critical.* Washington, D.C.: Congressional Research Service.

Moteff, John, and Paul Parfomak. 2004. *Critical Infrastructure and Key Assets: Definition and Identification.* Washington, D.C.: Congressional Research Service.

Mousseau, Michael. 2002–2003. "Market Civilization and Its Clash with Terror." *International Security* 27 (3): 5–29.

Mufson, Steven. 2001. "U.S. Adds Economic Weapons to Arsenal: Trade, Loans, and Aid Would Go to Allies in Terrorism Fight; Sanctions to Foes." *Washington Post,* September 18, p. A9.

Mulvenon, James. 2004. "Taiwan and the RMA." In Emily O. Goldman and Thomas G. Mahnken, eds., *The Information Revolution in Military Affairs in Asia.* New York: Palgrave.

Murray, Williamson. 1992. "The Influence of Pre-War Anglo-American Doctrine on the Air Campaigns of the Second World War." In Horst Boog, ed., *The Conduct of the Air War in the Second World War: An International Comparison.* New York: Berg.

Myers, Norman. 1993. *Ultimate Security: The Environmental Basis of Political Stability.* New York: W. W. Norton.

Narizny, Kevin. 2003a. "Both Guns and Butter, or Neither: Class Interests in the Political Economy of Rearmament." *American Political Science Review* 97 (2): 203–220.

———. 2003b. "The Political Economy of Alignment: Great Britain's Commitment to Europe, 1905–39." *International Security* 27 (4): 184–219.

National Commission on Terrorist Attacks upon the United States (9/11 Commission). 2004. *Final Report.* New York: W. W. Norton.

Nau, Henry R. 1995. *Trade and Security: U.S. Policies at Cross-Purposes.* Washington, D.C.: AEI Press.

Nelson, Jane. 2000. *The Business of Peace: The Private Sector as a Partner in Conflict Prevention and Resolution.* London: Prince of Wales Business Leaders Forum.

Newman, Edward. 2001. "Human Security and Constructivism." *International Studies Perspectives* 2 (3): 239–251.

Newnham, Randall E. 2002. *Deutsche Mark Diplomacy: Positive Economic Sanctions in German-Russian Relations.* University Park: Pennsylvania State University Press.

———. 2003. "'Nukes for Sale Cheap?' Purchasing Peace with North Korea." Paper presented at the annual meeting of the International Studies Association, Portland.

Nivola, Pietro S. 1997. "Commercializing Foreign Affairs? American Trade Policy After the Cold War." In Randall B. Ripley and James M. Lindsay, eds., *U.S. Foreign Policy After the Cold War.* Pittsburgh: University of Pittsburgh Press.

Nolt, James H. 1997. "Business Conflict and the Demise of Imperialism." In David Skidmore, ed. *Contested Social Orders and International Politics.* Nashville: Vanderbilt University Press.

Nossal, Kim Richard. 1994. *Rain Dancing: Sanctions in Canadian and Australian Foreign Policy.* Toronto: University of Toronto Press.

Nye, Joseph S., Jr. 2001–2002. "Seven Tests: Between Concert and Unilateralism." *National Interest* 66: 5–13.

———. 2002. *The Paradox of American Power: Why the World's Only Superpower Can't Go It Alone.* Oxford: Oxford University Press.

———. 2003. "U.S. Power and Strategy After Iraq." *Foreign Affairs* 82 (4): 60–73.

Oden, Michael. 1999. "Cashing In, Cashing Out, and Converting: Restructuring the Defense Industrial Base in the 1990s." In Ann R. Markusen and Sean S. Costigan, eds., *Arming the Future: A Defense Industry for the 21st Century.* New York: Council on Foreign Relations.

Office of the Undersecretary of Defense for Acquisition and Technology. 1996. *Report of the Defense Science Board Task Force on Information Warfare: Defense (IW-D).* November. Available at http://www.all.net/books/iwd/iwd.html#2.0.

O'Halloran, Sharyn. 1993. "Congress and Foreign Trade Policy." In Randall B. Ripley and James M. Lindsay, eds., *Congress Resurgent: Foreign and Defense Policy on Capitol Hill.* Ann Arbor: University of Michigan Press.

Ohlsson, Leif. 1999. "Environment, Scarcity, and Conflict: A Study of Malthusian Concerns." PhD diss., Department of Peace and Development Research, Göteborg University, Sweden.

Ohmae, Kenichi. 1994. *The End of the Nation State.* New York: Free Press.

Oneal, John R., Frances H. Oneal, and Zeev Maoz. 1996. "The Liberal Peace: Inter-dependence, Democracy, and International Conflict, 1950–1985." *Journal of Peace Research* 33 (1): 11–28.

Oneal, John R., and Bruce M. Russett. 1997. "The Classical Liberals Were Right: Democracy, Interdependence, and Conflict, 1950–1985." *International Studies Quarterly* 41 (2): 267–293.

———. 1999. "The Kantian Peace: The Pacific Benefits of Democracy, Interdependence, and International Organizations." *World Politics* 52 (1): 1–37.

Orentlicher, Diane F. 2004. "Unilateral Multilateralism: United States Policy Toward the International Criminal Court." *Cornell International Law Journal* 36 (3): 415–433.

Organski, A. F. K. 1958. *World Politics.* 1st ed. New York: Knopf.

———. 1968. *World Politics.* 2nd ed. New York: Knopf.

Organski, A. F. K., and Jacek Kugler. 1980. *The War Ledger.* Chicago: University of Chicago Press.

Orszag, Peter. 2003. "Homeland and the Private Sector: Testimony Before the National Commission on Terrorist Attacks upon the United States." November 19. Available at http://www.brookings.edu/views/testimony/orszag/20031119.pdf.

Papayoanou, Paul A. 1995. "Interdependence, Institutions, and the Balance of Power." *International Security* 20 (4): 42–76.

Pape, Robert A. 1996. *Bombing to Win: Air Power and Coercion in War.* Ithaca: Cornell University Press.

———. 1997. "Why Economic Sanctions Do Not Work." *International Security* 22 (2): 90–136.

———. 1997–1998. "The Limits of Precision-Guided Air Power." *Security Studies* 7 (2): 93–114.

———. 2003. "The Strategic Logic of Suicide Terrorism." *American Political Science Review* 97 (3): 343–362.

Patrick, Stewart. 2002. "Multilateralism and Its Discontents: The Causes and Consequences of U.S. Ambivalence." In Stewart Patrick and Shepherd Forman, eds., *Multilateralism and U.S. Foreign Policy: Ambivalent Engagement.* Boulder: Lynne Rienner.

Pearce, Fred. 2002. "Blood Diamonds and Oil." *New Scientist,* June 29, pp. 36–41.

Pearson, Frederic S. 1994. *The Global Spread of Arms: Political Economy of International Security.* Boulder: Westview.

Peet, Richard, and Michael Watts. 1996. *Liberation Ecologies: Environment, Development, and Social Movements.* London: Routledge.

Peluso, Nancy Lee, and Michael Watts, eds. 2001. *Violent Environments.* Ithaca: Cornell University Press.

Percival, Valerie, and Thomas F. Homer-Dixon. 1995. "Environmental Scarcity and Violent Conflict: The Case of Rwanda." Occasional paper, Project on Environment, Population, and Security. Washington, D.C.: University of Toronto, the Academy of Arts and Sciences.

Personick, Stewart D., and Cynthia A. Patterson, eds. 2003. *Critical Infrastructure Protection and the Law: An Overview of Key Issues.* Washington, D.C.: National Academies Press. Available at http://books.nap.edu/books/030908878X/html/7.html#pagetop.

Peterson, Paul E. 1994. "The President's Dominance in Foreign Policy Making." *Political Science Quarterly* 109 (2): 215–234.

Pharr, Susan. 1993. "Japan's Defensive Foreign Policy and the Policies of Burden Sharing." In Gerald L. Curtis, ed., *Japan's Foreign Policy*. New York: M. E. Sharpe.

"Picking the Locks on the Internet Security Market." 2001. Redherring.com, July 24.

Pierre, Andrew J. 1982. *The Global Politics of Arms Sales*. Princeton: Princeton University Press.

———, ed. 1997. *Cascade of Arms: Managing Conventional Weapons Proliferation*. Washington, D.C.: Brookings Institution Press.

Pierre, Andrew J., and Dmitri V. Trenin, eds. 1997. *Russia in the World Arms Trade*. Washington, D.C.: Carnegie Endowment for International Peace.

Pipes, Daniel. 2001–2002. "God and Mammon: Does Poverty Cause Militant Islam?" *National Interest* 66: 14–21.

Poe, Steven C. 1991. "Human Rights and the Allocation of U.S. Military Assistance." *Journal of Peace Research* 28 (2): 205–216.

Poe, Steven C., and James Meernik. 1995. "U.S. Military Aid in the 1980s: A Global Analysis." *Journal of Peace Research* 32 (4): 399–411.

Polachek, S. W. 1980. "Conflict and Trade." *Journal of Conflict Resolution* 24 (1): 55–78.

Posen, Barry R. 1984. *The Sources of Military Doctrine: France, Britain, and Germany Between the World Wars*. Ithaca: Cornell University Press.

———. 2003. "Command of the Commons: The Military Foundations of U.S. Hegemony." *International Security* 28 (1): 5–46.

Posen, Barry R., and Andrew L. Ross. 1996–1997. "Competing Visions for U.S. Grand Strategy." *International Security* 21 (3): 5–53.

Powell, Colin. 2002. "Campaign Against Terror." *Frontline* interview, PBS, June 7. Available at http://www.pbs.org/wgbh/pages/frontline/shows/campaign/interviews/powell.html.

President's Commission on Critical Infrastructure Protection. 1997. "Critical Foundations: Protecting America's Infrastructures." October. Available at http://www.ciao.gov/resource/pccip/Pccip_report.pdf.

Prime Minister's Commission on Japan's Goals in the Twenty-First Century. 2000. "Japan's Goals in the Twenty-First Century: The Frontier Within—Individual Empowerment and Better Governance in the New Millennium." Tokyo.

Prunier, Gérard. 1995. *The Rwanda Crisis: History of a Genocide*. New York: Columbia University Press.

Putnam, Robert. 1988. "Diplomacy and Domestic Politics: The Logic of Two-Level Games." *International Organization* 42 (3): 427–460.

Quester, George H. 1966. *Deterrence Before Hiroshima: The Airpower Background of Modern Strategy*. New York: Wiley.

Reich, Robert B. 1990. "Who Is Us?" *Harvard Business Review* 90 (1): 53–64.

Reinecke, Wolfgang H. 1997. "Global Public Policy." *Foreign Affairs* 76 (November–December): 127–139.

Reis, Sally. 1998. *Work Left Undone: Choice and Compromises of Talented Women*. Mansfield Center, Conn.: Creative Learning Press.

Rennack, Dianne E. 2003. *India and Pakistan: U.S. Economic Sanctions*. Washington, D.C.: Congressional Research Service.

Renner, Michael. 2002. *The Anatomy of Resource Wars*. Washington, D.C.: Worldwatch Institute.

Reno, William. 1998. *Warlord Politics and African States*. Boulder: Lynne Rienner.

————. 2000. "Shadow States and the Political Economy of Civil Wars." In M. Berdal and D. M. Malone, eds., *Greed and Grievance: Economic Agendas in Civil Wars.* Boulder: Lynne Rienner.

Ripley, Randall B., and James M. Lindsay. 1993. "How Congress Influences Foreign and Defense Policy." In Randall B. Ripley and James M. Lindsay, eds., *Congress Resurgent: Foreign and Defense Policy on Capitol Hill.* Ann Arbor: University of Michigan Press.

Ripsman, Norrin M. 2002. *Peacemaking by Democracies: The Effect of State Autonomy on the Post-World-War Settlements.* University Park: Pennsylvania State University Press.

Ripsman, Norrin M., and Jean-Marc F. Blanchard. 1996–1997. "Commercial Liberalism Under Fire: Evidence from 1914 and 1936." *Security Studies* 6 (2): 4–50.

————. 2000. "Contextual Information and the Study of Trade and Conflict: The Utility of an Interdisciplinary Approach." In Rudra Sil and Eileen M. Doherty, eds., *Beyond Boundaries? Disciplines, Paradigms, and Theoretical Integration in International Studies.* Albany: State University of New York Press.

Ripsman, Norrin M., and T. V. Paul. 2003. "Assessing the Uneven Impact of Global Social Forces on the National Security State: A Framework for Analysis." Paper presented at the annual meeting of the Central and Eastern European International Studies Association, Budapest.

————. forthcoming 2005. "Globalization and the National Security State: A Framework for Analysis." *International Studies Review* 7 (2).

Risse-Kappen, Thomas, ed. 1995. *Bringing Transnational Relations Back In: Non-State Actors, Domestic Structures, and International Institutions.* Cambridge: Cambridge University Press.

Robinson, Mary. 2003. "Human Rights and Corporate Accountability." Speech given at Fund for Peace, Washington, D.C., February 20. Available at www.fundforpeace .org.

Rodman, Kenneth A. 1997. "'Think Globally, Punish Locally': Nonstate Actors, Multinational Corporations, and Human Rights Sanctions." Paper read at the conference "Nonstate Actors and Authority in the Global System," University of Warwick, October 31–November 1.

Rogowski, Ronald. 1987. "Trade and the Variety of Democratic Institutions." *International Organization* 41 (2): 203–223.

"Romancing Big Steel." 2002. *The Economist,* February 14, p. 52.

Rosenau, James N. (1994). "New Dimensions of Security: The Interaction of Globalizing and Localizing Dynamics." *Security Dialogue* 25 (3): 255–281.

Rosenberg, Barbara Hatch. 2001. "Allergic Reaction: Washington's Response to the BWC Protocol." *Arms Control Today,* July–August. Available at http://www. armscontrol.org/act/2001_07-08/rosenbergjul_aug01.asp.

Ross, Michael L. 1999. "The Political Economy of the Resource Curse." *World Politics* 51 (2): 297–323.

————. 2000. "Does Resource Wealth Lead to Authoritarian Rule?" Paper read at the conference "The Economics of Political Violence," World Bank Research Group workshop, Princeton University, March 18–19.

————. 2001. *Timber Booms and Institutional Breakdown in Southeast Asia.* New York: Cambridge University Press.

————. 2003. "Natural Resources and Civil War: An Overview." Unpublished manuscript. August 15.

————. 2004. "How Do Natural Resources Influence Civil War? Evidence from Thirteen Cases." *International Organization* 58 (1): 35–67.

———. forthcoming. "What Do We Know About Natural Resources and Civil War?" *Journal of Peace Research.*

Rosso, Stephen J. Del, Jr. 1995. "The Insecure State: Reflections on 'the State' and 'Security' in a Changing World." *Daedalus* 124 (2): 175–207.

Rothkopf, David J. 2002. "Business Versus Terror." *Foreign Policy* 130: 56–64.

Rowe, David. 1999a. "Economic Sanctions Do Work: Economic Statecraft and the Oil Embargo of Rhodesia Reconsidered." In Jean-Marc F. Blanchard, Edward D. Mansfield, and Norrin M. Ripsman, eds., *Power and the Purse: The Political Economy of National Security.* London: Frank Cass.

———. 1999b. "World Economic Expansion and National Security in Pre–World War I Europe." *International Organization* 53 (2): 195–231.

Ruggie, John Gerard. 1982. "International Regimes, Transactions, and Change: Embedded Liberalism in the Postwar Economic Order." *International Organization* 36 (2): 379–415.

———. 1992. "Multilateralism: The Anatomy of an Institution." *International Organization* 46 (3): 561–598.

Rumsfeld, Donald. 2001. *Larry King Live* interview, CNN, December 5. Available at http://www.cnn.com/transcripts/0112/05/lkl.00.html.

Rushe, Dominic, and Lucinda Kemeny. 2003. "Trade Becomes the Next Battlefield." *Sunday Times,* March 23, p. 7.

Russett, Bruce. 1995. Foreward to James S. Sutterlin, *The United Nations and the Maintenance of International Security: A Challenge to Be Met.* Westport: Praeger.

Sachs, Jeffrey D., and Andrew M. Warner. 1995. *Natural Resource Abundance and Economic Growth.* Cambridge: Harvard Institute for International Development.

———. 1999. "The Big Push, Natural Resource Booms, and Growth." *Journal of Development Economics* 59 (1): 43–76.

———. 2001. "Natural Resources and Economic Development: The Curse of Natural Resources." *European Economic Review* 45: 827–838.

Sadowski, Y. M. 1993. *Scuds or Butter? The Political Economy of Arms Control in the Middle East.* Washington, D.C.: Brookings Institution Press.

Sampat, Payal. 2003. "Scrapping Mining Dependence." In Worldwatch Institute, *State of the World 2003.* New York: W. W. Norton.

Samuels, Richard J. 1991. "Reinventing Security: Japan Since Meiji." *Daedalus* 120 (4): 47–68.

Sanger, David E. 2003. "A Blink from the Bush Administration." *New York Times,* December 5, p. A28.

Schelling, Thomas. 1978. *Micromotives and Macrobehavior.* New York: W. W. Norton.

Schiesel, Seth. 2003. "Taking Aim at an Enemy's Chips." *New York Times,* November 20, p. G1.

Schlesinger, Stephen. 1998–1999. "The End of Idealism: Foreign Policy in the Clinton Years." *World Policy Journal* 15 (4): 36–40.

Schoultz, Lars. 1981. "U.S. Foreign Policy and Human Rights Violations in Latin America: A Comparative Analysis of Foreign Aid Distributions." *Comparative Politics* 13 (2): 149–170.

Schultz, Kenneth A., and Barry R. Weingast. 2003. "The Democratic Advantage: Institutional Foundations of Financial Power in International Competition." *International Organization* 57 (1): 3–42.

Schultze, Charles L. 1977. *The Public Use of the Private Interest.* Washington, D.C.: Brookings Institution Press.

Shapiro, Ian. 1996. *Democracy's Place.* Ithaca: Cornell University Press.

Sherman, Jake. 2002. "Options for Promoting Corporate Responsibility in Conflict Zones: Perspectives from the Private Sector." Paper read at the Permanent Mission of Luxembourg to the United Nations. New York: International Peace Academy.

Showalter, Dennis. 1973. "Soldiers into Postmasters? The Electric Telegraph as an Instrument of Command in the Prussian Army." *Military Affairs* 37 (2): 48–52.

Shugart, Matthew Soberg, and Stephan Haggard. 2001. "Institutions and Public Policy in Presidential Systems." In Stephan Haggard and Mathew D. McCubbins, eds., *Presidents, Parliaments, and Policy.* Cambridge: Cambridge University Press.

Silverstein, Gordon. 1997. *Imbalance of Powers: Constitutional Interpretation and the Making of American Foreign Policy.* New York: Oxford University Press.

Simon, Julian L. 1981. *The Ultimate Resource.* Princeton: Princeton University Press.

———. 1992. *Population and Development in Poor Countries.* Princeton: Princeton University Press.

Simon, Julian L., and Herman Kahn, eds. 1984. *The Resourceful Earth: A Response to Global 2000.* Oxford: Basil Blackwell.

Singapore 2000. 2000. Singapore: Ministry of Information and the Arts.

Singer, Peter W. 2001–2002. "Corporate Warriors: The Rise and Ramifications of the Privatized Military Industry." *International Security* 26, no. 3 (Winter): 186–220.

———. 2003. *Corporate Warriors: The Rise of the Privatized Military Industry.* Ithaca: Cornell University Press.

Smillie, Ian, Lansana Giberie, and Ralph Hazleton. 2000. *The Heart of the Matter: Sierra Leone, Diamonds, and Human Security.* Ottawa: Partnership Africa Canada.

Smith, D. 2001. "The Problem of Essentialism." In I. Skjelsbaek and D. Smith, eds., *Gender, Peace, and Conflict.* London: Sage.

Snyder, Jack. 1991. *Myths of Empire: Domestic Politics and International Ambition.* Ithaca: Cornell University Press.

———. 2000. *From Voting to Violence: Democratization and Nationalist Conflict.* New York: W. W. Norton.

Snyder, Scott. 1997. "North Korea's Nuclear Program: The Role of Incentives in Preventing Deadly Conflict." In David Cortright, ed., *The Price of Peace: Incentives and International Conflict Prevention.* Lanham: Rowan and Littlefield.

Solingen, Etel. 1998. *Regional Orders at Century's Dawn: Global and Domestic Influences on Grand Strategy.* Princeton: Princeton University Press.

Soo Hoo, Kevin J., Seymour E. Goodman, and Lawrence T. Greenberg. 1997. "Information Technology and the Terrorist Threat." *Survival* 39 (3): 135–155.

Spar, Deborah L. 1998. "The Spotlight and the Bottom Line: How Multinationals Export Human Rights." *Foreign Affairs* 77 (2): 7–12.

Spruyt, Hendrik. 2002. "The Origins, Development, and Possible Decline of the Modern State." *Annual Review of Political Science* 5: 127–149.

Staley, Eugene. 1937. *Raw Materials in Peace and War.* New York: Council of Foreign Relations.

Starks, Tim, and Martin Edwin Anderson. 2004. "Congress, Industry Both in Dismay over Homeland Security's Performance on Critical Infrastructure." *Congressional Quarterly's Homeland Security.* Available at http://www.ewa-iit.com/content.asp?sectionid=47&contentid=140.

Stein, Arthur A. 1984. "The Hegemon's Dilemma: Great Britain, the United States, and the International Economic Order." *International Organization* 38 (2): 355–386.

———. 1990. *Why Nations Cooperate: Circumstance and Choice in International Relations.* Ithaca: Cornell University Press.

Steurer, Reinhard. 2003. "The U.S.'s Retreat from the Kyoto Protocol: An Account of a Policy Change and Its Implications for Future Climate Policy." *European Environment* 13 (6): 344–360.

Stiglitz, Joseph E. 2003. *Globalization and Its Discontents*. New York: W. W. Norton.

Stohl, Rachel 2003. "Post–Sept. 11 Arms Sales and Military Aid Demonstrate Dangerous Trend." Center for Defense Information, January 14. Available at http://www .cdi.org.

Strandberg, Coro. 2002. *The Future of Corporate Social Responsibility*. Vancouver: VanCity Credit Union.

Strange, Susan. 1983. "Cave Hic Dragones: A Critique of Regime Analysis." In Stephen D. Krasner, ed., *International Regimes*. Ithaca: Cornell University Press.

———. 1996. *The Retreat of the State: The Diffusion of Power in the World Economy.* New York: Cambridge University Press.

Strange, Susan, and John Stopford. 1991. *Rival States, Rival Firms: Competition for World Market Shares*. Cambridge: Cambridge University Press.

Suliman, Mohamed. 1992. *Civil War in Sudan: The Impact of Ecological Degradation.* Berne: Swiss Peace Foundation and Center for Security Studies and Conflict Research.

———. 1993. "Civil War in the Sudan: From Ethnic to Ecological Conflict." *The Ecologist* 23 (3): 104–109.

———, ed. 1999. *Ecology, Politics, and Violent Conflict*. London: Zed Books.

Switzer, Jason. 2002. "Mining and Conflict: A Background Paper for the MMSD Workshop on Natural Resources and Conflict." London: IISD.

Taw, Jennifer Morrison, and Bruce Hoffman. 1994. "Operations Other Than War." In Paul K. Davis, ed., *New Challenges for Defense Planning*. Santa Monica: Rand.

Tenet, George. 2002. Testimony of George J. Tenet, director of central intelligence, before the Senate Select Committee on Intelligence. February 6.

Terashima, Jitsurô. 2002. "Washington Takes an Alarming Turn." *Japan Echo* 29 (4): 20–25.

Terriff, Terry, Stuart Croft, Lucy James, and Patrick M. Morgan. 1999. *Security Studies Today*. Cambridge, UK: Polity Press.

Thomas, Caroline. 1999. Introduction to Caroline Thomas and Peter Wilkin, eds., *Globalization, Human Security, and the African Experience*. Boulder: Lynne Rienner.

Thomas, Douglas. 2002. Testimony before the House Subcommittee on Government Efficiency, Financial Management, and Intergovernmental Relations. July 24.

Tierney, John. 2003. "A Popular Idea: Give Oil Money to the People Rather Than the Despots." *New York Times,* September 10, p. A9.

Tilly, Charles. 1989. *Big Structures, Large Processes, Huge Comparisons*. New York: Sage.

———. 1990. *Coercion, Capital, and European States, A.D. 990–1990*. Cambridge: Basil Blackwell.

Toffler, Alvin, and Heidi Toffler. 1993. *War and Anti-War*. New York: Warner.

Triplett, William C., III. 2000. "Potential Applications of PLA Information Warfare Capabilities to Critical Infrastructure." In Susan M. Puska, ed., *People's Liberation Army After Next*. Carlisle Barracks, Pa.: Strategic Studies Institute.

Trubowitz, Peter. 1998. *Defining the National Interest: Conflict and Change in American Foreign Policy*. Chicago: University of Chicago Press.

Tsalik, Svetlana. 2003. *Caspian Oil Windfalls: Who Will Benefit?* New York: Caspian Revenue Watch/Open Society Institute.

Tsebelis, George. 1995. "Decision Making in Political Systems: Veto Players in Presidentialism, Parliamentarism, Multicameralism and Multipartyism." *British Journal of Political Science* 25 (3): 289–325.

———. 2002. *Veto Players: How Political Institutions Work.* Princeton: Princeton University Press.

Tucker, Robert W. 2002. "The End of a Contradiction?" *National Interest* 69: 5–7.

Uchitelle, Louis, and John Markoff. 2004. "Terrorbusters Inc.: The Rise of the Homeland Security-Industrial Complex." *New York Times,* October 17. Available at www.nytimes.com.

United Nations (UN). 2004. *A More Secure World: Our Shared Responsibility—A Report of the Secretary General's High Level Panel on Threats, Challenges, and Change.* New York: United Nations. Available at http://www.un.org/secureworld.

United Nations Conference on Trade and Development (UNCTAD). 2003. *World Investment Report 2003: FDI Policies for Development: National and International Perspectives.* Geneva: UNCTAD.

———. 2004. *World Investment Report 2004.* Geneva: UNCTAD.

United Nations Development Programme (UNDP). 1994. *Human Development Report 1994.* New York: United Nations.

———. 2003. *Human Development Report 2003.* New York: Oxford University Press.

United Nations Global Compact. 2002. "Dialogue on Business in Zones of Conflict: Rapporteur's Report." New York: United Nations.

United Nations Population Division (UNPD). 2001. *Population, Environment, and Development: The Concise Report.* New York: United Nations.

———. 2002. *World Urbanization Prospects: The 2001 Revision.* New York: United Nations.

———. 2003. *World Population Prospects: The 2002 Revision.* New York: United Nations, February 26.

U.S. Defense Security Cooperation Agency. Various Years. "Foreign Military Sales, Foreign Military Construction Sales, and Military Assistance Facts." Washington, D.C.: Department of Defense. Available at http://www.dsca.osd.mil.

U.S. Department of Defense. 2003. "Department of Defense Almanac." September 2. Available at http://www.defenselink.mil/pubs/almanac/at_a_glance.html.

U.S. Department of Homeland Security. 2002. *The National Strategy for Homeland Security: Office of Homeland Security.* July 16. Washington, D.C.: Department of Homeland Security. Available at http://www.whitehouse.gov/homeland/book/nat_strat_hls.pdf.

———. 2004. "Homeland Security Budget in Brief, Fiscal Year 2005." Washington, D.C.: Department of Homeland Security. Available at http://www.dhs.gov.

U.S. Department of State. 2003a. "Congressional Budget Justification for Foreign Operations." Available at http://www.state.gov/m/rm/rls/cbj.

———. 2003b. "Country Reports on Human Rights Practices, 2002." Available at http://www.state.gov/g/drl/rls/hrrpt/2002.

———. 2003c. "World Military Expenditures and Arms Transfers, 1999–2000." February 6. Available at http://www.state.gov/t/vc/rls/rpt/wmeat/1999_2000.

U.S. General Accounting Office (GAO). 1996. *Information Security: Computer Attacks at Department of Defense Pose Increasing Risks.* GAO/AIMD-96-84. Washington, D.C.: General Accounting Office. Available at http://www.fas.org/irp/gao/aim96084.htm.

———. 2003a. *Critical Infrastructure Protection: Challenges for Selected Agencies and Industry Sectors.* GAO-03-233. Washington, D.C.: General Accounting Office, February.

————. 2003b. *Homeland Security: Voluntary Standards are Underway at Chemical Facilities but the Extent of Security Preparedness Is Unknown.* GAO-03-439. Washington, D.C.: General Accounting Office, March 14.

————. 2004. *Critical Infrastructure Protection: Improving Information Sharing with Infrastructure Sectors.* GAO-04-780. Washington, D.C.: General Accounting Office, July.

U.S. Public Law no. 107-56, Section 1016(e), "The USA Patriot Act." Available at http://www.whitehouse.gov/homeland/book/sect3-3.pdf.

U.S. Strategic Bombing Survey. 1945. *Overall Report (European War).* Washington, D.C.: Government Printing Office.

————. 1946. *The Effects of Strategic Bombing on Japan's War Economy.* Washington D.C.: Government Printing Office.

van Creveld, Martin. 1977. *Supplying War.* New York: Cambridge University Press.

————. 1991. *The Transformation of War.* New York: Free Press.

————. 1999. *The Rise and Demise of the State.* Cambridge: Cambridge University Press.

Vayda, Andrew P., and Bradley B. Walters. 1999. "Against Political Ecology." *Human Ecology* 27 (1): 167–179.

Väyrynen, Raimo. 1997. "Economic Incentives and the Bosnian Peace Process." In David Cortright, ed., *The Price of Peace: Incentives and International Conflict Prevention.* Lanham: Rowan and Littlefield.

Viner, Jacob. 1948. "Power Versus Plenty as Objectives of Foreign Policy in the Seventeenth and Eighteenth Century." *World Politics* 1 (1): 1–29.

Vlachos-Dengler, Katia. 2002. *From National Champions to European Heavyweights: European Defense-Industrial Capabilities Across Market Segments.* Santa Monica: Rand.

Vries, P. H. H. 2002. "Governing Growth: A Comparative Analysis of the Role of the State in the Rise of the West." *Journal of World History* 13 (1): 67–138.

Wackernagel, Mathis, et al. 2002. "Tracking the Ecological Overshoot of the Human Economy." *Proceedings of the National Academy of Sciences* 99 (14): 9266–9271.

Waever, Ole. 1995. "Securitization and Desecuritization." In Ronnie D. Lipschutz, ed., *On Security.* New York: Columbia University Press.

Walt, Stephen M. 1991. "The Renaissance of Security Studies." *Mershon International Studies Review* 41 (2): 211–239.

————. 2000. "Two Cheers for Clinton's Foreign Policy." *Foreign Affairs* 79 (2): 63–79.

————. 2001–2002. "Beyond bin Laden: Reshaping U.S. Foreign Policy." *International Security* 26 (3): 56–78.

Waltz, Kenneth N. 1970. "The Myth of Interdependence." In Charles P. Kindleberger, ed., *The International Corporation.* Cambridge: MIT Press.

————. 1979. *Theory of International Politics.* Reading, Mass.: Addison-Wesley.

————. 1993. "The Emerging Structure of International Politics." *International Security* 18 (2): 44–80.

————. 1999. "Globalization and Governance." *PS Online,* December. Available at www.apsanet.org.

————. 2000. "Structural Realism After the Cold War." *International Security* 25 (1): 5–41.

"War Allies Win Praise, Favors from President." 2003. *St. Petersburg Times,* May 7, p. 1A.

Watanabe, Akio. 2001. "Japan's Position on Human Rights in Asia." In Javed S. Maswood, ed., *Japan and East Asian Regionalism*. London: Routledge.

Watts, Michael. 2000. *Struggles over Geography: Violence, Freedom, and Development at the Millennium*. Cambridge, UK: Polity Press.

———. 2001. "Petro-Violence: Community, Extraction, and Political Ecology of a Mythic Commodity." In Nancy Lee Peluso and Michael Watts, eds., *Violent Environments*. Ithaca: Cornell University Press.

Weil, Carola. 2003a. "Lessons Not Learned, or the Wrong Lessons Learned, in Humanitarian Crises and International Protection." Paper read at a meeting of the American Political Science Association, Philadelphia, August 28–31.

———. 2003b. *People Versus Borders: Competing International Norms of Protection in Complex Humanitarian Emergencies*. PhD diss., College Park, University of Maryland.

Weimann, Gabriel. 2004. *Cyberterrorism: How Real Is the Threat?* Special Report no. 119. Washington, D.C.: U.S. Institute of Peace Press.

Weiner, Myron. 1994. "Security, Stability, and Migration." In Richard K. Betts, ed., *Conflict After the Cold War: Arguments on Causes of War and Peace*. New York: Macmillan.

Weiss, Thomas G. 1996. "Nongovernmental Organizations and Internal Conflict." In Michael. E. Brown, ed., *The International Dimensions of Internal Conflict*. Cambridge: MIT Press.

White House. 1996. Executive Order 13010. "Critical Infrastructure Protection." July 15. Available at http://frwebgate.access.gpo.gov/cgi-bin/getdoc.cgi?dbname=1996 _register&docid=fr17jy96-92.pdf.

———. 1998. *The Clinton Administration's Policy on Critical Infrastructure Protection: Presidential Decision Directive no. 63*. White paper. May 22. Available at http://www.nipc.gov/about/pdd63.htm.

———. 2001a. Executive Order 13228. "Establishing the Office of Homeland Security and the Homeland Security Council." Available at http://www.whitehouse .gov/news/releases/2001/10/20011008-2.html.

———. 2001b. Executive Order 13231. "Critical Infrastructure Protection in the Information Age." *Federal Register* 86, no. 202 (October 2001). Available at http://www.ciao.gov/news/eooncriticalinfrastrutureprotection101601.html.

———. 2002. *The National Security Strategy of the United States of America*. Available at http://www.whitehouse.gov/nsc/nss.pdf.

———. 2003a. Homeland Security Presidential Directive 7. "Critical Infrastructure Identification, Prioritization, and Protection." December 17. Available at http:// www.whitehouse.gov/news/releases/2003/12/print/20031217-5.html.

———. 2003b. *The National Strategy for the Physical Protection of Critical Infrastructures and Key Assets*. Available at http://www.whitehouse.gov/pcipb/physical _strategy.pdf.

———. 2003c. *The National Strategy to Secure Cyberspace*. February. Available at http://www.whitehouse.gov/pcibc/cyberspace_strategy.pdf.

———. 2003d. *National Strategy for Homeland Security: Office of Homeland Security*. Available at http://www.whitehouse.gov/homeland/book.

Whittington, Keith E., and Daniel P. Carpenter. 2003. "Executive Power in American Institutional Development." *Perspectives on Politics* 1 (3): 495–513.

Wildavsky, Aaron. 1966. "The Two Presidencies." *Trans-Action* 4 (December): 7–14.

Williams, Phil. 2002. "Transnational Organized Crime and the State." In Rodney B. Hall and Thomas J. Biersteker, eds., *The Emergence of Private Authority in Global Governance*. Cambridge: Cambridge University Press.

Williamson, Jeffrey G. 2001. "Demographic Change, Economic Growth, and Inequality." In Nancy Birdsall, Allen C. Kelley, and Steven W. Sinding, eds., *Population Matters: Demographic Change, Economic Growth, and Poverty in Developing Countries.* Oxford: Oxford University Press.

Wodele, Greta. 2004. "Panel Developing Infrastructure Protection Recommendations." *National Journal's Technology Daily,* April 14. Available at http://www.govexec.com/dailyfed/0404/041404tdpml.htm.

Wohlforth, William C. 1999. "The Stability of a Unipolar World." *International Security* 24 (1): 5–41.

Wood, Robert E. 1986. *From Marshall Plan to Debt Crisis: Foreign Aid and Development Choices in the World Economy.* Berkeley: University of California Press.

Woodrow Wilson International Center for Scholars and International Peace Academy. 2001. "The Economics of War: The Intersection of Need, Creed and Greed." Washington, D.C.

World Bank. 1997. *World Development Report: The State in a Changing World.* Washington, D.C.: World Bank.

———. 2003a. *World Development Indicators.* Washington, D.C.: World Bank.

———. 2003b. *World Development Report 2003: Sustainable Development in a Dynamic World.* Washington, D.C.: World Bank and Oxford University Press.

World Resources Institute. 2000. *World Resources 2000–2001.* Oxford: Elsevier Science.

World Wildlife Fund (WWF). 2002. *Living Planet Report 2002.* Gland, Switzerland: WWF.

Worldwatch Institute. 2003. *Vital Signs 2003.* New York: W. W. Norton.

Wu, Yuan-li. 1952. *Economic Warfare.* New York: Prentice-Hall.

Zakaria, Fareed. 1998. *From Wealth to Power: The Unusual Origins of America's World Role.* Princeton: Princeton University Press.

———. 2003. *The Future of Freedom: Illiberal Democracy at Home and Abroad.* New York: W. W. Norton.

Zanini, Michele, and Sean J. A. Edwards. 2001. "The Networking of Terror in the Information Age." In John Arquilla and David Ronfeldt, eds., *Networks and Netwars: The Future of Terror, Crime, and Militancy.* Santa Monica: Rand.

Zelikow, Philip. 2003. "The Transformation of National Security." *National Interest* 71: 17–28.

Zoellick, Robert B. 2001. "Countering Terror with Trade." *Washington Post,* September 20, p. A35.

The Contributors

Leo J. Blanken is a graduate student at the University of California, Davis. He is currently working on a dissertation using formal modeling to examine the political economy of imperialism.

Mark A. Boyer is professor of political science at the University of Connecticut and codirector of the GlobalEd Project. He is the former editor of *International Studies Perspectives,* a journal of the International Studies Association, and author or coauthor of five books, his most recent being *Defensive Internationalism: Providing Public Goods in an Uncertain World* (2004). He is also author of numerous refereed articles and book chapters on various aspects of international cooperation, teaching international studies, and negotiation.

Scott W. Brown is professor of educational psychology at the Neag School of Education at the University of Connecticut and codirector of the GlobalEd Project. He has published three books on issues related to educational psychology, and over 50 refereed journal articles and book chapters in the fields of educational psychology, educational technology, learning, and cognition. He has presented over 150 papers at professional conferences.

Michael Butler is an assistant professor of political science at East Carolina University. His most recent work has focused on just war and military intervention with published articles in the *Journal of Conflict Resolution* and the *Canadian Journal of Political Science.*

Peter Dombrowski is a professor in the Strategic Research Department of the U.S. Naval War College. He is also the editor of the Naval War College Press, which publishes the *Naval War College Review.* He is the author of over thirty journal articles, book chapters, and government reports. His book *Policy Re-*

sponses to the Globalization of American Banking was published by the University of Pittsburgh Press in 1996. He has served as coeditor of *International Studies Quarterly,* the flagship journal of the International Studies Association (ISA), and a term as chair of the ISA international political economy section. Among other awards, grants, and fellowships, he was a Federal Chancellor's Fellow with the Alexander von Humboldt Foundation. Dombrowski is currently completing a coauthored book, *Buying Transformation: Technological Innovation and the Defense Industry.*

Sue E. Eckert is a Watson Institute senior fellow and a visiting fellow at the Institute for International Economics in Washington, D.C., where her current research focuses on economic sanctions and electronic commerce. From 1993 to 1997 she was assistant secretary of commerce for export administration and administered a range of programs on U.S. export control and the defense-industrial base. Previously, she served on the professional staff of the U.S. House of Representative's Committee on Foreign Affairs, specializing in technology transfer, international trade, and national security and nonproliferation export-control issues. Eckert works extensively with business and non-profit groups as an independent consultant and lectures on foreign policy and national security decisionmaking issues.

Emily O. Goldman is associate professor of political science at the University of California–Davis and director of the University of California–Davis Washington Program. Her research focuses on U.S. strategic, military, and arms-control policy, strategy in peacetime, military innovation, the revolution in military affairs, defense transformation, and warfare in the information age. Her publications include *Sunken Treaties: Naval Arms Control Between the Wars* (1994), *The Politics of Strategic Adjustment* (1999), *The Diffusion of Military Technology and Ideas* (2003), and *The Information Revolution in Military Affairs in Asia* (2004). She has been the recipient of awards from the MacArthur, Olin, Pew, and Smith Richardson Foundations, and the U.S. Institute of Peace. She was a Secretary of the Navy Senior Research Fellow at the U.S. Naval War College in 1991–1992, and a residential fellow at the Woodrow Wilson International Center for Scholars in 2003–2004, writing a book on strategy under uncertainty.

Virginia Haufler is an associate professor in the Department of Government and Politics, University of Maryland, College Park. Her areas of expertise are international relations and international political economy. Her research focuses on issues of global governance and the role of the private sector, especially industry self-regulation and corporate governance. She is currently researching the evolution of international policy with regard to multinational corporations operating in zones of conflict. From 1999 to 2000, Haufler was a senior associate at the Carnegie Endowment for International Peace, where she directed a project on the role of the private sector in international affairs. She is a consultant to industry, nonprofits, and international organizations, and serves on the Executive Board of Women in International Security, a nonprofit organization for women in international affairs. Her major book publications include *A Public Role for the Private Sector: Industry Self-Regulation in a Global Economy* (2001), *Private Authority and International Affairs* (1999), and *Dangerous Commerce: Insurance and the Management of International Risk* (1997).

Steven W. Hook is an associate professor and graduate coordinator in the Department of Political Science at Kent State University. He has authored and edited several publications regarding a wide variety of aspects of foreign policy. His most recent publications include *Comparative Foreign Policy: Adaptation Strategies of the Great and Emerging Powers* (2002), "From Containment to Enlargement: U.S. Democracy Promotion After the Cold War" (2002), and "Privatizing Foreign Policy: Interest Groups and Sino-American Trade Relations" (2002). Hook is currently chair of the Foreign Policy Section of the American Political Science Association. He has also served as president of the International Studies Association–Midwest.

Natalie Hudson is a PhD candidate in political science at the University of Connecticut. She has recently published an article on gender mainstreaming and peacekeeping operations in *International Journal*.

Christopher W. Hughes is senior research fellow and deputy director at the Centre for the Study of Globalisation and Regionalisation, University of Warwick, UK. He was a former visiting professor at the Faculty of Law, University of Tokyo, and a research fellow at Hiroshima University. His research interests include Japanese security policy, Japanese international political economy, regionalism in East Asia, and North Korea's external political and economic relations. He is the author of *Japan's Reemergence as a "Normal" Military Power* (2004), *Japan's Security Agenda: Military, Economic, and Environmental Dimensions* (2004), and *Japan's Economic Power and Security: Japan and North Korea* (1999); coauthor of *Japan's International Relations: Politics, Economics, and Security* (2001); and coeditor of *New Regionalisms in the Global Political Economy* (2002) as well as *The Pacific Review*.

Paula R. Johnson is a PhD candidate in educational psychology at the University of Connecticut. Her most recent work, published and presented, focuses on leadership, gender, and computer-mediated communication.

Colin H. Kahl is an assistant professor in the Political Science Department at the University of Minnesota, a consultant for the U.S. government's Political Instability Task Force, and a 2004–2005 Council on Foreign Relations international affairs fellow. Kahl's research focuses on international security, civil and ethnic conflict, environmental politics, and U.S. foreign policy. He has published articles on demography, the environment, and violent conflict in a number of journals, including *International Security* and the *Journal of International Affairs,* and his book *States, Scarcity, and Civil Strife in the Developing World* is forthcoming.

Clarisse O. Lima is a PhD candidate in educational psychology at the University of Connecticut. Her research interests and most recent work, published and presented, focus on the digital divide, global citizenship education, and new literacies for the Internet.

Norrin M. Ripsman is an associate professor in the Political Science Department at Concordia University in Montreal, Canada. He was a Lady Davis postdoctoral research fellow in the Department of International Relations at the Hebrew University of Jerusalem in 1997–1998 and a Mershon Center (Ohio State University) postdoctoral fellow in international politics in 1998–1999. His primary research interests include the domestic sources of foreign security policy in democratic states, postwar peacemaking, constructing regional stability, and the political economy of national security. He is the author of *Peacemaking by Democracies: The Effect of State Autonomy on the Post-World-War Settlements* (2002) and a coeditor of *Power and the Purse: Economic Statecraft, Interdependence, and International Conflict* (2000).

David B. Rothstein is a PhD candidate in the Department of Political Science at Kent State University. In addition to his continuing his doctoral work, he serves as a research associate at Policy Matters Ohio, located in Cleveland.

Lars S. Skålnes is an assistant professor in the Department of Political Science at the University of Oregon. His publications include *Politics, Markets, and Grand Strategy: Foreign Economic Policies as Strategic Instruments* (2000), "From the Outside In, from the Inside Out: NATO Expansion and International Relations Theory" (1998), and "Grand Strategy and Foreign Economic Policy: British Grand Strategy in the 1930s" (1998).

Index

About the Book

Reflecting the growing interest among scholars and practitioners in the relationship between security affairs and economics, this new volume explores the nature of that relationship in the first decade of the twenty-first century.

Among the issues addressed in the book are the impact of the events of September 11, 2001, and of the U.S. response to those events. The authors also consider whether the challenges of the current security environment are in fact new, or instead more virulent manifestations of long-term trends and processes. The result is a state-of-the-art resource on the engagement between security studies and international political economy, intended to encourage further broadening and overlap of the research agendas of both fields.

Peter Dombrowski is a professor in the Strategic Research Department of the U.S. Naval War College's Center for Naval Warfare Studies.